Miriam Frenkel

"The Compassionate and Benevolent": Jewish Ruling Elites in the Medieval Islamicate World

Studies in the History and Culture of the Middle East

Edited by
Stefan Heidemann, Gottfried Hagen, Andreas Kaplony,
Rudi Matthee and Kristina L. Richardson

Volume 39

Miriam Frenkel

“The Compassionate and Benevolent”: Jewish Ruling Elites in the Medieval Islamicate World

Alexandria as a Case Study

A revised and updated edition, translated by Tzemah Yoreh

DE GRUYTER BEN-ZVI INSTITUTE

Despite careful production of our books, sometimes mistakes happen. Unfortunately, the series editor Kristina L. Richardson was misspelled in the original publication. This has been corrected. We apologize for the mistake.

ISBN 978-3-11-111067-7
e-ISBN (PDF) 978-3-11-071361-9
e-ISBN (EPUB) 978-3-11-071368-8
ISSN 2198-0853

Library of Congress Control Number: 2020943947

Bibliographic information published by the Deutsche Nationalbibliothek
The Deutsche Nationalbibliothek lists this publication in the Deutsche Nationalbibliografie; detailed bibliographic data are available on the Internet at http://dnb.dnb.de.

This volume is text- and page-identical with the hardback published in 2021.
Published in Hebrew as Ha-ohavim ve-ha-nedivim: ilit manhiga be-kerev yehudei aleksandria bi-yemei ha-beinayim © 2006 Ben-Zvi Institute, Jerusalem
Printing and binding: CPI books GmbH, Leck

www.degruyter.com

Contents

Introduction — XII

Acknowledgements — XXVII

Part I **Contexts**

Chapter 1
The Context of Time — 3
1 Tracing the Context — **3**
2 The Fatimid Era — **4**
3 The Ayyubid Dynasty — **22**

Chapter 2
The Context of Space — 29
1 Geographical Layout — **29**
2 The City's Confines — **29**
3 The Water System — **32**
4 The Harbor — **34**
5 The Topographical Features and Appearance of Alexandria in the Middle Ages — **36**
6 Internal Divisions — **37**
7 The Market and Mercantile Centers — **40**
8 Public Buildings — **42**
9 Synagogues — **45**
10 Residential Buildings — **46**
11 Alexandria: Gateway to the Magic of the Orient — **48**

Part II **The Community Leaders: Biographies**

Introduction — 53

Chapter 1
The Ben Yeshūʿā Family — 56
1 The Grandfather — **56**
2 Joseph b. Yeshūʿā the Judge — **57**

3 Yeshūʿā b. Joseph — 60

Chapter 2
Shelah b. Mubashshir Ben Nahum — 91
1 The Family — 91
2 First Years — 92
3 His Tenure as Judge — 94
4 A Communal Leader — 95
5 Shelah's Involvement in Extra-Communal Affairs — 101
6 Conclusion — 106

Chapter 3
Abraham b. Jacob al-Darʿī — 108
1 Amongst the Maghribi Merchants — 108
2 A Public Figure in the Alexandrian Community — 108
3 Relationship with Mevorakh b. Saʿadyah Nagid — 110
4 Al-Darʿī and the Palestinian Yeshivah — 112
5 The Family Connection — 113
6 Conclusion — 113

Chapter 4
Ārah̩ b. Nathan the Seventh (Musāfir b. Wahb) — 115
1 The Family — 115
2 Education — 115
3 Mercantile Activities — 116
4 Communal Work — 116
5 A Matter of Class — 116
6 Conclusion — 118

Chapter 5
Aaron b. Yeshūʿā the Physician Ibn al-ʿAmmānī — 119
1 Origins and Family — 119
2 Activities — 120
3 Wealth as a Lifestyle — 122
4 His Position in the Community — 123
5 Conclusion — 128

Chapter 6
Abū Naṣr b. Abraham — 130
1 Initial Forays into the Business World — 130

2 At the Nexus of Information and Relationships — 131
3 Commerce as a Conduit to Advocacy — 133
4 Activity within the Community — 134
5 Personal Profile — 137
6 Summary — 138

Chapter 7
Meir b. Hillel b. Ṣadoq — 140
1 Origins and Background — 140
2 Judge in Alexandria — 141
3 Tenure in Alexandria — 145
4 His Relationship with the Community — 147
5 Summary — 148

Chapter 8: Eleazar ha-Kohen b. Judah, Saʿd al-Mulk — 149
1 Background and Origin — 149
2 Judge and Leader — 149
3 The Leadership Crisis and Its Resolution — 152
4 Conclusion — 155

Chapter 9
R. Ephraim — 156
1 Background and Origin — 156
2 A Controversial Leader — 156
3 Summary: A Jannus-Faced Leader? — 158

Chapter 10
R. Pinḥas — 160
1 Background and Origin — 160
2 His Appointment — 161
3 Judge in Alexandria — 161
4 His Relationship with the Community — 165
5 Conclusion — 167

Chapter 11
Anatoly b. R. Joseph — 169
1 Background and Origin — 169
2 An Intellectual Portrait — 171
3 Judge in Alexandria — 172
4 Community Leader — 174

5 Conclusion — 177

Chapter 12
R. Samuel b. Jacob — 178
1 Acclimatization — 178
2 The Appointment Affair: A Rearguard Battle against the European Immigrants — 180
3 “The Beloved Judge” — 181
4 Conclusion — 183

Chapter 13
Isaac the Judge b. Ḥalfon — 184
1 Origin and Background — 184
2 Events Leading up to his Appointment — 184
3 Leadership with no Authority — 185
4 The Triumvirate — 188
5 R. Isaac and R. Abraham Maimuni — 190
6 Conclusion — 190

Chapter 14
Judah the Teacher b. Aaron the Physician Ibn Al-ʿAmmānī — 192
1 The Family — 192
2 Social Milieu and Family Ties — 192
3 Sources of Income — 194
4 Education and Skills — 196
5 Leading the Community — 198
6 Conclusion — 201

Part III **Towards a Characterization of the Jewish Leadership in Alexandria**

Chapter 1
Sources of Power — 205
1 Introduction — 205
2 The Yeshivah Period — 207
3 The Nagidate Period (1070–1130) — 211
4 Interlude (1130–1170) — 218
5 The Ayyubid Period (1170–1250) — 220

Chapter 2
Methods of Governance: Tools and Strategies — 227
1 Introduction — 227
2 Methods of Dissuasion, Punishment, and Execution — 227
3 Legal Tools: The Edict (*Taqqanah*) and the Restriction (*Seyag*) — 240
4 Mechanisms of Coercion — 244
5 Reconciliation and Persuasion — 247
6 Control of Resources: Appointments — 248
7 Controlling Financial Resources — 252
8 Control of Information — 259
9 Ties with the Muslim Regime — 261

Chapter 3
The Normative Understanding of Governance — 264
1 Introduction — 264
2 The Portrait of an Ideal Leader — 265
3 Responsibilities of the Leader — 269

Part IV **A Ruling Elite**

Introduction — 277

Chapter 1
Common Interests — 279
1 Shared Mercantile Interests — 279
2 Reciprocal Benefits — 280

Chapter 2
Systems of Training and Sorting — 282
1 Training Curricula — 282
2 Methods of Sorting and Culling — 284

Chapter 3
A Common Culture — 289
1 Torah Study — 290
2 Poetry — 295
3 Charity — 297
4 Lifestyle — 301

Chapter 4
Organizational Apparatus and Means of Communication — 304
1 Correspondence — **304**
2 Unofficial Meetings — **307**

Chapter 5 — 310
Conclusions — **310**

Bibliography — 311

Glossary of Terms — 326

Index — 327

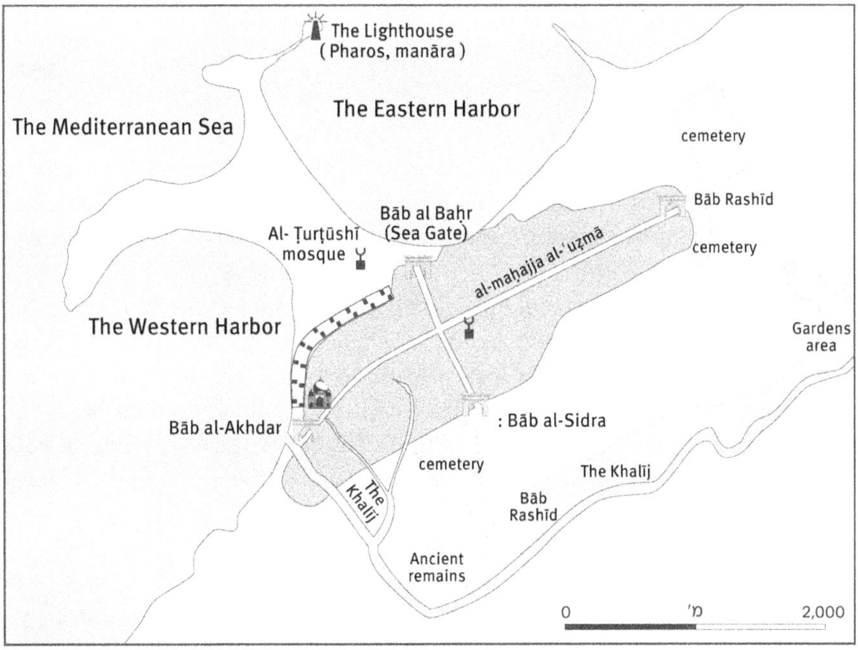

Alexandria during the Fatimid and Ayyubid eras

Introduction

1 Aims

"The Compassionate and Benevolent" is a monograph about the medieval Jewish community of the Mediterranean port city of Alexandria. In historical terms, it is a diachronic study, elucidating "processes" in a given socio-political arena over a defined period of time.

Alexandria as city or community, then, is not my subject here but rather the field of research through which I consider community relations and power dynamics in the medieval Jewish society of the Islamic lands. The nature of the Alexandrian Jewish community and the extent of its autonomy, both important topics in themselves, are not the focus of this book. My aim here is to present a well-defined micro-history and through it, to reveal some general truths as well.

In some instances, the book narrows its focus, attempting to provide a glimpse into the life stories, conducts and practises of contemporary private people. This is done in order to explore the intricate affiliations between individuals and groups and to better understand wider processes.

Our use of the term "Islamicate" rather than "Islamic" is crucial for this book. Coined by Marshall Hodgson in his seminal work *The Venture of Islam* (1974), the term "Islamicate" refers to the areas and societies ruled by Muslims, which may have included a Muslim majority, but that also included other significant non-hegemonic communities, who were full participants in the social, economic, cultural and intellectual activity and discourse of their time and space, in spite of their apparent second-class status ("protected peoples," *ahl al-dhimma*).[1] The term "Islamicate" represents the important truth that, alongside their idiosyncratic characteristics, all of these communities, Muslims, Jews and Christians, shared many cultural traits.

The Jewish community of Alexandria was an indispensable component of this medieval city. As such, its past does not constitute only part of Jewish history, but also reflects patterns and processes in medieval Islamicate society and culture.

---

1 Marshall Hodgson, *The Venture of Islam: Conscience and History in a World Civilization* (Chicago: The University of Chicago Press, 1974).

https://doi.org/10.1515/9783110713619-001

2 Why Alexandria?

The city of Alexandria is a fertile field for research on Jewish leadership. In the first place, Alexandria with its urban setting was a primary scene of activity under Islam. To a large extent the "urban spirit" dictated the character of the realm and its politics.[2] The Jews at this time formed a vital urban element and the centers of the ruling elites were located in the large central cities, rather than the villages and small towns of the periphery.[3] At the same time, Alexandria was not a capital city as such. Choosing to focus on a capital city, Cairo or Fustat, might have distorted the picture, because of the unique status, needs and characteristics of a capital city.[4] Alexandria, on the other hand, was a big enough city to provide the broad canvas needed for painting a clear and faithful portrait.

3 The Ruling Elite

Being ethnic and religious minorities, Jewish communities are frequently treated as monolithic entities, whose cohesive solidarity is highlighted and applauded. Nevertheless, the available sources, mainly those which originate from the Cairo Genizah, present themselves as voicing primarily a distinct segment within the Jewish community, that of its ruling elite.

The existence of elites that have a great deal of power and that act in a concerted fashion to preserve their status and continuity, aroused the interest of historians and social scientists already in the nineteenth century. Max Weber (1864–1920) connected the phenomenon to the increasing professionalization of modern society and to the rise of a professional bureaucracy,[5] whereas Karl Marx (1818–1883) viewed the ownership and supervision of the main means of production as the cause of the ability of a few to rule the many, and believed

2 Norman Stillman, "The Jews in the Urban History of Medieval Islam," in Ezra Fleischer, Mordechai A. Friedman and Joel. L. Kraemer (eds.), *Mas'at Moshe* (Jerusalem and Tel-Aviv: Bialik Institute, 1998), 246–255 [Hebrew]; Mark R. Cohen, *Under Crescent and Cross: The Jews in the Middle Ages* (Princeton: Princeton University Press, 2008), 188–197.

3 Stillman, "The Jews"; Cohen, *Under Crescent*, 188–197.

4 In Cairo there were relatively few Jews and most of them served as palace courtiers. The Genizah provides very little information about them. By the end of the era under discussion, Fustat continued to operate as the Jewish capital and foremost center for the Jews of Egypt and beyond. See Shelomo D. Goitein, *A Mediterranean Society: The Jewish Communities of the Arab World as Portrayed in the Documents of Cairo Geniza* (Berkeley, Los Angeles, and London: University of California Press, 1967–1994), 4: 10–12.

5 Reinhard Bendix, *Max Weber: An Intellectual Portrait* (London: Heinemann, 1960), 418 ff.

this to be a temporary stage of history. A group of Machiavellian thinkers ("the Elitists") opposed him and claimed that the existence of elites is necessary and unchanging: Robert Michels (1876–1936) spoke of the "iron law of oligarchy" and understood the phenomenon as a basic organizational need of every complex society, that has to delegate authority to a small and select group to take decisions in the group's name. In his words: "who says organization, says oligarchy."[6] Gaetano Mosca (1858–1941) also believed that the existence of elites was inevitable, and explained their supremacy by the "exalted" personal characteristics of elite members – such as were lacking among the masses – and their ability to act in an organized fashion: "A hundred men acting in harmony and agreement will overcome a thousand uncoordinated ones." Vilfredo Pareto (1848–1923) accepted these assumptions and added distinctions in the internal divisions between different kinds of elites ("lions" and "foxes"). His theory about the "circulation of elites" claims that elite status is not always inherited or protected by social institutions, but is preserved by constantly accepting new talented and deserving members. Since in democracies such a circulation does not happen, democracies tend to decay, unless new gifted persons manage to infiltrate the ranks of the elite.[7] Thorstein Veblen (1857–1929), on the other side, suggested that elites do little to advance the economy or general social welfare, and instead define themselves by their leisure and consumption.[8] In contrast to these classical theories, that blamed the masses themselves for being ruled by elites, in the 1950s studies began to be published that tended to present the masses as exploited and manipulated by the elites, who acted out of their own narrow interests.[9]

It seems that after the first two decades of the postwar period, interest in elites faded as most attention was given to new social parameters such as gender, ethnicity, and later on to post-colonial issues. A certain revival of the topic is

---

6 Robert Michels, *Political Parties: A Sociological Study of the Oligarchical Tendencies of Modern Democracy*, trans. Eden and Cedar Paul (Glencoe, Ill.: Free Press, 1949), 42.
7 Vilfredo Pareto, *Treatise of General Sociology, The Mind and Society* (NY: Harcourt, Brace & Co., 1935); Samuel E. Finer, *Vilfredo Pareto: Sociological Writings* (London: Pall Mall Press, 1966).
8 Thorstein Veblen, *The Theory of the Leisure Class* (NY: Penguin, 1994).
9 For the most central studies, see: Raymond Aron, "Social Structure and the Ruling Class," *British Journal of Sociology* 1 (1950): 1–16, 126–143; Siegfried F. Nadel, "The Concept of Social Elites," *International Social Science Bulletin* 8 (1956): 413–424; C. Wright-Mills, *The Power Elite* (NY: Oxford University Press, 1956); Geraint Parry, *Political Elites* (London: Allen & Unwin, 1969); Rupert Wilkinson, *Governing Elites: Studies in Training and Selection* (NY: Oxford University Press, 1969); Anthony Giddens, *The Class Structure of the Advanced Societies* (London: Hutchinson, 1973).

partially connected to the influential works by Pierre Bourdieu (1930 – 2002).[10] Bourdieu paid much attention to matters of power and to the ways inequality is achieved, preserved, and reproduced through elite tastes, associations, and dispositions. The new notions he introduced to the field, such as "cultural capital," "habitus," and "symbolic power," undermined earlier notions about the natural and necessary role of elites and provided new paradigms for the study of inequality.

The twenty-first century witnessed a revival of elite studies, most of them concerning the new elites in the United States [11] while others documented elite change, in post-communist countries.[12] But perhaps the most recent trend in elite studies concerns the emergence of transnational elites in face of the process of globalization. [13]

In the context of the present book, it may be worthwhile to mention also the work by E. Digby Baltzell (1915 – 1996) about the American elites, in which he provides detailed descriptions of the elites' human composition, ways of life, ca-

---

10 Pierre Bourdieu, *Distinction* (Cambridge, MA: Harvard University Press, 1984); idem, *Homo Academicus* (Stanford, CA: Stanford University Press, 1990); idem, *The Field of Capital Production* (NY: Columbia University Press, 1993); idem, *State Nobility* (Stanford: Stanford University Press, 1998).

11 The following is just a very partial list: Larry M. Bartels, *Unequal Democracy: The Political Economy of the Gilded Age* (Princeton: Princeton University Press, 2008); John Higley and Michael Burton, *Elite Foundations of Liberal Democracy* (NY: Rowman & Littlefield, 2006); Sven Beckert, *The Monied Metropolis* (NY: Cambridge University Press, 2003); Francie Ostrower, *Trustees of Culture* (Chicago: University of Chicago Press, 2004); Robert Frank, *Richistan: A Journey Through the American Wealth Boom and the Lives of the New Rich* (NY: Crown, 2007); David Rothkopf, *Superclass* (NY: Farrar, Strauss & Giroux, 2009); Jessica Holden Sherwood, *Wealth, Whiteness, and the Matrix of Privilege* (Lanham: Lexington Books, 2010); Gil Eyal, Ivan Szelenyi and Eleanor R. Townsley, *Making Capitalism Without Capitalists: The New Ruling Elites in Eastern Europe* (London: Verso, 2001); Crystal M. Fleming and Lorraine E. Roses, "Black Cultural Capitalists: African-American Elites and the Organization of the Arts in Early Twentieth Century Boston," *Poetics* 35 (2007): 368 – 387.

12 Heinrich Best, György Lengyel, and Luca Verzichelli (eds.), *The Europe of Elites: A Study into the Europeanness of Europe's Political and Economic Elites* (Oxford: Oxford University Press, 2012); John Higley and György Lengyel (eds.) *Elites after State Socialism* (Oxford: Rowman & Littlefield, 2000); John Higley, Jan Pakulski and Włoszimierz Wesołowski (eds.), *Postcommunist Elites and Democracy in Eastern Europe* (Basingstoke: Macmillan, 1998).

13 Christer Jönsson and Jonas Tallberg (eds.), *Democracy Beyond the Nation State? Transnational Actors and Global Governance* (Basingstoke: Palgrave Macmillan. 2010), 3 vols. The journal issue *Historical Social Research / Historische Sozialforschung*, 43.4 (2018), is also dedicated to this topic.

reers, and ethics.[14] In this informative and descriptive way, Baltzell brings these groups to light, delineates their boundaries and defines their nature. In my book I tried to follow a similar path, that is, to point out the very existence of such groups within Jewish society. Given the sweeping tendency to identify whole societies with their elite groups, especially in studies on Jewish history, I believe that even before trying to listen to the muted voices of the social margins: minorities, the poor, women, or children, it is worthwhile to put effort into exposing the elites and the ways they functioned.

Another source of inspiration for this book were the works by anthropologist Abner Cohen, who, by analyzing a variety of elites, has shown how elites that cannot organize themselves in an open and official manner manipulatively use the symbolic language of the society of which they are a part – such as values, myths and rituals – in order to solve their organizational problems.[15] Cohen's vision overlaps, to a large extent, with the conceptualization developed by Antonio Gramsci, according to which a deep and longstanding affinity exists between dominant social groups in a society and that society's political institutions. These institutions promote the particular interests of the group while making use of universalist rhetoric, which legitimizes social reality and the hegemony of the ruling group. [16]

Most of these studies were written in the social sciences. Hardly any historical studies have attempted to apply these rich theoretical frameworks to past societies. The elite group described in this book had its own particular political and economic interests, protected by an entire organizational system which aimed at securing its specific interests and at preserving its cohesiveness. The links which connected the various elite members were based on personal ties and were articulated in unofficial terms of friendship, love and kindness. "The compassionate and benevolent" are only part of the many titles with which members of the group used to address each other. The existence of this ruling elite group was never formally articulated, yet the implicit rules that dictated the nature of the

---

14 E. Digby Baltzell, *The Protestant Establishment: Aristocracy and Caste in America* (New Haven: Yale University Press, 1987); idem, *Philadelphia Gentlemen* (NY: Transaction, 1989); idem, *Sporting Gentlemen: Men's Tennis from the Age of Honor to the Cult of the Superstar*, (NY: Free Press, 1995); idem, *Puritan Boston and Quaker Philadelphia* (NY: Transaction, 1996).
15 Abner Cohen, *Two-Dimensional Man: An Essay on the Anthropology of Power and Symbolism in Complex Society* (London: Routledge & K. Paul: 1974); idem, *The Politics of Elite Culture: Explorations in the Dramaturgy of Power in a Modern African Society* (Berkeley: University of California Press, 1981).
16 Joseph V. Femia, *Gramsci's Political Thought: Hegemony, Consciousness, and the Revolutionary Process* (Oxford: Clarendon Press, 1981), 23–60.

informal political games played out in Jewish communities, as well as its patterns of leadership, seem both stable and steady. The leadership assumed the form of a wide network. The more connected a person was to others, and the more central his position in the network, the better his chances of acquiring a leadership position. The network comprised social, familial, economic, intellectual and commercial ties. It crossed geographical and communal boundaries and incorporated a steady pool of cosmopolitan members, who served as communal leaders at different stages of their lives in various places all over the Islamic world. Despite its wide geographical dispersion, this was a distinct and particular group, struggling simultaneously for its own interests as a group and for those of the wider Jewish society. All members of the ruling elite were engaged to some extent in commerce, and commercial links were an indispensable part of the network's connections, but not the sole ones. The network was made up out of very small circles, sometimes of no more than two merchants, but each merchant belonged to more than one circle and was thus able to serve as a link to several other circles. Each member actually stood at the center of a cluster of entangled circles, which all together constituted a ramified social and commercial network. The network covered a vast geographical range, from North Africa to India, and large quantities of merchandise and money circulated through it. The maintenance of the network was crucial to the continuance of this commercial machine and therefore commercial interests frequently overrode political, communal and religious conflicts. Members of opposing political fractions maintained their commercial relations even during seemingly dramatic disputes between Babylonians and Palestinians, Rabbanites and Karaites, locals and immigrants.

The book, hence, concerns the community leaders and its pacesetters. None the less, it does not aim to acclaim their grandeur, but to uncover their belonging to a distinct elite group and to expose the group's overt and covert strategies and apparatuses. This is perceived as an initial step towards revealing and giving voice to the silent marginal segments of medieval Jewish society, who hardly left any visible traces in history.

When first published in 2006, the book was one of the first works to depart from the traditional institutional approach applied to Jewish communal history. That approach depicted a pyramidal model of Jewish leadership according to which power emanated from formal and authoritative leading institutions—the Babylonian yeshivot, the Jerusalem Yeshivah, the exilarch, or the Nagid—down to the various communities with their appointed local leaders. Instead," The Compassionate and Benevolent" offered a horizontal model of networks, in which the main role was played not by institutions, but by human actors, with their struggles for power, intrigues, deals, and collaborations. It portrayed a cosmopolitan network of a leading elite with shared interests, which struggled to protect them and to maintain its privileged status.

Since the book's publication, additional studies have suggested other models to explain the organizing principles of medieval Jewish society in Muslim lands. Marina Rustow, in an influential article from 2008,[17] investigated the political culture of the Islamic East during the tenth to twelfth centuries using letters and petitions from the Cairo Genizah, which employ idioms referring to the exchange of benefit, reciprocal service, protection, oversight, patronage, and loyalty. Rustow identifies them as part and parcel of the same specialized vocabulary of patron-client relationships used in Arabic courtly literature written under Abbasid-Buwayhid rule. Although she observes that some of these terms went through devaluation over time, and others hardened into formulaic phrases, she views the parallels between Arabic courtly literature and everyday Genizah letters as a demonstration of the deep penetration of courtly etiquette into "other realms of relationships whose stability rested on the binding power of loyalty."[18] Rustow observes the reciprocal nature of court patronage during the tenth to twelfth centuries, in which the benefits and responsibilities exchanged on both sides were apprehended as mutually obligatory bonds. Upon analyzing the language of patronage, Rustow claims that idioms, such as benefit (*ni'ma*), service to one another (*khidma*), protection (*ri'āya, 'ināya*), and loyalty (*'ahd*) demonstrate "adherence to the social and linguistic forms of patronage,"[19] and although she admits that some of them were retained in an ossified mode, she believes that some others still held the original vigor of patronage relations, even outside the royal court, "by men and women, the literate and illiterate, courtiers, physicians, local leaders, judges, merchants, paupers, and the scribes who wrote for them—by anyone, in short, who asked for or received goods, services, or favors from anyone else."[20]

In the present book these affective idioms are apprehended as reflecting various kinds of ties, some of them hierarchical, but most of them are horizontal ties between equal members of a social ruling elite. Although they may, as claimed by Rustow, continue an older vocabulary, originally deployed to denote court patronage relationships (even if most of the terms themselves predate Islam), their usage in the context of the Genizha writings is engaged by and for an elite group

17 Marina Rustow, "Formal and Informal Patronage among Jews in the Islamic East: Evidence from the Cairo Geniza," *Al-Qanṭara* 29.2 (2008): 341–382.

18 Ibid., 343.

19 Ibid., 351.

20 Ibid., 352.

in order to bolster the informal ties that linked them together, and to preserve the group's cohesion.

In a later article from 2014, [21] Rustow refined her patronage model and offered a new paradigm for studying group coherence in pre-modern Mediterranean societies, including the Jewish society in the medieval Islamicate world. Based on Seth Schwartz's book on ancient Judaism,[22] Rustow proposes to adopt the analytical schema which posits reciprocity-based societies versus solidarity-based societies. While reciprocity-based relationships, which include various forms of patronage, take place face to face and do not take into consideration any wider group coherence, and therefore tend to create inequalities, solidarity-based societies emphasize group belonging and base themselves on shared ideology. Reciprocity-based societies are essentially hierarchical, while solidarity-based societies are relatively egalitarian, but separatist. She argues that between the tenth to the twelfth century, reciprocity was the dominant form of social relations among Jews of the Islamic east, and it shaped the relationships, not only between the leaders of the Jewish communities and their followers, but also among commercial magnates, as is manifested in the vocabulary of patronage used in Genizah documents and letters. From the twelfth century onward one can observe a tension between the patronage relationships still being practiced and an emerging ideology of solidarity, as is manifested in Maimonides' writings. I believe Rustow's analytical distinction between these two types of relationships, although still theoretical and lacking historical contextualization, may prove productive in the study of medieval Islamicate societies. Still, her paradigm treats the Jewish society as a monolithic entity and ignores class differentiation, which is the main argument in the present book. I hope this book shows clearly how an unofficial elite group within Jewish society managed to keep its own cohesiveness using "reciprocity relationships," to use Rustow's terminology and at the same time manipulating an ideology of national "solidarity," to use her terms again, for the same purpose.

In 2006, renowned economics professor Avner Greif published a book on the crucial role played by institutions in the modern western economy, in which he dedicated long pages to the trading practices employed by medieval Jewish mer-

---

21 Marina Rustow, "Patronage in the Context of Solidarity and Reciprocity: Two Paradigms of Social Cohesion in the Premodern Mediterranean," in: Esperanza Alfonso and Jonathen Decter (eds.), *Patronage, Production, and Transmission of Texts in Medieval and Early Modern Jewish Cultures* (Turnhout: Brepols, 2014), 13–44.

22 Seth Schwartz, *Were the Jews a Mediterranean Society? Reciprocity and Solidarity in Ancient Judaism* (Princeton NJ: Princeton University Press, 2009).

chants in Muslim lands, whom he calls "the Maghribis."[23] Greif considers the Genizah merchants to be the first to employ principal-agent relations in long-distance trade, in which "a reputation mechanism" substituted for institutional enforcement of law and control. In this coalition of merchants, Greif claims, any agent accused of dishonesty was shunned by the entire group. In this way, he argues, the "Maghribis" overcame the lack of state institutions of control, crucial for every successful long-distance trade venture. In spite of its success at the time, it was this system, according to Greif, that brought the Islamic world to a dead end and enabled European supremacy in global trade. While I am in no position to evaluate Greif's economic theory, and there is no place in this introduction for a discussion on the links he draws between the rise of Europe and a supposed decline of the Islamic economy,[24] nevertheless at the basis of Greif's theory lies a depiction of medieval Jewish life in Muslim lands which stands in sharp opposition to the way it is presented in this book. Greif speaks of a coalition of traders defined ethnically by their common origins in the Maghreb, which operated within a long-distant commercial network, while the present book portrays a network of members of a Jewish cosmopolitan ruling elite, defined socially and not ethnically, in which trade constituted just one aspect of its common interests, endeavors and culture. In several places, including in Alexandria itself, the Maghribis, or *Maghāriba*, as they are called in the Genizah documents, formed distinct identity groups, as did other groups of immigrants in the big Muslim cities. These were ad-hoc cliques intended to enhance their local interests, such as payment of the *jizya* tax or their roles in the local synagogue. Jews from the Maghreb immigrated to Egypt and to other countries in the Levant continuously from the ninth century, and perhaps even earlier, and there is no way to speak of one distinct group of "Jewish traders who left during the tenth century the increasingly politically insecure surroundings of Baghdad

23 Avner Greif, *Institutions and the Path to the Modern Economy: Lessons from Medieval Trade* (Cambridge: Cambridge University Press, 2006), 58–90. Earlier and later works by Greif also deal with this topic: idem, "Reputation and Coalition in Medieval Trade: Evidence on the Maghribi Traders," *Journal of Economic History* 49.4 (1989): 857–882; idem, "Contract Enforceability and Economic Institutions in Early Trade: The Maghribi Traders Coalition," *American Economic Review* 83.3 (1993): 525–548; idem, "The Maghribi Traders: A Reappraisal?," *Economic History Review* 65.2 (2012): 221–236.

24 See a detailed discussion of this issue in Jessica Goldberg, *Trade and Institutions in the Medieval Mediterranean: The Geniza Merchants and their Business World* (Cambridge: Cambridge University Press, 2012), 12–15 and esp. n. 30 for references to evaluations and continuations of Greif's economic theories. See also Jessica Goldberg, "Choosing and Enforcing Business Relationships in the Eleventh-Century Mediterranean: Reassessing the 'Maghribī Traders'," *Past & Present* 215.2 (2012): 3–40.

and initially emigrated to Tunisia ...which was controlled by the Fatimid Caliphate" and then moved to Egypt, when the Fatimids established their new capital in Cairo.[25] This conception follows, in a way, a theory developed by Moshe Gil, the great Genizah scholar and Greif's teacher, who believed that the *Maghāriba* not only formed a distinct commercial group in the High Middle Ages, but that they were the descendants of the Radhanites, a trade community of long-distance Jewish merchants of Persian origin whose astounding global trade routes are described in medieval Muslim administrative literature.[26] But Gil's stance is not supported by any source and is not accepted nowadays. On the other hand, the trading networks as presented in the Genizah documents were multiethnic organizations which included merchants of variegated origins.

Greif's thesis contradicts the main argument of this book in another way: while he considers a "multilateral reputation mechanism" to be the one and only criterion for acceptance or exclusion from the network, this book enumerates a series of criteria which determined an elite member's place in the network, the most important of which being one's location in the network and the number of links he managed to establish within it.

Jessica Goldberg's fascinating book from 2012[27] draws a comprehensive picture of medieval trade based mainly on merchants' letters from the Genizah. In her book she follows the mercantile activities of groups of Jewish merchants as they appear in the Genizah documents. One of her decisive conclusions is that there was no pan-Jewish web of trade in the Islamic world, and that not all Jewish merchants worked with one another. This was also my basic assumption in the present book. The cosmopolitan network of the Jewish ruling elite I present in the book, although allied by joint mercantile interests, was composed of many coalitions and partnerships of various sizes and of changing durability. Being members of a ruling elite did not mean belonging to an all-inclusive Jewish organization. As I explain in Part IV of this book, it did not even imply that all these members knew each other at all. Another claim made by Goldberg is that mercantile activity was not always compatible with religious community nor with family ties. To use her own words: "economic and religious geographies" were not the same. This conclusion apparently contradicts my claim that the Genizah letters reflect a cosmopolitan ruling elite, whose ties consisted

---

25 Greif, *Institutions*, 61.

26 Wolfhart P. Heinrichs et al. (eds.), *Encyclopaedia of Islam*, 2nd edition (Leiden: Brill, 1960–2005), s.v. "Rādhāniyya"; ʿUbaydallāh b. ʿAbdallāh Ibn Khurradādhbih, *Kitāb al-masālik wal-mamālik* (= *Liber viarum et regnorum*) (Leiden: Brill, 1889), 153–154; Moshe Gil, *Jews in Islamic Countries in the Middle Ages*, trans. David Strassler (Leiden: Brill, 2004), 615–697.

27 Goldberg, *Trade*.

of shared interests in commerce as well as in communal and religious leadership. But, while the fact that many people, at least during some part of their lives, conducted their family and communal lives in geographical regions that were not the same as that in which they conducted their mercantile activities, may point at the high level of mobility of this class, this actually does not negate my assertion that religious and communal leadership and involvement in long-distance and local trade were both ties that characterized and linked together a Jewish ruling elite. Moreover, Goldberg's assertion that local and inter-regional commerce were combined and promised many advantages, and the way she depicts the many profits of these combined belongings,[28] reinforce, from a commercial perspective, my claim about the common interests of the ruling elite.

Goldberg's book concerns trade in the medieval Mediterranean. It offers an innovative and elaborate picture of the ways, institutions and "geographies" of Jewish trade in the medieval lands of Islam. But, commerce provides a very limited view of society as a whole.[29] Trying to learn about a society only through the lens of trade is necessarily partial. While Goldberg's finds about the ways in which Jewish mercantile networks functioned do not actually contradict my main assertion in this book, but rather reinforce it, Goldberg herself, however, when explaining the class affiliation and social position of the merchants,[30] replicates Goitein's somewhat naïve depiction of a "bourgeoisie," which receives in Goldberg's work the quite anachronistic term of "the middling sort."[31]

---

28 Ibid., 355–357.

29 This resulted sometimes in partial interpretations of social phenomena. One case in point is the term *nās*, which Goldberg interprets as referring to the dignified local traders, while in many Genizah letters, which are not typically "merchants' letters," it is quite clear that the term is much wider, as I show in this book.

30 Goldberg, *Trade*, 38–50.

31 Here are just a few weak points for example: Goldberg asserts that "members of the middling sort occasionally became courtiers and high office-holders" (47–48), but these members were consciously trained and received an education that enabled them to occupy these positions. It was part of their *Bildung* and never happened "occasionally." In another place she explains that "other individuals through bad investments or loss of family might lose their foothold in this stratum" (47), but in this case Goldberg ignores the explicit preference of helping members of the elite (*bnei tovim*) who encountered financial problems over the "chronically poor," as they are termed by Mark Cohen. Another explanation asserts that "some individuals of modest origins rose into scholarly elite through brilliance" (47), but people outside the elite never received an education that allowed them to manifest their "brilliance." Yet another assertion claims that "business was understood as the necessary cost of maintaining a family's capital base... not as a source or motor for gaining social prestige" (48). But, how does this fit in with the phenomenon of academies bestowing titles on wealthy members of the community in return for financial support, mentioned on the same page?

My claim is that commerce in the Genizah society shared its codes, implicit laws and basic assumptions with larger systems and that it made use of the symbolic system of the surrounding culture. I propose that the various commercial networks of Genizah merchants constituted an indispensable part of a larger social network, which I call "the Jewish ruling elite," and that the literary skills and the behavioral toolkit of its members enabled them to join the group and to take part in its commercial and other activities. It is this elite class that is mainly represented in the Genizah documents, as its literate members were able to produce and to use written documents.

4 The Book's Structure

The book comprises four parts. **Part One** familiarizes readers with the contexts of the research and sets forth its perspectives. The context of time illuminates the external events—political, economic and demographic—that shaped the the Fatimid-Ayyubid period and largely determined it. The spatial context delineates the physical site of Alexandria where the actions and narratives take place. The city of Alexandria, its urban features and its history, serves in this book as a point of departure from which a cosmopolitan social network emerges.

Part Two, on prosopography, contains the chronologically arranged biographies of Alexandria's Jewish leaders in their public roles, with discussions of those who figured most prominently in the eyes of the community, and in their own eyes as well.

Both parts consider the evidential premises of the book, the scene of the action, leading figures, and the historical background.

Part Three analyses the characteristics and nature of Alexandria's Jewish leaders, the tools and strategies available to them, their sources of authority and how their roles and missions were viewed by contemporaries.

Part Four sums up the book, and presents the conclusion that the medieval Alexandrian Jewish leadership constituted an elite group, whose members derived their power mainly from their places in a wide-ranging cosmopolitan network. Explored here is the partially hidden apparatus which enabled the functioning of the elite group and guaranteed its cohesiveness. The shared concerns and the common culture that safeguarded the ruling elite members in their roles will be given special attention, as well as their often ambiguous modes of operation, and the correlation between their narrow interests and the welfare of the Jewish community as a whole.

5 The Genizah Documents

A wealth of documents from the Cairo Genizah supplied most of the sources for this book. Notwithstanding their fragmentary, selective, and haphazard nature, the documents abound with information, particularly as concerns the ruling elites who left a great many more records than any other segment of the Jewish society. Shelomo D. Goitein (1900 – 1985) has written lucidly and comprehensively about the rewards and limits of this unique corpus in his study of the Genizah.[32] Increasingly over the years, especially since the establishment of the Friedberg Genizah Project which provides scans of most Genizah collections, the Genizah texts have become essential for historians engaged in research concerning Jews in the lands of Islam. This is particularly so due to the monumental work of Goitein, who, to a large extent, cleared the way for future scholars.[33] However, the present study employs a new textual approach, and entails what Derrida has called double reading, namely, a primary reconstruction of the dominant meaning of the text in strict adherence to the principles of philology, and preferably through an awareness of context in comparison with other documents of the same type or by the same author. But beyond this type of primary reading, I have attempted here to seek deeper textual layers with a second reading in order to reveal their latent and unconscious content. Such a reading is based on the premise that all texts contain a subtext in as much as they are subject to the rules of discourse. Thus, a second reading makes it possible to reveal the written and unwritten assumptions and literary conventions that circum-

---

32 Goitein, *Society*, 1: 1 – 28.

33 Ibid., 23 – 25. Later historical writings that made greater use of Genizah material include Mark R. Cohen, *Jewish Self Government in Medieval Egypt* (Princeton: Princeton University Press, 1980); Moshe Gil, *In the Kingdom of Ishmael: Studies in Jewish History in Islamic Lands in the Early Middle Ages* (Tel Aviv: Tel Aviv University Press, 1997) [Hebrew]; Elinoar Bareket, *The Jewish Leadership in Fustat in the First Half of the Eleventh Century* (Tel-Aviv: The Diaspora Research Institute, Tel Aviv University, 1995) [Hebrew]; Menahem Ben-Sasson, *The Emergence of the Local Jewish Community in the Muslim World; Qairawan, 800 – 1057* (Jerusalem: Magness Press, 1996) [Hebrew]; Marina Rustow, *Heresy and the Politics of Community: The Jews of the Fatimid Caliphate* (Ithaca: Cornell University Press, 2008); Goldberg, *Trade*; Roxani E. Margariti, *Aden and the Indian Ocean Trade. 150 Years in the Life of a Medieval Arabian Port* (Chapel Hill: University of North Carolina, 2012); Arnold Franklin, *This Noble House: Jewish Descendants of King David in the Medieval Islamic World* (Philadelphia: University of Pennsylvania, 2013); Philip Ackerman-Lieberman, *The Business of Identity: Jews, Muslims, and Economic Life in Medieval Egypt* (Stanford: Stanford University Press, 2014); Eve Krakowski, *Coming of Age in Medieval Egypt: Female Adolescence, Jewish Law, and Ordinary Culture* (Princeton, NJ : Princeton University Press, 2017).

scribe the text.[34] I tried to apply this theory to the obscure medieval texts before us, revealed as it were through a glass darkly.

The corpus of a hundred Genizah documents, deciphered, transliterated and annotated, which constituted the basis for this book, are to be found in the original Hebrew version of this book. [35]

34 Jacques Derrida, *De la grammatologie* (Paris: Les Éditions de Minuit, 1967), 135, 144–145, 227–228. See also Miriam Frenkel, "Genizah Documents as Literary products," in Ben Outhwaite and Siam Bhayro (eds.), *"From A Sacred Source": Genizah Studies in Honour of Professor Stefan C. Reif* (Leiden: Brill, 2010), 139–155.
35 Miriam Frenkel, *"The Compassionate and Benevolent": The Leading Elite in the Jewish Community of Alexandria in the Middle Ages* (Jerusalem: Ben-Zvi Institute, 2006)

Acknowledgements

I would like to express my heartfelt gratitude to Dr. Tzemh Yoreh for his perceptive and accurate translation and to Dr. Leigh Chipman and Dr. Amir Mazor who did not only help with the copy editing but also with their professional and wise advices and with their most valuable comments. Last not least, I wish to thank the publisher and the editors, especially prof. Stefan Heidemann for including this book in the series *Studies in the History and Culture of the Middle East.* It was a truly great pleasure and honor to work with all of you.

Miriam Frenkel

https://doi.org/10.1515/9783110713619-002

Part I **Contexts**

Chapter 1 The Context of Time

1 Tracing the Context

It was Shelomo D. Goitein who coined the term “the Classical Genizah Period” in studies where he demonstrates that most of the documents in the corpus refer to a time between the 1020s and the mid-thirteenth century (1250),[36] a period during which two dynasties, the Fatimids and the Ayyubids, overlapped and influenced the course of history in Egypt and the Middle East. The eighty years of Ayyubid rule (1171–1250), despite some new features, was more of a transitional phase. The changes that took shape during the Fatimid era reached their culmination under the Ayyubids, while fateful new developments that would be of central importance centuries later for the Mamluks were just beginning to emerge.[37] Thus, following Goitein, it is possible to consider this 250-year period as a single unit of time with two main subdivisions, Fatimid and Ayyubid. While the history of these two dynasties has been studied by many fine scholars,[38] my own focus here will be on the city of Alexandria and the central events and developments that took place there during this period.

---

36 Goitein, *Society*, 1: 16–19. See also Goitein's plea for a periodization of Islamic history in general, where he suggests the years 850–1250 to be recognized as the era of “the Intermediate Civilization.” Shelomo D. Goitein, “A Plea for the Periodization of Islamic History,” *Journal of the American Oriental Society* 88.2 (1968): 224–228. A very similar periodization was adopted later by Marshall Hodgeson, who distinguishes the years 945–1258 as “the Earlier Middle Islamic Period”: Hodgeson, *The Venture of Islam*, 1: 96.
37 Goitein, *Society*, 1: 29–42.
38 For a general survey of the Fatimids, see Marius Canard, “Fatimids,” *Encyclopedia of Islam*, 2nd edition, *s.v.*; Paula Sanders, “Fatimids,” in Joseph R. Strayer (ed.), *Dictionary of the Middle Ages* (NY: C. Scribner's Sons, 1983), 5:24–30; Heinz Halm, “Die Fatimiden,” in Ulrich Haarmann (ed.), *Geschichte der arabischen Welt* (Munich: Verlag C.H. Beck, 1987), 166–199, 605–606; Michael Brett, *The Rise of the Fatimids: The World of the Mediterranean and the Middle-East in the Tenth Century CE* (Leiden: Brill, 2001); Paul Walker, *Exploring an Islamic Empire: Fatimid History and Its Sources* (London: IB Tauris 2002). For the history of the Ayyubids, see Andrew S. Ehrenkreutz, *Saladin* (Albany, NY: SUNY Press, 1972); R. Stephen Humphries, *From Saladin to the Mongols: The Ayyubids of Damascus, 1193–1260* (Albany, NY: SUNY Press, 1977); Yaacov Lev, *Saladin in Egypt* (Leiden: Brill, 1999); Samuel M. Stern, *Studies in Early Ismāʿīlism* (Jerusalem: Magness Press, 1983), 115–121.

https://doi.org/10.1515/9783110713619-003

2 The Fatimid Era

(a) The Age of Conquest (914–969)

In the year 969, during the days of al-Mu'izz (932–975), the fourth Imam, the Fatimid army under Jawhar completed its conquest of Egypt. In the center of Egypt, not far from Fustat, Jawhar established a new capital, al-Qāhira, to which he moved the court of the caliphate. Egypt became the center of the Fatimid Empire.

The conquest of 969, however, was preceded by several failed attempts. Alexandria, Egypt's main port, had been subdued time and again by the Fatimid army from the second decade of the tenth century onward. In the summer of 914, the first Berber troops of the Fatimid army landed in Alexandria and occupied the city. The Fatimid army under the command of the Imam Abū al-Qāsim completed the conquest in November. From Alexandria, Abū al-Qāsim continued along the west bank of the Nile and conquered vast areas as far as Fayyum. A counterattack by the Abbasid army forced Abū al-Qāsim to retreat to Alexandria where he entrenched himself, and in a fervent sermon at the central mosque, announced his intention of continuing the war with the Abbasids. An Abbasid onslaught forced his retreat from Alexandria in 915, but four years later, he seized it once again. In the spring of 921 the Abbasids re-conquered the city, and another Fatimid attempt to gain control was crushed in 935 by Ibn Ṭanj al-Ikhshīdī.[39] It was not until the spring of 973 that al-Mu'izz succeeded in regaining control of the city.

The Fatimid conquest of Alexandria is nowhere mentioned in Muslim historiography as a traumatic event. Quite the contrary, it is described in terms of harmonious cooperation between the victorious army and the local population. Thus, for example, the Egyptian historian Ibn Taghrībirdī writes:

> Al-Mu'izz delivered a sermon [before a delegation of local nobles that came out to greet him] in which he informed them that his aim was a blessed one, to maintain the jihad and justice and that he intended to seal his life with good deeds and to obey the command of his ancestor, the Messenger of God, Allāh's prayer be upon him and His greeting. He sermonized before them and spoke so exceedingly that some of them began to cry [with emotion]. To a group of them he even bequeathed robes of honor.[40]

---

39 Abū 'Umar Muḥammad al-Kindī, *Kitāb al-wulāh wa-kitāb al-quḍāh* (Leiden: Brill, 1912), 288–289; Abū al-Ḥasan 'Alī al-Andalūsī Ibn Sa'īd, *al-Mughrib fī ḥulā al-maghrib* (Cairo: n.p., 1953), 161; Al-Sayyid 'Abd al-'Azīz Sālim, *Ta'rīkh madīnat al-iskandariyya wa-ḥaḍāratuhā fī al-'aṣr al-islāmī* (Alexandria: Dār al-Ma'ārif, 1982), 175–177.

40 Jamāl al-Dīn Yūsuf Ibn Taghrībirdī, *al-Nujūm al-zāhira fī mulūk miṣr wal-qāhira* (Cairo: Dār al-Kutub al-'Ilmiyya, 1932), 4: 72.

Al-Muʿizz, it would seem, took a series of actions immediately after the conquest of the city, intended to win over the local leadership and ensure lasting tranquility. On the one hand he took care to lavish honors upon the local qadi, including a fine robe and a ceremonial procession with him on horseback through the city streets. Simultaneously, however, he appointed Ibn Abī Thawbān, one of his loyal followers from North Africa, as the new qadi of Alexandria, thereby setting the character of the new regime.[41]

(b) Hazy Origins (970–1020)

There is no available information about the local history of Alexandria during the early decades of Fatimid rule, neither in Muslim sources nor unfortunately, in the scanty Genizah findings of that period, the years when the Fatimid dynasty was established in Egypt. The reign of the Caliph al-ʿAzīz (975–996) was a period of relative political and economic stability, administrative organization, and military movement towards Syria and a considerable expansion of the army.[42] The Caliph al-Ḥākim bi-Amr Allāh was notorious for his inflammatory decrees against religious minorities,[43] yet we have no specific information about the effect of these decrees on the Jewish community of Alexandria. Evidence of this begins to emerge only in the days of Caliph al-Ẓāhir (1020–1035).

(c) An Era of Naval Battles (1020–1050)

From the documents in the Genizah we learn of almost continuous naval battles into the eleventh century. The fragmented epistle of Ismāʿīl b. Yūsuf Ibn Abī ʿUqba, written in Alexandria around 1030, describes a Byzantine attack on a fleet of merchant vessels en route from the Maghreb to the port of Alexandria:

> ... Until the ship of Ibn [...] arrived the enemy [...] for four days [...]. Only Ḥamza's ship. Five war vessels [...] ships in peace. Abū al-Dhahab is safe and sound. Later came Ḥamza's ship which had been attacked by the Byzantines and in it, three sailors and their captain arrived with the news that everyone on board of Hamza's ship was killed, and al-Ghazzāl was [also]

41 al-Kindī, *Kitāb al-wulāh*, 584, 587.
42 Yaacov Lev, *State and Society in Fatimid Egypt* (Leiden: Brill, 1991), 22–23.
43 Ibid., 34–36, 185–191.

> killed, may God have mercy on him. The Byzantines blocked their way with fire,[44] and cast vessel after vessel into the sea.[45]

Further information is found in the letter of Ephraim b. Ismāʿīl al-Jawharī, also writing in 1030 from Alexandria to Joseph Ibn ʿAwkal in Fustat. The letter tells of forced conscription to the war fleet (*qaṭāʾiʿ*) and of seizing merchant ships to supply war vessels.[46]

On the frontline of this naval battle against the Byzantines were pirates. At the beginning of the eleventh century there was a vast family network of Bedouin pirates, employed by the Fatimids to drive Byzantine ships away from their shores.[47] The pirates were extraordinarily active and took an enormous number of captives. Reports of Jewish captives are found among the Genizah letters, documenting the efforts of the community of Alexandria to ransom them. So, for example, we learn of a ship that "sailed, which is belonging to one of the Arabs, Jabāra b. Mukhtār, [in which] there were ten Jews from Anatolia";[48]a "captive woman they brought from the land of Edom";[49] a "ship that arrived from the land of Edom with many captives aboard";[50] the captive "R. Shabbetai son of R. Nathaniel from the land of Ana[tolia]"[51] and in a letter to the community of Mastaura in Greece, there is mention of our "captive brethren from among you."[52]

44 About the special Byzantine ships that shot "Greek fire" at them, see ibid., 105, n. 37. The Fatimid army would pelt the enemy with special oil containers (*qawārīr al-naft*) and set them on fire. In the Museum of Islamic Art in Cairo there is a display of such containers from the Fatimid period. See also David Ayalon, *Gunpowder and Firearms in the Mamluk Kingdom: A Challenge to a Mediaeval Society*, 2nd edition (London: Frank Cass, 1978); Salah Elbeheiry, "Les institutions de l'Egypte au temps des Ayyubides" (M.A. thesis, Universitè de Paris IV-Lille, 1972), 85–187.

45 ENA 3786r, ll. 22–27: Gil, *Kingdom*, no. 216.

46 TS 13 J 19.29r, ll. 16–21: Gil, *Kingdom*, no. 182; Menahem Ben-Sasson (ed.), *The Jews of Sicily 825–1068: Documents and Sources* (Jerusalem: Ben-Zvi Institute, 1991), no. 50 [Hebrew]. Forced conscription to naval service was quite common in Ayyubid times, see Lev, *State and Society*, 121.

47 See Goitein, *Society*, 1: 327–332; Archibald R. Lewis, *Naval Power and Trade in the Mediterranean, 500–1100 AD* (Princeton NJ: Princeton University Press, 1951), 204.

48 TS 13 J 14.20, ll. 15–16: Jacob Mann, *The Jews in Egypt and Palestine under the Fatimid Caliphs: A Contribution to Their Political and Communal History Based Chiefly on Genizah Material Hitherto Unpublished* (Oxford: Oxford University Press, 1969), 2: 87, no. 12. On Jabāra b. Mukhtār, see below, Part II, Chapter 1.

49 ENA 2804.9, l. 16: Mann, *Jews*, 2: 89, no. 14.

50 Ibid., l. 24.

51 TS 24.11 J 13, l. 16: Mann, *Jews*, 2: 91, no. 16.

52 TS 16.251, l. 14: Mann, *Jews*, 2:93, no. 18.

The prolonged war and the burden of ransoming so many captives oppressed and impoverished the Jewish community of Alexandria. Letters sent from the city are filled with complaints about the harshness of living conditions. Joseph b. Yeshūʿā, an Alexandrian, asks a friend in Fustat to send him a coat for the Day of Atonement (Yom Kippur) and complains that very few imports reach the city;[53] and a Palestinian cantor (*ḥazzan*) who was detained there grumbles about not receiving sufficient help and writes: "Had I known what my fate would be if I entered this port city, I would never have come here."[54] We also learn about the tribulations of the day from reports that seem to express relief, apparently in the aftermath of great stress and strain. So, for example, we see in the letter of Abū ʿAlī ʿImrān who writes from Alexandria at this time to his nephew Hārūn b. al-Muʿallim Jacob: "There is relief in the city, praise be to God, and conditions have improved."[55]

With the ascension of the Caliph al-Mustanṣir in 1035, a reign that lasted till 1094, longer than that of any other Fatimid caliph, Alexandria endured many ups and downs. Naval battles continued to rage throughout the 1040s and even worsened. Around 1045, Alexandria endured a double siege: the famous pirate Jabāra b. Mukhtār, who was also Amir of Barqa, together with his partner, Ibn Abī Yadū, surrounded the city and laid siege to it by land, while war ships attacked from the sea. A detailed description of this double siege, found in no other historiographical source, is provided by Nahray b. Nissim in a letter to Yeshūʿā b. Ismāʿīl al-Makhmūrī,[56] and by Mūsā b. Abī al-Ḥayy Khalīla in two letters to his trading partners, members of the Ṭāhertī family, in which he describes the horrors of the times from the perspective of a stranger, helplessly trapped in the city:

> We are stuck here, trembling in constant terror. For five days in a row I have not dared to step out [of the house] so fearful am I, because at the bazaar all who approach ask for bribes and other things too. May the Lord on high rescue us by His might. I fear that if the situation goes on in this way no one will be able to leave this year. By God, I regret that I spent the winter here, but there is nothing to be done about it. If travel were possible, by God I would not stay.[57]

53 TS 8 J 14r, ll. 15–17: Gil, *Kingdom*, no.186.
54 TS 20.28r, ll. 49–50.
55 TS 13 J 18.27, in the upper margins, partially translated by Goitein, *Society*, 3: 34.
56 TS 13 J 19.27v, ll. 5–7: Gil, *Kingdom*, no. 240; Ben-Sasson, *The Jews of Sicily*, no. 84. See also above, n. 11.
57 Bodl MS Heb c 28.34r, ll. 12–17: Gil, *Kingdom*, no. 458.

And in another letter he writes: “And I, by God, am unable to [...]. One day’s fear is more than enough for five. And in my heart, because of this, a fire burns.”[58]

A further indication is found in a letter from Joseph b. Shemaryah, the rabbinic judge, who writes in this period from Alexandria to Nahray b. Nissim in Fustat: “Later on we were beset by the same sorts of troubles and I was unable to set sail.”[59]

Hardships such as these were probably compounded by disease and plague, judging from the many contemporaneous notices of untimely deaths. One striking case disputed in the court of Alexandria in 1042 involved two sisters who had died prematurely and whose widowers contended their rights to marry the surviving youngest sister, though she was still underage.[60]

(d) Relief in the Wake of Distress (1050–1070)

In the year 1051 a particularly violent insurrection occurred in Alexandria. Members of the Banū Qurra tribe, who were originally from the al-Buḥayra region in the Nile Delta, but had settled in one of the new neighborhoods of Alexandria during the Muslim conquest, began to riot everywhere and briefly held the city. The vizier al-Yazūrī, [61] who came to power during this period, expelled them from the city and in their place, settled Banū Sunbās tribesmen from the town of Dārūm who had proven their loyalty to the Fatimids.[62]

Quite possibly it was al-Yazūrī’s hard-handed tactics that stopped the turmoil. In any event, reports from the early 1050s depict a bustling international city. Jacob b. Salmān wrote from Alexandria during this period to his sister in Qairawan, “There is much prosperity in the city.” Makhlūf b. Mūsā,[63] a Maghribi merchant who arrived in Alexandria tells in a letter about the intensive trade that

---

58 TS 12.402r, right hand margin Gil, *Kingdom*, no. 461.

59 ENA 2805.9r, ll. 6–7: Gil, *Kingdom*, no.733.

60 TS 13 J 8.31: Miriam Frenkel, *“The Compassionate and Benevolent”: The Leading Elite in the Jewish Community of Alexandria in the Middle Ages* (Jerusalem: Ben-Zvi Institute, 2006), no. 60 [Hebrew].

61 For the biography of Abū Muḥammad al-Ḥasan b. ʿAlī ʿAbd al-Raḥmān al-Yazūrī (vizier 1050–1058), see Leila S. Al-Imad, *The Fatimid Vizierate 969–1172* (Berlin: K. Schwarz, 1990), 181–183, and also Gil, *Kingdom*, 1: 333–334. For a comprehensive review of his regime and policies, see Hatim Mahamid, “The Fatimid Government from al-Mustanṣir to Ṣalāḥ al-Dīn 1036–1171” (M.A thesis, University of Haifa, 1988), 19–24 [Hebrew].

62 Taqī al-Dīn al-Maqrīzī, *al-Bayān wal-iʿrāb ʿammā nazala fī miṣr min al-aʿrāb* (Cairo: [n.p.], 1334/1916), 8–9.

63 ENA 2738.34v, ll. 19–29.

went on there: “As soon as I arrived in Alexandria, I took out the wares I had received from a Maghribi merchant in the service of others, not for profit, and I had not a moment’s rest.”[64] And the trade minister of Alexandria, Ibrāhīm b. Farāḥ, enthusiastically reports four new ships in the dockyard, “No finer ships than the four built this year in Alexandria.”[65] Joseph b. Yeshūʿā adds these details: “There have been numerous vessels in Alexandria this year and as many as 5,000 cargo-bearing ships have sailed from the port. Numerous indeed! Some of them are being repaired. Repairs on three of the ships have now been completed.”[66]

(e) Essential Features of Economic Growth (1050–1070)

Prosperity in Alexandria during this period was chiefly due to its far-reaching cosmopolitan trade network. Aside from the above-mentioned Maghribis, there was a considerable presence of European merchants in the port, who were organized in distinct professional groups. Thus, for example, Makhlūf b. Mūsā b. al-Yatīm writes in a contemporary letter that his son was forced to flee European wine merchants at the port of Alexandria to whom he had accrued a great many debts. These same merchants finally managed to lay hands on the father and bring him to trial before the qadi.[67]

Naval battles did not seem to hinder the city’s bustling economy. In 1052, warships entered the port of Alexandria and attacked merchant vessels anchored there, as described by Jacob b. Salmān al-Ḥarīrī, a merchant who was present at

---

64 TS 13 J 22.32r, ll. 4–7. The writer is referring here to informal commitments, a commercial partnership of the *muʿāmala* sort based on the trading of commercial benefits and various services among friends belonging to a social-commercial group. See Goitein, *Society*, 1: 164–179. The many services the writer was asked to perform for his Maghribi merchant friends in Alexandria attest to the lively trade between these two major commercial centers.

65 TS 13 J 22.32r, ll. 15–16: Gil, *Kingdom*, no. 543. And see also what al-Maqrīzī writes about the Fatimid dockyard (*dār al-ṣināʿa*) of Alexandria: Taqī al-Dīn al-Maqrīzī, *Kitāb al-mawāʿiẓ wal-iʿtibār fī dhikr al-khiṭaṭ wal-āthār*, 3 vols. (Beirut: Maktabat Iḥyāʾ ʿUlūm al-Dīn, 1959), 2: 377.

66 Moss. V 369 (=L52) r, ll. 8–9: Gil, *Kingdom*, no. 187.

67 TS 24.78r, in the margins. The wine merchants in this document are called “al-Rūm,” a generic term that made no distinction at that time between Christians from western Europe and Byzantine Christians, although it was at this precise time that Italian merchants and their ships were beginning to encroach upon Mediterranean trade in agricultural products like wine and cheese, increasing the likelihood that the reference here is to European merchants, most likely Italian rather than Byzantine. See David Jacoby, “Byzantine Trade with Egypt from the Mid-Tenth Century to the Fourth Crusade,” *Thesaurismata* 30 (2000): 27–28, 43–52, 35–46; Goitein, *Society*, 5: 43.

the scene: “Ten warships sailed into the port, each bearing a hundred troops ... And some say it was a fleet two hundred vessels strong ... firing upon all ships moored there.”[68]

Far from hindering trade, warfare seems to have enhanced and stimulated it. The presence of diverse troops in the city was a boost to the sale of goods, as the city's merchants clearly grasped. “The market has revived with the coming of the soldiers,” writes Faraḥ b. Joseph of Alexandria in the year 1056, [69] and the arrival of Bedouin troops saved the day for the pistachio trade from Aleppo, as Ismāʿīl b. Faraḥ testifies in a letter from Alexandria in the same year: “The ‘Ḥalabi’ (Aleppan pistachio nuts) is much in demand here among the Bedouins. Some of them, in the service of your lord (the vizier), long may he reign, have ventured as far as al-Buḥayra.”[70] And in a letter from the end of the same year he elaborates, “The ‘Ḥalabi’ sells quite well. What used to go for thirty-five now goes for thirty-eight.”[71]

Researchers tended to attribute the thriving economy of the Fatimid era to its liberal, laissez-faire policy,[72] but upon closer examination it becomes apparent that trade restrictions were heavy enough to burden merchants and impede their commercial dealings. A closer look at the letters of Alexandrian shippers from this era of impressive prosperity, 1050 – 1070, reveals such vigorous and oppressive interference on the part of the regime that merchants were forced to seek alternate trade routes. A case in point is the letter Ismāʿīl b. Faraḥ sent from Alexandria in 1056. After his signature he writes: “There is a shortage of water and foodstuffs are all but sold out, wheat goes for 3 gold in secret.”[73] The inculcation of Hebrew words, such as water (*māyīm*), wheat (*ḥiṭṭim*), and gold dinars (*zahōv*), in this Judaeo-Arabic message indicates that the authorities were scru-

68 TS 8 J 24.21r, ll. 6 – 7: Gil, *Kingdom*, no. 662; Ben-Sasson, *The Jews of Sicily*, no. 119; S. D. Goitein, *Letters of Medieval Jewish Traders* (Princeton NJ: Princeton University Press, 1973), no. 322.
69 TS 8 J 21. 17r, ll. 23 – 24: Gil, *Kingdom*, no. 518.
70 TS 13 J 16.19v, upper margin: Gil, *Kingdom*, no. 493; Ben-Sasson, *The Jews of Sicily*, no. 109. About Bedouin brigades under the Fatimids, see Yusuf. F. Hasan, *The Arabs in Sudan* (Edinburgh: Edinburgh University Press, 1967), 94 – 95.
71 TS 8 J 20.2r, l. 10: Gil, *Kingdom*, no. 494; Ben-Sasson, *The Jews of Sicily*, no. 108.
72 Goitein, *Society*, 1: 29 – 33; Eliyahu Ashtor, *A Social and Economic History of the Near East in the Middle Ages* (Berkeley: University of California Press, 1976); Abraham L. Udovitch, “Merchants and Amirs: Government and Trade in Eleventh Century Egypt,” *Asian and African Studies* 24 (1988): 53 – 72,; Susan Staffa, *Conquest and Fusion: The Social Evolution of Cairo 642 – 1850 AD* (Leiden: Brill, 1977), 61. But see lately Jessica Goldberg, *Trade and Institutions in the Medieval Mediterranean: The Geniza Merchants and their Business World* (Cambridge: Cambridge University Press, 2012), 164 – 179.
73 TS 13 J 16.19r, l. 28: Gil, *Kingdom*, no. 493; Ben-Sasson, *The Jews of Sicily*, no. 109.

tinizing commercial correspondence while the existence of a secret trade in wheat shows that there were heavy restrictions in place.[74]

However, such restrictions were generally applied in a private, informal manner by local officials with their own vested interests. The anonymous Amir of Alexandria in 1057 was a ship owner and merchant in his own right who carried out extensive trade with Jews.[75] This governor exploited his authority, inspecting the correspondence of Jewish merchants, as we see in a letter dated that year by Mūsā b. Abī al-Ḥayy Khalīla: "I entrusted a letter to the mail carrier as he was setting off but the Amir confiscated it, may God grant him good fortune."[76] When a convoy of seven merchant ships was forced to return from the port of Ra'́s al-Kanā'is, west of Egypt, to the port of Alexandria on account of a Byzantine naval attack, the Amir coerced all merchants to unload their cargos under penalty of arrest: "My lord the Amir tricked them into discharging their freight. Having already discharged part of it yesterday and today, they are now being tricked into discharging all that remains."[77]

Whether the Amir confiscated the unloaded cargo or doubled the duties to be paid on it, he aimed at exploiting his official position to the full and tyrannizing the merchants.[78] Thus, it would be difficult to attribute the economic boom in

---

74 About the Fatimids' systematic scrutiny of trade in wheat, see also Boaz Shoshan, "Fatimid Grain Policy and the Post of Muḥtasib," *IJMES* 13 (1981): 181–189; idem, "Grain Riots and the 'Moral Economy': Cairo 1350–1517," *Journal of Interdisciplinary History* 10 (1980): 459–478; Thierry Bianquis, "Une crise frumentaire dans l'Egypt fatimide," *JESHO* 23 (1980): 67–101; Lev, *State and Society*, 162–178. Disagreements among scholars over the motives behind Fatimid policies notwithstanding, the matter of the regime's militant intervention in trade is indisputable.

75 TS 8 J 27.2r, ll. 6–7: Gil, *Kingdom*, no. 447, which indicate that the governor was the owner of at least two large ships of the *qunbār* and *qārib* types used by Jewish merchants. For these terms see Goitein, *Society*, 1: 305–306. Copious material about his extensive commercial involvements, particularly with Jews, can be found in the archives of Nahray b. Nissim, and see Udovitch, "Merchants and Amirs," 61–65.

76 TS 8 J 27.2r, l. 2: Gil, *Kingdom*, no. 447.

77 ULC Or 1080 J 167r, ll. 10–11: Gil, *Kingdom*, no. 447. The term *tarsīm* used in these sentences means, in this context, warrants which officials were entitled to issue and in the course of which prisoners were required to pay the fees of the guards posted outside their doors under the warrant until the bill was paid in full. See Goitein, *Society*, 2: 371–372.

78 For more about the conflation of official roles and personal interests, see Udovitch, "Merchants and Amirs." Udovitch calls attention to this phenomenon but reaches the opposite conclusion: To his mind, it was the blurring of boundaries between the official and private realms that created an overlap between official mercantile activities and those of individual shippers and led to the laissez-faire policy of the Fatimids and their minimal involvement in trade. Jessica Goldberg, on the other hand, complicates the "free trade" zone theory, advanced by Goitein and Udovitch, and asserts that the Genizah merchants had to negotiate with two separate channels

Alexandria at this time, at least on a local level, to a consistent policy of laissez-faire on the part of the Fatimid regime. Moreover, prosperity was not sustained over a long period but occurred in short bursts interspersed with long periods of economic decline and depression.

Only one month after Faraḥ b. Joseph's optimistic letter informing Khalaf b. Sahl about the lively trade in Alexandria, he writes another with an altogether different view of the city's circumstances: "If you heard what state the merchants are in [...] Abū Saʿīd [Tāhertī] has sworn to his father that they are out of coin and all is lost. They know not where it went and whither they will go. Whatever leaves his gates, no matter the destination, perishes and is consumed. And if he stays at home he will starve to death."[79] Indeed, the great famine which hit Alexandria in 1056 left its indelible mark in many of the Genizah letters: "The city is in an abysmal state of depression. Bread is purchased in fear and trembling 'with swords and compassion'";[80] "the situation is critical, the roads are in disrepair [...] and nothing sells for more than food";[81] "starvation has taken hold [of the city]";[82] "the markets are paralyzed [...] There is nothing to buy here."[83] These swift changes in fortune and unstable market conditions made life in Alexandria chronically uncertain, as eloquently summed up by Ismāʿīl b. Faraḥ writing from Alexandria at the height of the crisis in 1056: "Don't be sad, God will bring relief. Only last year a person had to sell himself to buy anything and now it is somewhat [easier]. All the same no one knows what fate will bring in this place."[84]

(f) The Era of Anarchy (1070 – 1094)

By 1068, Alexandria had turned into a battlefield between black slaves, supporters of the Caliph al-Mustanṣir's mother, and the Turkish mercenaries gathered around the rebel Nāṣir al-Dawla Ibn Ḥamdān. The black soldiers took shelter be-

of power: governmental offices and patronage networks of courtiers. These could either promote the trade, or place burdens on the merchants or even create hazards for them. See Goldberg, *Trade*, 164 – 184.

79 TS 10 J15.15r, ll. 2 – 5: Gil, *Kingdom*, no.495. This letter was written in November 1056, just a month after the previous letter.

80 TS 10 J 20.10v, l. 11: Gil, *Kingdom*, no.491.

81 TS 8 J 20.2r, l.2; v., l. 2: Gil, *Kingdom*, no. 494; Ben-Sasson, *The Jews of Sicily*, no. 108.

82 TS 13 J 16.19, right margin, l. 2: Gil, *Kingdom*, no.493; Ben-Sasson, *The Jews of Sicily*, no. 109.

83 ENA 1822 A.47, ll. 6 – 7, 22 – 23.

84 TS 10 J 15.15, in the margins: Gil, *Kingdom*, no. 495.

hind the city walls; Ibn Ḥamdān and his army attacked, and eventually the black soldiers surrendered and were driven out by Ibn Ḥamdān who installed his Turkish supporters in their place. Even after 1070 and his defeat in Cairo at the hands of Ildegüz Asad al-Dawla, commander of the Turkish mercenary supporters of al-Mustanṣir, Ibn Ḥamdān found refuge in Alexandria. Conceivably there were Jews as well among Ibn Ḥamdān's supporters, at least those members of the merchant elite with whom he shared commercial ties and who often hired his ships to transport their goods.[85]

These events were accompanied by anarchy and vandalism which reached their peak with the pillaging of the great Fatimid royal library in Alexandria. Muslim sources relate that Lawāta Berbers who had allied themselves with Ibn Ḥamdān's army used the leather bindings of the books to repair their shoes and burned the paper.[86] For a long period of time, Alexandria and the entire coastal region formed a distinct autonomous entity, independent of the Fatimid domain and allied to the rival Abbasid Empire. The cancellation of weekly sermons in the name of the Caliph al-Mustanṣir and the delivery of black clothing and flags, symbols of the Abbasid Caliphate, to the city at the behest of Ibn Ḥamdān, are expressions of this.[87] The climate of insecurity throughout this period was reflected in numerous acts of looting by civilians during the heavy famines that cost so many lives in Alexandria. A vivid description of this state of chaos is given by the Muslim historian al-Maqrīzī: "And the mounting lawlessness and destruction in the city and the growing famine were such that people began to eat corpses and carcasses and ambush wayfarers in order to rob them, these and further terrors came in the wake of the wars and rebellions that have taken so many lives, only the Creator can count them."[88]

In 1070, Ibn Ḥamdān was murdered by Asad al-Dawla, the general of the Turkish forces who proceeded to subdue Alexandria and other regions previously ruled by Ibn Ḥamdān. Asad al-Dawla's ruthless exercise of power in Alexandria is described in Genizah letters from this period. Mevorakh b. Isaac writes

85 TS 13 J 26.8r, l. 17: Gil, *Kingdom*, no. 556; Ben-Sasson, *The Jews of Sicily*, no. 120.

86 al-Maqrīzī, *Khiṭaṭ*, 2: 53; idem, *Itti'āẓ al-ḥunafā' bi-akhbār al-ā'imma al-fāṭimiyyīn al-khulafā'* (Cairo: al-Majlis al-A'lā lil-Shu'ūn al-Islamiyya, 1967), 2: 294 ff. The Lawāta were a nomadic tribe who inhabited the western reaches of the Delta and the region of Libya. Maqrīzī recounts that the vast number of books they burned left enormous piles of ashes, the so-called "mounds of book" (*ṭalāl al-kutub*) in the Abiār region of the Delta. Some of the books found their way to different cities.

87 al-Maqrīzī, *Khiṭaṭ*, 2: 129; idem, *Itti'āẓ*, 106.

88 al-Maqrīzī, *Khiṭaṭ*, 2: 101.

from Alexandria in 1071 about the steep price of bread, the scarcity of clothing, and in summary: "There is no comfort in Alexandria."[89]

It was only in 1073 that al-Mustanṣir turned to Badr al-Jamālī, a manumitted Armenian slave, for help, and the latter vanquished Asad al-Dawla and his forces and returned the throne to al-Mustanṣir.[90] Badr al-Jamālī laid siege to Alexandria and managed to conquer it after a series of difficult battles. Muslim sources note that Badr al-Jamālī killed thousands of rebels in Alexandria after the conquest but did no harm to the townspeople themselves.[91]

Once he had overthrown Asad al-Dawla's regime, Badr al-Jamālī appointed the qadi Ibn al-Muḥayraq governor of Alexandria. However, the latter too revolted as head of an assembly of religious eminences and other local worthies. This time Badr al-Jamālī suppressed the insurrection at the start, arrested its leaders and even succeeded in seizing much property from them.[92] He appointed his eldest son, al-Awḥad Abū al-Ḥasan ʿAlī Muẓaffar al-Dawla, in Qadi Ibn al-Muḥayraq's place. The civil commotion of those years was accompanied by severe drought and economic instability, reflected in frequent changes of coinage.[93]

Nor did the subsequent appointment of al-Awḥad prevent further rebellion. In 1080 al-Awḥad led the Bedouin battalions against his father. The peace delegation Badr al-Jamālī sent to his son in an effort to stay the uprising proved of no avail and in the end Badr al-Jamālī sent an army to lay siege to the city. The month-long siege was exceedingly harsh and left its marks in many Genizah letters, including this one, written from Alexandria in 1080 by Solomon b. Nissim: "We have neither physicians nor medicines here nor anything else that might fortify the soul. I shall pray to God for deliverance."[94] Ḥayyim b. Eli ha-Kohen writes that same year: "It is impossible to send goods because our fellow merchants are unwilling to transport anything overland and there is little hope of receiving goods by sea, so I believe."[95] And Nathan b. Nahray reports likewise that "the city is paralyzed. There is no barter or trade anywhere here..."[96]

---

89 ULC Or 1080 J 264: Frenkel, *"The Compassionate and Benevolent"* [Hebrew], no. 100.

90 About Badr al-Jamālī (vizier 1073–1095), see Al-Imad, *The Fatimid Vizierate*, 96–109; Mahamid, "The Fatimid Government," 31–38; Cohen, *Jewish Self-Government*, 61–65 and esp. n. 45 for an extended bibliography about the man and his activities.

91 al-Maqrīzī, *Ittiʿāẓ*, 107.

92 Ibn Taghrībirdī, *Nujūm*, 5: 101.

93 TS Misc 25.70v, ll. 1–2: Gil, *Kingdom*, no. 472: "They experienced drought and the coins were changed twice." So writes Abraham b. Abī al-Ḥayy Khalīla to his brother Mūsā from Alexandria in the year 1075.

94 ENA 2747.10r, ll. 14–15: Gil, *Kingdom*, no. 646.

95 TS 13 J 16.2r, ll. 1–3: Gil, *Kingdom*, no. 792.

96 TS 1.610r, l. 21: Gil, *Kingdom*, no. 440.

Ultimately, the people of Alexandria surrendered and opened the city gates for Badr al-Jamālī. Al-Awḥad[97] was arrested and his abettors were fined. Muslim sources note that "Muslims and Copts alike" were subject to these fines,[98] and presumably Jews as well. Badr al-Jamālī used this money to restore the city's al-ʿAṭṭārīn mosque.[99] The reference to the Coptic share in the fine and its use in the restoration of the mosque underscores the Islamic character of Alexandria, and provides reasonable grounds for assumption that the city's protected minorities, Christians and Jews, had played a prominent role in the revolt.

After the death of Caliph al-Mustanṣir (1096), the rival pretenders to the throne, his son Nizār and the son of Badr al-Jamālī, al-Afḍal, abandoned their vicious struggle, known in later Muslim historiography as the "*nawba* (tragedy) of Alexandria,"[100] during which the city became a battlefield.[101] Nizār sought refuge there and Nāṣir al-Dawla Alptakīn, governor of Alexandria at the time; qadi Jalāl al-Dawla ʿAlī b. Muḥammad Ibn ʿAmmār; and the city's populace, all vowed allegiance to him. Thus, surrounded by loyal supporters, Nizār was invested as caliph with Fatimid pomp and ceremony.[102] Al-Afḍal aligned his troops against him, and went to war. The first battle ended in a crushing defeat for al-Afḍal and he was forced to retreat to Cairo. Nizār then expanded his domain over the entire coastal region with the support of Bedouin tribes from around Alexandria. Then, one year later, al-Afḍal struck again, laying siege to Alexandria and destroying its walls. This siege too left a mark in the Genizah letters: "Tradesmen all despair of me on account of the deadly pestilence and the siege," writes an anonymous merchant from Alexandria in 1094; he also complains about the "war taxes" he and his comrades were obliged to pay.[103] Ultimately, Nizār was forced to surrender and al-Afḍal conquered the city and put his opponents to death.[104]

97 Ibn Taghrībirdī, *Nujūm*, 5: 101, 119; al-Maqrīzī, *Ittiʿāẓ*, 2: 109; Jalāl al-Dīn al-Suyūṭī, *Ḥusn al-muḥāḍara fī akhbār miṣr wal-qāhira* (Cairo: IFAO, 1321/1924–5), 2: 131.
98 Ibid.
99 al-Maqrīzī, *Khiṭaṭ*, 2: 209. See also Sālim, *Ta'rīkh madīnat al-iskandariyya*, 191, who notes that a plaque inscribed with the date of the mosque's restoration remains in the mosque to this day.
100 Amīn al-Dīn ʿAlī Ibn al-Ṣayrafī, *al-Ishāra ilā man nāla al-wizāra* (Cairo: IFAO, 1923), 59.
101 On this struggle see al-Maqrīzī, *Khiṭaṭ*, 2: 276; Muḥammad b. ʿAlī Ibn Muyassar, *Akhbār miṣr*, ed. Henri Massé (Cairo: IFAO, 1919), 70; al-Maqrīzī, *Ittiʿāẓ*, 3: 27, 85; Mahamid, "The Fatimid Government," 40–42.
102 al-Maqrīzī, *Ittiʿāẓ*, 3: 13; al-Maqrīzī, *Khiṭaṭ*, 2: 154. About Fatimid ceremonial see Paula Sanders, *Ritual, Politics and the City in Fatimid Cairo* (Albany, NY: SUNY Press, 1994), 23–32; on the parasol, see ibid., 25–26.
103 TS 12.693r, ll. 9–10, 13–14: Frenkel, "*The Compassionate and Benevolent*" [Hebrew], no. 25.
104 About these events see al-Maqrīzī, *Ittiʿāẓ*, 3: 111–112.

These dramatic events are documented by a pilgrim from the Maghreb detained there for a long while due to the Crusader conquest of Jerusalem. In a letter he describes the difficulties he faced before the conquest of the city by al-Afḍal: "You know, sir, what we have been through these past five years; four years in a row pestilence and disease have raged, pauperizing men of property and killing vast numbers; entire families have succumbed to the plague."[105]

About the conquest of the city by al-Afḍal he writes:

> And I returned to Alexandria; we were under siege several times and the city was in ruins[...] and the uprisings; but all's well now. The Sultan [al-Afḍal], may Allāh make him great and victorious, has conquered it and meted out justice of a kind never witnessed before in the reign of any king throughout the world, for he levied not a single dirham from anyone.[106]

(g) The Reign of Al-Afḍal (1094–1143)

The stability of al-Afḍal's reign improved the lives of Alexandrian Jews. This is perhaps ascribable to the friendship between al-Afḍal and Mevorakh b. Saʿadyah who was named Nagid of the Jews of Egypt,[107] and to Mevorakh's close ties with the community of Alexandria, where he found refuge after being relegated from his position in Fustat.[108] Al-Afḍal bolstered the Jewish courts in Alexandria.[109] Members of the newly chosen local administration maintained particularly good relations with the Jewish community. In place of the qadi Ibn ʿAmmār, who had been a supporter of Nizār, al-Afḍal appointed Abū al-Ḥasan Aḥmad b. al-Ḥasan Ibn Ḥadīd, better known as Makīn al-Dawla. Ibn Ḥadīd was the first in a dynasty of qadis who served as judges and filled various other kinds

105 Bodl MS Heb b 11.7, ll. 38–42: Moshe Gil, *Palestine during the First Muslim Period (634–1099)* (Tel Aviv: Tel Aviv University and the Ministry of Defense Publishing House, 1983) [Hebrew], no. 575.

106 Ibid., ll. 18–22. This comment concerning al-Afḍal's leniency with respect to taxation probably refers to the heavy "war taxes" the city's inhabitants paid under Nizār; see n. 78. The affixed title "Sultan" to al-Afḍal's name is not unusual: the title was used to designate members of the administration far lower in rank than vizier. See for instance TS 20.177, ll. 11–12: Frenkel, *"The Compassionate and Benevolent"* [Hebrew], no. 37, where the local governor of Alexandria, Fakhr al-Mulk, was given the title "Sultan." On the loose sense of the term during the Ayyubid dynasty, see Humphries, *From Saladin to the Mongols*, appendix A, 365.

107 Concerning these ties, see Cohen, *Jewish Self Government*, 219–221.

108 Ibid., 214–217

109 TS 18 J 4.6: Frenkel, *"The Compassionate and Benevolent"* [Hebrew], no. 84.

of civil roles in Alexandria under the title Makīn al-Dawla.[110] This qadi, who was the undisputed ruler of the city,[111] bestowed protection[112] on the Jews of Alexandria and even intervened on their behalf in a number of situations. Thus, for instance, Nagid Mevorakh's representative in Alexandria remarks that "the judge offered counsel" to the Jews of the community and mediated between them and the clerk in charge of the poll tax.[113] The poll tax imposed by Makīn al-Dawla was so low that Jews still considered his rates exemplary many years later.[114] And when the community elder was slandered, the qadi himself interrogated witnesses in a way that generally favored the accused and opposed the religious sages who wished to convict the Jewish elder.[115]

The new governor appointed by al-Afḍal, Amir Fakhr al-Mulk, likewise maintained exceptionally cordial relations with the Jewish inhabitants of Alexandria. When he entered the city he was welcomed by a ceremonial delegation of them, and he promised to protect them and even hailed the Nagid Mevorakh in a festive address "before the nations of the world" which was understood by the people as "praise for Israel."[116] Evidently Fakhr al-Mulk fulfilled the hopes placed in him by the Jewish community. Throughout his rule he kept up a close correspondence with Mevorakh the Nagid and when asked, never refused to intercede on behalf of the Jewish community.[117]

Nevertheless, the Genizah documents reveal grave economic hardships and issues of security during al-Afḍal's reign, which lasted till the death of the Caliph al-Ḥāfiẓ in 1143. In a letter to Āraḥ b. Nathan, sent from Alexandria towards the end of the eleventh century, the addressee is requested to hurry up and send all the wheat in his possession because conditions are so dreadful no one can earn

110 This qadi belonged to the Banū Ḥadīd family, a Mālikī family from Toledo, Spain, who had settled in Alexandria during the second half of the eleventh century, and whose members rose to prominence especially during the second half of the twelfth century. See S. Abd al-Aziz Salem, "D'Alexandrie à Almeria. Les Banu Khulayf : Une famille alexandrine au Moyen Age," *Revue de l'Occident Musulman et de la Mediterranée* 46 (1987): 64–70.

111 He served as overseer of finances (*nāẓir al-amwāl*) and amassed an incredible fortune.

112 TS 13 J 22.23: Frenkel, *"The Compassionate and Benevolent"* [Hebrew], no. 73. The term for protection is *murāʿa*.

113 TS 20.177: Frenkel, *"The Compassionate and Benevolent"* [Hebrew], no. 37.

114 ULC Or 1080 J 258: Frenkel, *"The Compassionate and Benevolent"* [Hebrew], no. 99. In 1141 Rayḥān, the vizier's slave, promised to procure a royal edict for the Jews ensuring that the *jizya* tax would not deviate from the rate fixed by al-Makīn.

115 TS 13 J 13,24: Frenkel, *"The Compassionate and Benevolent"* [Hebrew], no .61.

116 TS 20.177: Frenkel, *"The Compassionate and Benevolent"* [Hebrew], no. 37; TS 24.21: Frenkel, *"The Compassionate and Benevolent"* [Hebrew], no. 38.

117 TS NS J 24: Frenkel, *"The Compassionate and Benevolent"* [Hebrew], no. 88. Ibid., his intervention to free Jewish prisoners without a fine.

a living.[118] Another letter from that period describes the total suspension of trade in the city.[119] Samuel b. R. Judah ha-Bavli requests that the books he has ordered be sent to him directly to Alexandria in order to avoid the perils of the road.[120]

Similarly, beginning in the third decade of the twelfth century, reports of disease and plague[121] as well as exorbitant prices, riots and anarchy began to circulate.[122] In a letter from 1137, Abū Naṣr b. Abraham describes the utter exhaustion suffered by so many of the city's inhabitants due to the prolonged and intensifying hardships: "As for the situation here, I pray to God that He will unburden us soon because this has been going on for too long and the people are worn out."[123]

(h) Days of Hatred (*sin'ūt*) (1140 – 1150)

The early 1140s saw a new governor appointed in Alexandria,[124] this time a merchant who used his position unrestrainedly to confiscate the goods of Jewish traders.[125] Moreover, his rule coincided with such violent outbreaks of anti-Jewish hatred that dignitaries from Alexandria beseeched the court Jews of Cairo to solicit government help in halting the riots.[126] The riots of Alexandria apparently ensued from the general mood of anarchy as described by Abū Naṣr in his letter:

---

118 TS 13 J 19.4: Frenkel, *"The Compassionate and Benevolent"* [Hebrew], no. 68.

119 ENA NS 2.1.6: Frenkel, *"The Compassionate and Benevolent"* [Hebrew], no. 14.

120 TS 13 J 11.8: Shelomo D. Goitein, "Early Testimonies from the Geniza about the Jewish Community of Salonica," *Sefunot* 11 (1971 – 1978) = *The Book of Greek Jewry*, 1: 11 – 13.

121 Bodl MS Heb b 13.52 (2834). Nathan b. Judah writes from Alexandria to the brothers Bnei Ẓemaḥ concerning the dire plague (*wakhām*) then raging.

122 Bodl MS Heb c 28.31r, ll. 8 – 9: Frenkel, *"The Compassionate and Benevolent"* [Hebrew], no. 2. See also ENA 2806.14, a small fragment of a legal document from Alexandria, dated 1135 where the following is written between the lines: "and times are tough"; and also ENA NS 21.14: Frenkel, *"The Compassionate and Benevolent"* [Hebrew], no. 17, in which Ḥalfon b. Nethanel complains in 1137 about the interminable hardships.

123 ENA NS 21.14v, ll. 11 – 12: Frenkel, *"The Compassionate and Benevolent"* [Hebrew], no. 17.

124 TS 12.290: Frenkel, *"The Compassionate and Benevolent"* [Hebrew], no. 22. Abū Naṣr b. Abraham wants to deliver a letter of recommendation to the governor (*wālī*) of Alexandria, "the old one if he is still there, or perhaps the new *wālī*."

125 TS 13 J 15.20.

126 TS 12.290: Frenkel, *"The Compassionate and Benevolent"* [Hebrew], no. 22. Abū Naṣr b. Abraham asks Moses b. Japheth ha-Levi Sanī al-Dawla to write a letter to the qadi Ibn ʿAwf, asking him to put a stop to the *sin'ūt*. About this term, see Goitein, *Society*, 2: 277 – 279.

"The situation here is disgraceful, the mob attacks decent people and any tot sticks his tongue out and curses."[127]

A conspicuous and powerful figure in those days was the Mālikī jurist (*faqīh*) Ibn ʿAwf, considered the greatest Islamic jurist of Alexandria alongside the *faqīh* al-Salafī.[128] This legal sage maintained commercial ties with Jewish merchants[129] but is nonetheless referred to in one of the Genizah documents as having "oppressed the Jewish community of Alexandria."[130]

Mounting religious jealousy is evinced in the case of Judah ha-Levi, the poet who stopped in Alexandria around that time on his pilgrimage to the Holy Land and found himself accused of religious incitement against Islam. Only his lofty status and the intercession of the community's *dayyan* (religious judge) on his behalf saved him from a trial and imprisonment. Prominent in the case were the *ṣāhib khabar*, chief of the secret police, and his emissaries (*rusūl*) who terrorized Judah ha-Levi and his attendants.[131] The center-stage position in the city now taken by public figures who had once played only minor roles in it,[132] is indicative of the social climate and growing mistrust towards religious minorities of Alexandria.

(i) The Twilight Era (1154–1171)

In its final years the Fatimid dynasty was ruled consecutively by three underage caliphs, al-Ẓāfir (1149–1150), al-Fā'iz (1154–1160) and al-ʿĀḍid. Fatimid rule as such no longer existed and amid the lingering power struggles between viziers and district governors, the Alexandrian rulers took an active role. For many

127 TS 12.290: Frenkel, *"The Compassionate and Benevolent"* [Hebrew], no. 22.
128 His full name was Abū Ṭāhir Ismāʿīl b. Makkī b. ʿĪsa Ibn ʿAwf al-Zuhrī al-Iskandarānī, and he boasted a glorious lineage going back to ʿAbd al-Raḥmān b. ʿAwf, one of the Prophet's companions. Al-ʿAwfiyya, the madrasa (religious house of study) that Ibn ʿAwf headed, was one of the first two Sunni madrasas founded in Egypt (in 1138). He died in 1188. See al-Suyūṭī, *Ḥusn al-muḥāḍara*, 1: 213–214; Lev, *Saladin*, 16–17.
129 TS 12.290r, l. 9: Frenkel, *"The Compassionate and Benevolent"* [Hebrew], no. 22.
130 Moss. A VII 154.2 (L222) v, ll. 3, 10: Frenkel, *"The Compassionate and Benevolent"* [Hebrew], no. 19. See also TS 16.272r, l. 30: Frenkel, *"The Compassionate and Benevolent"* [Hebrew], no. 30, where he is referred to as taking his place among the legal sages (*majlis fuqahā'*).
131 ULC Or 1080 J 258: Frenkel, *"The Compassionate and Benevolent"* [Hebrew], no. 99; TS 13 J 14.1: Frenkel, *"The Compassionate and Benevolent"* [Hebrew], no. 62.
132 See Yaacov Lev, "The Suppression of Crime, the Supervision of Markets, and Urban Society in the Egyptian Capital during the 10th and the 11th Centuries," *Mediterranean and Historical Review* 3 (1988): 77–79; Goitein, *Society*, 2: 371.

years Najm al-Dīn Ibn Maṣāl served as governor of Alexandria and the al- Buḥayra region.[133] With al-Ẓāfir's ascendence to the throne, Najm al-Dīn was appointed vizier and engaged in many harsh battles against his enemy Ibn Salār, who also served as governor of Alexandria and was an adherent of al-Ẓāfir's elder brother.[134] Nevertheless, during the 1150s Alexandria enjoyed a fairly stable and prosperous period. Japheth b. Shelah who arrived in the city from Sicily around this time writes his impressions of the new surroundings to the great merchant, Joseph ha-Kohen: "And the city is powerful, beautiful and blessed."[135]

Still, the endless battles eventually left their mark. Throughout al-Fāʾiz's caliphate, the *wālī*, Amir Ṭarkhān b. Salīf b. Ṭarīf and his brother Ismāʿīl waged a series of fierce wars against their rival, the vizier Ṭalāʾiʿ b. Ruzīk.[136] Eventually both were defeated and put to death. The clashes turned Alexandria into a ghost town, as described by someone newly arrived from Fustat: "When we reached the city a battle was raging between the two groups, members of the Lakhm tribe [the Arabs] and the black skins [the Ravens]. A hundred of them have already died. The governor has left the city which has been deserted, locked and bolted, the best of its stores all looted."[137]

During al-ʿĀḍid caliphate, Ḍirghām Ibn ʿĀmir, commander of the Maghreb forces, went to war with Shawār Ibn Mujīr.[138] At Shawār's request, Nūr al-Dīn Ibn Zangi, overlord of Aleppo and Damascus, sent auxiliary troops under the command of Asad al-Dīn Shīrkūh, thus defeating Ḍirghām and enabling Shawār to take office as vizier.[139] However, when Shawār ascended to the vizierate in 1164, he turned his back on Shīrkūh and banished him from Egypt. Shīrkūh re-

133 On Najm al-Dīn Muḥammad b. Maṣāl, a rich merchant from the city of Lukk, in the region of Libya, who was one of Najm al-Dīn's main supporters and was appointed vizier in 1149, see al-Maqrīzī, *Ittiʿāẓ*, 3: 11–12; al-Maqrīzī, *Khiṭaṭ*, 2: 154; Al-Imad, *The Fatimid Vizierate*, 193–194.

134 On ʿAlī b. al-Salār (vizier 1149–1153), see al-Maqrīzī, *Ittiʿāẓ*, 3: 196; Maqrīzī, *Khiṭaṭ*, 2: 339; Al-Imad, *The Fatimid Vizierate*, 194. For a detailed summary of the battles between the two, see Mahamid, "The Fatimid Government," 62–63.

135 TS 16.344.

136 Ṭalāʾiʿ b. Ruzīk served as vizier between 1156–1160. See ʿAlī b. Aḥmad Ibn al-Athīr, *al-Kāmil fī al-taʾrīkh* (Leiden: Brill, 1870), 9: 75; al-Maqrīzī, *Ittiʿāẓ*, 3: 257–258; Ibn Taghrībirdī, *Nujūm*, 5: 345; Al-Imad, *The Fatimid Vizierate*, 195.

137 TS 10 J 31.6.

138 On Shawār b. Mujīr al-Saʿdī (vizier 1162 and again 1164–1168), see Shams al-Dīn Ibn Khallikān, *Wafayāt al-aʿyān wa-anbāʾ abnāʾ al-zamān* (Beirut: Dār al-Thaqāfa, 1968), 2: 439–448; Al-Imad, *The Fatimid Vizierate*, 195.

139 Jamāl al-Dīn Muḥammad Ibn Wāṣil, *Mufarraj al-kurūb fī akhbār banī ayyūb* (Cairo: Maṭbaʿat Jāmiʿat Fuʾād al-Awwal, 1953), 1: 150–151; Shihāb al-Dīn Abū Shāma, *Kitāb al-rawḍatayn fī akhbār al-dawlatayn* (Cairo: Lajnat al-Taʾlīf wal-Tarjama wal-Nashr, 1956), 2: 364.

newed the war at full force and appealed for help to Amalric, Crusader King of Jerusalem, whose armies were amassed in Ashkelon. A huge battle ensued in 1167 between Shawār's forces on the one side, augmented by the Crusader army, and on the other side, the great Syrian army, led by Shīrkūh and a young commander named Ṣalāḥ-al-Dīn al-Ayyubī (Saladin). The heavy siege and the famine that ensued took a heavy toll and many people died or fled the city.

The government of Alexandria was unequivocal in its support. The *wālī*, Najm al-Dīn Ibn Maṣāl,[140] maintained close ties with Shīrkūh and even sent him a large supply of arms. The battle ended in victory for Shīrkūh, and Alexandria's leaders, including the *wālī* Najm al-Dīn Ibn Maṣāl, the qadi al-Ashraf Ibn al-Ḥabbāb and al-Rashīd b. al-Zubayr, threw open the city gates for Shīrkūh and even presented him with money and weapons.[141] Shīrkūh expressed appreciation by declaring that he would install himself in Alexandria and make it his capital, but fearful of a Crusader attack from the sea, he left and named Ṣalāḥ al-Dīn as his representative and second-in-command. The Crusader attack was not long to come. That very year the combined forces of Shawār and the Crusaders assailed the city and laid siege to it. The chronicler William of Tyre, later Archbishop of Tyre and chancellor of the Crusader Kingdom of Jerusalem,[142] describes the protracted battle and siege of Alexandria in great detail: The fleet blockaded the river and prevented supplies from reaching the city while the infantry destroyed the surrounding towns and villages to prevent help from reaching the besieged population. According to William of Tyre, the inhabitants themselves, skilled merchants not soldiers, tried to end the siege and its horrors:

> What is there to say? Every day more fighting, more sentry-guards slain at the city walls, incessant robberies, night terrors and most of all, a lack of provisions have brought the people to a point of despair. That is why they preferred to surrender the city and sell themselves into slavery than become victims of cruel starvation. There were whispers at first and then loud declarations that the strangers who had brought this terrible calamity upon them [Shīrkūh's men] should be expelled from the city and an agreement reached to remove the siege and allow the city to return to its past condition of freedom and honor.[143]

140 See above, n. 133.
141 Abū Shāma, *Kitāb al-rawḍatayn*, 2: 426–427.
142 For his biography, see William of Tyre, *A History of Deeds Done Beyond the Sea*, translated and annotated by Emily A. Babcock and August C. Krey (NY: Columbia University Press, 1943) 1: 3–49.
143 Ibid., 2: 338.

Muslim sources, on the other hand, present a different account. The Alexandrians, they say, fully supported Ṣalāḥ al-Dīn and fought side by side with his forces and only after Shawār bribed Shīrkūh did he return to Syria. Either way, Shawār's reconquest of Alexandria brought retribution against the old leaders and the selection of new ones.[144] In 1168, Amalric once more invaded Egypt. The Fatimid caliph appealed to Nūr al-Dīn for help this time, and the latter dispatched a large army under Shīrkūh to defeat the Crusaders. The victorious Shīrkūh remained in Egypt and was appointed vizier, only to die a few months later. He was replaced by the nephew who had fought at his side, Ṣalāḥ al-Dīn, who quickly gained support and influence. In a 1171 sermon delivered at the mosque in the name of the Abbasid caliph, the rival of the Fatimids, the new vizier gave voice to his hope of liberation. The death of Caliph al-ʿĀḍid, which occurred days later, marked the end of the Fatimid dynasty in Egypt and the beginning of a new era, and the reign of the Ayyubid dynasty, founded by Ṣalāḥ al-Dīn.[145]

The transition from the Fatimid to the Ayyubid era was fraught with confusion for the Jewish community of Alexandria.[146] Their sense of despair found expression in the contemporaneous writing of Manasseh the Alexandrian teacher: "The hardships of this time will not escape the notice of his Majesty, may his name be exalted."[147]

3 The Ayyubid Dynasty

The Ayyubid dynasty lasted a mere eighty years, yet it marked a turning point in Egyptian history. Egypt's position as an administrative center was reinstated after years of anarchy under the Fatimids. Moreover, the establishment of a Sunni dynasty and the restoration of orthodox Sunni Islam led to changes in the status of religious minorities.

---

144 Abū Shāma, *Kitāb al-rawḍatayn*, 2: 468; William of Tyre, *History*, 2: 342–343: William recounts that the sultan held a grand triumphal procession through the courts of the city, complete with orchestras and choruses, and that the citizens "trembled with fear." He exacted tribute and heavy taxes, meted out harsh punishments to some, gifts and rewards to others. The fines he imposed were so hefty that special clerks were appointed to claim them.
145 On the rise of Ṣalāḥ al-Dīn and his seizure of control over Egypt see Lev, *Saladin*, 53–107.
146 See Part II, Chapter 8.3: Conclusions.
147 TS 24.27v, l. 24: Frenkel, *"The Compassionate and Benevolent"* [Hebrew], no. 39.

(a) Years of Consolidation (1171–1175)

The early years of Ṣalāḥ al-Dīn's reign brought hardship to Alexandria. Time and again the Crusader armies attempted to bring down Egypt's new government, abetted by residual supporters of the Fatimids. In 1174, Alexandria was attacked by the army of William II, the Norman king of Sicily, in league with the city's Fatimid sympathizers and loyal Ismaʿīlī forces from Syria, according to Muslim sources. Ṣalāḥ al-Dīn uncovered the conspiracy and foiled it just in time. The Sicilian fleet, caught unawares, landed on the shores of Alexandria with a large force and launched a vigorous assault.[148] After a battle lasting five days, the fleet was defeated and returned to whence it came. Muslim sources emphasize the active role played in this by the Alexandrians themselves, who rallied to the side of Ṣalāḥ al-Dīn's army against the Christian invaders, but their inconsistent accounts of the number of Alexandrians killed in battle raise doubts as to their veracity.[149]

(b) The Reign of Ṣalāḥ Al-Dīn (1171–1193)

After the early years of consolidation, Egypt as a whole and Alexandria in particular enjoyed an extended period of economic prosperity.[150] Ṣalāḥ al-Dīn, who

---

148 Ibn Wāṣil, *Mufarraj al-kurūb*, 2: 12–13; Taqī al-Dīn al-Maqrīzī, *Kitāb al-sulūk li-maʿrifat duwal al-mulūk* (Cairo: Lajnat al-Ta'līf wal-Tarjama wal-Nashr, 1934), 1: 55–56; Ibn al-Athīr, *al-Kāmil fī al-ta'rīkh*, 1: 211, Abū Shāma, *Kitāb al-rawḍatayn*, 4: 164; William of Tyre, *History*, 2: 399. And for a more detailed account, see William of Tyre in Old French translation, *L'Estoire de Eracles empereur et la conquest de la Terre d'Outremer*, which is in fact the anonymous French source of the period. About this source, see John H. Pryor, "The *Eracles* and William of Tyre: An Interim Report," in *The Horns of Hattin*, ed. Benjamin Z. Kedar (Jerusalem: Ben Zvi Institute and Israel Exploration Society, 1992), 270–294. About the viewpoint of historians on Sicily under the Normans see David Abulafia, *Italy, Sicily, and the Mediterranean, 1100–1400* (London: Variorum, 1987), 45; Donald Matthew, *The Norman Kingdom of Sicily* (Cambridge: Cambridge University Press, 1992), 279; Lev, *Saladin*, 164–165, n. 14.
149 The figures vary between seven hundred killed and (according to Ibn Wāṣil, see *Mufarraj al-kurūb*, 2: 13) and seven (in the estimation of Abū Shāma, see *Kitāb al-rawḍatayn*, 2: 599). For further details: Lev, *Saladin*, 164–165, n. 14.
150 Andrew S. Ehrenkreutz, *Saladin* (Albany, NY: SUNY Press, 1972), 101–105, 168–169, 172; Jonathan Phillips, *The Life and Legend of the Sultan Saladin* (New Haven and London: Yale University Press, 2019); Anne-Marie Eddé and Jane Marie Todd, *Saladin* (Cambridge, MA: Belknap Press, 2011).

visited the city four times between 1175–1186,[151] strove to transform it into his main naval base in the campaigns against the Crusaders. On his first visit he gave an order to repair the city walls,[152] a project that was completed by the time of his second sojourn there in 1181,[153] during which he enjoined the rebuilding of the fleet and established a special bureau of naval affairs into which he poured tax revenues from extensive areas in Egypt.[154] Also associated with the reign of Ṣalāḥ al-Dīn is the recasting of the city in a Sunni-Muslim style. The surge of public building in Alexandria at this time was intended primarily for this purpose and most of the new buildings served as religious institutions, mosques, religious colleges (madrasa), lodging houses for travelers, bath houses and public hospitals for pilgrims and students from abroad.[155]

(c) Alexandria as a Sunni City

The city's reinforced Sunni-Muslim character had far-reaching consequences for relations between the Muslim authorities and Alexandria's religious minorities. The Fatimid rulers of Egypt, Isma'īlīs governing a Sunni majority, had seen fit to countenance religious pluralism and allow maximum autonomy to the various groups under their dominion,[156] whilst the Sunni regime that followed concerned

---

151 Claude Cahen, "La chronique des Ayyubides d'al-Makin b. al-Amid," *BEO* 15 (1955–57), 130.

152 Abū Shāma, *Kitāb al-rawḍatayn*, 2: 486; Ibn Wāṣil, *Mufarraj al-kurūb*, 1: 199; al-Maqrīzī, *Khiṭaṭ*, 2: 171.

153 'Imād al-Dīn Ibn Kathīr, *al-Bidāya wal-nihāya fī al-ta'rīkh* (Cairo: Maṭba'at al-Sa'āda, 1932), 12: 296; Ibn Wāṣil, *Mufarraj al-kurūb*, 2: 112; Abū Shāma, *Kitāb al-rawḍatayn*, 2: 289. A reference to these visits is likewise found in the Genizah. A letter by R. Eleazar refers twice to Ṣalāḥ al-Dīn's departure from the city as a significant date. See TS 16.272v, l. 18: Frenkel, *"The Compassionate and Benevolent"* [Hebrew], no. 30: *wa-lamā kharaja al-sulṭān* (and when the Sultan left), and ibid., line 26: *wa-ba'd maḍā al-sulṭān* (and after the sultan left).

154 See Lev, *Saladin*, 166–168; al-Maqrīzī, *Sulūk*, 1: 73.

155 al-Maqrīzī, *Sulūk*, 1: 76; al-Maqrīzī, *Khiṭaṭ*, 3: 169; Muḥammad b. al-Ḥusayn Ibn Jubayr al-Kinānī, *Riḥlat Ibn Jubayr* (Beirut: Dār Ṣādir, 1964), 42. See too Yehoshua Frenkel, "Political and Social Aspects of Islamic Endowments (*awqāf*): Saladin in Cairo (1169–73) and Jerusalem (1187–93)," *BSOAS* 62/2 (1999): 20–30.

156 See Goitein, *Society*, 1: 31; Samuel M. Stern, *Studies in Early Isma'ilism* (Leiden: Brill/Jerusalem: Magness Press, 1983), 85–95. On alternative explanations for the liberal attitude of the Fatimids towards other religions as issuing from the very nature of Ismā'īlī belief rather than from tactical-political motivations, see Azim A. Nanji, "Portraits of Self and Others: Isma'ili Perspectives on the History of Religions," in *Mediaeval Isma'ili History and Thought*, ed. Farhad Daftary (Cambridge: Cambridge University Press, 1996), 153–160; Farhad Daftary, *The Ismā'īlīs:*

itself with the internal affairs of all religious groups, including those of the Jewish community.[157] The new policy is sharply reflected in two typical Genizah documents: the first is a perplexing account dating from the first decade of the Ayyubid dynasty, about the appointment of rival candidates for the position of *dayyan* (a judge in a rabbinical court), ostensibly an internal matter, in which the Muslim authorities of the city meddled. The Amir of Alexandria, Fakhr al-Dīn and the local qadi, ʿAbd al-Karīm al-Bīsānī, each backed a different candidate; the latter's candidate proclaimed himself "messiah" at a special court session attended by the greatest Muslim legal sages and the qadi of the city.[158] The second document concerns a local *dayyan* who appealed to the *muḥtasib*, the Muslim clerk in charge of markets and public morals, when an Alexandrian Jew denigrated his religion in public.[159]

(d) Alexandria, a Cosmopolitan City

Alexandria, a city with an ever-dynamic populace, underwent a transformation. An altogether strange new element of European merchants joined the city's heterogeneous population. Trade with Europe had been greatly disrupted as a consequence of the Crusades, and in order to revive it, Ṣalāḥ al-Dīn granted traders from the mercantile cities of Italy permission to settle in Alexandria. The influx of new inhabitants provoked much social turmoil, leading to the popular uprising of 1190, when an angry mob attacked the European ships docking in the port.[160] Then, in 1217, as many as thirty thousand merchants, according to Muslim sources, took to the streets and went on a wild rampage.[161]

In the Jewish community, too, a change took place in 1212 with the arrival of three hundred or more Jewish immigrants from Christian Europe. Although not all of them settled in Alexandria, there is no doubt that their presence was a cause of consternation for the Jewish community, as evident in the panicky words of Judah Ibn al-ʿAmmānī: "Seven rabbis, great sages, have reached us ac-

Their History and Doctrines (Cambridge: Cambridge University Press, 2007), 2–30; Lev, *State and Society*, 180–198.

157 On the Ayyubid policy of religious oppression and discrimination against minorities in the early days of their rule as compared to the policy of Ḥākim bi-Amr Allāh, see Lev, *Saladin*, 187–193.

158 TS 16. 272: Frenkel, "*The Compassionate and Benevolent*" [Hebrew], no. 30.

159 TS 16.231: Frenkel, "*The Compassionate and Benevolent*" [Hebrew], no. 29.

160 al-Maqrīzī, *Sulūk*, 1: 90.

161 Ibid., 175; al-Maqrīzī, *Khiṭaṭ*, 1: 306.

companied by a hundred others, men, women and children, seeking bread [...] Most of the community is in dire straits for lack of income, and now these great expenses have fallen to them. We shall see how things work out."[162]

(e) "A Place Stabilized"

In the years 1200–1202 Alexandria was beset by famine, water scarcity, pillage and plague.[163] Famine and plague severely diminished the city's population. Judah Ibn al-ʿAmmānī counts forty beggars in 1212 among the permanent residents of Alexandria who obtained their sustenance from community institutions. In his capacity as scribe of the community's rabbinical court, Judah would record the number of charity recipients each week, so his figures are undoubtedly accurate. This low figure points to the dramatic drop in population during this period.[164]

Nonetheless, early thirteenth-century Alexandria was regarded as an island of stability in a war-ravaged world. Such a view is apparent in a letter written by Maimonides to the *dayyan* of Alexandria, R. Pinḥas, when he heard that the latter was planning to quit his post and leave the city: "And I have heard that you wish to return to Christian lands in your distress for the people. I caution you not to do so. Would you leave the place well stabilized for places beleaguered by troops?"[165] And indeed, the key battlefields of this period were far from Egypt's borders. Moreover, a series of peace treaties signed by al-ʿĀdil, brother and heir of Ṣalāḥ al-Dīn, with the Crusader King Amalric, safeguarded the period of tranquility until his reign ended in 1218.

162 TS 12.299v, ll. 16–17: Shelomo D. Goitein, *Palestinian Jewry in Early Islamic and Crusader Times in the Light of the Genizah Documents* (Jerusalem: Yad Ben-Zvi, 1980), 339–343 [Hebrew]. For Goitein's commentary, see ibid.

163 ENA NS 19.10r, ll. 14–16; v. ll. 1–7, 3–8: Frenkel, *"The Compassionate and Benevolent"* [Hebrew], no. 16.

164 TS 12.299v, lines 16–17, Goitein, *Palestinian Jewry*, 339–343

165 Yitzhak Shailat, *The Letters and Essays of Moses Maimonides: A Critical Edition of the Hebrew and Arabic Letters of Maimonides* (Maaleh Adumim: Ma'aliot, 1987), 2: 450, no. 450: letter to R. Pinḥas [Hebrew].

(f) Waning Towards the End (1218–1219)

With the succession of al-Kāmil Muḥammad to the throne in 1219, the Crusades resumed, this time on the very borders of Egypt: King Louis IX of France (St. Louis) entered the Fifth Crusade and decided to attack the heart of the Ayyubid Empire, the land of Egypt. In 1219 his armies laid siege to the port city of Damietta,[166] and as a result Alexandria too began to prepare defenses for a prolonged invasion, using forced labor to dig a deep ditch around the city. The fear of being summoned into forced labor rings loud and clear in the Genizah letters: "The city is beset by the digging of the moat. The city is cut off and forced labor [...]. The city is cut off and no one can show himself without being taken to the moat."[167]

The battles must have reached the outskirts of the city, judging from the letters of contemporaries which speak of casualties in the vicinity of the canal that connected the Nile to the city (*khalīj*):" The city is paralyzed, there is no trade. [...] No one can leave by sea or by land [...] else they will be killed. And many have been killed in the *khalīj*."[168] As the war drew on, there were economic concerns as well: "The markets have all been shut down. There is no one buying or selling anymore,"[169] relates a letter from Alexandria written in 1219. And a former treasury clerk complains that he has been forced to hire out his son as a tailor's apprentice for half a dirham a week and adds, "Bread costs a dirham and a half and is barely fit to eat."[170]

The bread shortage and exorbitant prices caused social upheavals and rioting, as described in a letter from Alexandria: "On the second day of the holiday there was a terrible uprising on account of the bread. People searched in vain throughout the city until the Lord brought relief at the end of the day [...]. The Amir and the supervisor of the markets (*muḥtasib*) rode out, wishing to burn the bread-sellers because of the bread."[171]

---

166 Peter M. Holt, *The Age of the Crusades: The Near East from the Eleventh Century to 1517* (London: Longmann, 1985), 63.
167 TS 8 J 20.26r, lines 1–2, 6–7.
168 TS 13 J 17.23r, lines 8, 11.
169 TS 13 J 17.23v, line 9.
170 TS 16.286r, ll. 14, 15–17: Frenkel, *"The Compassionate and Benevolent"* [Hebrew], no. 31.
171 TS 12.305r, ll. 7–10. The term *khabbāzūn* can signify bread-sellers, bakers or bakery owners. For a comprehensive discussion on their role and status in the Fatimid city, see Lev, *State and Society*, 164–166.

Added to these calamities, another plague spread though Alexandria and all of Egypt in the early thirteenth century, accompanied by severe drought and famine. Muslim sources report a vast number of deaths in Alexandria. The qadi of Alexandria, these sources insist, led prayers at seven hundred funerals in a single day.[172] The plague decimated the population and caused citizens to flee in droves, to North Africa in particular.[173]

(g) The End of an Era

The year 1249 marks the end of an era. During that year Alexandria came under threat from King Louis IX and his forces when they succeeded in capturing Damietta and began to advance towards Cairo. The Ayyubid sultan al-Ṣāliḥ died and not a year passed before his heir, al-Muʿaẓẓam Tūrānashāh, was murdered by Mamluk soldiers from the Baḥriyya battalion. These same Mamluks succeeded soon after in halting the advance of the Crusader armies, and became the rulers of Egypt for the next three hundred years.[174]

172 Ibn Taghrībirdī, *Nujūm*, 2: 174; al-Suyūṭī, *Ḥusn al-muḥāḍara*, 2: 175; ʿAbd al-Laṭīf al-Baghdādī, *Kitāb al-ifāda wal-iʿtibār fī umūr al-mushāhada wal-ḥawādith al-muʿāyana bi-arḍ miṣr* (Cairo: Maṭbaʿat Wādī al-Nīl, 1870), 57.
173 Ibid.
174 Holt, *The Age of the Crusades*, 65–66, 82–83.

Chapter 2 The Context of Space

The chapter concerns the urban space, in which the events and developments discussed later on took place. Using a wealth of information from two types of sources, the accounts of medieval travelers to the region and mutually supportive Genizah documents, we endeavor to reconstruct the city's topography, its appearance and its image in the eyes of contemporaries.

1 Geographical Layout

Alexandria is conveniently located on a Mediterranean harbor near the upper tip of the western arm of the Nile (Rashīd). To the south lies Lake Mariyūṭ (Gk. Mariotis), which is linked to the Nile by a series of canals.[175] North of the harbor lies the island of Pharos, site of the famous lighthouse of Alexandria, which obstructs the winds and tidal flows. To the west the city borders on the western desert.[176]

2 The City's Confines

(a) The Wall

The wall of medieval Alexandria contained only half the area of the early Hellenistic city which had greatly diminished over time. To the west, it formed a boundary with the desert[177] and was crucial to the city's defensive system. Repeatedly attacked, particularly from the sea on the northern side, the wall was repaired and restored by al-Mutawakkil during the Abbasid era, by Ibn Ṭūlūn, and Ṣalāḥ al-Dīn in 1174.[178]

The five main gates of Alexandria were:

175 The reeds that grew on the banks of this lake were considered particularly fine for making styluses. See Bodl MS Heb c. 13.20 (Gil, *Kingdom*, 673). Nahray b. Nissim places an order for some fine "Mariotis reeds."

176 For a more extensive discussion of Alexandria's unique location between several areas with very different types of production, see Miriam Frenkel, "Medieval Alexandria—Life in a Port City," *Al-Masāq* 26.1 (2014): 5–35, esp. 9.

177 William of Tyre, *History*, 2: 335: "Behind the wall and adjacent to it sprawls a large, uninhabitable desert."

178 See Part I, Chapter 1.3 (b): The Reign of Ṣalāḥ al-Dīn (1171–1193).

https://doi.org/10.1515/9783110713619-004

Bāb-al-Sidra, the jujube gate: the southern gate, the mainland entrance to the city. Through it, travelers would pass and pay tariffs on goods sent to Fustat.[179]

Bāb Rashīd: the eastern gate which led to the Rashid [Rosetta] Gate and Fuwa, where tolls and tariffs were also collected.[180]

Bāb al-Baḥr, the sea gate: the northern gate which led to the port.[181]

Bāb al-Bahār (the spice gate) or Bāb al-Qarāfa (the cemetery gate): the western gate through which caravans from the Maghreb and the interior would pass.

Bāb al-Akhḍar, the green gate: another northern gate, open only on Fridays, which led to the sprawling cemeteries of the city.[182]

These were the old Hellenistic gates to city, and their state of preservation was noted in amazement by al-ʿAbdarī, a traveler from the Maghreb who visited the city in 1289:

> Among the wonders and marvels I beheld was the soundness of the old gates, undamaged despite their colossal height, with magnificent capitals and ashlars perfectly hewn, every segment, every lintel and threshold carved from a single block. And what's most striking is how such a block could have been mounted despite its immensity. And the passing ages have left the gates unchanged, unmarked, but beautiful and bright, their side facades perfect works of masonry, iron-plated without and consummately crafted within.[183]

179 See Goitein, *Letters*, 258, n. 6. Genizah documents referring to Bāb Sadra: GW XXXVI (Goitein, *Letters*, 58); 29 ULC Or 1080 (Frenkel, *"The Compassionate and Benevolent"* [Hebrew], no. 97); TS 10 J 14:11 (Frenkel, *"The Compassionate and Benevolent"* [Hebrew], no. 51); TS 13 J 21.25 (Frenkel, *"The Compassionate and Benevolent"* [Hebrew], no. 71); TS 24.67 (Frenkel, *"The Compassionate and Benevolent"* [Hebrew], no. 40).

180 Bāb Rashīd is mentioned in the following documents: BM Or 5542.22r, l. 7 (Gil, *Kingdom*, 169); Bodl MS Heb d 47.62r, l. 5 (Gil, *Kingdom*, 184); TS 12.355r, l. 20 (Gil, *Kingdom*, 487); TS 24.67; 20r, line 28 (Frenkel, *"The Compassionate and Benevolent"* [Hebrew], no. 40). In most of these documents Bāb Rashīd is mentioned with regard to its various tolls and tariffs.

181 Benjamin of Tudela, *The Itinerary of Benjamin of Tudela*, ed. and trans. Marcus N. Adler (London: Frowde, 1907), 104: "And its courtyards are so evenly aligned in the market places [*shukot*] that one can see a mile unobstructed from Rashīd gate to Sea gate."

182 The latter three gates, though never mentioned in Genizah documents, are mentioned by Ibn Baṭṭūṭa who visited Alexandria in 1326. See Muḥammad b. ʿAbdallāh Ibn Baṭṭūṭa, *Riḥlat Ibn Baṭṭūṭa al-musammāt tuḥfat al-niẓār fī ghrāʾib al-amṣār wa-ajāʾib al-asfār* (Beirut: Dār al-Kutub al-ʿIlmiyya, 1983), 28; see also P. Kahle, "Die Katastrophe de mittelalterichen Alexandria," *Mélanges Maspero IIII. Orient Islamique* (Cairo: IFAO, 1940), 137–154, for descriptions of the gates by European travelers during the Mamluk period.

183 Abū ʿAbdallāh al-ʿAbdarī, *Riḥlat al-ʿabdarī al-musammāt al-riḥla al-maghribiyya* (Rabat: Jāmiʿat Muḥammad V, 1968), 91. For a more elaborate description of the gates, see Frenkel, "Medieval Alexandria," 9–13.

(b) The Garden Areas

On the outskirts of the city, between the walls and beyond them, lay tracts of farmland and cultivated gardens where the inhabitants of the city would stroll and refresh themselves. This fact is evident from a Sabbath sermon on the verse from Song of Songs, "A garden enclosed is my sister, my bride." The sermon was delivered at a time when "youths would go out during the holidays to the gardens and vineyards" and the preacher adjured them "to refrain from the habit of idling in the nearby orchards and irrigation canals within the Sabbath perimeter (*teḥum*)."[184] Another bit of evidence comes from an 1103 lease for a vegetable garden, a property defined as "a garden on the west bank of the canal (*khalīj*) beyond the city limits."[185]

We also find a description of a beautiful garden on the banks of the *khalīj* in a verse by a contemporary Muslim poet, Ẓāfir al-Ḥadād (d. 1138).[186] There were also many Nile-fed groves on the banks of Lake Mariyūṭ and around the village of Mariyūṭ, where Alexandrians would often go to fish and take their ease.[187] These well-tended parks were a source of wonder and pride for the citizens of Alexandria. In his description of the Crusader siege of 1174, William of Tyre lingers over a description and does not conceal his pain at the destruction of the gardens in the course of the siege:

> Around the city thick as woodland spread flowering gardens with every sort of fruit-bearing tree and healing shrub. The sight of such a magical oasis beckoned passersby to find rest and tranquility therein. Our soldiers invaded the orchards en masse in search of material for their siege machines. [...] The orchards were despoiled and alas, nothing remained of their former beauty. With the signing of the peace treaty, the inhabitants lamented this devastation, deeming it the most grievous of all their injuries.[188]

---

184 TS 13 J 19.7, ll. 11–13. The sermon is attributed to R. Pinḥas; thus his words reflect the city's appearance in the thirteenth century. See also the afterword to Part II, Chapter 10.5: Conclusion.
185 DK2r, ll. 3–4. This contract in Arabic script concerns two Christians, the Alexandrian Marzūq b. Mufarraj al-Naṣrānī and the Alexandrian Zurayq b. Makhlūf al-Naṣrānī, the lessees, and the Muslim owner of the garden, Abū ʿAlī Ḥamūd al-Yamīnī.
186 Salem, "D'Alexandrie à Alméria," 216.
187 al-Maqrīzī, *Khiṭaṭ*, 1: 300.
188 William of Tyre, *History*, 2: 337.

3 The Water System

The city's water supply derived from two sources: rainwater cisterns and water from the Nile piped into the inhabitants' homes by means of a sophisticated underground pipe system left over from the Ptolemaic period. Ibn Jubayr, the famous Muslim traveler who visited Alexandria in 1178, notes in his journal: "The water flows underground through all quarters and streets and wells side by side in a row."[189]

> The city is situated fifty-six miles from the river but during flood season some of the water flows to the city through irrigation canals. This water is carefully conserved in large cisterns used solely for this purpose by residents throughout the year. Some of the water is channeled through underwater pipes to irrigate the orchards beyond the city.[190]

Since it was situated some distance from the branch of the Nile, Alexandria was dependent for its water supply on a man-made canal leading from the river to the city. This canal, called the *khalīj* or *khawr* in medieval times, was built during the Greco-Roman period and often stood in need of overhauling and maintenance since it was inclined to become clogged. When the canal was not operational during the low phase of the Nile, the city suffered serious water shortages – a phenomenon often attested to in the letters of the Genizah, as we find in this one describing the great famine of 1200: "No water reaches the wells."[191]

The canal streamed drinking water and water for irrigation and also served as the main artery of transport between Alexandria and Fustat and other cities in the Nile Valley. The exit and entrance to the *khalīj* were official transit stations where travelers had to pay a special toll fee called *wājib al-khawr.*[192] Fees varied according to the value of the goods or at the whim of the toll collectors, as evident from huge discrepancies amongst them. Thus, for example, Saʿdān b. Thābit paid sixteen dirhams for a shipment of caraway seeds in the year 1130,[193] whereas thirty years later there were some who paid a whole dinar.[194]

Toll collectors at the transit stations had a free hand: a poor merchant short of money was charged the full fee and had to leave an enormous load of kohl

189 Ibn Jubayr, *Riḥla*, 41.
190 William of Tyre, *History*, 2: 335.
191 ENA NS 19.10v, ll. 2–3: Frenkel, *"The Compassionate and Benevolent"* [Hebrew], no. 16.
192 ULC Or 1080 J 178r, l. 27. See also Goitein, *Letters*, 258, n. 8.
193 Bodl MS Heb c 28.55, l. 22: Goitein, *Letters*, 58.
194 TS 10 J 31.6r, ll. 19–21: Frenkel, *"The Compassionate and Benevolent"* [Hebrew], no. 58. The payment was probably only for the entrance, not for shipment of any goods.

with them as a security deposit against full payment of his debt.[195] In one of his letters, Judah Ibn al-ʿAmmānī recounts the terrible anguish suffered by R. Joseph al-Baghdādī who was not only publicly shamed and banished from the city but received rough treatment from the toll collectors of the *khalīj*.[196]

Since the *khalīj* was open only during the high-water season and was blocked during the lengthy low-water phase, its re-opening was eagerly anticipated while its closing was awaited with some trepidation, as this determined the rhythm of city life and the revenue of many of the inhabitants. The threat of the *khasr al-khalīj* (the low-water phase of the canal)[197] loomed constantly over the heads of merchants and citizens alike. We find many echoes of this in the Genizah letters. Abraham b. Abū Zikrī reports from Alexandria that "No more trips will be possible now due to the *khalīj*."[198] Abū Nāṣir b. Abraham writes early in the twelfth century that he will be unable to ship his wheat till the *khalīj* is once again in full flow.[199] Judah b. Joseph ha-Kohen makes this recommendation to his business partner in Alexandria: "Go up to Fustat while the *khalīj* is still 'working'."[200] Abraham b. Fakhr of Alexandria gives this reason for not visiting his son in Fustat: "I am in Alexandria waiting for the *khalīj* to get here, with God's help";[201] while Samuel b. Aaron urges his partner to hurry up and fetch his goods from Alexandria: "You know that soon the ways will be sealed off again and I will be stuck in Alexandria with the shipment."[202] Attempts to cross the *khalīj* on foot during the low-water phase often proved disastrous. Mūsā b. Abī al-Ḥayy Khalīla, mired there for thirty days with a shipment of linen, wrote to his partner, Nahray b. Nissim: "Frightful winter conditions, slippery and sludgy, made it impossible to deliver the merchandise. The animals were stuck there till Wednesday. [...]. It was on account of the mud that the goods failed to reach the merchants' quarters."[203]

---

195 TS 12.434r, l. 15: Frenkel, *"The Compassionate and Benevolent"* [Hebrew], no. 23.
196 TS 24.67v, l. 40: Frenkel, *"The Compassionate and Benevolent"* [Hebrew], no. 39.
197 TS NS J 328, in the margins, ll. 4–5.
198 ENA 2727.
199 TS 13 J 22.31: Frenkel, *"The Compassionate and Benevolent"* [Hebrew], no. 74.
200 TS 8 J 20.8r, l. 4.
201 TS 13 J 24.17r, ll. 21–23.
202 TS 13 J 21.8, in the right-hand margin.
203 Bodl MS Heb d 66.54r, l. 5; Gil, *Kingdom*, 704. More about the water system in Frenkel, "Medieval Alexandria," 13–16.

4 The Harbor

The harbor was the city's principal locus of activity. There were, in fact, two harbors in Alexandria, dating back to Ptolemaic times: an eastern harbor and a western one separated by a causeway—seven stadia long and thus called the Heptastadion—stretching from the lighthouse to the shore. Originally the eastern harbor encompassed a smaller harbor known as the Royal Harbor which served the imperial flotilla but was not in use during the Middle Ages. The entry to the eastern harbor, hazardous and difficult to navigate, was intended for ships from Christian and other infidel lands while the western harbor, secured by iron chains, was designated for the sole use of Muslim ships.[204]

The entrance to the harbor or "sea gate" was shut every night and re-opened in the morning. A description in a letter sent from Alexandria in 1057 says: "Towards nightfall I heard the sea raging and I said in my heart: 'Surely no ships will put out to sea.' But when I awoke at dawn they were opening the gate and I saw that the ships had sailed."[205] In charge of the gate was an appointed official called in Hebrew sources *baʿal ha-sheʿarim*, meaning "the gate's owner" (doubtless a translation from the Arabic *ṣāḥib al-bāb*), who apparently supervised the comings and goings in the harbor and was authorized to issue special permits. This is evident from a letter dispatched in 1027 by Joseph b. Yeshūʿā, who writes of a special tariff the community had been obliged to pay the gate keeper so he would allow a released Jewish captive to enter the harbor and board a ship that was sailing back to his own country: "When the time came for him to sail home we counted out two and a half gold pieces for the gatekeeper."[206] In addition to the gate keeper, sources also mention a type of official known as the sea gate scribe (*kātib bāb al-baḥr*), evidently charged with copying and writing out all the documents that pertained to entering and leaving the harbor.[207]

There were Jews among these harbor officials too, as we find in a letter written in the twelfth century by a government official who was being held captive: "My father served the realm of Alexandria as sea gate keeper for fifteen years

---

204 For a detailed description of harbor life, see Goitein, *Society*, 1: 339–346; Claude Cahen, *Makhzūmiyyāt: Études sur l'histoire economique et financiere de l'Égypte medieval* (Leiden: Brill, 1977), 155–157.

205 Bodl MS Heb d 66.54r, l. 5: Gil, *Kingdom*, 70.

206 TS 24.29. Cf. Cahen, *Makhzūmiyyāt*, 285.

207 Ms Stras 4110.88r, l. 7–8: Gil, *Kingdom*, 714. In evidence here are commercial alliances between Jewish merchants and the sea gate copyist. On the complexities of the harbor administration see Cahen, *Makhzūmiyyāt*, 155–157.

when most of the merchants came from the lands of Edom [Christendom], in the west and the east."[208]

The famous lighthouse of Alexandria (*manāra, manār, fanār*),built by the Ptolemaic kings and considered one of the Seven Wonders of the ancient world, was still in use during the Middle Ages and continued to be a source of fascination for the historians, geographers and travelers of the age.[209] Benjamin of Tudela devoted much space in his otherwise laconic writings to the lighthouse and its use by contemporaries: "The lighthouse is visible at a distance of a hundred miles by day and by night, and when the keeper lights the beacon, mariners bound for Alexandria see it from afar and sail in its direction."[210]

The lighthouse served as a symbolic gateway between the open sea and the territorial waters of Alexandria. Passengers regarded the safe docking of their ships at the lighthouse the conclusion of their journey—as we see in the effusive words of thanks offered by Judah b. Joseph from the deck of his ship when it dropped anchor under the lighthouse: "I am under the lighthouse now, praised be God for turning matters to the good. And may the Lord bring a favorable outcome and inscribe and keep me and all of Israel from harm."[211]

Irresponsible crews dumped their cargos as they passed "under the lighthouse," and considered themselves to have done their duty this way,[212] while vessels waiting to embark gathered in the waterway between the harbor and the open sea: "Two ships from Alhambra which had anchored under the lighthouse sailed off together in the morning after Friday," reads a letter from Alexandria,[213] and Salāma b. Mūsā al-Safāqṣī writes to Nahray b. Nissim: "We have

---

208 Bodl MSS Heb c 28.53, ll. 25–27: Mann, *Jews*, 2: 273–274, no. 13.

209 Aḥmad b. Abī Ya'qūb al-Ya'qūbī, *Kitāb al-buldān* (Leiden 1891), 338; Abū 'Alī Aḥmad Ibn Rusta, *Kitāb al-a'lāq al-nafīsa* (Leiden: Brill, 1881–1882), 7: 37; Abū al-Ḥasan 'Alī al-Mas'ūdī, *Murūj al-dhahab wa-ma'ādin al-jawhar fī al-ta'rīkh* (Cairo: n.p. 1958), 1: 373; Muḥammad b. 'Alī Ibn Ḥawqal, *Kītāb ṣūrat al-arḍ* (Leiden: Brill 1938), 151; Shihāb al-Dīn Yāqūt al-Ḥamawī, *Mu'jam al-buldān* (Beirut: n.p., 1995), 1: 183; Ibn Jubayr, *Riḥla*, 14–15; al-Maqrīzī, *Khiṭaṭ*, 1: 155; Al-'Abdarī, *Riḥla*, 91–93. See also Asin-Palasios, who quotes the highly detailed description of a visit to Alexandria by a Spanish pilgrim from Malaga, Yūsuf b. Muḥammad al-Balawī b. al-Shaykh al-Mālikī in his book Kītāb Alif-Ba (see Miguel Asín-Palacios, "Una descripción nueva del Faro de Alejandría," *al-Andalus* 1 (1933): 241–300). Likewise, Évariste Lévi-Provençal ("Une description arabe inédite du Phare d'Alexandrie," *Mélanges Maspero IIII*, 161–171), quotes a long passage describing the lighthouse by Abū 'Ubayd al-Bakrī, preserved in the fourteenth century Maghrebi writer Muḥammad b. 'Abdallah b. 'Abd al-Mu'min al-Khimyarī al-Sibtī's book *Kītāb al-rawḍ al-mu'ṭār fī 'ajā'ib al-aqṭār.*

210 Benjamin of Tudela, *Itinerary*, 105.

211 ULC Or 1080 J 35r, l. 4: Gil, *Kingdom*, 156.

212 TS 10 J 19.9r, ll. 22–23: Gil, *Kingdom*, 180; Ben-Sasson, *Jews of Sicily*, 56.

213 TS NS J 324, ll. 5–6.

decided to set sail no matter what. We are presently at anchor under the lighthouse."[214]

5 The Topographical Features and Appearance of Alexandria in the Middle Ages

Medieval Alexandria preserved the appearance of the classical Hellenistic city:[215] eight streets intersecting at right angles, incorporating a checkerboard pattern. This urban design with long and straight broad avenues was rare enough by then in the lands of Islam to cause visitors to Alexandria between the tenth and thirteenth centuries to be struck with amazement. Benjamin of Tudela writes: "The streets are wide and straight, so that a man can look along them for a mile from gate to gate."[216]

The buildings too, constructed out of enormous blocks which had survived from ancient times were immensely impressive to medieval travelers. Ibn Jubayr opens the chapter on his travels to Alexandria titled "Some Remarks on the History of Alexandria and Its Sights" with these words:

> And I shall begin by remarking on the beauty of the city's design and the size of its buildings, with avenues broader than I have ever seen and buildings taller, more ancient and majestic [...]. And with my own eyes I beheld there marble columns and entablatures of an inconceivable height and breadth and grace. One may even on occasion find columns so tall that the very air cannot hold them. And no one knows what their purpose might be and why they were placed there. And we were told that in the distant past they supported special dwellings for philosophers and magistrates of that age and Allāh knows what. Belike they were intended for stargazing.[217]

Al-ʿAbdarī, in a long paean of rhyming prose also sees fit to remark: "A city of capacious squares, pillars of perfection and stately habitations."[218]

The colossal stone exteriors seem to have created such a dazzling effect in the Mediterranean sunlight that it overwhelmed travelers and gave rise to a whole range of traditions about the city where one cannot tell night from day

214 TS 10 J 4.2r, ll. 11–12: Gil, *Kingdom*, 747. More about the harbor in Frenkel, "Medieval Alexandria," 16–19.
215 See E.J. Owens, *The City in the Greek and Roman World* (London and NY: Routledge, 1991), 30–50; Yāqūt, *Muʿjam*, 1: 186.
216 Benjamin of Tudela, *Itinerary*, 104.
217 Ibn Jubayr, *Riḥla*, 14.
218 Al-ʿAbdarī, *Riḥla*, 90.

and whose citizens walk around with black cloths over their eyes to keep from being blinded by the glare. The Muslim geographer Yāqūt al-Ḥamawī who describes Alexandria in the early thirteenth century cites these traditions, and adds: "As for the glare, it is there to this day," attributing the phenomenon to the gleaming white stone-block walls.[219]

An enormous avenue called *al-maḥajja al-ʿuẓmā* (the Great Royal Road) ran through the center of the city from the west gate to the east gate, while another central road traversed it linking the north gate to the south gate. In the center of the city, on one side of *al-maḥajja al-ʿuẓmā* was the *qaṣaba* quarter, apparently a market area with shops and stalls lining the main avenue. The long, narrow design of this quarter, typical of markets, is probably what gave it its name, meaning "reed."[220]

6 Internal Divisions

The internal division of the city into sub-districts is insufficiently clear. Genizah documents refer to *nāḥiyya*, *ḥāra*, *khaṭṭ* and *zuqāq*, but we have no way of ascertaining what these terms denote with respect to urban features and dimensions.[221] The process of Arabization undergone by Alexandria in the wake of the Muslim conquests left its mark in many of toponyms which pertain to the tribes that settled there at that time – for instance, Nāḥiyyat Banī Ḥusayn.[222] The city retained vestiges of its ethnic past till the end of the eleventh century: entire quarters were inhabited by single tribes or homogeneous groups of settlers from particular regions,[223] but over time these divisions became blurred. For example, Nāḥiyyat Banī Ḥusayn, a name indicative of an entirely Arab-Muslim population, is the neighborhood where the home of the Christian Yūḥannā b. Munajjā stood between a house belonging to a priest and the home of a Jew

219 Yāqūt, *Muʿjam*, 1:185–186. The traditions cited were mentioned by Ibn ʿAbd al-Ḥakam as early as the ninth century. See ʿAbd al-Raḥmān Ibn ʿAbd al-Ḥakam al-Qurayshī, *Futūḥ miṣr wal-maghrib wal-andalus* (Leiden: Brill, 1960), 42.

220 Ibn ʿAbd al-Ḥakam, *Futūḥ miṣr*, 42; al-Suyūṭī, *Ḥusn al-muḥāḍara*, 1: 37.

221 See Goitein, *Society*, 4: 13. *Ḥāra:* TS 12.254, right margins (Gil, *Kingdom*, 532); BM Or 5542.9v, l. 6 (Gil, *Kingdom*, 488; Ben-Sasson, *Jews of Sicily*, 107). *Nāḥiyya:* TS Ar 30.30. *Khaṭṭ:* TS AS 150.1, ENA 154, TS 8 J 6.14. TS 10 J 15.5r, ll. 14–15: Zuqāq al-Māḥāl (Gil, *Kingdom*, 490).

222 TS Ar 30.30, a lease agreement from 1132 for a house in Nāḥiyyat Banī Ḥusayn. On the course of Arab settlement in Alexandria, see Ibn ʿAbd al-Ḥakam, *Futūḥ miṣr*, 130.

[198] See above, Part I, Chapter 1.2 (d): Relief in the Wake of Distress (1050–1070).

named ha-Kohen (al-Kūhān).[224] And in 1158, Khaṭṭ Bīr Jābr was no longer a strictly Arab-Muslim quarter either, being the residential address of the mother of the Jew Berākhōt b. Abraham, next door to which, so notes the address written on a letter, stood the Babylonian Synagogue.[225] Another house in the neighborhood belonged to a Jew, named Abū al-Maʿānī al-Masjūnī[226] and adjoining it was the house of a Christian priest by the name of Makārim.

This is how the term *ḥārat al-Yahūd* as mentioned in various documents should be understood.[227] In light of the basic structure of the ancient city, it is quite possible that this was the site of the "Delta Quarter," the original Jewish quarter of Hellenistic times.[228] During the period under consideration this quarter was still populated mainly by Jews. In some Genizah letters, the quarter is typically referred to as al-Ḥāra, *the* neighborhood. When Mardūk b. Mūsā seeks someone to help him with the household and look after him in old age, he looks for a suitable person, a Jew it would seem, in the *ḥārat al-Yahūd.*[229] Nevertheless, with the rising integration of the city's ethnic quarters, it is likely that members of other ethnic groups resided in *ḥārat al-Yahūd*, as did the Jews in various other neighborhoods of Alexandria.[230]

Another oft-mentioned quarter in Genizah documents is al-Qamra, an old, well-established neighborhood and possibly identical to *ḥārat al-Yahūd*, with many Jews among its residents identified as al-Qamrī.[231] One letter speaks of a Jewish student who came to study in Alexandria and found temporary lodgings there.[232] In another letter a Jewish relative is invited to visit family members in

---

224 TS Ar 30.30, the aforementioned lease in n. 222, names the lessee as Bishr b. Ezekiel, a Jew.

225 ENA 154 (2588).

226 TS AS 150.1, a release clause for a tenancy agreement from the thirteenth century written by the *dayyan* Solomon b. Zechariah which willingly freed the landlord from obligations and restraints.

227 TS 12.254, right margins (Gil, *Kingdom*, 532); BM Or 5542.9v, l. 6 (Gil, *Kingdom*, 488; Ben-Sasson, *Jews of Sicily*, 107); ENA 2738.6v, ll. 11–12 (Gil, *Kingdom*, 337).

228 This quarter was situated on the shore, east of the royal palace. See Victor A. Tcherikover, *The Jews in Egypt During the Hellenistic-Roman Age in the Light of the Papyri* (Jerusalem: Magness, 1963), 21, n. 32.

229 TS 12.254 in the margins (Gil, *Kingdom*, 532): "My children have left the house [...] and there is no one to bring me water and I need someone to serve me but have found no one in the *ḥārat al-Yahūd.*"

230 This was in fact the situation in Greco-Roman times as well. See Tcherikover, *Jews in Egypt*, 21, n. 32.

231 TS NS J 36, Frenkel, *"The Compassionate and Benevolent"* [Hebrew], no. 90: Ḍiyāʾ b. Joseph al-Qamrī.

232 TS 10 J 12.16, in the address; the wistful letter, filled with concern, was sent by a mother to her son *al-shaykh* Abū al-Maḥāsin al-tilmīdh al-Miṣrī.

Alexandria and stay in al-Qamra.[233] This quarter seems to have been a bustling center, and during the reign of Ṣalāḥ al-Dīn when the authorities wanted to punish and publicly condemn a Jew for impiety, the royal police would display him in the teeming streets of al-Qamra and chastise him before the crowds.[234] It was a popular meeting place, too. "My heart was unceasing in its concern for you," writes Abraham b. Sahlān to his friend in Alexandria, "until Faṣil arrived and told me he had come upon you safe and sound in Qamra."[235]

Besides being a residential area, al-Qamra accommodated hostels, workshops and markets.[236]A twelfth-century letter, addressed from "Barakāt b. Harūn b. al-Kūzī, the silk vendor's shop, al-Qamra, Alexandria,"[237] invites a friend to stay in al-Qamra, assuring him that he will be able to make a living there, with silk-weavers, dyers and market criers all in great demand.[238]

Jews inhabited yet another quarter called al-Qarāfa (the cemetery). The Muslim geographer Yāqūt mentions this in his topographical dictionary, mainly in connection with a neighborhood of the same name in Fustat. About the neighborhood in Alexandria he notes only that it is "a place in Alexandria."[239] Al-Qarāfa was known as the ancient burial grounds in the south-western corner of the city which laid beyond the medieval wall.[240] There is no information about an inhabited area in the vicinity other than that referred to in a query sent to Maimonides about a bill of sales for the "judge's house in the port city, may God bless it, in al-Qarāfa," belonging to members of the Ibn al-ʿAmmānī family. The house is described as a domicile, parts of which were permanently rented out, a possible indication that al-Qarāfa was a residential area. The position and wealth of the landlords, the Ibn al-ʿAmmānī family, suggests that al-Qarāfa was not the backwater one might assume it to have been considering the scant attention Yaqūt pays it in his book.[241]

233 TS 10 J 18.3, ll. 7–8: *wa-asaʿa in kāna yumkinuka an tajī tataʿayyash fī al-Qamra:* "And if you come now you could earn a living in Qamra."
234 TS 16.23, l. 21.
235 TS 16.6v, l. 1–2.
236 See above in this section.
237 TS 13 J 36.11.
238 TS 10 J 18.3, lines 11–12.
239 Yāqūt, *Muʿjam,* end of the entry on al-Qarāfa.
240 ʿAlī b. Abī Bakr al-Harāwī, *Kītāb al-ishārāt ilā maʿrifat al-ziyārāt* (Damascus: IFAO, 1953), 47.
241 *Letters and Essays of Moses Maimonides*, 2, responsa 2: a document from 1205. On the Ibn al-ʿAmmānī family and their wealth, see below, Part II, Chapter 5.

We find yet another indication that there were residential neighborhoods near the cemetery in a bill of sale for a house in the vicinity of the catacombs (*khaṭṭ al-Dayāmīs*), most likely the ancient necropolis of Alexandria.[242]

7 The Market and Mercantile Centers

The largest mercantile center in Alexandria was situated, as mentioned earlier, in the heart of the city along the main avenue. The market was split up into secondary districts named after the different trades plied there: *sūq al-ṣagha*, the goldsmiths' market,[243] *sūq al-asākifa*, the cobblers' market,[244] *sūq al-ṣaraf*, the money changers' market,[245] and *sūq al-ʿaṭṭārīn*, the perfumers' market.[246] Nevertheless, as Goitein has noted, the names of the markets did not always correspond to their designated trades, and each market district included various kinds of trade and merchandise.[247] The bustling life of the market took place in different "houses" as well. Such a "house" (*dār*) in fact comprised a wide array of buildings organized as a *sūq* in every way and performing all necessary aspects of commercial life: money-changing, the signing of business contracts and partnerships, the payment of taxes and tariffs, the storage of goods, mail de-

242 TS 8 J 6.14v – a bill of sale from the year 1214: Sitt al-Ukhūwah b. Futūḥ hereby sells an eighth of the house in Khaṭṭ al-Dāyamīs to her brother Ephraim. On the necropolis and the catacombs of Roman Alexandria, see Françoise Dunand, "Pratiques et croyances funéraires en Egypt romaine," in *Aufstieg und Niedergang de roemischen Welt, II*, ed. Wolfgang Haase (Berlin: De Gruyter, 1995), 18.5: 3223. For more about Alexandria's appearance and construction, see Frenkel, "Medieval Alexandria," 19–23.

243 ENA 154 (2558)v: the letter of Abraham b. Berākhōt b. al-Ḥājja from Būsh (south of Cairo) to the store of Abū Zikrī Judah b. Isaac in the Sūq al-Sāgha (sic, rather than *ṣāgha*).

244 TS 8 J 19.7: Amram b. Nathan sends a letter to the market stall of Ismāʿīl b. Abraham al-Tūnī (the tuna seller), the fishmonger in the al-Asākifa (cobblers' market) of Alexandria.

245 . TS Ar 30.30: Bishr b. Ezekiel, *al-munādī fī sūq al-ṣaraf* (the crier in the money changers' market); GW IXr, l. 43: Frenkel, "*The Compassionate and Benevolent*" [Hebrew], no. 18; TS 20.121, Frenkel, "*The Compassionate and Benevolent*" [Hebrew], no. 34, with a vivid description of commercial dealings in that market.

246 TS 8 J 4.15, court case in 1098: Hillel b. Bunyās al-ʿAṭṭār (the perfume seller] gives testimony about an argument that erupted between two Syrian merchants, "I was in Alexandria at my father's shop in Sūq al-ʿAṭṭārīn."

247 Goitein, *Society*, 4: 26–28. See also above, nn. 244, 246: the tuna fishmonger's shop was situated in the cobblers' market while the perfumer's father's shop was actually in the perfumers' market.

livery, with rooms for public auctions and stalls, stores and workshops.[248] The houses were named for their main line of merchandise. In Alexandria we find "the House of Linen" (*dār al-katān*), most prominently;[249] "the House of Precious Stones" (*dār al-jawhar*);[250] "the House of Almonds" (*dār al-lūz*);[251] "the New House" (*al-dār al-jadīda*);[252] "the Blessed House" (*al-dār al-mubāraka*);[253] and Dār Mānak, used primarily as a customs house for exports from Alexandria: any merchant who wished to export goods from the city had to go through this house with a special pass and pay the duties imposed, which is perhaps why the place is so often mentioned in the letters of Alexandrian merchants.[254] The *qālūṣ* where linen and other bulky goods were traded is mentioned only once, apparently because it was not especially active at the time, as evidenced by a letter from Salāma b. Mūsā who felt it necessary to send instructions on how to get there to his correspondent, Judah Ibn Sighmār.[255] Another commercial site in Alexandria is referred to in the Genizah letters as *al-ṣaffayn*, meaning the two rows, a reference to its appearance: a colonnade that evidently enclosed stores and other buildings. The *ṣaffayn* of Alexandria is described as a place for storing and preserving goods[256] and also served as a brokerage[257] where accounts were drawn up and debts collected.[258]

---

248 Goitein, *Society*, 1:194–195, 4:26–27, and there see a physical description of a system of such medieval buildings in a 'house' in Fustat, *dār al-jawhar* (House of the Precious Stones).
249 Phi 390; TS 10 J 11.7; ENA 2738.6; TS 10 J 20.16; TS 12.379; TS 2.66; TS 8 J 22.8 (Gil, *Kingdom*, 337).
250 ENA 2805.17: Gil, *Kingdom*, 551. It seems that mother-of-pearl was also treated there. See ENA 2805.17r, ll. 9–10: "I'll buy you mother-of-pearl of the kind produced in *dār al-jawhar*."
251 TS 13 J 17.2r, l. 6: Gil, Kingdom, 400. On the importance of the almond trade see Goitein, *Society*, 4: 246.
252 TS 13 J 3.4: Frenkel, *"The Compassionate and Benevolent"* [Hebrew], no. 59. In 1143 the goods of a Jewish merchant who drowned off the shore of Alexandria were removed from there by the official Muslim overseer of estates, *ṣāḥib mawārīth al-goyyim*, to the Rabbinical Court of Alexandria.
253 TS 8 J 21.29: Gil, *Kingdom*, 464, where cargo from the port was unloaded and deposited in 1063.
254 Bodl MS Heb d 75.20; TS Ar 18 (1) 101 (Gil, *Kingdom*, 449); TS 12.335 (Gil, *Kingdom*, 487); ENA 3616.29 (Gil, *Kingdom*, 118); TS J 2.66 (Gil, *Kingdom*, 272); Bodl MS Heb d 46.62 (Gil, *Kingdom*, 184); BM Or 5563.19 (Gil, *Kingdom*, 185); ENA 2738.6 (Gil, *Kingdom*, 337); TS 13 J 17.7 (Gil, *Kingdom*, 808). About the meaning and Greek origin of the place, see Goitein, *Society*, 4:27.
255 INA D 55.14r, in the margins, l. 4: Gil, *Kingdom*; Ben-Sasson, *Jews of Sicily*, 11 – *al-qālūṣ, wa-huwa bi-l-qurb minka, min baytika* (the *qālūs* is nearby, close to where you live). On the meaning of the name and the origins of this institution see Goitein, *Society*, 4:29.
256 TS 8 J 18.21r, l. 8: Gil, *Kingdom*, 770. A consignment of leather (*nit'*) awaits Jacob b. al-Qābisī at the Ṣaffayn.
257 Ibid., l. 12: *al-samsār allādhī fī al-ṣaffayn* – the brokerage at al-Ṣaffayn.

8 Public Buildings

(a) The Fatimid Period

Public buildings and their architectural style often embody doctrines or beliefs. Indeed, since the approach to construction in the public sphere changed from one dynasty to the next, we should distinguish between the monuments created during the Fatimid and Ayyubid eras.

Because our knowledge of building in Alexandria under the Fatimids comes mostly from later Muslim sources, hostile to the Fatimid dynasty itself[259]and therefore, hardly inclined to extoll the beauties of its architecture or to glorify the memory of the Fatimid caliphs, the picture they create is in all likelihood misleading and distorted. Nevertheless, we may assume that the Fatimids put most of their resources and efforts into the construction of al-Qāhira, their new capital, and virtually abandoned Alexandria. In any case, the few public buildings we know of dating from the Fatimid era are Sunni religious buildings built in opposition to the Fatimid-Isma'īlī Caliphate, and certainly not typical of Fatimid Alexandria.

Madrasas, the Muslim Schools for Religious Learning

By the twelfth century there were two Sunni madrasas in Fatimid Alexandria: al-ʿAwfiyya and al-Salafiyya. The first of these, founded by the vizier Riḍwān Ibn al-Walkhashī in 1138, was named after the head of the Alexandrian Mālikī school who was director of the madrasa, Shaykh Abū al-Ṭāhir Ibn ʿAwf. This madrasa stood on the main avenue, *al-maḥajja al-ʿuẓmā'*, apparently in an area that was part of the *sūq*.[260] The other madrasa, al-Salafiyya, was founded in 1143

---

258 GS 10 J 9.21r, l. 14: Gil, *Kingdom*, 315. "I went over the al-Ṣaffayn account (*ḥisāb al- Ṣaffayn*)." See also Goitein, *Society*, 1:194. More about the commercial centers of Alexandria, see Frenkel, "Medieval Alexandria," 23–26.

259 See Lev, *State and Society*, 6–7; Sanders, *Ritual, Politics and the City.*

260 The Mālikī school had a powerful standing in Alexandria due to its Maghribi origins, the large Maghribi population of the city, its proximity to the Maghreb and the waves of Maghribi immigrants who settled near the harbor. See Subhi Y. Labib, "al-Iskandariyya," *Encyclopedia of Islam*, 2nd edition, 4:640 *s.v.* About Madrasa al-ʿAwfiyya, see al-Maqrīzī, *Ittiʿāẓ*, 3: 139; Abū al-ʿAbbās Aḥmad b. ʿAlī al-Qalqashandī, *Ṣubḥ al-aʿshā fī ṣināʿat al-inshā'* (Cairo: Dār al-Kutub, 1913), 10: 458. On Shaykh Abū Ṭāhir Ismāʿīl b. Makkī b. ʿIsā Ibn ʿAwf al-Zuhrī al-Iskandarānī who died in 1190 and had the privilege of being Ṣalāḥ-al-Dīn's teacher of ḥadīth, see Abū ʿAbdallah b. ʿUthmān al-Dhahabī, *al-ʿIbar fī ḥabar man ghabar* (Kuwait: Dā'irāt al-Maṭbūʿāt

by ʿAlī Ibn Salār, governor of Alexandria, and named after the Shāfiʿī scholar who taught there, Abū al-Ṭāhir Aḥmad al-Salafī.[261]

Mosques

We know of three great mosques built in Alexandria under the Fatimids: the al-Ṭurṭūshī mosque, the al-Muʾtaman mosque and the Jāmiʿ al-ʿAṭṭārīn. The first of these was built in 1125 at the initiative of a Spanish Mālikī legal sage, Abū Bakr al-Ṭurṭūshī (Ibn Abī Randaqa). The mosque stood outside the city walls, beside the gate that led to the harbor.[262] This unusual choice of location was in no small measure an expression of the Mālikī legal sage's criticism of the Ismaʿīlī-Fatimid regime. From this mosque, facing the sea, the ascetic al-Ṭurṭūshī could watch the harbor, Alexandria's nerve center and the meeting place with foreign cultures and their imported luxuries, which epitomized for him the evil corruption of the Fatimids. Al-Ṭurṭūshī used to clash repeatedly with customs officials, ship-owners and sailors in the harbor and those who frequented the harbor undoubtedly regarded the nearby presence of his Mālikī mosque as a provocation.[263]

---

wal-Nashr, 1960), 4: 242; al-Suyūṭī, *Ḥusn al-muḥāḍara*, 1: 214; Jamāl al-Dīn al-Shayyāl, *Aʿlām al-Iskandariyya fī al-ʿaṣr al-islāmī* (Cairo: Dār al-Maʿārif, 1965), 112–125.

261 See al-Maqrīzī, *Iʿttiʿāẓ*, 3: 144. On the Shāfiʿī scholar Abū Ṭāhir ʿImād al-Dīn Aḥmad b. Muḥammad b. Aḥmad al-Iṣfahānī al-Jarwānī al-Salafī, who died in Alexandria in 1185 and was buried there, see Tāj al-Dīn al-Subkī, *Ṭabaqāt al-shāfiʿiyya* (Cairo: Maṭbaʿat al-Bābī al-Ḥalabī, 1935/1324), 4: 45; al-Suyūṭī, *Ḥusn al-muḥāḍara*, 1: 165. About the subversive anti-Ismāʿīli aspect of the founding of these two madrasas, see al-Maqrīzī, *Ittiʿāẓ*, 3: 167, 198; Georges Vajda, "La Mašyaḥa d'Ibn al-Ḥaṭṭāb al-Rāzī: Contribution a l'histoire du sunnisme en Egypte fatimide," *BEO* 23 (1970): 21–99. For the madrasas and Alexandria see also Gary Leiser, "The Madrasa and the Islamization of the Middle East. The Case of Egypt," *Journal of the American Research Center in Egypt* 22 (1985): 29–47.

262 al-Maqrīzī, *Ittiʿāẓ*, 3: 125. About the legal scholar Abū Bakr al-Ṭurṭūshī of Spain (1081–1059), author of *Sirāj al-mulūk*, who settled in Alexandria and was related by marriage to the legal scholar Ibn ʿAwf, see al-Suyūṭī, *Ḥusn al-muḥāḍara*, 1: 213. See also Jamāl al-Dīn al-Shayyāl, *Jamāl al-Dīn Abū Bakr al-Ṭurṭūshī: al-ʿālim al-zāhid al-thāʾir* (Cairo: n.p., 1968). For a concise discussion of his life and figure see Joseph Drory, *Ibn al-ʿArabī of Seville: A Journey in the Land of Israel (1092–1095)* (Ramat Gan: Bar-Ilan University, 1993), 59–63 [Hebrew]; Lev, *Saladin*, 118, 119.

263 al-Ṭurṭūshī himself justified his presence in Alexandria with the need to guide lost souls and spread the true message of the Quran to the masses (*mukhālaṭat al-nās*). On the sailors who tried to throw him in the sea due to his unusual prayer rituals, see Maria I. Fierro, "La polémique à propos de *rafʿ al-yadayn fī l-ṣalāt dans al-Andalus*," *Studia Islamica* 65 (1987): 83–84. About his quarrels with the customs collectors at the harbor and his writings arguing against the purchase of goods from Christians and Jews, see Drori, ibid.

Other mosques were established as madrasas in the busy commercial quarters of the city. The al-Mu'tamin mosque was built by al-Mu'tamin, then governor of Alexandria, on the Great Royal Road, *al-maḥajja al-ʿuẓmā*, in 1126.[264]

Inside the perfumers' market, Sūq al-ʿAṭṭārīn, stood the largest and most famous mosque of the time, called Jāmiʿ al-ʿAṭṭārīn. This mosque was restored and renovated by Badr al-Jamālī in 1086, and was thus also known as the New Mosque, *al-masjid al-jadīd*. It was built in the style of Spanish and North African mosques, with a luxurious garden in the courtyard.[265] It is in fact the only religious building we know of in a manifestly Fatimid-Ismaʿīlī style, which was used by the Fatimid administration to promulgate the Ismaʿīlī version of the faith through its distinctive call to prayer and weekly sermons.[266]

(b) The Ayyubid Period

Our knowledge of public buildings in Ayyubid Alexandria derives from two main sources: the enthusiastic report of a contemporaneous Muslim traveler, Ibn Jubayr, who visited the city during the reign of Ṣalāḥ al-Dīn; and the books of the historian Maqrīzī, in the Mamluk period, which preserve the works of earlier writers.[267] According to these two sources, Ayyubid Alexandria had seen a tremendous surge in public building and this was no doubt reflected in the general ambiance of the city. In the words of Ibn Jubayr:

> This city owes its splendor and virtues to its ruler [Ṣalāḥ al-Dīn], meaning the madrasas and hostels (*maḥāris*) for students and pilgrims who arrive from distant lands where each can find a place to live and a madrasa in which to study the subject of his interest [...]. And the Sultan's interest in foreigners and wayfarers was such that he had bath houses built for them in which they bathed to their hearts' content and also hospitals to care for the sick and he appointed doctors for them.[268]

---

264 Salem, "D'Alexandrie à Alméria," 228–229.

265 See Muḥammad b. Qāsim al-Nuwayrī al-Iskandarānī, *Kitāb al-ilmām bi-l-aʿlām fīmā jarat bihi al-aḥkām wal-umūr al-maqaḍiyya fī waqʿat al-iskandariyya* (Hyderabad: Da'irat al-Maʿārif al-ʿUthmāniyya, 1970), 103.

266 Al-Nuwayrī (ibid.) writes that "when the Shiʿite government ceased to be and the Sunni government took its place, public gatherings and Friday sermons in this mosque were discontinued because they were of an Ismaʿīli kind."

267 About al-Maqrīzī's importance as a historical source of the Ayyubid period, see Lev, *Saladin*, 43–44.

268 Ibn Jubayr, *Riḥla*, 15–16.

al-Maqrīzī repeated this information in his book, but from his words we can understand that new buildings were going upon the west side of the city, near al-Qarāfa Gate.[269]

Sources also speak of a vast number of mosques in the city but the numbers seem too exaggerated to be true.[270] Ibn Jubayr's description indicates a cluster of three or four mosques side by side and the mosque itself being a complex (*murakkaba*), which included a group of buildings besides the mosque: a madrasa and a law court, and perhaps other sorts of religious buildings as well.[271]

Benjamin of Tudela mentions many inns: "Every nation has an inn (*funduk*) of its own."[272] But it is quite possible that these inns functioned within pre-existing buildings which had been converted for the purpose – as was done by many members of the Ayyubid elite to buildings and municipal properties in Cairo and Fustat.[273] Perhaps this is why their presence was inconspicuous and did not attract the attention of other travelers.

9 Synagogues

Genizah documents specify at least two synagogues in Alexandria between the twelfth and thirteenth centuries. In the eleventh century, Āraḥ b. Nathan reports to the *Nagid* Mevorakh that he read his epistles aloud at "both synagogues."[274] At the beginning of the thirteenth century, Sa'adya b. Berākhōt of Alexandria sends Maimonides a query about the morning prayer "held hitherto [1201] at the two synagogues,"[275] while the man responsible for the charity fund in Alexandria writes to Abraham Maimuni about a scandalous rumor that had been spread on Sabbath "in both synagogues."[276] Then too, when the judge Samuel ha-Dayyan died at the end of the thirteenth century, the elders consulted the people of "both synagogues" about the appointment of a new judge.[277]

269 Maqrīzī, *Sulūk*, 1: 76; Maqrīzī, *Khiṭaṭ*, 3: 169. Maqrīzī locates the new madrasa next to Turānshāh's tomb in the Qarāfa, which is on the west side of the city.
270 Ibn Jubayr estimates 8,000 to 12,000 mosques. See Ibn Jubayr, *Riḥla*, 17.
271 Ibid.
272 Benjamin of Tudela, *Itinerary*, 106.
273 Lev, *Saladin*, 108–114.
274 TS 24.21v, l. 54: Frenkel, *"The Compassionate and Benevolent"* [Hebrew], no. 38.
275 Maimonides, *Responsa*, 1:202, no.118. See also ibid., 2: 485–486, no. 259, and in another question from Sa'adyah b. Berākhōt during the same century: "At first it was instituted (*nitkan*) at the small synagogue and later on transferred to the big synagogue."
276 TS 10 J 16.6, ll. 9–13: Frenkel, *"The Compassionate and Benevolent"* [Hebrew], no. 54.
277 TS 13 J 21.20, ll. 13–14.

The documents refer to "the big synagogue" *(al-kanīsa al-kabīra),*[278] which was the synagogue of the Palestinian Jews (*kanīsat al-Shāmiyīn)*[279] and "the small synagogue" *(al-kanīsa al-ṣaghīra),*[280] which was the smaller Babylonian synagogue (*kanīsat al-ʿIrāqiyīn).*[281] We know that the Babylonian synagogue was located in the mixed neighborhood of Bīr Jabr,[282] most likely a few steps away from the Palestinian synagogue, for when a highly popular guest preacher arrived in town, the two congregations merged together at the Babylonian synagogue over the Sabbath to hear his sermon.[283]

This synagogue was an imposing structure with a courtyard large enough to accommodate a not inconsiderable crowd, since it was customary to assemble around the deceased in the courtyard for the recitation of prayers.[284] At the beginning of the thirteenth century, a special domed structure for this purpose was added inside the courtyard.[285]

10 Residential Buildings

The wealth accumulated in Fatimid times by the religious and commercial elites of the city gave rise to stately mansions whose architecture, enormous size and height and splendid gardens inspired works by contemporary poets. Ibn Qalāqis,

278 BM Or 5542.26.

279 TS 13 J.17, l. 7 – a cancelled promissory note from 1033: "the big synagogue known as Shāmiyīn."

280 TS NS J 183, a document dissolving a partnership in 1240; TS G 2,102, a note written by R. Joseph Rosh ha-Seder in 1198, in the margins of a book he authored on prayer practice. See Mordechai A. Friedman, "Objections to Prayer and Prayer Customs of the Land of Israel as reflected in the Responsa found in the Genizah (Responsa of R. Yosef Rosh ha-Seder)," in Shulamit Elitzur et al. (eds.), *Knesset Ezra: Literature and Life in the Synagogue* (Jerusalem: Ben Zvi Institute, 1990), 74, 85, 89 [Hebrew]; idem, "A Cry of Destruction about the Cancellation of the Saying of Piyyutim: A Request to Address the Sultan," *Pe'amim: Studies in Oriental Jewry* 78 (1999): 129, n. 2 [Hebrew].

281 Abraham Maimuni, *Responsa*, ed. Abraham H. Freiman and Shelomo D. Goitein (Jerusalem: n.p., 1938), 182, no. 106: The year 1235.

282 ENA 154 (2558): a letter from 1158 sent to the address "Bīr Jabr, Kanīsat al-ʿIrāqiyīn." In Arabic letters the address reads: *kanīsat al-Yahūd* (congregation of the Jews), indicating that there were Christian churches in the neighborhood as well.

283 TS 16.149: Frenkel, *"The Compassionate and Benevolent"* [Hebrew], no. 28.

284 Maimonides, *Responsa*, 2: 308–309, no. 151.

285 ENA NS 19.10r, l. 21–27: Frenkel, *"The Compassionate and Benevolent"* [Hebrew], no. 16. See also Goitein, *Society*, 5:550, n. 195, who believed this to have been a Palestinian custom. For more about public buildings, see Frenkel, "Medieval Alexandria," 26–30.

an Alexandrian poet of the Fatimid era wrote a panegyric to the palace of Banū Ḥalīf, an enormously wealthy family of qadis.[286] The opulent palace of the qadi Makīn al-Dawla with its fabled water fountain was immortalized in Muslim historiography.[287] The Jewish elite also lived in sumptuous homes, decked with gardens and fountains. Judah ha-Levi paid homage to the home of Aaron Ibn al-ʿAmmānī in some of his poems.[288] There were celebrated mansions in Ayyubid Alexandria as well. The qadi of Alexandria, Abū al-Makārim Ibn al-Ḥabbāb (d. 1201), for instance, owned a magnificent palace by the Sea Gate.[289]

These mansions were apparently built in a certain characteristic style. It is said that when the brother of Ṣalāḥ al-Dīn, Taqī al-Dīn Ibn Ayyūb, left Alexandria and settled in al-Ḥamā (Syria), he built a splendid residence in the "Alexandrian manner." Al-Nuwayrī, who reports this, provides a fairly detailed description, owing to which we have a general idea of what an Alexandrian mansion looked like: It consisted of a grand hall (*majlis*) for entertaining with folding double doors, a ventilation system built into the facade (*ṣadr*) of the building with a kind of broad chimney which filtered fresh air from the roof into every part of the home (*bādhanj, malqaf*).[290] Two closed narrow chambers (*kumm*, pl. *akmām*) branched off from the grand hall. The entrance to the hall was through a broad open vestibule (*qāʿa*) with parallel stone benches (*ṣuffa*) on either side. Adjacent to the house was a kind of pavilion made of light material which al-Nuwayrī calls "a temporary house" (*ʿaraḍī*) and which had large windows overlooking the gardens of the *khalīj*.[291]

A lease of the home of Ibn al-ʿAmmānī of Alexandria, preserved in a query submitted to Maimonides, includes a description of the four-story mansion: On the ground floor (*sufl*) were the women's quarters (*ḥuramiyya*) and another large room. Above were another three floors of living quarters and a top floor (*ʿulwu*) with a hidden door (*bāb al-sirr*] and a kitchen (*maṭbakh*).[292] A description of a mansion similar in structure and detail is found in a lease agreement from 1132. It too includes a large *qāʿa* and a women's apartment (*qāʿa ḥuramiyya*), as well as a "new room," a cistern (*ṣihrīj*), a well (*bīr*) and a garden.[293]

---

286 Aḥmad b. Muḥammad al-Maqqarī, *Nafḥ al-ṭīb fī ghuṣn al-andalus al-raṭīb* (Cairo: Maṭbaʿat al-Bābī al-Ḥalabī, 1949), 4: 24; Salem, "D'Alexandrie à Alméria," 215.
287 Maqrīzī, *Ittiʿāẓ*, 2: 381 3: 91.
288 See Part II, Chapter 5.3: Wealth as a Lifestyle.
289 Salem, "D'Alexandrie à Alméria," 252–253.
290 See also Goitein, *Society*, 4: 65–78.
291 Al-Nuwayrī, *Kitāb al-Ilmām*, 4: 49.
292 Maimonides, *Responsa*, 1: 2–3, no. 2.
293 TS Ar 30.30.

Of course, not all the city's homes were so grand. The homes described here were the exception, yet they lent the city an air of wonderment that magnetized visitors and served as a model for homes of a similar style and structure but with more modest dimensions.[294]

11 Alexandria: Gateway to the Magic of the Orient

The grandeur of Alexandria in the eyes of travelers and visitors from around the Muslim world seemed a remnant of splendor from a vanished past,[295] yet travelers from Europe were captivated particularly by the gateway to what they saw as the opulence of the orient. For travelers from around the Muslim world, the entrance through a crowded, bustling harbor gate was a most unpleasant experience, as described by Ibn Jubayr:

The first thing we witnessed upon arriving is that the Sultan's officials boarded our ship in order to inventory its cargo. And all Muslims aboard were listed by name and appearance and land of origin, and asked what goods or money they had with them [...] and on the shore stood policemen and officials charged with conveying all cargo to the Bureau (diwān). The passengers were called one by one to display their belongings and the *dwwān* was stiflingly crowded. A thorough search of every item, large or small, was conducted, and they stuck their hands in their belts in case something was concealed therein. And then they made them swear that they had nothing more with then than what had been found. And during all this many of the travelers' items went missing because they had passed through so many hands and it became more oppressive until at last they were released from this shameful and humiliating situation.[296]

Nevertheless, for travelers from European Christendom the incredible abundance in the port was a source of great wonder. As Benjamin of Tudela writes: "Alexandria is a commercial market for all nations. Merchants come thither from all the Christian kingdoms...and merchants of India bring thither all kinds of spices and the merchants of Edom buy of them. And the city is a busy one and full of traffic."[297] William of Tyre, who was born in Jerusalem,

294 See, for instance, ENA 2806.2, a rental agreement for a house lease in the amount of just seven dirhams, which included a *qāʿa* and a top floor (*ʿulwu*) as well. For more about residential buildings, see Frenkel, "Medieval Alexandria," 30 – 32.

295 See above, Part I, Chapter 2.5: The Topographical Features and Appearance of Alexandria in the Middle Ages.

296 Ibn Jubayr, *Riḥla*, 13.

297 Benjamin of Tudela, *Itinerary*, 106, no. 26.

but was of western European ancestry and identified culturally with western Christendom, writes in the same spirit:

> Whatever its needs are, Alexandria procures them from over the sea in great abundance That is why Alexandria is renowned for acquiring more goods of every kind than any other seaport in the world. All that is lacking in our part of the world: spices, pearls, the treasures of the east, vessels from strange ports, arriving from India, Sheba, Western Ethiopia and Persia and nearby lands [...] And that is why people flock there in such profusion from east and west, and Alexandria serves as an open market fair for both worlds.[298]

The magic of fabled Alexandria and its effect on western Christians manifested in the behavior of the Crusaders who captured it briefly in 1167, as described by William of Tyre: "The Christians enjoyed wandering through the city which had heretofore been the object of their lust. They gazed at the ports and the walls and collected stories and other lore from which, upon their return, they could weave tales for their friends and refresh the minds of their listeners in pleasing conversation."[299]

298 William of Tyre, *History*, 2: 336.
299 Ibid., 338.

Part II The Community Leaders: Biographies

Introduction

The second part of this book is a prosopographic study of the individuals who led the Alexandrian community in the period under consideration. Prosopography is an exegetical methodology of social and political history, which focuses on the individual – not as an objective in and of itself, but rather as a means to disclosing the collective portrait of a given society. It seeks to accomplish this through the production of a series of individual biographies and the amalgamation of many case studies, assuming that the individual is a point at which diverse historical forces converge, and therefore through the study of individual actors, the social apparatus of which they are a part may be revealed. By studying individual biographies, light is shed upon the institutional, cultural, emotional and intellectual lives of the entire group.[300] Prosopographical methods are not uniform; they are dependent upon the quality of the sources at the historian's disposal. Scholars of medieval Jewish history do not have at their disposal organized biographical handbooks, such as the onomastica routinely used by scholars of antiquity, nor the profuse biographical dictionaries that serve scholars of Islamic culture so well.[301] The vast majority of documents at my disposal originate in the random and heterogeneous Genizah collections.[302] It was the haphazard nature of these materials that dictated my methodology. Individual biographies were not readily accessible; rather, they needed to be painstakingly constructed, brick by brick, from disparate material found on site. There was no way to ask the same consistent questions in each case, and to cast specific data into set biographical molds, since the information that the Genizah documents provide is completely random. Therefore, in this part of the book I collected every possible shred of material from any source I could, in an effort to reconstruct a coherent and logical life story. I hope this eventually turned out to be an advantage, as it prevented me from duplicating ready-made medieval bio-

300 Claude Nicolet, "Prosopographie et histoire sociale: Rome et l'Italie a l'époque républicaine," *Annales, Economies, Societés, Civilisations*, 25.2 (1970): 1209–1229; André Chastagnol, "La prosopographie, méthode de recherché sur l'histoire du Bas-Empire," *Annales, Economies, Societés, Civilisations*, 25.2 (1970), 1229–1235; Lawrence Stone, "Prosopographie," *Daedalus*, 100.1 (1971): 46–75.
301 On the use made of this discipline for the study of antiquity, see Nicolet, "Prosopographie et histoire sociale"; for its role in the study of Muslim societies, see: Jacqueline Sublet, "La prosopographie arabe," *Annales* 25.2 (1970): 4–79. Petry's book on Mamluk Cairo is a typical example of a prosopographical study. See Carl F. Petry, *The Civilian Elite of Cairo in the Later Middle Ages* (Princeton NJ: Princeton University Press, 1981).
302 About the characteristics of the Cairo Genizah, see Goitein, *Society*, 1: 1–28.

https://doi.org/10.1515/9783110713619-005

graphical patterns, as so often happens in historical writings. Following Clifford Geertz, who considered cultural studies to be an exegetical science in search of meaning,[303] I chose to use an exegetical methodology,[304] based on an in-depth reading of the extant texts and impregnating them with meaning by means of a consistent and reasonable system of decoding. Like LaCapra, I assume that archival documentation, which is seemingly transparent and factual, includes various layers of knowledge and may contain many subtexts.[305] Therefore, instead of a quantitative collection of sometimes meaningless data, I attempted to engage in qualitative analysis, which ultimately yielded a collection of biographies, admittedly partial, but each one contributing another dimension to our portrait of the past.

The biography of the individual is an integration of his personal/private and political/public dimensions, particularly in the society under discussion, in which the two aspects cannot be separated. This methodology of integrating the personal biography and the individual's societal persona is a *post facto* match with the methodology developed by the philosopher and historian Jean-Paul Sartre. Sartre advocated for intermittently employing both "horizontal and vertical" readings of the biography and of social methodology, arguing that knowledge of one leads to knowledge of the other and that the societal collective and the individual mutually illuminate one another:

> The group bestows its power and its efficacy upon the individuals whom it has made and who have made it in return, whose irreducible particularity is one way of living universality. Through the individual the group looks back to itself and finds itself again in the opaqueness of life as well as in the universality of its struggle. Or rather, this universality takes on the face, the body, and the voice of the leaders whom it has given to itself; thus, the event itself, while a collective apparatus, is more or less marked with individual signs; persons are reflected in it to the same extent that the conditions of the conflict and the structures of the group have permitted them to be personalized.[306]

A basic issue which had to be decided upon before undertaking this project is that of selection, or in other words: who would be included in this collection of biographies. Unlike biographical handbooks, wherein the author selected a special group of people and grouped them together as a defined and refined societal category, the Genizah documents did not undergo any conscious selection

303 Clifford Geertz, *The Interpretation of Cultures* (NY: Basic Books, 1973), 5, 10.
304 See Dominick LaCapra, *History and Criticism* (Ithaca NY and London: Cornell University Press, 1985).
305 Ibid.
306 Jean-Paul Sartre, *Search for a Method*, trans. Hazel Barnes (NY: Knopf, 1963), 79, 130.

process. The texts that made their way into the Genizah deal with large segments of the population, and were not sorted in any way, and thus *prima facie* I had to make my own decisions as to inclusion and exclusion.

My first and most basic criterion for selection was necessarily the dearth of material that the Genizah yields about any one person. Data about an individual, interesting as it may be, is not useful if one cannot combine this data into some sort of coherent biography. I could therefore include only individuals who are featured to a sufficient extent in the Genizah so as to reconstruct a biographical portrait of some sort, even if this portrait is partial and lacunose.

Other criteria were determined by the project's focus: the community in Alexandria. In this project I only included people who lived in the city on a regular basis, and for whom Alexandria was the main site of their activity, for at least part of their lives. I did not include people who owned houses and property in the city, or people who lived there intermittently, such as merchants who would come to Alexandria on business for limited periods of time.

The biggest difficulty, however, was in defining who was part of the ruling class. The nature of Genizah society, which almost completely lacked markers of legal status,[307] magnified the problem. As we shall see below, the ruling class were not necessarily entitled to their status in the legal sense. Rather, they constituted an entirely unofficial group, and for this reason, one finds in the Genizah collections individuals who were politically active in the community, whether they held official positions or titles or not. *Post facto* it becomes clear that the Genizah was self-selecting. It naturally preserved first and foremost the documents of those in the upper classes. These people, who were literate bibliophiles, who were active and prominent in the community, left their mark in the Genizah more than anyone else.

This collection of biographies is organized chronologically, under the assumption that an individual's personal story reveals the story of the society of which he is a part, and thus a series of personal biographies may reflect historical processes that the collective underwent as well. The fragmentary nature of the information provided by the Genizah sometimes creates the need to fill gaps with hypothetical extrapolations. Weaving a coherent tapestry requires one to use patches of this nature. I tried to base them on similar cases, or to draw upon our general knowledge of the nature of the Genizah collection.

307 Goitein, *Society*, 2: 42, 65; 4: 5.

Chapter 1 The Ben Yeshūʿā Family

One local family led the Alexandrian community until the last third of the eleventh century. The information available to us, all of which is drawn from the Cairo Genizah, pertains for the most part to the last of the leaders from this family: Yeshūʿā b. Joseph. This is not necessarily an indication of his importance as a leader or significant aspects of his governance; rather it derives from the fact that his tenure as leader overlapped with the renewal of the Ben Ezra Synagogue, and it was there and at that time that the texts which one day would constitute the Cairo Genizah were deposited. Thus, Yeshūʿā b. Joseph's documents were collected in the nascent Genizah and survived.[308] We are constrained to view the two generations prior to Yeshūʿā from his later perspective, and the further we are from Yeshūʿā's time period, the murkier our knowledge of these earlier figures is.

1 The Grandfather

We know nothing about the grandfather except that he was a judge (*dayyan*) in Alexandria, and that he was not entitled to the designation "Fellow" (*ḥaver*), a title which the Yeshivah of the Land of Israel (hereafter: Palestinian Yeshivah) bestowed upon his grandson in the fullness of time. In a missive the Head of the Yeshivah (Gaon) sent to the Alexandrian community in 1025, he writes about Yeshūʿā: "It would have been appropriate for him to thank God for he was granted something that neither his father nor his grandfather were granted."[309] The Head of the Yeshivah hints here at the title "Fellow" (*ḥaver*), which the Yeshiva bestowed upon Yeshūʿā, and incidentally we learn that in the first decades of the eleventh century, at the very latest, and over the course of at least three generations, the Ben Yeshūʿā family was involved in the governance of the Alexandrian community. The first member of this family known to us, however, is shrouded in mystery, we only know he existed.

308 On the circumstances of the construction of the Genizah chamber in the Ben Ezra synagogue, see Goitein, *Society*, 1: 18; idem, *Palestinian Jewry*, 46–47.
309 TS 13 J 16.16, ll. 14–16: Gil, *Palestine* [Hebrew], no. 74, no. 63.

https://doi.org/10.1515/9783110713619-006

2 Joseph b. Yeshūʿā the Judge

(a) Chronological Framework

The first document pertaining to this leader is the certificate of his reappointment as the *muqaddam*[310] of the Alexandrian community. This certificate of authority, which was written in Arabic script, was published in honor of the Fatimid Caliph al-Mustanṣir's ascension in 1036.[311] The document enumerates the heads of the Palestinian Yeshivah in whose time Joseph served as *muqaddam*. The first of the leaders mentioned is Josiah, who died in 1025, but since the document is missing part of its beginning, it is likely that prior leaders were mentioned.[312] It is thus assumed that Joseph served in this capacity beginning in the last years of the tenth century or the first years of the eleventh century.

Joseph served as a judge for many years: In 1042 he is referred to in the opinion of the Muslim qadi as "He who is known by the title 'judge'."[313] Only in a missive from 1055 is he mentioned in conjunction with blessings for the dead, such as "Let his memory be a blessing," "Let his resting place be in Eden."[314] One can thus surmise that Joseph died not earlier than the fifth decade of the eleventh century, meaning that he served as a judge in Alexandria for about fifty years.

(b) His Position

The extent of Joseph b. Yeshūʿā's authority and responsibilities as the *muqaddam* of the Alexandrian community, as they were viewed by the Muslim rulers, are formulated clearly in his certificate of appointment and included:

1. The authority to pass judgment on the basis of Jewish law, and specifically family law.
2. The power to make community appointments. The certificate mentions only two types of positions: the liturgical-administrative sphere (i.e. cantors in

310 On the role of the *muqaddam* as appointed leader of the community, see Goitein, *Society*, 2: 68–75.
311 TS NS 320.45: Goitein, *Palestinian Jewry*, 77–78. For the circumstances of the document's writing, see ibid., 52.
312 Goitein (ibid., 78, nn. 1–3) believes that the two *geonim* who preceded Josiah appointed Joseph as judge *(dayyan)*, but he does not explain on what grounds he bases his conclusion.
313 TS 13 J 8.31: Frenkel, *"The Compassionate and Benevolent"* [Hebrew], no. 60.
314 TS 24.56, ll. 33, 38: Gil, *Palestine* [Hebrew], no. 355.

the synagogues),[315] and the financial sphere: "a person who shall administer what was donated to them." This refers to the community's funds and its property derived from donations and bequests. The appointment of these positions was under the full authority of the *muqaddam*, who could fire the people he appointed if he saw fit.

3. Punitive authority: "And if one of them objects [...]." Unfortunately, the document is abruptly truncated and we are unable to ascertain what punitive measures the *muqaddam* could employ.

The Muslim rulers saw the *muqaddam* as the leader of the local community responsible for adjudication, administration, and religious ceremonies. In order to invest his position with authority, the rulers granted him official recognition and provided him with the means to execute his decisions. One should note that there is no evidence in this document for conceiving of the *muqaddam* as an intermediary between the Jewish community and the Muslim rulers, or as a community advocate in matters which required intercession.

(c) Actual Activities

The few Genizah documents that pertain to Joseph b. Yeshūʿā do not allow us a wide survey of his activity within the community, but they are sufficient to offer us some hints. Three out of the four documents dealing with his tenure offer evidence that much of his attention was focused upon securing funds for the ransoming of captives – an area which was not officially within the purview of his authority as the *muqaddam*.[316] The fourth document is a court record from 1042, which deals with a complicated case of "reciprocal marriage" (*taʿwīḍ*) upon

315 In the original: *ḥazzānim*. The cantors fulfilled many administrative functions in the community beyond their liturgical role. It is likely that this term comprehended the various offices of community government. On the important status of the cantors in the Jewish communities of the Islamic world, see Leo Landman, "The Office of the Medieval Hazzan," *JQR* 62 (1972): 246–276; Goitein, *Society*, 2: 223; idem, *Palestinian Jewry*, 89, n. 25; Eliyahu Ashtor, "Aspects of the Character of the Jewish Community in Medieval Egypt," *Zion* 30 (1965): 63 [Hebrew].

316 TS 10 J 15.16: Frenkel, *"The Compassionate and Benevolent"* [Hebrew], no. 53. This is the opening, in flowery Hebrew, of a letter in Joseph b. Yeshūʿā's handwriting, sent to an unidentified community, and forms a preface to a request for help in raising funds, apparently for the ransoming of captives. TS 24.29 (Mann, *Jews*, 1: 367–370) and Bodl MS Heb a f.28 (2873) (Arthur Cowley, "Bodleian Geniza Fragments," *JQR OS* 18 [1906], 250–254) are two letters addressed to the leader of the Palestinian community in Fustat, Ephraim b. Shemaryah, both requesting help for the ransoming of captives.

which he adjudicated. The added Arabic letters on the back of the document indicate that final judgment in this complicated case was not rendered in Joseph's court, but was eventually brought before the Muslim qadi.[317]

(d) Sources of His Authority

Until the last third of the eleventh century, the position of *muqaddam* in Alexandria was for life and was hereditary, passing from father to son. Joseph was invested in this position only after the death of his father. In the truncated sentence at the beginning of his certificate of appointment it states: "[...] his death, and afterwards Joseph ha-Kohen was appointed." This, in spite of the fact that at the end of Joseph's life, his son Yeshūʿā was the *de facto* leader and that it was the son who determined community policy and penned the letters upon which his father's official signature appeared. In 1042, however, when a case was brought before the Muslim qadi, which the Jewish court had not succeeded in adjudicating, the qadi required that the elderly Joseph give formal testimony at the time of the trial. Joseph was thus still the official judge of the community, despite his great age, and despite the fact that in reality it was his son who led.[318] It is thus apparent that at this time the position of judge in Alexandria was hereditary and that the authority with which this position was invested passed from father to son. We shall see below, however, that the source of this authority was somewhat unstable and the subject of intense controversy within the community.[319]

(e) Joseph b. Yeshūʿā's Image

In the Genizah documents pertaining to his tenure, all indications point to a communal perception of Joseph b. Yeshūʿā as a beloved and popular leader who was accepted and valorized both in the Alexandrian community and by the Palestinian Yeshivah. At the end of his days, when his son Yeshūʿā administered communal matters on his behalf with his approval and with the support of

317 TS 13 J 8.31: Frenkel, "*The Compassionate and Benevolent*" [Hebrew], no. 60, and see the summary of the document in Goitein, *Society*, 3: 74, n. 34.
318 TS 13 J 8.31: Frenkel, "*The Compassionate and Benevolent*" [Hebrew], no. 60.
319 See below, Part II, Chapter 1.3 (b): The Opposition.

the Gaon of the Palestinian Yeshivah, the son's policies led to dissatisfaction amongst certain segments of the community. They complained about him to the head of the Palestinian Yeshivah, and publicly claimed that his father's leadership was better: "A letter from the community, God preserve it, has come to me, and in it they complain about the conduct of R. Yeshūʿā ha-Kohen, who is among them, claiming that his father's ways were better than his."[320] Even after Joseph's death, a different Gaon, Daniel b. Azaryah, mentions his affection for the father, whom he loved while the latter was alive: "And I attest, on my father's life, may the spirit of God guide him, that I love this fellow [= Yeshūʿā b. Joseph] and I loved his father, may he rest in Eden."[321]

This being said, one should note that the two statements above were written after Joseph's death when he no longer led the community, and they evince no small measure of nostalgia.

3 Yeshūʿā b. Joseph

(a) An Alexandrian "Prince"

Yeshūʿā b. Joseph was trained from a young age to step into his father's shoes as the leader of the Alexandrian community, and a substantial percentage of the letters penned in the father's name were written by the son,[322] or were sent in the name of both Joseph and Yeshūʿā: "From me and from R. Yeshūʿā the adept, my precious one."[323]

During the years 1038–1042, while his father was still alive, and was still the official *muqaddam* and judge of the community,[324] Yeshūʿā held the title of *ḥaver,* granted to him by the Palestinian Yeshivah, thus becoming the first judge in Alexandria to hold this prestigious title and position. This took place at the time of the controversy between the Gaon Solomon b. Judah and his rival Nathan

---

320 TS 13 J 14.16: Gil, *Palestine* [Hebrew], no. 74; Frenkel, *"The Compassionate and Benevolent"* [Hebrew], no. 63. This is the response sent by the Gaon of the Palestinian Yeshivah, Solomon b. Judah, to the complaint made by the Alexandrians.

321 TS 24.56: Gil, *Palestine* [Hebrew], no. 355. A letter from Daniel b. Azaryah from 1055, to Abraham ha-Kohen b. Isaac Ibn al-Furāt, in which the crisis in the Alexandrian community is also mentioned.

322 See above, n. 318.

323 TS 10 J 15.16: Frenkel, *"The Compassionate and Benevolent"* [Hebrew], no. 53.

324 On this title, see Gil, *History of Palestine*, 506.

b. Abraham.[325] The Gaon who granted him this title was likely Solomon b. Judah, who in the fullness of days was revealed as Yeshūʿā's advocate and protector. It is reasonable to assume that with this boon the Gaon wished to establish for himself a measure of power in the Alexandrian community, since Yeshūʿā stood to inherit his father's position. The father remained alive, however, for a number of years following his son's elevation by the Palestinian Yeshivah.

Yeshūʿā, in the first part of his tenure, was hence the *de facto* leader of the community. He administered local matters and depended upon the support of the head of the Palestinian Yeshivah. In the background, however, was his aged father, who in the eyes of the Muslim authorities was still considered "the Judge" and according to members of the community, was the epitome of a cherished leader to whom they looked up. Their criticism against Yeshūʿā was in contrast to his father who was "better than him."[326] Even the head of the Yeshivah, who supported Yeshūʿā and promoted him, felt the need to respond to the complaints of the community, not only in a letter rebuking Yeshūʿā, but also in a missive to his father: "And regarding your first communication, we have written to him and chastised him, and we have written to his father, and here is our letter to you."[327] His official title *ḥaver* was granted to him by the Gaon on the basis of references which attested to his worth, but also and perhaps especially contrasted him with his father: "All unanimously value him more than his father, and say he is greater than his father, and it is on the basis of this testimony that the Yeshiva's leaders bestowed upon him the title of *ḥaver.*"[328]

It is thus apparent that Yeshūʿā b. Joseph's social milieu nurtured and groomed him, and attached to him a set of expectations befitting an heir apparent destined to fill his father's shoes after the latter's death.

(b) The Opposition

The process of "inheritance" described above was seen as customary and was a societal norm, but it was not to be taken for granted, and there was opposition to it on more than one occasion.

---

325 On this conflict, see Moshe Gil, *A History of Palestine, 634–1099*, trans. Ethel Broido (Cambridge: Cambridge University Press), 669–719.

326 See above, Part II, Chapter 1.2 (e): Joseph b. Yeshūʿā's Image.

327 TS 12.238, ll. 17–18: Gil, *Palestine* [Hebrew], no. 73.

328 Ibid., ll. 12–13.

The Rival

Shelah b. Moses the Cantor was one of the more noteworthy individuals who challenged this custom. Shelah's signature as the representative of the community appears side by side with Joseph b. Yeshūʿā the Judge's signature on a legal document written on behalf of the community to the Muslim judiciary.[329] This is to say that Shelah was one of the more powerful people amongst the leaders of the community, besides Joseph the Judge.[330] Being the cantor, he occupied a central position of power in the community apparatus. It is thus not at all surprising that a short time after Yeshūʿā was granted the title of "Fellow of the Yeshivah" – a title which bolstered his standing in the community – Shelah the Cantor also tried to gain this title and to strengthen his position as a potential heir to the leadership.

"The Meek Shall Inherit the Earth"

Shelah the Cantor succeeded in building around him an opposition of a populist nature; it coalesced around the claim that Yeshūʿā's leadership was detached and aloof from the community. "Meekness" (*tawāḍuʿ*) was a central issue when it came to the opposition to Yeshūʿā: The Gaon Solomon b. Judah emphasized Yeshūʿā's "meekness" in his response to those who opposed Yeshūʿā and presented him as gifted with perspicacity and moderation, meekness and wisdom.[331] Yeshūʿā himself emphasized his gift of meekness. This is apparent in a letter of reference addressed to the Alexandrian community, which stated: "R. Yeshūʿā, the fellow, may the Merciful one preserve it, the son of our master Joseph, may heaven be his resting place, came before us, and we saw that he is meek and God-fearing to the extent that we are pleased on his behalf and on your behalf that such a man will be among you."[332]

A comparison between the handwriting of this "letter of reference" and other documents penned by Yeshūʿā b. Joseph evince a great deal of similarity, and cause one to suspect that this letter was written by Yeshūʿā himself as part of his struggle to establish himself as leader. One should note that the fabrication of documents was not exceptional in the political atmosphere of the time. Thus,

---

329 TS 13 J 8.31: Frenkel, *"The Compassionate and Benevolent"* [Hebrew], no. 60.

330 See above, n. 315.

331 TS 13 J 14.16: Gil, *Palestine* [Hebrew], no. 74; Frenkel, *"The Compassionate and Benevolent"* [Hebrew], no. 63.

332 TS 13 J 28.21: Shelomo D. Goitein, *Jewish Education in Muslim Countries Based on Records from the Cairo Genizah* (Jerusalem: Ben-Zvi Institute and The Hebrew University, 1962), 192–193 [Hebrew].

for example, when the Gaon Solomon b. Judah received the letter of complaint against Yeshūʿā, he first made sure to check the handwriting of the letter and to compare it to the attached signatures. He then voiced his suspicions publicly: "You, the signatories, sign your names in the same handwriting as the person who penned this missive, and who shall say that this reflects their will?"[333] In other words, most of the signatures were added by the same person who wrote the document and the Gaon is doubtful whether they were "collected" with the signatories' knowledge.

If, indeed, we are dealing with a letter that was purposely forged by Yeshūʿā, this is a golden opportunity to comprehend what sort of public persona Yeshūʿā wished to present to the community. But even if this letter was penned by his supporters, one may assume that it was written with his approval and that it accurately reflected the public image he preferred. In any case, it is clear that Yeshūʿā wished to earn legitimacy on the basis of his personal attributes: "Humility and fear of God" were the main qualities that he wished the community to believe he possesed. Yeshūʿā and his supporters probably sought to present him in this way to counter the claims that he was proud and aloof. Daniel b. Azaryah Gaon[334] states this explicitly: "I advised him, to none other than R. Yeshūʿā the Fellow, may the Merciful One grant him life, that he should conduct himself with grace and that he should change the prevailing negative opinion about him, which was mentioned above. For it has been his custom to sit upon his lofty cathedra and be proud."[335]

A measure of aloofness and of distance is apparent in Yeshūʿā's words when he describes the members of his community: "The people do not know the legal minutiae and they go against the court, they twist all that is adjudicated and embolden the defendants in order to stir up anger."[336] In another letter, which he had written in an attempt to prevent Daniel b. Azaryah's visit to Alexandria for fear that members of the community would confront him and humiliate him, he states the following: "God knows that if I had the influence, I would release him [=Daniel b. Azaryah] from the burden of all Jews. But the Merciful One pardons those under constraint."[337]

333 TS 12.328, ll. 15–16: Gil, *Palestine* [Hebrew], no. 73; Frenkel, *"The Compassionate and Benevolent"* [Hebrew], no. 80.

334 On this Gaon, see Gil, *History of Palestine*, 719–739; Goitein, *Palestinian Jewry*, 132–188.

335 TS 24.56r, right margin, l. 18; v, l.1: Gil, *Palestine* [Hebrew], no. 355.

336 Bodl MS Heb c 13.20v, ll. 9–10: Gil, *Kingdom*, no. 673.

337 Bodl MS Heb b 3.16v, ll. 14–17: Gil, *Kingdom*, no. 671; Frenkel, *"The Compassionate and Benevolent"* [Hebrew], no. 1. On "Jews" meaning members of the local community, see Goitein, *Society*, 2: 67.

The opposition to Yeshūʿā b. Joseph's leadership derived then from the tension between the populist elements of the community and the entrenched family of leaders, which had become distant and aloof.

Betwixt Babylonians and Palestinians

Despite its populist origins, the opposition to Yeshūʿā morphed into a well-known political tableau with familiar protagonists. It originally coalesced around a political rival (Shelah b. Moses the Cantor) but was soon characterized by the dichotomous paradigm of Babylonian and Palestinian rivalry.[338] Shelah the Cantor's supporter and spokesman was the leader of the Babylonian community in Fustat, Sahlān b. Abraham. He demanded of the Gaon Solomon b. Judah that his protégé also be made a "fellow": "The great and honored holy teacher R. Sahlān, may the Rock preserve him, has asked in writing regarding the cantor, may God protect him, that he too should be granted the title 'fellow.'"[339] R. Yeshūʿā's supporters, on the other side, were the heads of the Palestinian community, as we shall see below in detail.[340]

A Persistent Rivalry

The rivalry between Yeshūʿā and Shelah the Cantor was not short-lived. After Shelah's death, his son continued the struggle. In a letter from 1066, written by Ibrāhīm b. Farāḥ, one of Yeshūʿā's supporters, to Judah b. Moses Ibn Sighmār, he mentions the son of the cantor, who sends malignant epistles against him: "I have already dispatched a letter to you in the hands of the letter bearer, Manṣūr, and with it is a note from the son of the cantor [...] in which he maligns me [...]. I ask that when my master the Nagid and my master the Fellow, may God permit their majesty to endure, arrive, you shall be so good as to read the letter before them so that they may know that this man bears malice in his heart towards me."[341]

Shelah the Cantor's struggle against Yeshūʿā's leadership was thus a protracted campaign, which went through reversals and different phases. An internal skirmish amongst the local leadership morphed into a popular conflict between community members and an out-of-touch hereditary leadership, and

338 Gil, *History of Palestine*, 515–516; Bareket, *Jewish Leadership*, 81–90.
339 TS 13 J 14.16, ll. 17–18: Gil, *Palestine* [Hebrew], no. 74; Frenkel, *"The Compassionate and Benevolent"* [Hebrew], no. 63.
340 See below, Part II, Chapter 1.3 (c): Sources of Support, in the section: The Fustat Leaders.
341 TS 13 J 26.8r, ll. 4–10: Gil, *Kingdom*, no. 556.

finally translated into the conventional pattern of a struggle between Palestinians and Babylonians, which continued for more than one generation.

(c) Sources of Support

Shelah the Cantor was not the only party who benefited from powerful interests both within the community and outside of it. Yeshūʿā b. Joseph did as well. He represented and was supported by internal and external power brokers, as we shall delineate below.

The Geonim, the Heads of the Palestinian Yeshivah

Solomon b. Judah Gaon was Yeshūʿā's key supporter. He nurtured and promoted Yeshūʿā, and provided his tenure as leader with the necessary legitimacy. In an unprecedented move, he granted him the title "Fellow of the Yeshivah" when his father, the judge, was still alive, and at the same time refused to grant his rival, Shelah the Cantor, the same title. This gesture, which took place at the height of the inheritance struggle, was of vital importance, and it determined the outcome in favor of Yeshūʿā. This being said, it is evident that the head of the Yeshivah made some effort to demonstrate neutrality and minimize the value of his intervention. To a letter of complaint sent by members of the community, for example, he responded:

> In the letter written in the month of Kislev you protest against his eminence the great and holy master R. Yeshūʿā ha-Kohen who was ordained as a fellow by the heads of the Yeshivah after they ascertained that he was worthy, and that he was decent, and that no bad thing had ever been heard about him from those among you, from amongst your community as well as from outside visitors, all of them praise him [...]. And it was upon this that the heads [of the Yeshivah relied] when they ordained him as a fellow. [It was expected that he would] act humbly and bear their affliction and strife, we did not appoint him to be a burden unto them [...]. It has already been said that many of you are inclined to support him.[342]

And in another letter he states: "Otherwise, we do not force him upon you. If he conducts himself among you with 'humility,' this is well and good. He is your son and it is from your mouths that he sustains himself."[343] Regarding Abraham b.

342 TS 12.238, ll. 7–17: Gil, *Palestine* [Hebrew], no. 73.
343 TS 13 J 14.16, ll. 16–17: Gil, *Palestine* [Hebrew], no. 74; Frenkel, *"The Compassionate and Benevolent"* [Hebrew], no. 63.

Sahlān's request to bestow the title of "Fellow" upon Shelah the Cantor as well, he answers: "There is no way to do this at this time, since both the chief judge, may the Rock preserve him, yours truly, and everyone else, concur that this is how it is properly done. And everyone agrees to pray upon he who carries the title 'fellow.'"[344]

In other words, the Head of the Yeshivah Solomon b. Judah tried very hard to obfuscate his personal responsibility for choosing Yeshūʿā as the leader. He did this in two ways: He presented the choice of Yeshūʿā as the choice of members of the community, who had accepted him and who had recommended him freely without any coercion. He also minimized his role in choosing Yeshūʿā and passed the responsibility on to the chief judge and the other leading members of the Yeshiva. He also took pains to demonstrate impartiality. He referred to Shelah the cantor as "his great and honorable holiness, our teacher and master Shelah the Cantor, who is desirable and worthy to be entitled *ḥaver*,"[345] He thus hinted that Shelah was also worthy of this desired title and at the same time excoriated Yeshūʿā's aloofness and conduct, stating unequivocally: "This is shameful."[346]

One should note that the appointment of local leaders was one of the main responsibilities of the Gaon, as was clearly articulated in the official letter of appointment granted to him by the caliph himself, which makes Solomon b. Judah's emphasis upon an impartial façade in the case at hand very apparent. It must be said, though, that Yeshūʿā's conduct does reflect a good deal of independence from the Gaon, as is evinced in the complaint levelled at him by members of the community, which claimed that he disdained the title granted to him.[347]

In Daniel b. Azaryah's tenure as Head of the Yeshivah, Yeshūʿā continued to lead the Alexandrian community and to be the focal point of controversy and scandal. In the course of one of the more tempestuous crises, Yeshūʿā was forced to leave Alexandria and find sanctuary in Fustat, where he sought protection from his detractors. The Head of the Yeshivah, Daniel b. Azaryah, was his main supporter, and ultimately diffused the crisis, allowing Yeshūʿā to return to Alexandria. Daniel interceded directly and responded forcefully to the letters of complaint against Yeshūʿā, vociferously denying all allegations against him.

344 TS 13 J 14.16, ll. 19–21.
345 Ibid., ll. 2–3.
346 Ibid., 14.
347 See above, Part II, Chapter 1.1: The Grandfather.

In a letter to Abraham Ibn al-Furāt[348] in which Daniel reports to him regarding the actions he undertook on behalf of Yeshūʿā as the crisis unfolded, one may discern very obvious undertones of anger against the opposition: "And with regard to everything that happened in Alexandria, I did not ignore it when it was occurring, [and I did] as much as I could. And when I arrived in Fustat you know how I sanctioned his detractors. Because I swear upon my life, they disdained custom and desecrated the commandments."[349]

One may assume that the sanctions the Head of the Yeshivah imposed against Yeshūʿā's enemies were very harsh, since he saw fit to characterize their behavior as anti-religious and as a desecration, no less. He continues to elaborate upon his actions in the affair: "And when letters detailing what happened to our honored fellow, may the Merciful One preserve him, arrived, I wrote back immediately, and vehemently disagreed, and I instructed him that he should not get involved between him [Yeshūʿā] and his rivals, and that he should not write to them, and I forbad him to do so under any circumstance, and I sent other more forceful letters afterwards." [350]

Daniel b. Azaryah Gaon, brought the full force of his authority to bear on behalf of Yeshūʿā. To this end he employed one of his primary tools for wielding authority: the written declaration. Initially he published a letter to the community, a pamphlet that was meant to hang in the synagogue so that everyone in the community could see it. In it he dismissed all the accusations against Yeshūʿā, and attempted to preserve Yeshūʿā's good name, guaranteeing him his public support. Afterwards he sent personal letters to Eli b. Amram, another Yeshivah fellow and the head of the Palestinian community in Fustat,[351] and to others whom he identified as involved in the dispute, and authoritatively forbade them from involving themselves further in the affair demanding that they stop sending letters. By forbidding them to write letters, the Gaon actually cut off the opposition's main conduit of influence and propaganda, while he himself could continue to use it in his advocacy on Yeshūʿā's behalf.

---

348 On Abraham Ibn al-Furāt, who was a royal physician at the Fatimid court and deeply involved in the affairs of the Yeshivah and the communities, see Gil, *History of Palestine*, 724–725; Goitein, *Palestinian Jewry*, index, *s.v.*; Goitein, *Society*, 5: 263–264.

349 TS 24.56, 1, ll. 39–42: Gil, *Palestine* [Hebrew], no. 355.

350 TS 24.56r, right margins, ll. 1–9.

351 About Eli ha-Ḥaver b. Amram, see Goitein, *Jewish Community*, 144–153; Goitein, "HaRav: An Obscure Chapter in the History of the Palestinian Gaonate, with an Appendix: A Letter by 'the Daughter of the Head of the Yeshiva'," *Tarbiẓ* 45 (1987): 64–75; Gil, History of Palestine, §779; Cohen, *Jewish Self-Government*, 203, 233.

In the following letter. Daniel demonstrates his high regard and even his love for Yeshūʿā,[352] but a close reading of the text reveals that his attitude vis-à-vis Yeshūʿā was somewhat ambivalent. Following Abraham Ibn al-Furāt's unalloyed praise of Yeshūʿā, Daniel b. Azaryah responds with the following:

> May the Redeemer offer you encouragement, I understood what you wrote, regarding our important fellow R. Yeshūʿā, may the Merciful One grant him life, the son of R. Joseph ha-Kohen the Judge, may his memory be for a blessing, and your praise of him regarding his regular interest in your affairs and his words of encouragement, and his love of you and his frequent advice as you describe in the continuation [of your letter]. Firstly, I shall say that your attempt to steer his affairs in the right direction is entirely acceptable, for it is advisable to adhere to your valuable advice and blessed counsel. This is doubly true since you are now a man whose prestige is a boon to us and whose great and elevated status sustains us.[353]

Daniel b. Azaryah agrees that one should "steer R. Yeshūʿā's affairs in the right direction," or in other words intercede on his behalf, first and foremost since he wished to placate Ibn al-Furāt. Ibn al-Furāt's close relationship with the Fatimid authorities as the court physician made him a central and very powerful figure in the politics of the Jewish community,[354] and Daniel b. Azaryah himself sought him out and wished to derive benefit from Ibn al-Furāt's elevated status in the court. Daniel b. Azaryah says this in the letter without any attempt at obfuscation; the phenomenon of seeking the support of court Jews was considered self-evident and complimentary to those of elevated status and there was no reason to hide it, as is quite clear in the style of the above quoted communication.[355] The implication of the letter, however, is that the sought-after intimacy with Ibn al-Furāt was the Gaon's primary consideration when he agreed to help Yeshūʿā, rather than his great love of the community leader. It is true that Daniel b. Azraryah declares his love for Yeshūʿā later in the letter, but one notes the hidden caveat: "And I attest on my father's life, may the spirit of God guide him, I love this fellow and I love his father, may he rest in Eden."[356] The reference to the father, seems to be out of place and somewhat surprising in this context. This was probably the Gaon's way to indicate that this purported "love" is mostly for the

352 See above, Part II, Chapter 1.2 (e): Joseph b. Yeshūʿā's Image.
353 TS 24.56r, ll. 32–38: Gil, *Palestine* [Hebrew], no. 355.
354 See above, n. 348.
355 Daniel uses the term *jāh* here. On this multifaceted and complex term in Judeo-Arabic and Muslim cultures, see Goitein, *Society*, 5: 255–260. One of the definitions he adduces there is "a position of power and influence, obtained in very different ways and used for a large variety of causes." See also Marina Rustow, "Formal and Informal Patronage."
356 TS 24.56r, l. 38: Gil, *Palestine* [Hebrew], no. 355.

father and not for Yeshūʿā himself. Indeed, a more explicit reservation regarding Yeshūʿā's conduct and character appears immediately afterwards: "It has been his custom to sit upon his lofty cathedra and be proud in it and to act against the duties that are inherent to [his elevated status]."[357]

Daniel b. Azaryah Gaon actively and uncompromisingly supported Yeshūʿā the local leader, despite his reservations regarding his character and his conduct. This policy was due to a number of considerations, some of them short-term factors – such as his desire to appease those who had the ear of the Muslim authorities – and some others more fundamental such as the perpetuation of the Yeshivah's customary support of the existing hereditary leadership.

This ambivalent relationship is also apparent in how Yeshūʿā related to Daniel b. Azaryah as is reflected in Yeshūʿā's letter to his friend and business partner, Judah b. Moses Ibn Sighmār.[358] It is apparent that this letter was preceded by another exchange between the two, and in this earlier exchange matters were discussed which were not supposed to reach the ear of Daniel b. Azaryah. Judah Ibn Sighmār, however, did not try very hard to keep the letter secret as instructed by Yeshūʿā, and the letter eventually reached Daniel b. Azaryah, who read it and did not appreciate what was said therein at all.[359]

We do not know what was written in this secret letter that caused Daniel b. Azaryah to be so angry, though one may assume that Ibn Sighmār and Yeshūʿā's collusion and conspiracy behind his back by means of letters did not indicate a great deal of loyalty. One may perhaps assume that the letter had to do with his intention to visit Alexandria. In 1060 Daniel b. Azaryah embarked on a journey to Egypt,[360] and probably wished to include Alexandria in his itinerary. Hosting the head of a Yeshivah in the community required a great deal of financial outlay and labor, and at the time of the planned visit the community was in dire financial straits due to the significant sums of money spent on the ransoming of captives.[361] Moreover, significant opposition to Daniel b. Azaryah existed in the Alex-

357 TS 24.56v, ll. 1–2.

358 Bodl MS Heb b 3.16: Gil, *Kingdom*, no. 671; Frenkel, *"The Compassionate and Benevolent"* [Hebrew], no. 1. Gil is of the opinion that the letter was composed in 1040 and reflects the controversy between the Gaon Solomon b. Judah and Nathan b. Abraham, but Judah Ibn Sighmār, to whom the letter is addressed, only reached Egypt around 1050 (see Cohen, *Jewish Self-Government*, 116), while in 1060/1 Daniel b. Azaryah was in Egypt and it is likely that he wanted to visit Alexandria, too.

359 Bodl MS Heb b 3.16r, ll. 4–6.

360 See Gil, *History of Palestine*, §892.

361 Bodl MS Heb b 3.16r, ll. 20–25: Gil, *Kingdom*, no. 671.

andrian community, and Yeshūʿā learned that certain figures were planning to harass him during his stay:

> These people, however, trust what Abū Saʿd says, may God fail to preserve him. He promised them that when my lord the head of the Yeshivah arrives they would surround him and do with him as they wished. I believe that after I wrote what I wrote and after he answered what he answered, that he shall abstain [from this course of action]. For he is, may God preserve him in perpetuity, an honorable leader [...] lest he be ridiculed.[362]

In other words, Yeshūʿā tried to prevent the visit not only due to the logistical difficulties, but also out of consideration for the head of the Yeshivah, and his desire to prevent Daniel's embarrassment. For this reason, he asked Judah Ibn Sighmār to explain in advance to Daniel b. Azaryah the limits of his power in the community if the latter insisted on coming.[363] It seems that the visit did, in fact, occur, and that the scenario which Yeshūʿā foresaw did take place. In a written testimony, recorded in the Alexandrian court many years later, we read that a number of people cursed Daniel b. Azaryah while he was in Alexandria, and that in retaliation he excommunicated them.[364]

The relationship between Yeshūʿā and Daniel b. Azaryah is revealed as multi-faceted. In the purely personal realm it was characterized by suspicion and mutual lack of trust, and it does not seem that the two were close. Indeed, there was virtually no direct communication between the two, and no personal correspondence between them survives. Daniel did, however, send letters to Yeshūʿā, such as his official rebuke of the latter, delivered in response to the complaints of the community against him,[365] but these were official letters and indirect messages sent through intermediaries. This being said, it was clear to both of them that they were on the same side, and thus their political identification dictated their loyalties at times of crisis. Daniel b. Azaryah rescued "the Fellow of the Yeshivah" and "the Judge" of the Alexandrian community from a communal uprising, and Yeshūʿā attempted, ineffectively, to prevent "the Head of the Yeshivah" from enduring derision and ridicule. One may say that their joint interest

---

362 Bodl MS Heb b 3.16r, ll. 12–16.

363 See above, Part II, Chapter 1.3 (b): The Opposition, in the section: "The Meek Shall Inherit the Earth."

364 A witness document from 1079. See Gil, *History of Palestine*, 589, without mentioning the document's shelf-mark.

365 See above, Part II, Chapter 1.2 (e): Joseph b. Yeshūʿā's Image; Bodl MS Heb b 3.16r, ll. 10–11: Gil, *Kingdom*, no. 671, where a letter from the Gaon that Yeshūʿā kissed and placed on his head is mentioned.

in preserving the stability of the regime and its traditional framework overrode their personal disagreements.

It is apparent from the body of written material studied above that the head of the Yeshivah's authority was perceived as first among equals. His personal authority was not that of a sole ruler, but rather the authority of a governing body, which coordinates and acts in tandem. The correspondence also indicates a symbiotic system in which the head of the Yeshivah and the local leader help and support one another. It seems likely that the source of this support is the mutual interest of both in preserving the governing *status quo*. At this point in time and in this case their considerations are systemic and bereft of personal inclinations and preferences.

The Fustat Leaders

The internal politics of the Alexandrian community was intimately connected with the leadership of the Fustat community, though no official dictate required it. We have already noted above the deep involvement of Sahlān b. Abraham, one of the leaders of the Babylonian community in Fustat,[366] in the popular uprising against Yeshūʿā's leadership.

Yeshūʿā, in contrast, was friendly with the head of the Palestinian community in Fustat, Ephraim b. Shemaryah. It was to him that Yeshūʿā directed requests for financial aid in the name of "the community of Alexandria,"[367] ad-

366 See above, Part II, Chapter 1.3 (b): The Opposition, in the section: Betwixt Babylonians and Palestinians; Bareket, *Jewish Leadership*, 177–176; Gil, *History of Palestine*, §807. Bareket and Gil believe that Sahlān spent a long time in Alexandria and therefore considered it right to intervene also in the community's internal conflicts. In my opinion, Sahlān only spent brief periods in Alexandria, for business purposes, as was common among the merchants of the time. Even the letter that Bareket mentions (ENA 4020.18) deals with matters of trade and his intention to return quickly to Fustat, whereas the identification of the letters to the Fustat community on the subject of the emancipation of captives is not at all certain (in Bareket's own words: "The assumption that it was Sahlān who wrote the letters for Joseph ha-Kohen and his son Yeshūʿā is based on the identification of the handwriting, and still requires absolute proof."). See Bareket, ibid., n. 42. Gil and Bareket's hypothesis as to a lengthy stay of Sahlān's in Alexandria seems to be due to the desire to explain his apparently odd involvement in the internal affairs of the Alexandrian community. However, such involvement was characteristic of the close ties between the two communities; see Abraham L. Udovitch, "A Tale of Two Cities: Commercial Relations between Cairo and Alexandria during the Second Half of the Eleventh Century," in Harry A. Miskimin, David Herlihy and Abraham L. Udovitch (eds.), *The Medieval City* (New Haven and London: Yale University Press, 1977), 143–162.
367 See Mann, *Jews*, 2: 88–91, nos. 14, 15, 16 (no. 14 was also published by Elinoar Bareket, *The Jews of Egypt, 1007–1055* [Jerusalem: Ben-Zvi Institute, 1995], 71 [Hebrew]).

dressing him officially as a the head of the Fustat community : "To our brethren of the community who live in Tzoʿan Mitsraim,[368] and especially to our honored teacher, Epraim fellow of the great Sanhedrin, may the Rock preserve him, the son of our honored and holy teacher Shemaryah, may his soul rest in peace, and to all the elders and scholars, from your beloved friends, the Alexandrian community."[369] In matters that required special attention, however, Yeshūʿā was not reluctant to exploit his personal friendship with Ephraim b. Shemaryah. Thus, for example, when Shabbetai b. R. Nethanel, a distinguished captive from Byzantium released together with other captives, wished to fulfill his dream and make a pilgrimage to Jerusalem, Yeshūʿā helped by providing him with an intimate letter requesting aid, addressed to Ephraim b. Shemaryah, in furtherance of this goal. The letter was intended to be read by Ephraim personally, as the signature indicates: "Your beloved friend and companion Yeshūʿā ha-Kohen b. R. Joseph the Judge."[370]

Although Abraham b. Sahlān, the leader of the Babylonian community in Fustat, sought to undermine Yeshūʿā's position while Ephraim b. Shemaryah who was the head of the Palestinian community was his friend and supporter, this does not indicate that Yeshūʿā was the representative of the Palestinian community in Alexandria and consequently benefited from the support of their leader in Fustat. The internal politics of the community were a good deal more complex. An indication of this, perhaps, is that Ephraim b. Shemaryah's successor, Eli b. Amram, who also belonged to the Palestinian community, not only ceased to support Yeshūʿā, but actually adopted policies inimical to him, and sought to undermine his position. In furtherance of this hostility against Yeshūʿā, he cooperated with local rivals, which ultimately led to Daniel b. Azaryah's intervention and request to cease and desist.[371] What led to Eli's attempt to depose Yeshūʿā? The key to this question likely lies in the special political situation in Fustat following Eli's appointment and the struggle which preceded it. Eli's rival for this position was "the Rav" Judah ha-Kohen b. Joseph, the revered Maghribi religious leader , who had the support of central Maghribi figures such as Nahray b. Nissim, Judah Ibn Sighmār,[372] and the very influential court physician, Abraham Ibn

---

368 צוען מצרים was the biblical name ascribed in official documents and letters to Fustat.

369 Mann, *Jews*, no. 15, ll. 1–4.

370 TS 13 J 24.11: Mann, *Jews*, no. 16.

371 See above, Part II, Chapter 1.3 (c): Sources of Support, in the section: The Geonim, the Heads of the Palestinian Yeshivah.

372 See Goitein, "HaRav"; Gil, *History of Palestine*, 265–266; Goitein, *Jewish Community*, 144–155.

al-Furāt.[373] These activists in "the Rav's" faction were also Daniel b. Azaryah's key supporters when he sought to become the head of the Yeshivah. As we shall see below, Yeshūʿā b. Joseph was close to these people and was identified as part of their faction. It thus stands to reason that when Eli succeeded in his campaign to become the leader of the Fustat community and defeated "the Rav," he wished to appoint his own supporters in Alexandria in Yeshūʿā's place.[374] He harnessed the political clout that had led to his victory over "the Rav" to undermine Yeshūʿā in Alexandria, and very likely joined forces with local populist elements in the city, who had opposed Yeshūʿā from the beginning. These are the local "opponents" (*khuṣūm*) who Yeshūʿā mentions in his letter to Daniel b. Azaryah.[375]

We thus find that the leaders of the Fustat community had a vested interest in interfering and influencing the appointment or deposal of the Alexandrian leader, Yeshūʿā b. Joseph, since he was an actor in the political game. This struggle was not restricted to one community or one campaign, and included the triangle of the Palestinian Yeshivah, the Fustat community, and the Alexandrian community. For this reason, in order to properly understand the position of community leader, we must venture beyond the framework of the local community and consider the broader politics of the time. We shall attempt to unravel the ties that linked this pan-communal faction and analyze Yeshūʿā b. Joseph's relationship with each of the key figures individually.

The "Faction"

A faction is an unofficial spontaneous group of people, which coalesces around a specific one-time goal, and whose existence is usually short-lived. Since it has no ideological focus, it transcends the borders of class, camps, parties, and ideological groups. Joining different communal factions is motivated by individual aspirations regarding objects of competition or dispute – and is not determined by previous social obligation, such as filial obligations or religious sympathies.

---

373 See above, n. 348.

374 See Gil, *History of Palestine*, §§378, 779, 891, 893. On "the Rav" and his special status among the Maghribis, see Goitein, "HaRav."

375 On the popular elements, see above, Part II, Chapter 1.3 (b): The Opposition, in the section: "The Meek Shall Inherit the Earth." For Daniel b. Azaryah's letter, see Part II, Chapter 1.3 (c): Sources of Support, in the section: The Geonim, the Heads of the Palestinian Yeshivah.

This being said, a faction may become institutional and turn into an official organized group.[376]

A number of detailed analyses have been published regarding the ways in which the faction under consideration coalesced with the goal of appointing Daniel b. Azaryah as the head of the Yeshivah and their unified attempt to prevent the appointment of Eli b. Amram as the leader of the Fustat community.[377] In what follows we shall scrutinize Yeshūʿā b. Joseph's ties with each of the members of "the Rav's" faction and attempt to understand the relationship between the supporters, in order to determine whether the definition above fits. Was there an ideological backdrop or basic social commitments at the basis of this association, or was it a group that coalesced for one specific purpose?

"The Rav" Judah ha-Kohen b. Joseph

The great prestige of "the Rav" amongst the Maghribi Jews in Fustat, and the potent combination of legal authority and political clout made him the obvious candidate to succeed Ephraim b. Shemaryah, as leader of the Jewish community of Fustat. The intrigue surrounding this appointment led to the forming of a political faction of which Yeshūʿā b. Joseph was a member. Yeshūʿā had no direct correspondence with the Rav, and when he wanted to ask him a legal query, he needed Nahray b. Nissim to function as intermediary: "And now I ask of you to inquire with our master the Rav and tell me what is preferable." On another occasion Yeshūʿā had asked "the Rav" a question through Nahray, but Nahray got mixed up and sent Yeshūʿā "the Rav"'s answer to someone else's question. Yeshūʿā responds: "This was not the question I asked and had sent to you."[378]

Though Yeshūʿā sent "the Rav" legal queries, he did not see him as a decisive authority and did not hesitate to disagree with his rulings. Regarding a question Yeshūʿā had about levirate marriage, "the Rav" stated unequivocally: "In this day and age one is commanded to perform levirate marriage rather than re-

376 See Ted C. Lewellen, *Political Anthropology* (Westport, CT: Praeger, 1983), 110–111; Moshe Shokeid, "Clans Indeed? Family and Political Factions in the Adaption to the Moshav," in Moshe Shokeid and Shlomo Deshen (eds.), *The Intercultural Experience: A Reader in Anthropology* (Jerusalem and Tel Aviv: Schocken, 1998), 196–197; Ralph W. Nicholas, "Factions: A Comparative Study," in Michael Benton (ed.), *Political Systems and the Distribution of Power* (London and NY: Routledge, 2011), 21–61; Bernard Siegal and Alan Beals, "Pervasive Factionalism," *American Anthropologist* 62 (1960): 394–417; Raymond Firth, "Introduction to Factions in India and Overseas Indian Society," *British Journal of Sociology* 8 (1958): 291–295.
377 See above, nn. 371–373.
378 Bodl MS Heb c 13.20r, l. 10; v, l. 13: Gil, *Kingdom*, no. 673.

lease the parties." Yeshūʿā responded to this that "there are some levirs who should perform levirate marriage and there are some levirs that should be released, for the majority of the people today do not intend to redeem the name of the dead in this way, and the elders and the judge in all places have permission to intercede with him [the levir]."[379] It seems likely that Yeshūʿā's request for "the Rav"'s opinion was due to the political situation in which he found himself, and to his desire to maintain the relationship and the correspondence with Nahray b. Nissim and other members of the faction, rather than any respect for "the Rav"'s legal authority. Indeed, after completely disregarding "the Rav"'s ruling, Yeshūʿā insists on sending him his greetings: "And please bow down most humbly before our teacher 'the Rav' on my behalf."[380]

Abraham Ibn Al-Furāt

Abraham ha-Kohen b. Isaac Ibn al-Furāt, also known as "the Lord of the Congregation" (*sar ha-ʿedah*), was a significant political powerbroker, though it is not known whether he held any official position.[381] His power likely derived from his close relationship with the Muslim authorities in his capacity as the court physician of the governor of Ramla and from his wealth.[382] Ibn al-Furāt was also related through family ties to the priestly heads of the Yeshivah and to Solomon b. Judah Gaon. He was actively involved in the controversy between Solomon b. Judah and Nathan b. Abraham regarding the leadership of the Yeshivah,[383] and was likely the driving force behind the faction seeking to appoint "the Rav" to the leadership of the Fustat community. Ibn al-Furāt was also one of the most important supporters of Daniel b. Azaryah and helped him become the head of the Yeshivah. Daniel valued his support greatly and sought his help and fellowship on a regular basis. Ibn al-Furāt extended his support to Yeshūʿā b. Joseph as well and helped him as much as possible. In a letter to Daniel b. Azaryah, he requests that the latter direct his attention to Yeshūʿā, who

379 Bodl MS Heb c 13.20r, ll. 16, 21–23. On the problem of the levirate, see Mordechai A. Friedman, *Jewish Polygyny in the Middle Ages: New Documents from the Cairo Genizah* (Jerusalem: Mossad Bialik, 1986), 129–151 [Hebrew]; Friedman, "The Commandment of Pulling off the Sandal Takes Precedence over the Commandment of Levirate," *Teudah* 13 (1997): 35–66 [Hebrew].
380 Bodl MS Heb c 13.20v, l. 23: Gil, *Kingdom*, no. 673.
381 Bareket claims that Ibn al-Furāt served as *ra'īs al-yahūd* with an official appointment by the Fatimid caliph; this is her own opinion which requires justification and evidence. See Elinoar Bareket, "Abraham ha-Kohen the Physician Ben Isaac," *HUCA* 71 (2001): 1–19 [Hebrew]. In any case, even according to Bareket, Ibn al-Furāt was not appointed before 1055.
382 See Gil, *History of Palestine*, §§ 779, 893; Bareket, "Abraham ha-Kohen."
383 Gil, ibid.; Bareket, ibid.

faced a political crisis in his community. He adds words of praise regarding Yeshūʿā and notes Yeshūʿā's enduring loyalty towards him. He tells Daniel that Yeshūʿā took care of all of his business in Alexandria, was attentive to his position, and was eager to offer his considered advice.[384] In other words, Yeshūʿā is described by Ibn al-Furāt as his Alexandrian delegate or representative. Or put another way, in Ibn al-Furāt's political network – which encompassed Palestine, Egypt, and North Africa – Yeshūʿā functioned as his point man in Alexandria. Ibn al-Furāt returned the favor by coming to Yeshūʿā's aid and employing his valuable connections on Yeshūʿā's behalf when it was needful.[385]

Abū Zikrī, Judah b. Moses Ibn Sighmār

Abū Zikrī was a merchant of Tunisian origin and a scion of a wealthy and learned family who were very influential in Tunisia. He was the representative and spokesperson of the Tunisian Jews in Fustat. Though he held no official office, he was very involved in communal affairs at this time. He regularly donated money to the Palestinian Yeshivah, and was granted the honorary title "Elect of the Yeshivah" (*beḥir ha-yeshivah*). Abū Zikrī assisted quite regularly in the ransom of captives and was close with the Ben Saʿadyah family, the family of the Negidim (heads of the community) in Egypt. He was a student of "the Rav" and studied law under him.[386]

Abū Zikrī and Yeshūʿā forged an intimate relationship and were part of the same social milieu.[387] From the letter Yeshūʿā sent Abū Zikrī,[388] it is apparent that their ties were multi-faceted: (a) In the mercantile sphere – Abū Zikrī is asked to come to the aid of Yeshūʿā's envoy and help him buy merchandise in Fustat. (b) In the communal sphere – Abū Zikrī was involved in the transfer of

---

384 See above, Part II, Chapter 1.3 (c): Sources of Support, in the section: The Geonim, the Heads of the Palestinian Yeshivah. The content of Abraham Ibn al-Furāt's letter to Daniel b. Azaryah, in which he praises Yeshūʿā and supports him unreservedly, is known to us from its quotation in the Gaon's response.

385 Ibid.

386 On Abū Zikrī Judah b. Moses Ibn Sighmār, see Goitein, *Society*, 1: 158–159; Cohen, *Jewish Self-Government*, 116–117.

387 See ENA NS 18.35v, l. 11: Gil, *Kingdom*, no. 537. This is a letter by Labrāṭ b. Moses Ibn Sighmār, from Susa, to his brother Judah Ibn Sighmār in Alexandria, in which he sends regards to Yeshūʿā.

388 Bodl MS Heb b 3.16: Gil, *Kingdom*, no. 671; Frenkel, *"The Compassionate and Benevolent"* [Hebrew], no. 1.

funds to Alexandria for the ransom of captives. (c) In the political sphere – it is apparent that both men belonged to the same faction:

> I was very surprised at your negligence regarding the letters, which were read by my master the head of the Yeshivah [= Daniel b. Azaryah], may the Rock preserve him, and he was angered as you described in your letter. I appreciate your benevolence in correcting the mistake that occurred. For I am grateful for your benevolence in every situation, though I must note that I read the letter you sent me in the presence of the Shaykh Abū Isḥāq, and I ripped it up in front of him, until there was nothing left of it, though there was nothing in it that one need fear, but I wanted to fulfill your instructions in this matter [...]. No one knows about the letters that came to me and nothing is left of them.[389]

This letter hints at an intricate system of clandestine correspondence between the two, a correspondence that was so regular that a code of conduct developed regarding the secrecy of the communications. One had to read the letters in the presence of a third person from the same faction, and if the author of the letter requested it, one had to destroy the letter upon reading it, once again in the presence of a third party – even if there was actually no sensitive information therein. This code of conduct implies the existence of a faction, that operated in secret, but was also semi-established. Yeshū'ā's explicit rebuke of Abū Zikrī indicates that he regarded the latter as an equal.

It seems that Abū Zikrī was closer to Daniel b. Azaryah than Yeshū'ā, and functioned as Yeshū'ā's go-between when he wished to correspond with Daniel. We noted above that Yeshū'ā turned to Abū Zikrī in order to prevent the Gaon's visit in Alexandria, and was asked to explain to him the difficulty inherent in such a visit: "And I ask you, may God preserve you, that if you see that the Gaon [= Daniel b. Azaryah] is adamant in his desire to travel here [= Alexandria], that you tell him what my predicament is here, so that he will not imagine that it is possible for me to adequately host him in Alexandria. For if [he nevertheless comes], I will not apologize to him."[390] In other words, Abū Zikrī is seen by Yeshū'ā as close enough to the Gaon that he could warn him regarding the delicate situation Yeshū'ā was in, and convince him not to come. In the same letter Yeshū'ā alludes to an alliance between Abū Zikrī and the head of the Yeshivah: "For it is your way, my lord, to 'renew this pact' with him [Daniel b. Azaryah]."[391]

389 Bodl MS Heb b 3.16r, ll. 4–10, 19.
390 Ibid., v, ll. 14–15. My translation differs from Gil's.
391 Ibid., r, l. 16.

Nahray b. Nissim

Nahray b. Nissim was a merchant and banker of Maghribi origin and one of the dominant figures in Fustat of this time period. As a public figure, Nahray was one of Daniel b. Azaryah's confidants, and the latter bestowed upon him many titles, such as "Fellow," "Rav," and "Elect of the Yeshivah." Later Nahray was one of the most ardent advocates of Daniel b. Azaryah's son, David b. Daniel. Nahray was one of "the Rav's" (Judah ha-Kohen b. Joseph) most faithful students and one of his biggest supporters, though he issued his own rulings as well.[392]

Nahray's involvement, as a banker and public figure, in the ransom of captives connected him to Yeshūʿā. In a letter written by Yeshūʿā and addressed to Nahray, the latter was asked to embark on a fundraising campaign on behalf of the captives for whom the Alexandrian community could not raise enough money to secure their release and to support them.[393] As noted above, Nahray was the intermediary between Yeshūʿā and "the Rav" when legal questions arose in the Alexandrian court and Yeshūʿā wished to know "the Rav's" opinion.[394]

Yeshūʿā's correspondence with Nahray b. Nissim relates to communal matters, but his letters also reveal a personal relationship. The two collaborated in the mercantile sphere as *muʿāmala* partners. This type of partnership was not formal, but it was quite consistent and included a variety of services the partners undertook for each other. Their collaboration is reflected in Yeshūʿā's request in the letter alluded to above: "Let me know all your desires and needs, for I am happy to grant them."[395] This phrase is a known formula between merchants in *muʿāmala* partnerships, though it is usually written in Arabic. The formulaic statement indicates a willingness to continue the collaboration.[396] Other indications of this business relationship are Yeshūʿā's reference to a debt he owed Nahray after selling fabric on his behalf in Alexandria.[397] In a memorandum sent to Alexandria, Nahray asks that Yeshūʿā deal with books he sent to a copyist: "The

392 On him, see Moshe Gil, *Jews in Islamic Countries in the Middle Ages*, trans. David Strassler (Leiden: Brill, 2004), §392–399. See also: Goldberg, *Trade*, 56–64. On his activity on behalf of "the Rav," see Gil, *History of Palestine*, §891.

393 TS 12.338: Gil, *Kingdom*, no. 672.

394 See above, Part II, Chapter 1.3 (c): Sources of Support, in the section: "the Rav" Judah ha-Kohen b. Joseph.

395 TS 12.338, 2, ll. 21–22: Gil, *Kingdom*, no. 672.

396 On the *muʿāmala* and how it worked, see Goitein, *Society*, 1: 164–169.

397 TS 12.338, 2, ll. 22–23: Gil, *Kingdom*, no. 672. At the same time, it should be noted that Nahray had business relations at the same level with Shelah the Cantor b. Moses, Yeshūʿā's political rival. See TS 13 J 17.1, ll. 15 ff.: Gil, *Kingdom*, no. 537.

teacher owes me eleven codices, five of them larger codices, and six of them in two different formats. Please appoint R. Yeshūʿā to deal with this entire matter until its completion."[398]

They also shared an intellectual interest. When he writes to Nahray, Yeshūʿā employs a high register and poetic language, while Nahray asks him to send him special pens from Alexandria manufactured from reeds which grow on the banks of Lake Mariotis:[399] "And [I ask you to] remember regarding the pens from Mariotis reeds, for at this time [of year] they are still wet, and they do not cut them until the month of Av at the time of the grape harvest, and I will send for them and when they are brought to me I will cut the pens and then deliver them to you."[400] It seems then that the pens, which were the working tools of these two intellectuals who wrote prolifically, were also a joint interest that bolstered their mutual relationship..

Summary

The people mentioned above were connected to each other in a variety of ways, at different levels of intimacy: personal friendship, mercantile ties, professional ties, legal-intellectual ties, and political ties. This web of relationship tied people of different origins and various locales together. A good many of them were of Maghribi descent, but the web included also Abraham Ibn al-Furāt the Egyptian, who spent a great deal of time in Palestine; Yeshūʿā b. Joseph, a scion of an Alexandrian family who had lived there for many years, and Daniel b. Azaryah of Baghdad, who was connected to the Palestinian Yeshivah. One may assume that the group coalesced as a political faction in order to achieve concrete and discrete goals, but lasted a long time afterwards and underwent some degree of institutionalization, which was expressed in agreed-upon behavioral codes.

Yeshūʿā b. Joseph was thus active in this extra-communal political faction, along with central figures in the Jewish world whose activities spanned the Fatimid empire, and especially the triangle that spanned the Maghreb, Egypt and Palestine.[401] His activity had direct ramifications upon his appointment as community leader and his ability to persevere at his position. One may say that a

398 TS 12.379, 2, ll. 3–4: Gil, *Kingdom*, no. 276.

399 See above, Part I, Chapter 2 (b): The Garden Areas.

400 Bodl MS Heb c 13.20v, ll. 21–18: Gil, *Kingdom*, no. 673.

401 See also Menahem Ben-Sasson, "The Ties of the Maghrebis to the Land of Israel, 9th-11th centuries," *Shalem* 5 (1987): 31–82, where the author draws a similar picture, which he reached from a systematic study of center-periphery relations.

great deal of his clout derived from his membership in this powerful extra-communal faction.

(d) Spheres of Activity

In this section I will not deal with Yeshūʿā's official duties as judge and leader of the Jewish community of Alexandria, but rather I shall attempt to identify the spheres in which he was most active.

Presiding as Judge

Yeshūʿā b. Joseph functioned as supreme judge,[402] though the Genizah reveals very little of his activities in this sphere. The little that may be gleaned suggests an innovative jurist, who steadfastly maintained his position even while in the minority. His independence is revealed in the case of a widow who objected to a levirate marriage to her brother-in-law. This case is described in a letter Yeshūʿā sends to Nahray b. Nissim.[403] The widow vigorously opposed a union with her husband's brother, who was already married to another woman, but he refused to release her, and insisted on the levirate marriage. The elders designated by the court to persuade the widow to relent got nowhere, and the situation was exacerbated by those who urged the brother not to give in either. As noted above, in response to Yeshūʿā's query R. Judah ha-Kohen of Fustat, "the Rav," ruled that the legal obligation of levirate marriage superseded the command of release. Yeshūʿā himself, however, opined that in this case one should not compel the widow to marry against her will so that she wouldn't be "led astray." He revealed sensitivity to the young widow's plight, and was sympathetic to her desire not to be a second wife against her will. In his letter to Nahray b. Nissim, he requests that the latter "cajole the Rav," or in other words, explain to him the uniqueness of the situation, so that he would change his ruling and prevent discord.[404]

---

402 See ENA NS 18.35v, l. 11: Gil, *Kingdom*, no. 537. Labrāṭ b. Moses Ibn Sighmār writes from Susa to his brother Judah Ibn Sighmār in Alexandria, and send regards to "R. Yeshūʿā *bei din.*"
403 Bodl MS Heb c 13.20: Gil, *Kingdom*, no. 673. See above, Part II, Chapter 1.3 (c): Sources of Support, in the section: "The Rav" Judah ha-Kohen b. Joseph.
404 On the difference between valent criteria and formal ones in the interpretation of the law, see Moshe Halbertal, *Interpretive Revolutions in the Making: Values as Interpretative Criteria in Jewish Law* (Jerusalem, Magness Press, 1997), 15–22.

Correspondence

As noted above, Yeshūʿā administered communal correspondence even when his father was still the *de jure* leader,[405] and thus he was at the crux of community activity. As the administrator, he could introduce himself to the central figures at all the important loci of power such as the Palestinian Yeshivah, the community in Fustat and other Jewish groups.

The Ransoming of Captives

The ransoming of captives was a critical issue in Alexandria at this time. As a central port, Alexandria was the main place where captives were brought, and it was here that the mercantile side of human trafficking took place. The ransoming the captives was a burdensome liability upon the public purse and was a central aspect in the day-to-day administration of the community.[406]

Fundraising

The ransoming of captives was primarily a financial matter and required fundraising and pecuniary resources. Some part of the financial burden fell upon the Alexandrian community. Yeshūʿā's efforts were focused on fundraising outside of the community. Some of the money was raised through the donations of other communities by means of the communal charity apparatus, with the community leader or another public figure as the intermediary. The Fustat community provided a good deal of the funds, and Yeshūʿā oversaw the correspondence on this subject with the leaders of this community. In his letters addressed to Ephraim b. Shemaryah, the head of the Fustat community, Yeshūʿā requests that he collect funds for the purpose of freeing captives.[407] Later it was Nahray b. Nissim who was the head of the community, and Yeshūʿā corresponds with him as well. In a letter from 1050 he asks him to raise the necessary sum of

---

405 See above, Part II, Chapter 1.3 (a): An Alexandrian 'Prince'.
406 See Goitein, *Society*, 1: 327–332, 1: 137–138; Miriam Frenkel, "'Proclaim Liberty to Captives and Freedom to Prisoners': The Ransoming of Captives by Medieval Jewish Communities in Islamic Countries," in Heike Grieser and Nicole Priesching (eds.), *Gefangenenloskauf im Mittelmeerraum; Ein intereligiöser Vergleich*, Hildesheim, Zurich and NY, Georg Olms Verlag, 2015, 83–97. For a general and more comprehensive discussion of the emancipation of prisoners, see below, Part III, Chapter 2.7 (b): Fundraising Campaigns; and Part IV, Chapter 3.3: Charity.
407 ENA 2804.9: Mann, *Jews*, 2: 88–89, no. 14, with an incorrect shelf-mark; TS 13 J 4.11: Mann, *Jews*, 2: 91, no. 16, with an incorrect shelf-mark; TS 16.347: Frenkel, *"The Compassionate and Benevolent"* [Hebrew], no. 33.

money from community members, including a meticulous calculation of the total, and a detailed log of his negotiations with the slave traders.[408]

Funds were procured from other communities as well. Yeshūʿā's custom was to send special emissaries to the more rural communities and provide these emissaries with letters. Thus, for example, Joseph al-Aḥwal, a community dignitary, was sent by Yeshūʿā to the communities of the Rīf (the countryside of the Delta) with flowery letters requesting funds.[409]

A central source of funds was private donors, men of finance, who had the ear of the Muslim authorities and usually dwelt in Fustat and Cairo. Private benefactors of this type would sometimes donate such large sums, that entire communities could not match their donations. One of these men was Nethanel ha-Kohen,[410] whose central role in the emancipation of captives is apparent from the following letter:

> Afterwards his emissary came to the seat of our great and mighty one, his holiness our teacher and master, Nethanel ha-Kohen, the esteemed dignitary and lord, may God grant him life and bless him, and with him was one of the captives with an offering. He accepted it from our hands with grace and aplomb, and reciprocated with a gift of his own worth more than one and a half times the original. Afterwards he sent for the other captive and weighed out money for him in the sum of thirty-three and a third gold coins. He provided them with clothing and dressed them and gave them provisions for the journey. He then sent them to someone else who gave them the fare for the voyage and they went on their way happy and grateful for all that was done on their behalf, and he did not ask the community to give them even one loaf of bread.[411]

And in another letter: "This is for our elder the honorable R. Nethanel ha-Kohen and for the rest of the holy community [...] succor. R. Nethanel answered, do not relate to this until the money comes [...]. I will take care of this matter as you wish to the best of my ability, and God will grant success."[412] Nethanel ha-Kohen was, at this time, such a dependable donor to the cause that the fundraisers took his contribution for granted: "And you may depend upon the munificence of our God and upon the honorable elder R. Nethanel ha-Kohen the son

408 TS 12.338v: Gil, *Kingdom*, no. 672.

409 Bodl MS Heb c 13.16, ll. 20–21: Gil, *Kingdom*, no. 671; Frenkel, "*The Compassionate and Benevolent*" [Hebrew], no. 1.

410 Bareket is of the opinion that Nethanel ha-Kohen bore the title of *raʾīs al-yahūd*, but this still needs to be proven. See Bareket, "Abraham ha-Kohen."

411 TS 13 J 14.20, ll. 1–18: Mann, *Jews*, 2: 87.

412 TS 13 J 20.25, ll. 2–14: Mann, *Jews*, 2: 88.

of our R. Eleazar, for it rests with him."[413] A figure often mentioned in conjunction with Nethanel ha-Kohen is David ha-Levi b. Isaac,[414] who is called upon in another letter: "We ask the mighty lord [...] according to his custom, that he should direct the elder [...] may he live forever, to send thirty-three gold [coins] [...] and it is our humble entreaty that the mighty lord [...] we wrote this letter to him so that he might [...] so that he would benefit from the fruits of his generosity in this world and earn the balance in the world to come."[415]

Rewarding the Benefactors

Proper expressions of gratitude for the generosity of benefactors was one of Yeshūʿā's responsibilities: "And we prayed mightily before our God on his behalf in the presence of the entire congregation, and we have also made it our practice to pray for him in the presence of our community on every Sabbath in both synagogues, and we have not failed to praise him."[416] And in a letter to David ha-Levi b. Isaac he states: "And at every moment we offer a prayer to the Lord our God to vouchsafe the life of our master and lord, and we ask of him [...] to hasten the coming of the Messiah [...] so that Israel shall dwell peacefully and he shall [...] be elevated upon a blessed throne and [...]."[417] In other words, Yeshūʿā b. Joseph was attentive to public expressions of gratitude towards benefactors, which included public commendation and special prayers on their behalf in the synagogues. A partial description of these paeans of praise are found in another letter addressed to Shemaryah b. Ephraim:

> And we took out the scrolls and the cantors stood [...] both great and small, and concerning our friend and master, Fellow of the Yeshivah [...] our teacher David ha-Levi b. Isaac [...] may the Rock preserve him and our brothers the Dustaris [...] according to his elevated status and R. Abraham b. [...] to save you from all harm [...] and may you find tranquility [...] and we also blessed R. Ṣadoq ha-Levi b. Levi and our R. Abraham b. David Ibn Sighmār the delight of the Yeshivah, may the Merciful One preserve him.[418]

---

413 ENA 4020.44, ll. 6–7: Mann, *Jews*, 2: 92 (Mann does not mention the shelf-mark, and the line numbers there are 27–28, because he combined two fragments without saying so); Frenkel, *"The Compassionate and Benevolent"* [Hebrew], no. 11.

414 Bareket believes that he bore the title of *raʾīs al-yahūd*. See above, n. 410.

415 ENA 4020.44, ll. 8–10, 14–17: Mann, *Jews*, 2: 92 (line numbers are 29–31, 35–39); Frenkel, *"The Compassionate and Benevolent"* [Hebrew], no. 11.

416 TS 13 J 14.20, ll. 9–11: Mann, *Jews*, 2: 87.

417 ENA 4020.45, ll. 18–20: Mann, *Jews*, 2: 92, no. 17; Frenkel, *"The Compassionate and Benevolent"* [Hebrew], no. 11. Mann omitted a few lines in his transcription, see ibid., appendix.

418 ENA 2804.11: Mann, *Jews*, 2: 89–90, no. 15; Frenkel, *"The Compassionate and Benevolent"* [Hebrew], no. 10. Mann's shelf-mark is incorrect and his reading is incomplete.

Negotiation with the Captors

Attempting to secure the ransoming of captives included bargaining with the captors or with the captives' owners, which was often quite exhausting and dangerous, as we shall see below. In a letter to Nahray b. Nissim, Yeshūʿā describes the tough negotiations he conducted with merchants from Amalfi, who had purchased three Jews captured by Byzantine soldiers, and wished to sell them to the Jewish community of Alexandria: "The owner of one them said to us: 'I shall take sixteen gold coins as the advance payment, I shall give you half a gold coin as a gift, and you shall give me sixteen gold coins.' The other two said: 'For the two [captives] we shall not accept anything lower than thirty-six gold coins.' And yet we continue to try."[419] In another letter, Yeshūʿā's personal exchanges with the pirates are briefly summarized. These exchanges took place via correspondence as well as face-to-face.

> Why not take from me [the same sum] as your relative Yabqā b. Abī Razīn took [...]. By us an Edomite slave is worth twenty gold coins, now bring [this sum] [...] and take your coreligionist and depart. We said that we cannot do this thing [...] since it would be unreasonable, and our sages decreed that "one does not redeem captives for a higher sum than they are worth in consideration of the greater good of the world."[420]

In these lines Yeshūʿā briefly delineates his negotiations with Mukhtār b. Jabāra, the Amir of Barqa, who was also the *de facto* leader of the pirates in the southern Mediterranean.[421] He offered him the same sum as he had paid the Amir's relative, the pirate Yabqā b. Abī Razīn.[422] Mukhtār stubbornly requested a higher than usual sum for the Jewish captives. He was willing to release a Byzantine (Edomite) slave for the lower sum, but no Jews. Yeshūʿā replied that he could not pay the higher price since it was religiously interdicted. The active verbal forms employed in this letter corroborate the hypothesis that Yeshūʿā himself undertook the negotiations with Mukhtār, and beforehand with the latter's relative Yabqā b. Abī Razīn. Yeshūʿā describes the circumstances under which he negotiated as harsh: "We went to his tents and sat in the dryness by the sea and in the icy night [...] while we were with him we questioned him and spoke to him about many things."[423] In other words, Yeshūʿā undertook to go to Mukhtār's desert tents; the protracted and difficult negotiations took place in foreign territory and in inauspicious environs. It appears that Yeshūʿā was quite adept at bargain-

419 TS 12.338, ll. 9–13: Gil, *Kingdom*, no. 672.
420 TS 13 J 20.25, ll. 11–18: Mann, *Jews*, 2:88, no. 13.
421 See Goitein, *Society*, 1: 327–328.
422 On Yabqā b. Abī Razīn, see Mann, *Jews*, 1: 89–91; Goitein, *Society*, 1: 328.
423 TS 13 J 20.25, ll. 5–6: Mann, *Jews*, 2:88, no. 13.

ing. He compares the suggested price to previous payments he made to other pirates, and finally he resorts to the ultimate argument: He cannot pay a premium over the normal price since it is religiously interdicted. The use of such a stratagem is indicative of the mutual respect the parties had for one another. Even the Muslim pirate, whose only interest was profit, was expected to respect the commandments of the other's religion.

The pirates also saw Yeshūʿā as a known address for negotiating these matters. When they had Jewish captives, they let him know while still in transit, prior to their arrival at the port of Alexandria. The letters were addressed directly to Yeshūʿā, who was expected to represent the community in the negotiations: "I have received a letter from Mukhtār the Arab, who told me that he had sent his son Jabāra."[424] And in another letter: "And afterwards a rumor was heard that a ship belonging to one of the Arabs, Jabāra b. Mukhtār, had set sail and upon it were twenty Jews from the land of Anatolia, and it had arrived at a place called Ramāda, on the way to the Maghreb, and no one had believed it until the letter came to us."[425]

Remuneration

The reward for the difficult task of emancipating captives was significant. Firstly, the extensive correspondence with the wealthy benefactors who had the ear of the Muslim authorities, and the ability to publicly acknowledge their munificence, led to a closer relationship with these important powerbrokers. Moreover, there was no true distinction between the copious amount of money earmarked for the emancipation of captives and the personal business dealings of those who dealt with freeing them. The money that was stockpiled was used as an open reservoir of funds, freely available at almost any time for freeing captives or for business. The lack of distinction between private business needs and public interests that characterized Yeshūʿā's fundraising is evident in the following case.

In 1050 Yeshūʿā b. Joseph directed a group of captives from Alexandria to Fustat. The group was accompanied by Abraham al-Ṣiqillī, who was Yeshūʿā's junior business partner. Abraham was paid for this journey and was reimbursed for travel expenses such as hiring riding animals. His wages as special envoy were generously covered by Judah Ibn Sighmār, a personal friend and associate

424 Ibid., l. 15.
425 TS 13 J 14.20, ll. 15–18: Mann, *Jews*, 2:87, no. 12.

of Yeshūʿā's.[426] In the course of the lengthy voyage from Alexandria to Fustat, however, Abraham al-Ṣiqillī passed through many communities. Since he was furnished with a letter requesting funds written by Yeshūʿā and accompanied on his journey by a band of weary captives, he succeeded in raising a considerable amount of money for the captives and was able to cover both his wages and his travel expenses. Al-Ṣiqillī's expectation for this additional income was championed by Yeshūʿā b. Joseph, who asked his benefactor Judah Ibn Sighmār, not to request that al-Ṣiqillī turn over the funds, but rather to "favor" the emissary as was "his good custom," in other words – to let him keep the extra money he raised. According to the mercantile logic of the time, one did not let money lay fallow,[427] but rather one invested it in merchandise, which was what Yeshūʿā wanted. Since the emissary was bound for Fustat and had funds at his disposal, he was asked to go to the Perfumers' Quarter (*murābaʿat al-ʿaṭṭārīn*) in Fustat and make some small purchases on behalf of Yeshūʿā: "Two qirat worth of fine musk, one qirat worth of fine clove seeds, one qirat worth of nuts, one qirat worth of aloewood, one qirat worth of pumpkin seeds, and one qirat worth of fine saffron."[428] Yeshūʿā would cover the cost of these purchases upon al-Ṣiqillī's return, but in the meantime the money should be used profitably. Abraham al-Ṣiqillī was still a novice and not yet proficient in mercantile customs, and this venture to Fustat would be a great opportunity for him to gain some hands-on experience in these sorts of transactions and familiarize himself with the merchants of the Perfumers' Quarter. In Fustat al-Ṣiqillī would be accompanied by Judah Ibn Sighmār, who would lend him his experience and good name,[429] and would advise him in his initial forays into mercantile activity.

These instructions were all included in a letter Yeshūʿā sent Judah Ibn Sighmār.[430] Yeshūʿā shares his plans with no attempt at obfuscation, since the funds raised on behalf of the captives were viewed in the same way as a bank deposit and using the money was seen as prudent, for in this way the deposit would keep its value.[431]

---

426 See above, Part II, chapter 1.3 (c) Sources of Support, in the section: Abū Zikrī, Judah b. Moses Ibn Sighmār.

427 On this mercantile logic, see Goitein, *Society*, 1: 200.

428 Bodl MS Heb b 3.16r, right margins, l. 9 and upper margins, l. 3: Gil, *Kingdom*, no. 671; Frenkel, "*The Compassionate and Benevolent*" [Hebrew], no. 1.

429 In the original: *jāh*. On this term, see above, n. 55.

430 Bodl MS Heb b 3.16r, l. 24; 2, l. 3: Gil, *Kingdom*, no. 671.

431 On the common practice of hiding and camouflaging letters, see above, Part II, Chapter 1.3 (b): The Opposition. In contrast, with regard to the community's monies there was a careful separation and meticulous and detailed register of every item of income and expenses. See Goitein, *Society*, 2: 101.

Hospitality

As the leader of the community Yeshūʿā b. Joseph considered it proper to host scholars who found themselves in Alexandria, even when the visit was unofficial or unexpected. Moses b. Joseph Ibn Kaskīl happened to pass through the Alexandrian port, and though Yeshūʿā did not know of him beforehand, he hosted him for five days. That time period was sufficient for Yeshūʿā to gain a favorable impression of Ibn Kaskīl's considerable talent and knowledge and to become friends with him. Upon departure he provided him with a letter of reference to Eli b. Amram, the leader of the Fustat community.[432] At the time of the visit Ibn Kaskīl was probably still a young scholar, as is apparent in Yeshūʿā's benediction: "May God grant that many of his age be like him."[433]

We already saw above that the responsibility for hosting Daniel b. Azaryah, the Head of the Palestinian Yeshivah also fell upon the shoulders of Yeshūʿā. Hosting a Yeshivah head and community leader was a challenging task, and as we alluded to above, it was a challenge that Yeshūʿā was afraid to undertake, and tried to avoid.[434]

(e) Other Activities

Intellectual Ties

Yeshūʿā b. Joseph was an erudite intellectual, at least according to his perception of himself and his social persona. Many of his letters are written in a poetic register and with a fair deal of sophistication, and he frequently employs Talmudic expressions.[435] From the evidence we have of his legal activity, which is unfortunately scant, Yeshūʿā is revealed as a very confident jurist with full command of the legal sources, and as one who does not hesitate to disagree with other people's rulings.[436]

---

432 TS 13 J 11.2: Gil, *Kingdom*, no. 674.
433 Ibid., ll. 12–13.
434 See above, Part II, Chapter 1.3 (c): Sources of Support, in the section: The Geonim, the Heads of the Palestinian Yeshiva.
435 For example, Bodl MS Heb b 3.16v, ll. 16–17 (Gil, *Kingdom*, no. 671; Frenkel, "*The Compassionate and Benevolent*" [Hebrew], no. 1): אנוס פטריה רחמנא ; TS 12.338, esp. r, l. 3 (Gil, *Kingdom*, 673): his letter to Nahray; Bodl MS Heb c 13.2r, ll. 14, 17, 19, 20, 23: Gil, *Kingdom*, no. 673.
436 See above, Part II, Chapter 1.3 (c): Sources of Support, in the section: "The Rav" Judah ha-Kohen b. Joseph; and Part II, Chapter 1.3 (d): Spheres of Activity, in the section: Presiding as Judge.

It was stated above that Yeshūʿā prompted his image as a knowledgeable person and highlighted his intellectual prowess. In a letter of reference which he "procured," he sought to sculpt his public persona as an erudite religious leader. "And he [Yeshūʿā] presented a sermon before us, and he was as a bubbling brook of knowledge regarding everything about which he spoke."[437] The scathing criticism he directed at others reveals Yeshūʿā to have had a high opinion of himself. Referring to the community's elders, he once said: "For there are those among us who are not familiar with legal intricacies,"[438] which implies that he himself had full command of legal minutiae.

From his place as the leader of the community, Yeshūʿā cultivated intellectual ties that went beyond his local environs. We have already noted his cerebral interactions with Nahray b. Nissim,[439] but perhaps a more noteworthy relationship in the same vein was his association with the Sephardic scholar Moses b. Joseph Ibn Kaskīl. The relationship between Nahray and Yeshūʿā was a relationship between equals, whereas Yeshūʿā's association with the Sephardic intellectual, who passed through Alexandria and was Yeshūʿā's guest for a number of days, was more characteristic of a patron-protégé association. Yeshūʿā was the elder "fellow," the leader of the community and a judge, whereas Ibn Kaskīl was still a young scholar.[440] Immediately upon Ibn Kaskīl's arrival in Alexandria, Yeshūʿā tried to ascertain the man's worth. Yeshūʿā was primarily interested in his analytic abilities and his intellectual acumen:

> I peeked into his rooms, and behold they are all bursting like a pomegranate with wisdom and understanding. His erudition is the most weighty [element of his intellectual acumen],

---

437 TS 13 J 28.21, right margins, ll. 1–5: Frenkel, *"The Compassionate and Benevolent"* [Hebrew], no. 80. Yeshūʿā desires to emphasize his rhetorical ability, *dibbur*; the breadth of his knowledge, "like an overflowing fountain"; its comprehensiveness, "in every field" – in accordance with the contemporary Muslim inclination to encyclopedism along the lines of the *adab* literature. See Francesco Gabrieli, "Adab," *Encyclopedia of Islam*, 2nd edition, *s.v.*, and more extensively on the development of the term over time, in Carlo-Alfonso Nallino, *La littérature arabe des origins à l'époque de la dynastie ummayade*, trans. Charles Pellat (Paris: Maisonneuve, 1950). See also Charles Pellat, "Variations sur le theme de l'adab," *Corréspondence d'Orient-Études* 5–6 (1964): 19–37, on *adab* literature's purpose of fashioning the average Muslim in the fields of religion, morals and literature; and Gérard Lecomte, *Ibn Outayba (mort en 276/889): L'homme, son oeuvre, ses idées* (Damascus: n.p., 1965), pointing to the indelible bond between *adab* and religious literature. This image is also suited to the qualities of the ideal man in Jewish society. See Goitein, *Society*, 5: 415, 426, 428, 431.

438 Bodl MS Heb c 13.20v, l. 9: Gil, *Kingdom*, no. 673.

439 See above, Part II, Chapter 1.3 (c): Sources of Support, in the section: Nahray b. Nissim.

440 TS 13 J 11.2, ll. 12–13, 20–21: Gil, *Kingdom*, no. 674.

> and he also fears God and is exceedingly humble. And if I ask him anything from the Bible, the Mishnah, the Talmud, or secular subjects, I find him replete with wisdom.[441]

It is apparent that Yeshūʿā was enchanted by Ibn Kaskīl's intellectual capacity. He especially valued his great knowledge of all religious subjects: "Bible, Mishnah, and Talmud." Evidently, he also appreciated his familiarity with secular subjects, and the general breadth and depth of his knowledge: "the rooms are bursting like pomegranates," "[he is] replete with wisdom." After Yeshūʿā ascertained the worth of this guest, he expressed his approval and his acceptance by inviting him to stay in Alexandria. Moreover, he announced Ibn Kaskīl's arrival to the head of the Fustat community, Eli b. Amram, and thus he promulgated the news of his coming to the scholarly community at large, a community of which both Yeshūʿā and Eli b. Amram were members.

Ties with the Non-Jewish World

Yeshūʿā b. Joseph served as a link between members of the Jewish ruling elite and the local Muslim authorities in Alexandria. When the Nagid Mevorakh b. Saʿadyah, in Fustat wished to rent a vineyard belonging to the Amir of Alexandria, Abū Manṣūr, it was Yeshūʿā who was asked to deliver the offer, accompanied by a letter of reference, to the Amir.[442] This presents Yeshūʿā as the intermediary between the Jewish leadership in Fustat, when they wished to secure personal privileges, and representatives of the Muslim rulers in Alexandria. It is likely that these ties promoted his status as the leader of the community.

(f) The End of Tenure

We do not know how Yeshūʿā's tenure as leader ended. The last document penned by him is the letter of reference to the Alexandrian community, which he apparently wrote himself. In this document a separate reference letter from Elijah b. Solomon Gaon,[443] who was the head of the Palestinian Yeshivah between

---

441 Ibid., ll. 9–12.
442 Bodl MS Heb c 3.16v, ll. 3–6: Gil, *Kingdom*, no. 671; Frenkel, "*The Compassionate and Benevolent*" [Hebrew], no. 1. Gil's interpretation and dating of this document differ from mine; see ibid., appendix.
443 TS 13 J 28.21, margins, ll. 6–12: Frenkel, "*The Compassionate and Benevolent*" [Hebrew], no. 80.

1062–1083,[444] is alluded to. This indicates that 1062 is the *terminus post quem* for Yeshūʿā's termination. In the same document a further dispute in the Alexandrian community is alluded to, involving Yeshūʿā's leadership.[445] It thus stands to reason that Yeshūʿā did not pass away while serving as the head of the community, but rather was ousted from his position. Indeed, the next community leader was not a scion of this Alexandrian dynasty and came from a different family altogether.

Yeshūʿā b. Joseph, the last scion of a local dynasty that ruled over the Jewish community of Alexandria during several generations, was deeply engaged not only with local affairs, but also with the politics of the Palestinian Yeshivah. His communal activities were entangled with a dense web of personal relationships with central key figures in contemporary commerce and religious-intellectual life, such as Abraham Ibn al-Furāt, Judah Ibn Sighmār, and Nahray b. Nissim, and "the Rav". Their relationships combined political interests, mercantile endeavors, intellectual and personal ties.

444 See Gil, *History of Palestine*, 741–746.

445 TS 13 J 28.21, margins, ll. 4–11: Frenkel, *"The Compassionate and Benevolent"* [Hebrew], no. 80.

Chapter 2 Shelah b. Mubashshir Ben Nahum

1 The Family

Shelah (Sahl) b. Mubashshir was the scion of one of the most powerful families of Alexandria, the Ben Nahum family. His father, Mubashshir Ben Nahum, was one of the community's distinguished notables. In 1029 the father's signature appears together with the signatures of other dignitaries, who served as the representatives of the Jewish community in Alexandria and its spokesmen, in a letter to the community of Fustat.[446] In 1042 Mubashshir's name is included in a list of elders who attend testimony in the court of Yeshūʿā b. Joseph.[447]

The Ben Nahum family were involved in extra communal politics. They were adamantly and actively opposed to Daniel b. Azaryah, and were at the forefront of the opposition to his visit in 1060.[448] A legal testimony from Alexandria dated to 1079 states:

> Our revered and elder teacher R. Muvḥar, the son of our teacher R. Ṣedaqa, may Heaven be his abode, came before us and said: I was in the hall of the esteemed Zaʿīm al-Mulk in Alexandria. ʿImrān and Ezra the sons of Bashīr Ben Nahum were present there, and I sued them for the [campaign] of defamation they lead these days, and in the course of the discussion I mentioned the excommunication declared by our master Daniel, the Head of the Yeshiva, may his blessed and unsullied memory be for a blessing, against their family. The aforementioned ʿImrān said: "May God grind the bones of Daniel" – may ʿImrān's mouth be filled with soil – and his brother, Ezra, said: "Amen."[449]

The opposition fomented by the Ben Nahum sons against the visit of Daniel b. Azaryah ended with the latter's excommunication of the family. Even twenty years later, the family was still stirring up opposition to such an extent that they were brought to trial. Muvḥar b. Ṣedaqa, the man who prosecuted them, easily infuriated them enough to curse the memory of Daniel b. Azaryah, who

---

446 Bodl MS Heb a 3.28: Cowley, "Bodleian Geniza Fragments," 250 – 254. This is a letter dated 1028, in Yeshūʿā b. Joseph's handwriting.
447 TS 13 J 8.31: Frenkel, *"The Compassionate and Benevolent"* [Hebrew], no. 60.
448 See above, Part II, Chapter 1.3 (c): Sources of Support, in the section: The Geonim, the Heads of the Palestinian Yeshivah.
449 TS Misc 23, f. 3r: Gil, *Palestine* [Hebrew], no. 531. My translation differs slightly from Gil's.

https://doi.org/10.1515/9783110713619-007

had passed away seventeen years before, and recorded their statements, along with other testimony, probably with the intention of bringing them to trial.[450]

ʿImrān and Ezra were likely Shelah's cousins.[451] Shelah was especially close to his uncle Bashīr, the father of the two, and they cooperated on public ventures even before Shelah was appointed judge. Shelah relates in a letter from 1071 how he and his uncle helped a family in crisis in Alexandria and how they both travelled to Fustat to plead before the leadership regarding the poor and destitute of their city.[452]

Other members of the family are mentioned, mostly in connection with their mercantile activities.[453]

2 First Years

Between 1065–1077, Shelah did not yet serve as judge. In documents from this period he signs: "Shelah b. Mubashshir *n"n* [= his soul at rest]," without any official title. Nevertheless, he was already deeply involved in communal activity, which was mainly directed to social causes.

A letter penned by Shelah in 1065 addressed to Nahray b. Nissim,[454] wherein he relates his involvement in the deliverance of aid to a widow and her orphans, gives us a window into his social activism. Essentially, it is a thank-you note to Nahray for making sure that the widow received the merchandise and money

450 See ibid., later in the document. It follows from this that cursing and verbal attacks were considered judicable offences, even – and perhaps mainly – towards those no longer among the living.

451 ʿImrān Ben Nahum is also mentioned as a middleman in Alexandria, responsible for transferring letters from there to Salonica. See TS Ar. 53.37, ll. 33–34 (Shelomo D. Goitein, "The Jewish Communities of Saloniki and Thebes in Ancient Documents from the Cairo Genizah," *Sefunot* 11 (1971), 15–17 [Hebrew]).

452 TS 13 J 17.5, ll. 6–7, 18–19: Frenkel, *"The Compassionate and Benevolent"* [Hebrew], no. 67.

453 TS 8 J 18.27: Gil, *Kingdom*, no. 773. Jacob Ben Nahum is mentioned there as conducting commercial business with Nahray b. Nissim between Tripoli and Fustat, by means of merchant colleagues situated in Alexandria. David Ben Nahum and Isaac Ben Nahum are also mentioned as having commercial ties with Nahray b. Nissim, similarly conducted between Fustat, Tripoli, and Alexandria. See TS 10 J 20.3 (Gil, *Kingdom*, no. 690); TS 13 J 25.8 (Gil, *Kingdom*, no. 691); see also TS 8 J 5.1 (Gershon Weiss, "Legal Documents Written by the Court Clerk Halfon b. Manasse (dated 1100–1138): A Study in the Diplomatics of the Cairo Geniza," unpublished PhD diss., [University of Pennsylvania, 1970], 97–100), Joseph b. Samuel Ben Nahum's will from 1114, indicating extensive wealth. The family also had branches in Fustat and other cities. See Goitein, *Society*, 5: 167, n. 229.

454 ENA 2805, f. 2a: Gil, *Kingdom*, no. 790.

owed to her deceased husband. Shelah had requested Nahray's help in assisting the widow recover her husband's property. When the husband's merchandise had arrived, Shelah had made sure that it was handed over to the widow, collected the bill owed to her husband, and transferred the balance to the widow. Finally, he made sure that Nahray was ritually compensated in benedictions and praise: "God, blessed be His name, knows of my prayers on your behalf on holidays and on special occasions, and of my prayers of merciful intercession on behalf of your parents. May it come to pass, that the Most High shall answer these prayers on your behalf and grant you a rich reward in heaven."[455]

Despite holding no office, he represented the poor people of Alexandria vis-à-vis the leadership in Fustat. In furtherance of these causes he travelled to Fustat and confronted the *ra'īs* Judah b. Sa'adyah, as he attests to in this letter:[456]

> Regarding the leader's (*ra'īs)* anger directed at me, and his heavy heart, I have no advice. May the Most High judge between us and those who curtail our rights. We are people who journeyed to Fustat to further the cause of the poor of our city. We did not unduly burden anyone, and we did not spread dissent in the community, nor did we commit any "crime."[457]

In addition to his social activities at this time, Shelah was part of the regular cohort serving on the court in Alexandria. On a court document from 1074,[458] he is listed as one of the corroborating witnesses. In another instance he is the signatory upon the dissolution of a partnership in 1077.[459] On both documents he signs: Shelah son of R. Mubashshir *n"n* [may his soul rest], and in an embellishment to the signature he adds: "May he live forever." with no indication to any official status in court. It is only from 1079 that he adds the title "the Judge" to his signature.[460]

---

455 Ibid., ll. 5–6, 13.

456 On this title as one of Judah b. Sa'adyah's and its significance, see Cohen, *Self-Government*, 169–170.

457 ENA 2805, f. 2a, ll. 16–20: Gil, *Kingdom*, no. 790.

458 TS 28.6 c: Frenkel, *"The Compassionate and Benevolent"* [Hebrew], no. 41. This is a compensation bill (*avīzāriyya*), in which a woman appoints a guardian, in order to sue her mother and sister for the property she had left with them when she emigrated from Alexandria to the Maghreb. The document was written in Zuwaylat al-Mahdiyya and executed in Alexandria.

459 TS 16.138, a bill dissolving the partnership between Joseph b. Isaiah al-Dhahabī and Khalaf b. 'Azrūn.

460 TS 10 J 4.9 + TA 12.8, an *avīzāriyya* bill from 1079, in which the slave-woman Sitt al-Rūm, who was freed shortly before her master's death, appoints a representative to collect a debt on her behalf. There he signs as Sahl the judge son of R. Mubashshir *n"n*.

3 His Tenure as Judge

Between 1079–1103, Shelah served in an official capacity on the court, first as an associate justice, then as chief justice. Three documents which he signed as a witness survive from his tenure as an associate justice. The first is the certification of a court document from 1079, which he witnessed.[461] The second document is a collaboration of the Fustat and Alexandria courts. It is a compensation bill from 1088, A woman who was abandoned by her husband in Alexandria appointed an advocate to prosecute the case against her husband who was in Fustat. The other signatures on this bill are those of Mariut ha-Kohen b. Joseph and Eli ha-Kohen, who served as a *parnas* (welfare official) in Fustat, and confirms the identity of the woman.[462] The third document is a marriage certificate (*ketubba*), in which Shelah's signature appears next to that of Mawhūb b. Aaron the Cantor.[463]

Around the year 1100, as he begins to use the title *Beit dīn*, Shelah is appointed chief justice in Alexandria.[464] On a case from 1101 he signs "Shelah *Beit dīn*, son of Mubashshir, may his soul rest." His co-signatories are Job b. David ha-Levi, the Judge, and Mariut ha-Kohen b. Joseph, whose signature is the last one [465] In another document written a little while afterwards there is reference to "the court of the honored Shelah"; this is a case from Fustat, which documents a disagreement between Alexandrian merchants. This case was first brought before Shelah, but was retried in Fustat, and the witnesses, who were called again to testify, state: "I have appeared in the past before Shelah, and I am now repeating what I said then." Similarly: "I have already appeared

461 Ibid.
462 ENA 4010.19.
463 TS 12.677.
464 On the title *Beit dīn*, referring to the chief justice and signifying a professional judge appointed to lead the court, see Goitein, *Society*, 2: 314–315.
465 Usually, the last signature on a court's act is that of the most senior signatory. See Goitein, *Society*, 2: 313. The last signature on this document is that of Mariut, even though Shelah was already in office as chief justice. The reason for this is apparently Mariut's special status as the son of Joseph ha-Kohen, who had been the chief justice of the Palestinian Yeshivah's court and the cousin of Evyatar Gaon, and bore the title of "Fellow" (*ḥaver*) of the Yeshivah. On Joseph ha-Kohen b. Solomon, see Gil, *History of Palestine*, §§889, 897. Gil mentions another son of Joseph's who came to Alexandria, named Abū al-Barakāt Solomon. It seems that Mariut is yet another son of his, since his identity and family are written in the document unequivocally. Another possibility is that since Mariut served as chief justice in Alexandria before Shelah (see above, n. 162), it may be that for a while Alexandria had two chief judges in office at the same time. This is in contradiction to Goitein's view (Goitein, *Society*, 2: 315).

before Shelah and given my statement, and it has been recorded in a court deed before three [judges] namely Shelah b. Mubashshir, our master R. Mawhūb the Cantor, the expert and supporter of the Yeshivah, son of R. Aaron, and our master R. Mariut ha-Kohen the Fellow, son of the great and holy master R. Joseph, the chief justice." Finally the court in Fustat arrives at a verdict: "We, the court, have decided that the suit brought by Ezekiel before the court of Shelah was[...]."[466] which points at Shelah's stature as the chief justice of Alexandria.

4 A Communal Leader

It is very difficult, in fact it is nearly impossible, to distinguish between the communal activities of a local leader and his position and activities in the inter-communal system. In what follows, we shall, nevertheless, endeavor to focus mainly on the communal aspects of Shelah's leadership and survey his policies as they pertain to the local sphere.

(a) Shelah and "the Maghribis" (al-*Maghāriba*)

At the time of Shelah's tenure a dynamic and quite distinct community composed of recently arrived settlers from the Maghreb formed in Alexandria. This group attempted to keep separate organizational bodies, especially when it came to the payment of taxes to the Muslim authorities. They felt that the established community was attempting to have them pay more than their fair share, and exerted a great deal of effort to pay taxes separately and directly to the authorities – without the communal apparatus' intervention. This situation led to frequent crises, which sometimes involved actual violence. The events that led to one such crisis are described in some detail in a letter by one of the Maghribi leaders, Benayah b. Mūsā, to Nahray b. Nissim:

> [...] Until the situation deteriorated. They would regularly set traps for us surreptitiously, and cause us untold harm. Then, last summer when "our friends" (*aṣḥābuna*) were demanded [to pay] dinars, and I suspected that they intended to perform a despicable act and implement their designs, I went, together with five other Maghribis, to the judge and I prostrated myself before him and said to him: "Take from each one of us what you see fit." We each paid him on time, and did not tell any of them. And it was difficult for

466 TS 20.121, ll. 4–5, 28–31, 47–48: Frenkel, *"The Compassionate and Benevolent"* [Hebrew], no. 34.

> them that it took place in this way. And when the most recent due date was upon us, we went to the judge and I asked him, kissing his feet, that we shall do as we did before since we feared them and since there is little justice to be had, and because they wished us malice in their heart...and we paid our debt and we left with the qadi's signature and his seal upon a decree commanding that no one was to speak with us [regarding this matter]. And when they saw that this was the case, they broke the scales in half and said: "The residents of Alexandria are poor" and they once again quarreled with us. And a letter had come from our master the Head [*ra'īs*= Mevorakh b. Sa'adyah], may his majesty be elevated, and we discussed the matter before the judge. I said to him: "Enough with the avarice." And he listed all the people and collected what God had ordained, and required that all who draw breath must pay.[467]

We are thus privy to a series of prolonged quarrels, the focus of which was the Maghribis' refusal to pay their share of taxes as dictated by the established leadership. They preferred to pay their taxes directly to the Muslim qadi, and to this end they enlisted the Muslim authorities and managed to procure an edict forbidding the Jewish community from approaching them with any demands. Shelah b. Mubashshir was the prime instigator of this protracted struggle, as Benayah himself relates:

> Ben Nahum went to the synagogue. And no one from our group knew of it. And he did unto me the same thing he has been wont to do for so long. He appointed a man to walk through the markets and proclaim: "We have done the following regarding this situation." And when our Maghribi friends heard of this, it was very difficult for them and they did not tolerate it at all, and great commotion ensued, which defies succinct description.[468]

The public announcement that circulated in the streets and marketplace, as described in this letter, was an explicit attempt at belittlement and ridicule.[469] One must therefore understand Shelah's actions as a public ceremony of disparagement targeting Benayah.

This was not, however, a personal spat between Shelah and Benayah. The entire Ben Nahum family was involved, including Nissim, Shelah's son, who played an important role in this campaign, as Benayah b. Mūsā attests: "And worst of all, Nissim and Ibn Galina did what no one else had dared, and said:

---

467 TS 13 J 23.3r, l. 13; right margins, l. 2: Frenkel, "*The Compassionate and Benevolent*" [Hebrew], no. 75.

468 Ibid., right margins, l. 2 – upper margins, l. 5.

469 See Shelomo D. Goitein, "The Local Jewish Community in the Light of the Cairo Geniza Records," *JJS* 12 (1961): 149.

We are the leaders [of the community] and we excommunicate [you]."[470] In another letter from this period, the disagreement is described explicitly as a struggle between the Ben Nahum family and the *Maghāriba*: "The matters between the *Maghāriba* and the Ben Nahum family are unsatisfactory."[471]

The Ben Nahum family was only the vanguard of this struggle of an entire group of the Alexandrian community. Shelah's pilgrimage to Fustat to plead with the leadership on behalf of the poor people of Alexandria was described above, but was actuality an advocate for a distinct segment of the community, a group that defined itself in localized terms. These "inhabitants of the city" coalesced as part of the protracted struggle with the new Maghribi expatriates, who had only recently relocated to Alexandria, in an attempt to force them to pay taxes through the community apparatus. Shelah was the forceful and undisputed leader of this group, as attested to by a member of the opposition: "They have one leader, we have one hundred."[472]

The opposition consisted of a cohesive group of Maghribis who stood together with Benayah. In his letters Benayah emphasizes that the persecution was impersonal and directed to the Maghribi transplants as a group: "There is no possibility for a stranger to dwell in their midst in peace";[473] and more explicitly: "What was done was not done only to me, but to all strangers."[474]

Despite this tense state of affairs, the Ben Nahum family collaborated closely with a number of Maghribi merchants. Thus, for example, Abū Joseph Jacob Ben Nahum was a partner in a group of merchants, which included Mūsā b. Abī al-Ḥayy Khalīla, a known Maghribi merchant from Alexandria, and Nahray b. Nissim, who was also of Maghribi origin. It should not surprise us, therefore, that in a business letter from Mūsā b. Abī al-Ḥayy to Nahray, he deemed it appropriate to inform him of Ben Nahum's situation.[475] Abū Joseph Jacob Ben Nahum's primary responsibility was the transfer of merchandise, mainly bundles of dinars, from the Maghreb to Nahray in Fustat.[476] These types of services were an element

470 TS 13 J 23.3, 2, ll. 9–10: Frenkel, *"The Compassionate and Benevolent"* [Hebrew], no. 75. On Jacob b. Galinā see ENA NS 2.6, 2, l. 17: Frenkel, *"The Compassionate and Benevolent"* [Hebrew], no. 14.

471 ENA NS 2.6, 2, ll. 9–11: Frenkel, *"The Compassionate and Benevolent"* [Hebrew], no. 14.

472 ENA NS 2.6v, ll. 12–13: Frenkel, *"The Compassionate and Benevolent"* [Hebrew], no. 14.

473 Ibid., r, right margins, ll. 7–8.

474 Ibid., v, l. 14.

475 TS 8 J 27.2r, l. 13: Gil, *Kingdom*, no. 447. See also the collection of letters by Mūsā b. Abī al-Ḥayy Khalīla in Gil, *Kingdom*, nos. 444–467.

476 AIU VII E 193r, l. 6: Gil, *Kingdom*, no. 450.

of the informal *muʿāmala* business partnership,[477] and thus one may assume that Jacob Ben Nahum was a partner in this *muʿāmala*, the members of which were mostly Maghribi merchants, and some of them Maghribis from Alexandria, who fought with his family so persistently. Below we shall illustrate the special relationship between Shelah and the Maghribi merchant Nahray b. Nissim, as well as with "the Rav" Judah ha-Kohen, who was the spiritual leader of the Maghribi community in Fustat.[478] At this stage it is difficult to explicate the contradictory behavior of Shelah and his family regarding the Maghribi community, especially in front of their persistent mistreatment of the Maghribis, as depicted by Benayah b. Mūsā above, including public ridicule in the form of announcements in the marketplaces, speaking dubiously of Benayah's loyalty to the Nagid, the seizure of property, levying a "communal tax" more than once, and even excommunication.[479]

(b) Shelah and the Local Jews of Alexandria

As was mentioned above, Shelah began his public work as an advocate for the weak and the needy in the Alexandrian community,[480] but his tenure as chief judge led to much strife and dissatisfaction. He had a difficult time exerting his authority upon the more violent and reactionary members of the community. Thus, for example, a certain crook who attempted to sow discord between a widow and her son in order to gain control over her property, completely ignored the repeated court summons Shelah sent to him.[481] Two letters requesting aid, written at the time of his tenure, are not addressed to him, but rather to the leadership in Fustat, completely bypassing his authority. One letter addressed to the dignitary Eli ha-Kohen b. Yaḥyā is from a mother in Fustat, Ḍiyā b. Joseph, begging for help to secure her son's release from jail.[482] The son, Fāḍil, was involved in a conflict with a violent litigant. Their case had first come before the Jewish

477 On the *muʿāmala*, see also above, Part II, Chapter 1.3 (c): Sources of Support, in the section: Nahray b. Nissim.
478 See below, Part II, Chapter 2.5 (c): Shelah and "the Rav," and (d): Shelah and Nahray b. Nissim.
479 TS 13 J 23.3r, right margins, ll. 2–5; 2, ll. 1–2, 4–5, 9–10: Gil, *Kingdom*, no. 605; Frenkel, "*The Compassionate and Benevolent*" [Hebrew], no. 75. See also below, Part IV, Chapter 1.1: Shared Mercantile Interests.
480 See above, Part II, Chapter 2.2: First Years.
481 TS 13 J 16.3: Frenkel, "*The Compassionate and Benevolent*" [Hebrew], no. 66.
482 TS NS J 36: Frenkel, "*The Compassionate and Benevolent*" [Hebrew], no. 90.

court led by Shelah, who acquitted him, as the mother writes: “My son Fāḍil, who is my only child, had a conflict with Abū Sa‘d b. Shardāna, and the case was tried in the Jewish court. The leader of the Jews wrote them letters of acquittal.”[483] The litigant continued to harass her son until he managed to have him incarcerated. The mother’s letter addressed to the dignitary asks him to provide her with a letter of reference (*ruq‘ah*) from the Nagid Mevorakh to the qadi, asking him to release her son. In other words, the verdict of the Jewish court led by Shelah was worthless when faced with the forceful behavior of the litigant, and the mother was required to find other alternatives in order to help her son. In her distress, she addresses the true powerbrokers, who lived in Fustat and not in Alexandria.

The second letter was also written by a woman and addressed to the Nagid Mevorakh. Jalīla b. Abraham writes in her name and in the name of her orphaned children, but not about Shelah’s powerlessness. Her accusation is more serious: She claimed that Shelah and his son, R. Nissim, collaborated with her deceased husband’s business partners to steal her husband’s property and the money guaranteed by her *Ketubba* (marriage contract).[484] Shelah is depicted in this letter as someone who, far from protecting the weak and downtrodden, exploited them and made joint cause with their abusers.

The Head and the litigants mentioned above cheated me and I don’t know how... They appropriated all the property and brought it to Alexandria. When the property got here, the *ra‘īs* put his hands on it and screamed at me saying: “This Muslim, your husband owes him property worth thirty-six dinars, and he laid claim to it, and it is apparent to me that he is speaking the truth.”

And later on in the letter: “Afterwards the Head and his son Nissim said: ‘We must not acquiesce to this woman’s demands. We shall sell [this property] and divide the proceeds, each according to his claim.”[485] The woman also accuses Shelah of deliberately lying to the qadi and making no mention of her position: “The Head came to him and said: ‘Yes, O Qadi, this man is indeed truthful and she owes him thirty-six dinars, he is trustworthy and speaks the truth, and the

483 Ibid., ll. 11–14.
484 TS 28.19: Frenkel, *“The Compassionate and Benevolent”* [Hebrew], no. 42. Nissim Ben Nahum, one of Shelah’s three sons, is mentioned in additional documents: TS 12.627, where *‘urs Nissim b. Nāḥūm* (the marriage of Nissim Ben Nahum) is referred to; ULC Or 1080 J 109, a letter from 1109 to the *ḥazzan* of Damietta; ENA 2740.3, in which the two other sons, Mubashshir and Isaac, are also mentioned; ENA 4020.59, in which the sons Nissim and Mubashshir are mentioned.
485 TS 28.19, ll. 17–18, 22–25, 27–29: Frenkel, *“The Compassionate and Benevolent”* [Hebrew], no. 42.

woman has already said: 'As for me, my husband has nothing'. You should take the money and pay her and me."[486]

In this case, Shelah is accused of very serious crimes. Not only did he not protect the poor and the widows, he made common cause with the oppressive powerbrokers – so he could take a portion of the inheritance for himself. He did not hesitate to cheat and to lie, and to take advantage of the widow's weakness and his position in the community vis-à-vis the Muslim authorities, in order to lay claim to property and money. Indeed, there are further hints of dissatisfaction and serious allegations against his leadership. A very fragmentary letter, of which only the right half survives states: "'The Head, our teacher R. Shelah the Judge[...]the community oppressively and with little consultation[...] b. Joseph and his brothers who are known as 'the sons of Nahum'[...]cases before the court with testimony that is not[...]"[487] Though most of the letter is missing, one may glean from the little that survived that the Ben Nahum family were accused by members of the community of despotism and inadequate leadership.

Corroboration of this is found in another letter that Shelah himself wrote to the Nagid Mevorakh, in which he is explicit about people in the community who attempt to undermine him and malign him: "[...] regarding those who seek help against me when I have done no wrong. I exert considerable efforts on their behalf and they exert considerable efforts in slandering me and harming me[...] the Almighty God who reads hearts and minds will give to each according to his just due, as it is written.[488] This letter also confirms that Shelah's brothers were deeply involved in the leadership of the community: "It is not hidden from our magnificent lordship, may he live forever, the matter of his servants, my brothers Shaltiel and Joseph[...]and they also carry the burden of the community and advocate on its behalf and they also bear the responsibility in my place, for I am a sick man, and have no more strength."[489]

Shelah's leadership is thus revealed as a family enterprise. His son Nissim and his two brothers Joseph and Shaltiel shared power with him, and in certain situations actually governed in his place. Though Shelah helped the poor, the orphans, and the widows on many occasions, and liked to present himself as the representative of the destitute in the city, in reality the weak and the needy of Alexandria energetically opposed his leadership and that of the entire Ben Nahum family. This lack of legitimacy led to expressions of dissatisfaction and vehement protest by members of the community, encouraged violent elements

486 Ibid., ll. 54–56.
487 TS NS J 334, ll. 8–11: Frenkel, *"The Compassionate and Benevolent"* [Hebrew], no. 93.
488 TS 16.24: Frenkel, *"The Compassionate and Benevolent"* [Hebrew], no. 27.
489 Ibid., ll. 13–14, 16–18.

to act presumptively and forcefully, and other elements to bypass his local authority and seek redress among the leaders in Fustat.

5 Shelah's Involvement in Extra-Communal Affairs

(a) Ties with the Palestinian Yeshivah

From the very beginning, Shelah's doings were not confined to the local community and were inextricably tied to the activities of the Palestinian Yeshivah. Shelah was one of the seven members who led the Yeshivah, and was entitled "the Sixth."[490] The deep involvement of the Ben Nahum family in the Yeshivah's affairs was already mentioned above, and especially their unyielding opposition to the leadership of Daniel b. Azaryah and his son David b. Daniel.[491] Shelah himself was also part of this campaign. Around 1085, when, beside Alexandria, David b. Daniel controlled all the Jewish communities along the coastal cities of Palestine, Shelah wrote a long and detailed opinion piece in which he proved, using biblical prooftexts, that the coastal town of Ashkelon is considered to be part of the Land of Israel. This was not simply punditry, but rather a learned polemic against the assertions of David b. Daniel's supporters, who claimed in response to those who rebuked them regarding the takeover of the coastal cities, that these cities, and especially Ashkelon, were not part of the Land of Israel. Shelah publicly announced the purpose of this opinion piece: "And I needed [to do] this, for I was scandalized by those who say that Ashkelon is in truth a Philistine city [and not part of the Holy Land]."[492] He explicitly remarks that he spoke about this matter to the Gaon Evyatar, the head of the Yeshivah, and goes so far as to quote him: "We mentioned this matter before our master the Gaon and he has stated that[...]." We thus learn from here of his personal relationship with the Gaon Evyatar.

Even after 1094, when the Palestinian Yeshivah was forced to relocate to Tyre and its status began to decline, Shelah continued to depend on its support. When he encountered financial difficulties after his brother's silk shop was subjected to competition from silk merchants from Syria, and his leadership was

490 On the organization and structure of the Palestinian Yeshivah, see Gil, *History of Palestine*, 505–508.
491 See above, Part II, Chapter 2.1: The Family.
492 TS 16.24r, ll. 4–6: Frenkel, *"The Compassionate and Benevolent"* [Hebrew], no. 27, and see Gil, *History of Palestine*, §906.

under harsh scrutiny from members of the community,[493] the Palestinian Yeshivah came to his succor and granted him a letter of reference and protection. The document is very badly preserved, but the gist is quite clear:

> And moreover we announce our desire and yearning to alleviate the[...]humble and the regular custom [...] Despite this, when we arrived [...]to the city of Alexandria as was required... we found[...]Shelah the Fellow and Judge, son of Mubashshir, may heaven be his abode, and his brothers, may their Rock preserve them, serving the community[...] their ability to do[...]and to buy there not by force, but because of some lack[...] but they call[...]the silk shop in Alexandria when[...]unworthy people who seek to evict them from their shop.[494]

(b) Shelah's Ties with the Nagid Mevorakh b. Saʿadyah[495]

It was already stated above that in the first days of Mevorakh b. Saʿadyah's Nagidate, Shelah locked horns with him in a bitter struggle. Shelah made the journey to Fustat with his uncle to advocate on behalf of the poor of Alexandria, whose rights had been trampled on, in his opinion. This battle was connected to the campaign the Ben Nahum family was waging against the Maghribi merchants over separate taxation of the different groups in the community.[496] Shelah's protest aroused a great deal of resentment and ire in the Nagid. Shelah and the Nagid's family at that time were rivals in two opposing camps. The figure who supported Shelah at the time was none other than Moses ha-Kohen Sanī al-Dawla, Mevorakh's bitter rival. Shelah's confrontational stance is very apparent in the letter, in which he articulates a strong unyielding position against Mevorakh b. Saʿadyah.[497] This quarrel devolved into a severance of ties between Shelah and the established "inhabitants of the city" of Alexandria on one side

493 See above, Part II, Chapter 2.4 (b): Shelah and the Local Jews of Alexandria.

494 Moss. VII 137, ll. 12–17: Gil, *Palestine* [Hebrew], no. 548. Gil dated the letter there to 1071 on the basis of the letters 'ת'ת'ל'א written in the margins, next to the signature, but what is written there does not appear to be the date but rather the remains of lines that were written in the margin and erased. The affair of the silk shop and the complaints against Shelah and his brothers also took place in a later period, certainly after 1094. See above Part II, Chapter 2.4 (b): Shelah and the Local Jews of Alexandria.

495 On Mevorakh b. Saʿadyah's Nagidate, which was divided into two different periods (1079–1082, 1094–1111), see Cohen, *Self-Government*, 171–177, 213–271.

496 See above, Part II, Chapter 2.4 (a): Shelah and "the Maghribis" (*al-Maghāriba*). It is possible that this hostility is also connected to Shelah's vehement opposition to David b. Daniel, who at this time received the protection and shelter of Mevorakh. See Cohen, *Self-Government*, 181; Gil, *History of Palestine*, 753–754.

497 TS 13 J 17.5r, ll. 15–17: Frenkel, *"The Compassionate and Benevolent"* [Hebrew], no. 67.

and Mevorakh b. Saʿadyah and his Maghribi friends on the other. In the fullness of time, this severance was referred to in the collective communal memory as "the disagreement." Benayah b. Mūsā, one of the Maghribi leaders writes:[498] "No one did more for him [for Mevorakh] than I did and your uncle ʿAwāḍ, may God have mercy upon him, did, regarding his [Mevorakh's] 'disagreement' with them [=with Shelah and his camp]."[499] Even in 1159, two generations later, Judah b. Nathan recalled the event and described it in these words: "And he [Mevorakh b. Saʿadyah] travelled from Alexandria to Fustat. And then there was the "disagreement" between him and the Ben Nahum family. And Sanī al-Dawla was an advocate for the Ben Nahum family."[500]

The relationship between Shelah and the family of the Nagids shifted one hundred and eighty degrees in Mevorakh's second term in office (1094–1111). A Maghribi merchant living in Alexandria describes the final stage of the disagreement, and explains why in the end the interests of the Ben Nahum family overrode those of the Maghribi merchants: "And it was because our master the lord of lords [= Mevorakh b. Saʿadyah] was at that point inclined favorably to them [= to the Ben Nahum family]."[501]

Indeed, during Mevorakh's second term as Nagid, he was favorably inclined towards Shelah and his family. At that time, Shelah was granted a major promotion in the judicial hierarchy. He began to serve as a regular judge on the court and then as chief justice, even though he was on the bench together with Mariut ha-Kohen, a judge with many titles and a great deal of prestige.[502] Shelah's court at the time was under the authority of the Nagid and was granted a permanent charter from him. This is made explicit in a bill dated 1101: "The bill delineated above was duly invested in the permanent court...my lord Mevorakh, the Master of the Court, the Nagid of all Nagids, the Pillar of all of Israel."[503] We have already noted that a legal dispute adjudicated in Shelah's court was tried again in Fustat.[504]

Shelah owed his appointment to the bench to Mevorakh b. Saʿadyah. A close and very involved relationship began to develop between the two, without any distinction between the public and the private spheres. The two regularly collaborated in the mercantile realm. Thus, for example, we hear about a shipment of

---

498 TS 13 J 23.3v, ll. 3–4: Frenkel, *"The Compassionate and Benevolent"* [Hebrew], no. 75.
499 See above, Part II, Chapter 2.4 (a): Shelah and "the Maghribis" (*al-Maghāriba*).
500 TS 10 J 6.5r, ll. 8–9: Frenkel, *"The Compassionate and Benevolent"* [Hebrew], no. 48.
501 ENA NS 2 I 6v, ll. 19–20: Frenkel, *"The Compassionate and Benevolent"* [Hebrew], no. 14.
502 See above, Part II, Chapter 2.3: His Tenure as Judge.
503 TS 20.129. See Cohen, *Self-Government*, 242, n. 106.
504 See above, Part II, Chapter 2.3: His Tenure as Judge.

dinars sent by Mevorakh to Shelah.[505] On another occasion, when his brothers Joseph and Shaltiel's business was in dire straits, Shelah turned to Mevorakh to help them out.[506] Both public and private funds were exchanged between the two at different times. Shelah recounts a dispute between a number of heirs, that reached the qadi and the governor. Shelah, who was worried that the inheritance would be seized by the Muslim authorities, sold the merchandise and deposited the money with Mevorakh.[507] In times of financial stress in the community, Shelah took advantage of his close relationship with the Nagid, and made a personal request for money.[508]

Shelah acted as Mevorakh's representative in Alexandria. It is Shelah who was responsible for the ritual manifestations of loyalty to the Nagid, and Shelah hardly ever missed an opportunity to do it. A meeting in Fustat between the Nagid and the elders, for example, was an important enough occasion to organize a festive prayer in the Nagid's honor at the synagogue in Alexandria:

> It became known to me[...]regarding your meeting with the elders in Fustat, may God continue to preserve them, together with your son, the lord and chief Abū al[...]may God grant him long life, and may God grant you His Torah and His shelter, and we thanked God Almighty for this, I and the entire community, and I took out the Torah scrolls and prayed with steadfast devotion to God Almighty.[509]

Shelah frequently consulted with Mevorakh and fully coordinated his actions with him, even regarding internal community matters. When he encountered difficult cases,[510] or when he failed in compelling criminals to bow to the authority of the court, he always saw fit to report this to Mevorakh, both in official mem-

505 ENA 4020.59: Frenkel, *"The Compassionate and Benevolent"* [Hebrew], no. 12. This is a letter written by Shelah to Yeshūʿa b. Japheth in which he asks for information about what happened to the dinars that Mevorakh sent him via Yeshūʿā. This letter was written during the second period of Mevorakh's Nagidate, after 1094, since Mevorakh is referred to here as *sar ha-sarim*, "prince of princes." On Mevorakh's titles and the estimated dates that he received them, see the table in Cohen, *Self-Government*, 264–265. In contrast, the letter refers to only two of the three sons of Shelah mentioned in later letters, thus is may be assumed that it was written between 1095–1110. The discussion there is not of a gift sent by Mevorakh to Shelah, as Cohen thought (ibid., 242, n. 107), since later in the letter Shelah speaks explicitly of debts that he hopes to collect.
506 TS 16.24: Frenkel, *"The Compassionate and Benevolent"* [Hebrew], no. 27.
507 ENA 2740.3: Frenkel, *"The Compassionate and Benevolent"* [Hebrew], no. 9.
508 TS Misc. 27.19r, ll. 12–13: Frenkel, *"The Compassionate and Benevolent"* [Hebrew], no. 87.
509 TS 16.24, ll. 1, 3–7: Frenkel, *"The Compassionate and Benevolent"* [Hebrew], no. 27.
510 See ENA 2740.3, esp. ll. 12–13: Frenkel, *"The Compassionate and Benevolent"* [Hebrew], no. 9. This is a complicated inheritance dispute that almost reached the qadi's court. Shelah detailed in this letter to the Nagid how he had dealt with the case.

oranda of the community, penned by the elders, and in personal letters to Mevorakh.[511]

We thus find that at the same time that the power of the Palestinian Yeshivah waned and the Nagid in Egypt became more central, Shelah began to switch loyalties and depend more and more upon the Nagid's support. A mutual relationship between Shelah and the Nagid developed, which was based upon favors and services rendered, and in which the personal and public spheres were indistinguishable.

(c) Shelah and "the Rav"

Only the preface to one letter written by Shelah b. Mubashshir to "the Rav" Judah ha-Kohen, survives.[512] Nevertheless, the style and tone of the letter reflect extensive ties between the two. A four-line poem is appended to the beginning of the letter, likely composed by Shelah himself. The letter itself is written in a celebratory and poetic register. Shelah refers to himself in the address and in the body of the letter as "his student" (*tilmīdhuhu)*, which may reflect a student-teacher relationship between the two. In the letter Shelah informs "the Rav" that the latter's brother is due to arrive in Fustat in order to help Shelah and his brother.[513] The lines of the poem allude to the travails and harassment endured by Shelah:

> Greetings to whom [...] my many foes
> He who with his grievance alleviates my pain
> My foes overcame me plotting behind my back
> Their arrow unerringly released upon the beloved of my heart

The opening line of the letter, where the motif of peace is repeated a number of times, may perhaps allude to the hopes and prayers of the writer, who is at odds with his community: "Peace from the Lord of peace, who makes peace in His heavenly abode, let [peace] be upon all [...]."[514]

---

511 TS 13 J 16.3, ll. 21–22: Frenkel, "*The Compassionate and Benevolent*" [Hebrew], no. 66. This is about a scoundrel who managed to make mischief between a widow and her son in order to gain control of her property.

512 TS 10 J 15.8: Frenkel, "*The Compassionate and Benevolent*" [Hebrew], no. 52.

513 Ibid., ll. 10–11.

514 Ibid., l. 6. On the distress referred to here, see above, Part II, Chapter 2.4 (a): Shelah and "the Maghribis" (*al-Maghāriba*).

It is thus apparent that "the Rav" was not only Shelah's spiritual mentor, but also his political ally, and he quickly came to Shelah's succor when the latter encountered problems within his community.

(d) Shelah and Nahray b. Nissim

The relationships between Shelah and Nahray b. Nissim are revealed in a letter Shelah wrote Nahray.[515] Bequests, wills, and helping the widows and orphans of Alexandria are the focus of the communication. Nahray and Shelah, who at the time was yet to be appointed as judge of Alexandria, act – in tandem with other figures[516] – as part of a well-connected and intricate network dedicated to these matters. They corresponded on a regular basis and were careful to pass along as much information as possible. In the letter at hand at least three cases of bequests and wills are discussed, as well as the large sums of money at stake in these matters.[517]

6 Conclusion

The most noteworthy characteristic of Shelah's tenure as leader is the great shift in his approach over time. He began as a bellicose leader, a scion of a well-established family with roots in Alexandria and as the spokesperson of a particular group in Alexandria. In this earlier period, borne as he was upon a wave of xenophobic particularism, Shelah did not hesitate to clash with the Nagid in Fustat. Later, at the end of his tenure, he is obviously doing the Nagid Mevorakh b. Saʿadyah's bidding. In the final years of his tenure, evidence accumulates regarding corruption and degradation amongst Shelah and his family, a venality that was reflected in the shady use of public funds and outright cheating. These tendencies lead to the delegitimization of his leadership.

During all the years of his career, Shela was involved with powerful key figures outside the local community of Alexandria, be they the official heads of the Jews in the Fatimid state, like the Gaon and the Nagid, or influential persons like Nahray, and the "Rav." His connections with these powerful persons crossed the

---

515 ENA 2805, f. 2a: Gil, *Kingdom*, no. 790, and see above, Part II, Chapter 2.2: First Years.
516 ENA 2805, f. 2a, ll. 2, 20: Gil, *Kingdom*, no. 790.
517 See above Part II, Chapter 2.2: First Years; 2.4 (a): Shelah and "the Maghribis" (*al-Maghāriba*). Nahray had close commercial relations with other members of the Ben Nahum family, like Jacob Ben Nahum (Gil, *Kingdom*, nos. 691, 773) and David Ben Nahum (Gil, *Kingdom*, no. 690).

boundaries between groups that were traditionally conceived as rivals, like the local Alexandrians and the *Maghāriba*.

Chapter 3 Abraham b. Jacob al-Darʿī

1 Amongst the Maghribi Merchants

Abraham b. Jacob al-Darʿī's origins were in the Darʿa Valley of Morocco, as his name indicates. His initial mercantile ventures in Egypt involved trade in precious stones and silk between Fustat and Alexandria. At that time, he was a member of Nahray b. Nissim's mercantile circle. In a letter from the beginning of the 1060s Nathan b. Nahray gives his regards to members of this group, and Abraham b. al-Darʿī is counted among them.[518] Al-Darʿī occasionally flouted the commercial standard code of conduct, which irked his fellows. Yeshūʿā b. Ismāʿīl writes of a transaction involving trade in dinars, in which al-Darʿī made a tidy profit whilst employing unconventional methods, but in the end he lost a good deal of his dinar shipment and a large sum of money. Yeshūʿā b. Ismāʿīl does not hide his *schadenfreude* in his letter: "Allow me to relate to you what 'his misconduct led to'[...] and afterwards God punished him and did not save any of it [of the shipment of dinars]. And I say: 'Blessed be He in whose justice there is no distortion '."[519]

A further allusion to the discomfiture that al-Darʿī caused may be found in Nathan b. Nahray's letter to his cousin Nissim b. Nahray. Just like al-Darʿī, Nathan wished to sell corals (*marjān*), which arrived at the port of Alexandria, but he did not wish to collaborate with al-Darʿī; in fact Nathan extracted an oath from Nissim, that he should tell R. Abraham nothing about this transaction.[520]

2 A Public Figure in the Alexandrian Community

Beginning in 1096, after Mevorakh b. Saʿadyah ascended to the Nagidate for a second time, al-Darʿī became a key figure in the internal politics of the Alexandrian community. Though al-Darʿī was not considered an easy or reliable person to work with in the mercantile realm, his role as mediator and negotiator is not

518 TS 10 J 16.18: Frenkel, *"The Compassionate and Benevolent"* [Hebrew], no. 55. The other merchants mentioned by name are Abū Sahl Manasseh ha-Kohen, Nahray's brother-in-law; Abū al-Bishr, Abū Zikrī b. Manasseh, and Ismāʿīl al-Qalaʿī.

519 ENA 2805.12r, ll. 2, 8–9: Goitein, *Palestinian Jewry*, 186–187.

520 DK XVIIIr, ll. 13–15; v, l. 3: Frenkel, *"The Compassionate and Benevolent"* [Hebrew], no. 6.

https://doi.org/10.1515/9783110713619-008

in dispute. In a letter in which Benayah b. Mūsā describes "the disagreement" in Alexandria between the Maghribi newcomers and the more established "inhabitants of the city,"[521] he sees fit to mention that R. Abraham al-Darʿī was present in the city at the time.[522] One may infer that al-Darʿī's presence was critical to the resolution of divisions within the community.

Abraham al-Darʿī was the advocate of the unfortunate in the community, as is readily apparent from the following case: A violent inhabitant of Barqa induced a young orphan to steal a valuable Torah scroll from his widowed mother in order to finance a partnership of selling wine with him. The widow succeeded in galvanizing the community against her son and recovered the Torah scroll. As the struggle progressed, she gave the scroll to the man she trusted for safekeeping, this being none other than Abraham al-Darʿī. As a letter recounts: "And the widow came screaming in protest until she succeeded in placing him before the community [for judgment], and in stirring up the authorities against him, and she recovered the Torah scroll, and gave it to R. Abraham al-Darʿī, may God preserve him, for safekeeping."[523]

It is at this time that we also find al-Darʿī's signature on a substantial number of legal documents. These signatures indicate that he served as a regular member of the court in Alexandria.[524] Al-Darʿī also served as Mevorakh b. Saʿadyah's representative (*nāʾib*) in Alexandria.[525]

Al-Darʿī passed away before his time, under mysterious circumstances. He accused his political opponent, Nathan b. Judah, of poisoning him – an accusation that continued to plague Nathan many years after the events.[526]

---

521 TS 13 J 23.3: Gil, *Kingdom*, no. 650; Frenkel, *"The Compassionate and Benevolent"* [Hebrew], no. 75. See above, Part II, Chapter 2.4 (a): Shelah and "the Maghribis" (*al-Maghāriba*).

522 Ibid., r, l. 18: R. Abraham al-Darʿī was present – *wa-kāna R' Avraham al-Darʿi ḥāḍir.*

523 TS 13 J 16.3r, ll. 9–10: Frenkel, *"The Compassionate and Benevolent"* [Hebrew], no. 66. The phrase "galvanizing the communities against him" is *wa-aqamat*(sic) *ʿalayhi al-hība* in the original. For the complex connotations of the term *hība*, see Cohen, *Self-Government*, 248–250.

524 TS 8.142: a sliver of the bottom part of a court document dealing with a monetary disagreement in Alexandria, from 1096. Al-Darʿī's signature there is clear: [Ab]raham b. Jacob *n.b.t.* Darʿī; JNUL 4 577.3, a bill of testimony from Alexandria, dated 1103; TS 13 J 7.11, where he has signed a court document from Denia in Spain, executed in Alexandria in the late 1090s; ENA NS 18.34, where he has signed a *Ketubba* from Alexandria, dated to around 1100.

525 On his special relationship with the Nagid, see below, in the next section.

526 On this affair, see the late letter written by Nathan b. Judah in the middle of the twelfth century, in which he reconstructs the events: TS 10 J 6.5: Frenkel, *"The Compassionate and Benevolent"* [Hebrew], no. 48, and see below, in the following section.

3 Relationship with Mevorakh b. Saʿadyah Nagid

Al-Darʿī owed his position in Alexandria directly to Mevorakh b. Saʿadyah Nagid. The consolidation of his position in the public sphere occurred only after 1094, when Mevorakh returned to the Nagidate. Only one letter, which al-Darʿī sent to Mevorakh, survives, and though it is our sole testimony to the relationship between the two, its style and tone suggest a frequent and fairly regular correspondence between them. In this letter al-Darʿī apprises the Nagid of the goings on and developments in the community. In particular, and most pointedly, al-Darʿī's news focused on the displays of loyalty and proper respect for the Nagid in Alexandria. Thus, for example, the account of a new Amir's arrival in Alexandria revolves entirely around the presentation of Mevorakh's letter of recommendation to the Amir and the praise the new Amir heaped upon Mevorakh:

> And when the Shaykh Abū al-Ḥusayn arrived, he gave him the letter of recommendation from your enduring eminence. He [the Amir] sent for me and invited me and the elders of the community and sustained our hopes and promised us a great deal, and furthermore said: "It is my responsibility to care for you because of the two eyes of this lord [= Mevorakh b. Saʿadyah]." And the members of the community thanked you for your interest in them, and were glad and prayed for your eminence, and on behalf of your son. May God hear [their prayers] and grant you a long life of comfort and joy.[527]

In the same way, news of a reduction of the poll tax focuses in Abraham's letter entirely on the expressions of gratitude and loyalty of the community vis-à-vis the Nagid, whom they credited with this discount:

> The situation of the destitute has improved with regard to the poll tax. The judge and the governor instructed the tax official and the supervisor to attend to the poor and they [= the poor] pray for his eminence and his son. May God answer their prayers and may what was written come to pass: "Fear not, for I am with you; Be not frightened, for I am your God."[528]

Even the arrival of a visitor from Tripoli is seen by al-Darʿī as an opportunity to wage a propaganda campaign on behalf of the Nagid:

> And I wish to let you know, that this man, al-Zanātī, who came from Tripoli, regarding whom I have already written your eminence, when he arrived in Alexandria, thanked your eminence before the nations of the world and prayed for you and thus Israel was praised. May God grant him further honor and greatness.

527 TS 20. 177, ll. 12–19: Frenkel, "*The Compassionate and Benevolent*" [Hebrew], no. 37.
528 Ibid., ll. 23–27. Isaiah 41:10, trans. *JPS Hebrew-English Tanakh: The Traditional Hebrew Text and The New JPS Translation* (Philadelphia: Jewish Publication Society, 1999).

The type of information al-Darʿī conveyed to Mevorakh indicates that he functioned as the Nagid's representative in Alexandria, and was supposed to apprise the Nagid of public opinion and the level of support for the latter's leadership, in the community and outside of it. It is apparent that al-Darʿī made a great effort to appease the Nagid with positive news.

Another letter corroborates that Mevorakh did indeed see al-Darʿī as his representative in Alexandria. This is a late letter, from the 1150s. Its author, Nathan b. Judah,[529] pieces together events from fifty years before: "And he [= Mevorakh b. Saʿadyah] asked me at that time to correspond with him. Darʿī was his representative [= *nāʾibuhu*] in Alexandria and it was difficult for him that I would correspond with the Nagid."[530] Later in the letter, Judah b. Nathan relates numerous incidents of harassment, persecution, and even attempted murder by al-Darʿī, the background of which was his great jealousy of Judah b. Nathan's close relationship with the Nagid. The following case, from an unexpected source, illustrates the nature of the complex relationship between al-Darʿī and the Nagid. The public and the private spheres are intertwined here in a way that makes it virtually impossible to disentangle. Nathan b. Judah describes the cynical manipulation of al-Darʿī's feelings by the Nagid, and al-Darʿī's great dependence upon him:

> The *raʾīs* [= Mevorakh b. Saʿadyah] was accustomed to misleading him in a rather remarkable way: If a letter from his representative in Alexandria, in other words, from al-Darʿī, would arrive, the Nagid would delay it, and al-Darʿī would become jealous and inimical towards me. Afterwards the *raʾīs* would say to al-Darʿī: "Any letter that I write to you, if he [Nathan b. Judah] should ask for a copy, you should give him one." And the enmity would be redoubled. And al-Darʿī, has twice tried to dispose of me, "and God has not allowed him to harm me."[531]

The jealousy that the Nagid managed to incite in al-Darʿī led him to perform a series of desperate acts, which are indicative of his great dependence upon the former. Nathan b. Judah relates, among other things, that:

> Afterwards when he was on his deathbed, he told his wife: "I know that he [Nathan b. Judah] met the messenger I sent to the doctor. The doctor wrote me a prescription, and as he was returning with my prescription, he [Nathan b. Judah] took it and substituted a

---

529 Nathan b. Judah, who was probably an interesting person in his own right, left only this single letter in the Genizah, which does not provide sufficient material to draw a portrait of him.
530 TS 10 J 6.5r, ll. 9–10: Frenkel, *"The Compassionate and Benevolent"* [Hebrew], no. 48.
531 Ibid., r, ll. 11–16. Genesis 31/7.

> different prescription. And because I prepared the medicine according to the counterfeit prescription, I am now close to death."[532]

These words were apparently written by al-Darʿī's opponent, and thus one may suspect them of prejudice and subjectivity. It must be noted, however, that if one considers this in conjunction with the man's dependence upon the Nagid, and considering that this was written fifty years after the events – when al-Darʿī was no longer among the living and did not pose a threat to the author – even if we do not accept Nathan b. Judah's version at face value, it suggests a complex relationship, which features a desperate dependency and intense feelings.

4 Al-Darʿī and the Palestinian Yeshivah

Al-Darʿī was not known to hold any official title that would indicate an affiliation with the Palestinian Yeshivah. This being said, he adopted an active stance in the great struggle for the leadership of the Yeshivah that took place between Evyatar and David b. Daniel, as a supporter of David.[533] When Evyatar's son[534] arrived for a visit in Alexandria, he did his best to disparage him and to humiliate him. We learn this from a late letter written by Nathan b. Judah in which he describes the incident: "Afterwards, during the visit of the sons of our lord Evyatar, may his memory be for a blessing, to Alexandria, he suffered every sort of despicable act at the hands of al-Darʿī. And I was consumed with rage and I wrote an edict against him [against al-Darʿī]."[535]

The division in the Alexandrian community between the supporters of Evyatar on the one hand and his detractors on the other was destined to continue for more than one generation. After al-Darʿī's death, his brothers-in-law found out about the edict put out by Nathan b. Judah against al-Darʿī, and sued him for defamation.[536] Hence, the rivalry regarding the leadership of the Palestinian Yeshivah, affected and shaped internal divisions inside the Alexandrian community.

---

532 Ibid.

533 On this struggle, see Gil, *History of Palestine*, §§902–916; Cohen, *Self-Government*, 178–212.

534 It is not clear if this refers to Elijah or to Ṣadoq. On both of them, see Gil, ibid.

535 TS 10 J 6.5r, ll. 21–22: Frenkel, *"The Compassionate and Benevolent"* [Hebrew], no. 48.

536 Ibid., v, ll. 10–13.

5 The Family Connection

Al-Darʿī married a local woman, the daughter and scion of one of the established families of Alexandria. As was the case with other settlers from the Maghreb, marriage was the way by which one could integrate into the community.[537] Before his death al-Darʿī saw fit to accuse Nathan b. Judah of his impending demise in his wife's hearing,[538] a move that was intended to mark his main rival and to galvanize his wife's family to continue waging his battles after his death. Indeed, his two brothers-in-law, his wife's siblings, rose to defend his honor and continued his campaigns after his death, as is apparent in Nathan b. Judah's writings:

> And after I wrote the edict against al-Darʿī in response to his defamation of our master, may his memory be for a blessing [= Evyatar], a copy of the edict remained in my possession for some time. And when I sent it with that polluted man, Ibn Isḥaq, to his great eminence, may his honor be elevated, Ibn Isḥāq went to al-Darʿī's brothers-in-law and informed them. Both of them testified against me. One of them testified that I had altered the doctor's prescription, as I mentioned above, and the other testified that I had written the prescription myself[...] and al-Darʿī's brothers-in-law, when they heard that I had sent the edict, were greatly disturbed, and they both testified against me.

In other words, when the messenger Ibn Isḥāq wished to publicize the wrongs perpetrated against al-Darʿī, he turned without hesitation to those he saw as al-Darʿī's supporters and the perpetuators of his cause, his two brothers-in-law. And indeed, the two came to his defense and sued Nathan b. Judah in court.

6 Conclusion

Abraham al-Darʿī rose from amongst the Maghribi merchants who immigrated to Egypt. He paved his way to a position of leadership in the community by means of a strategic marriage to a local family. His integration into this family determined his place in local politics, which was divided along the lines of the struggle for the leadership of the Palestinian Yeshivah, and determined his support for David b. Daniel. Al-Darʿī made a name for himself in community politics as a trustworthy intermediary who could help with compromises between the opposing camps. His far-flung mercantile ties, a supportive family, and his skills as an arbitrator helped him pave his way and survive as a leading and influential person in the Alexandrian community. Although he had no official position of

537 See Gil, *History of Palestine*, §§370 – 384.
538 See above, Part II, Chapter 3.3: Relationship with Mevorakh b. Saʿadyah Nagid.

leadership, he was deeply involved in the politics of the Palestinian Yeshivah, and later on, he functioned as the Nagid Mevorakh's *nāʾib* or representative in Alexandria. A major source of his power was his direct and immediate relationship with the Nagid. If we accept Nathan b. Judah's account, or at least the gist of it, we may surmise that this relationship was also the source of his weakness. His complete dependence upon the arbitrary whims of one man locked him in a tangle of conflicting emotions, which led to his untimely end.

Chapter 4 Āraḥ b. Nathan the Seventh (Musāfir b. Wahb)

1 The Family

Āraḥ was a scion of a highly distinguished family of Palestinian origin. His father was one of seven leading members of the Palestinian Yeshivah and held the honorable title "The Seventh";[539] his brother Abraham b. Nathan held the same position, as well as the title of "Beloved of the Academy." Between the end of the eleventh and beginning of the twelfth centuries, Āraḥ was a dignitary in Fustat, an associate of the Nagid Mevorakh b. Saʿadyah and had a close relationship with the Muslim authorities.[540] Some degree of familial ties existed between Āraḥ and the Ben Saʿadyah family of Nagids, if one may judge on the basis of a letter Moses, son of Judah b. Saʿadyah wrote to him, wherein he referred to himself as *qarībuhu* (his relative).[541]

2 Education

Āraḥ did not bear any official title at any yeshivah. Never the less, his elevated use of language in which he tended to incorporate Hebrew words and biblical verses, as well as a mellifluous and rich Hebrew paean he wrote for an eminent figure,[542] attest to his learning and education. The vestiges of a letter written in Arabic script addressed to "Abū al-Faḍl b. Hibat Allāh, the head of the communities,"[543] indicate a very good command of Arabic, to the extent that he felt it easier to communicate in this language even with fellow Jews.[544]

---

539 *Ha-sheviʿi ba-Ḥavurah.* ENA 4010.28v, l. 1: Gil, *Palestine*, 42.
540 On him, see Cohen, *Jewish Self-Government*, 130–131.
541 TS 13 J 19.4, the address *shākir tafaḍḍulihi qarībuhu Moshe b. Abū Zikrī* (thanking his graciousness, his relative Moshe b. Abū Zikrī): Frenkel, *"The Compassionate and Benevolent"* [Hebrew], no. 68; see also Cohen, *Jewish Self-Government*, 137, n. 111.
542 TS 13 J 14.19: Frenkel, *"The Compassionate and Benevolent"* [Hebrew], no. 64.
543 On this title, see Goitein, *Society*, 2: 75–77.
544 TS Ar. 39.126: Frenkel, *"The Compassionate and Benevolent"* [Hebrew], no. 86. The fact that no further Arabic-script letters written by Jews one to another have been found can be attributed to the character of the Cairo Genizah, which has preserved mainly Hebrew-script writings, rather than to this custom being uncommon.

https://doi.org/10.1515/9783110713619-009

3 Mercantile Activities

Āraḥ was a professional merchant and personally embarked on long trade voyages. Moses b. Judah expressed in one of his letters concern that Āraḥ not depart without a friend to accompany him on his journey (*rafīq*), and offered himself as a partner on his next trip.[545] Āraḥ himself writes to his brother Abraham, letting him know that he has returned safely from an arduous voyage.[546]

4 Communal Work

Although we don‘t know of any official communal position held by Āraḥ, he certainly considered himself obliged to contribute to the community by virtue of his familial and social connections. In a letter to his brother Abraham, he urges him to immediately pass a letter along from a high Muslim official bearing the name Ḥusām al-Mulk to the qadi Makīn al-Dawla, recommending that he respect the rights of the Jews: "His honor is undoubtedly familiar with the enmity (*sin'ūt*) of the Alexandrians, therefore do not delay this matter for any reason whatsoever."[547]

5 A Matter of Class

The need to help the Jews in Alexandria was evidently one of Āraḥ's favored causes. This being said, one does note a modicum of aloofness and reserve in Āraḥ's attitude towards the community. Thus, for example, in a letter to his brother he describes a drunken brawl that erupted in Alexandria, which ended with the intervention of the Muslim authorities and a disagreement between members of the community and the *muqaddam* who led them – it is readily apparent that his sympathies lie with the *muqaddam*.

> There was a serious uproar and the governor came…if there had been a different *muqaddam* in town, he would not have succeeded in doing what this *muqaddam* did. They took a group of people and put them in jail, and the *muqaddam* succeeded in getting

545 TS 13 J 19.4r, ll. 4–5; v, l. 3: Frenkel, "*The Compassionate and Benevolent*" [Hebrew], no.68. On the *rafīq* see Goitein, *Society*, 1: 347–349.
546 TS 13 J 22.23, ll. 5–7: Frenkel, "*The Compassionate and Benevolent*" [Hebrew], no. 73.
547 Ibid., ll. 15–16. On the qadi al-Makīn see, Part I, Chapter 5.3. On the term *sin'ūt*, see Goitein, *Society*, 2: 278.

> them out without the forfeiture of any money on their part. The Creator, may he be extolled, shall protect this man whose help preserves this community [...]and though he only did good work on their behalf, they repaid him by coming up and complaining about him to [...] regarding all they had done. These [individuals] may be counted as slanderers. He took them to the Sultan because they had vilified him and because of their shouts at night.[548]

Ārah̩ scolded the community members for being angry at their *muqaddam*, who had involved the Muslim authorities and had had them jailed, and saw their complaints as incomprehensible ingratitude. In another case, Ārah̩ viewed populist expressions of support for the Nagid Mevorakh as rowdy, and inappropriate. When members of the community took the letter of the Nagid that they had with them and paraded it in the streets, in a raucous procession, Ārah̩ considered their behavior so unacceptable that he took the step of turning to the chief of police in the city, requesting that he put a stop to the ceremony. He called for the letters of the Nagid to be read in an orderly fashion in the synagogue. He also turned to his brother Abraham for help in this matter. His aversion to the popular ceremony and his clear preference for the code of conduct practiced by the Muslim elite – which emphasized the decorous reading of letters in public – is readily apparent: "When a valuable letter from the Nagid makes it into the hands of my Lord Fakhr al-Mulk [the Amir of Alexandria], may God guarantee his success, he kisses it and lays it on his eyes. The Jews, however, drag it from place to place. I have informed you of this so that you would be able to act in any way you see fit. Peace." [549]

The description of the ceremony in his letter, which is replete with negative expressions, betrays the full extent of his aversion:

> And on the second day, the ninth of the month of Kislev, groups of people would pass by, and exclaim that they had a letter from our master the lord of lords, may his magnificence be elevated, and they would gather together in bunches and would waive the letter – and in their midst there was the "shrew," the filthy one – and they would cackle in the markets and in the houses until I could take it no more.[550]

548 TS NS J 24r, ll. 8–19: Frenkel, *"The Compassionate and Benevolent"* [Hebrew], no. 88.
549 Ibid., r, upper margins, ll. 5–10. On the use of the term *yehudim* (i.e., Jews) to refer to ordinary people, see Goitein, *Society*, 2: 63–64.
550 TS NS J 24, r, ll. 23–26: Frenkel, *"The Compassionate and Benevolent"* [Hebrew], no. 88, and see the appendix there for the possibility that the document was used for magical purposes.

6 Conclusion

Āraḥ b. Nathan, a wealthy merchant from Alexandria, held no official position in the community. Despite this, his family background, his skills, his education, and his social ties, identify him as a member of the community's ruling elite, and, indeed, he conducted himself as such. Āraḥ worked on behalf of the community, employing his social and familial ties and his status. Nevertheless, his letters betray strong alienation towards the local Jews alongside admiration of Islamic etiquette.

Chapter 5 Aaron b. Yeshūʿā the Physician Ibn al-ʿAmmānī

1 Origins and Family

Aaron Ibn al-ʿAmmānī was a scion of a family of cantors and physicians originating in Amman. His roots in the Land of Israel are emphasized in multiple paeans Judah ha-Levi wrote in his honor, during his sojourn in Alexandria. The following are just a few examples: "You hail from the Temple of the Lord"; "[You are] the source, whose waters flow from the Temple"; "A voice calls to Aaron and his sons proclaiming / you came from the mountain of myrrh [= the Temple Mount] to convey your many flairs / you are the fitting recipients of all verse and song"; "[You are a] Jerusalemite, heir to holiness / passed down from ancient fathers / Holy people coming from the Temple / their birthplace upon mountains of balsam"; "The rock from which they [= the Ben Yeshūʿā family) were hewed is the Temple of the Lord." In some poems he even refers to Aaron as "Ben Zion" (= son of Zion).[551]

Aaron Ibn al-ʿAmmānī's origins in the Land of Israel was certainly significant for Judah ha-Levi, himself a future pilgrim to the Holy Land, but this pedigree was also very central to the Ibn al-ʿAmmānī family's public activity. Aaron's five sons are repeatedly mentioned as working in tandem with him in a united family enterprise. Judah ha-Levi regularly mentions Aaron Ibn al-ʿAmmānī together with his sons. Inhis letter to Samuel b. Hananyah the Nagid he writes: "O he who extolled me and anticipated my every need, he and his sons."[552] And in the poem *Golden Bells and Pomegranates* he proclaims: "A voice calls

---

551 On the Ibn al-ʿAmmānī family, see Amir Mazor and Efraim Lev, "Dynasties of Jewish Physicians in the Fatimid and Ayyubid Periods," *Hebrew Union College Annual* 89 (2018): 221–260. On the Ibn al-ʿAmmānī dynasty, see 240–246. See also Hayyim Schirmann, "Poets Contemporary with Mose [sic] Ibn Ezra and Yehuda ha-Levi (III)," *Studies of the Research Institute for Hebrew Poetry in Jerusalem* 6 (1946): 265, n. 1 [Hebrew]; Goitein, *Society*, 2: 245, n. 21; Hayyim Brody (ed.), *Dīwān des Abū-l-Ḥasan Jehuda ha-Levi* (Berlin: Mekitze Nirdamim, 1894–1930), no. 27, l. 8 [Hebrew]; ibid., no. 67, ll. 3, 23–25; no. 32, ll. 11–14; no. 33, l. 23; the title "Ben-Zion," no. 70, l. 37]. See also Moshe Gil and Ezra Fleischer, *Yehuda ha-Levi and his Circle* (Jerusalem: Magness Press, 2001), 139, n. 140 [Hebrew]. For Judah ha-Levi's Alexandrian poems, see Yehoshua Granat, "The Mixed Blessings of the Western Wind: Ambiguous longings in Halevi's Alexandrian Poems of Welcome and Farewell," in Alison Salvesen, Sarah Pearce, and Miriam Frenkel (eds.), *Israel in Egypt The Land of Egypt as Concept and Reality for Jews in Antiquity and the Early Medieval Period* (Leiden: Brill, forthcoming).

552 *Diwan*, 1, letter 2, ll. 30–31.

https://doi.org/10.1515/9783110713619-010

to Aaron and his sons proclaiming..."[553] In the poem *Where is God's glory?*, the poet offers encouragement to the community of Alexandria and promises:

> She shall not fear bereavement or widowhood/ for his descendants sit upon his throne / She shall dwell securely / as the community members assemble to ascend to his court and to his house of learning / let their minds be as one so that his flock / shall not stray from its pasture and enclosure / Aaron and his sons will set it right / each according to his appointed task and burden.[554]

In other words, Ibn al-ʿAmmānī's sons were seen as his heirs and successors, as a team of shepherds responsible for the well-being of the herd, which is the community. This is especially apparent in the poem *The choicest of spices*, dedicated to Aaron and his sons, where each of them is extolled separately, and as a group they are described as "the five enterprising sons / Aaron the holy one's children / wise and precocious, called to duty / ready to assume the throne / to ascend to their father's lofty dais."[555] The sons are thus described as his obvious inheritors, ready to continue in their father's path. Since this is a panegyric written in honor of Aaron Ibn al-ʿAmmānī, one must assume that the depiction of his children as partners in the governance of the community and as his future heirs was intended to conform to his aspirations, and reflects the critical importance he ascribed to his origins and the position of his sons.

2 Activities

Aaron was a physician like his father. His son Judah's signature was "Judah the Teacher son of R. Aaron the Physician."[556] Allusions to his profession may be found in Judah ha-Levi's poetry: "He brings comfort with his diligence and his healing/ a doctor he is and his medicines are a tree of life."[557] Also: "He contends with the angels of death / his sword unsheathed, he parries their thrusts / he is almost like Aaron who stopped the contagion / and heals the afflicted / with his potions, his spices, his veritable elixirs."[558] It is likely that he was a court physician for the government, and he was certainly employed in some capacity by the

553 Ibid., no. 67, l. 23.
554 Ibid., no. 2, ll. 15–22.
555 Ibid., no. 33, ll. 18–21.
556 See Mann, *Jews*, 2:305.
557 *Diwan*, 1, no. 2 (Where is God's glory), ll. 10–11.
558 Ibid., no. 70 (Beautiful voice), ll. 47–51. On his status as a physician, see also Goitein, *Society*, 2: 245; Gil-Fleischer, *Yehuda ha-Levi*, 139, nn. 136, 138.

authorities, since Judah ha-Levi refers to him as "lord" (*sar*) and speaks of his "courtly position." (*misrah*).[559] In a letter to him Judah ha-Levi remarks that "he has ten shares in the king."[560]

Aaron was himself a liturgical poet, and some of his compositions survive in the Cairo Genizah.[561] We know that he responded to Judah ha-Levi's panegyrics[562] and composed his own paeans to Samuel b. Hananyah Nagid, since Judah ha-Levi wishes both of them: "You should revel in his position and he should revel in your mellifluous composition, may God cause you to be together."[563] Aside from this, it seems quite likely that Aaron Ibn al-ʿAmmānī was involved in the book business. In a letter sent to Abū Saʿd al-ʿAṭṭār in Fustat, he expresses concern over five volumes that he had sent him through emissaries, but had not heard back about their safe arrival. Since he is careful to note the number of volumes and the fact that they were written on parchment, one may assume that they were sent to Abū Saʿd for mercantile purposes.[564]

---

559 For example, *Diwan*, 1, letter 1, ll. 5, 31, 62–63; no. 67, l. 17; no. 70, l. 77 and more.

560 *Diwan*, 1, letter 1, l. 38. 2 Samuel 19/44.

561 See Schirmann, "Poets." Another *piyyut* of his for the day of Passover is Bodl 2084.1, and see also Alexander (Sandor) Scheiber, "Unbekannte Gedichte von Aaron Ibn al-Ammani, dem Freunde Jehuda Hallevis," *Sefarad* 27 (1967): 269–281. Gil-Fleischer, *Yehuda ha-Levi*, 141, n. 153, list ninety manuscripts that contain poems and fragments of poems by him, according to the data of the Genizah Research Project for Hebrew Poetry, founded by the Israel Academy of Sciences and the Humanities; Sarah Cohen, *The Poetry of Aaron al-ʿAmmānī: A Critical Edition* (Jerusalem: Mekize Nirdamim, 2008; (in Hebrew).

562 See Schirmann, "Poets," 265–288; Gil-Fleischer, *Yehuda ha-Levi*, 208–209.

563 *Diwan*, 1, letter 1, 86–87. For an appraisal of the poor literary value of these *piyyutim* and on Judah ha-Levi's gently mocking attitude to Ibn al-ʿAmmānī's artistic abilities, see Goitein, *Society*, 2: 259, n. 101; Gil-Fleischer, *Yehuda ha-Levi*, 141–142. To Goitein's words (ibid.) it should be added, that despite all his surviving poems being liturgical, we know that he also composed secular ones. In contrast, see Yahalom's view that Egyptian Jewry had little interest in secular poems, since it was a "basically conservative society" (Joseph Yahalom, "Poetry and Society in Egypt: Their Relationship as Reflected in the Attitude to the Secular Poetry of Judah ha-Levi," *Zion* 45 (1980): 289 [Hebrew]). See also Gil-Fleischer, *Yehuda ha-Levi*, who agree with Yahalom's opinion, but qualified this by saying that at the same time, "the illustrious among them often wrote poems in honor of those more illustrious." On the role of poetry in the service of the elite, see below, Part IV, Chapter 3.2: Poetry.

564 TS 13 J 14.25: Frenkel, *"The Compassionate and Benevolent"* [Hebrew], no. 65. The variety of the books is very impressive, and includes biblical exegesis (on the book of Ezekiel), *yotzrot* poems by Ibn Abitur, Dioscorides' *De Materia Medica* and *Halakhot Gedolot.*

3 Wealth as a Lifestyle

Aaron Ibn al-ʿAmmānī surrounded himself with luxury and adopted a lifestyle which flaunted his wealth. We learn this mostly from the poems and letters of Judah ha-Levi, who attests that he succumbed to the extravagance he indulged in as a guest of Aaron's. His magnificent house, the beautiful garden and the fountain in its midst are all described in Judah ha-Levi's poetry.

> The most fragrant oils and balsam / the choicest spices and delicacies / a sculpted garden with a fountain in its midst / in a gentle valley and by a flowing brook / a mosaic floor in an enchanted glade / tiled in gold / the waters of the vale empty upwards [...] above a canopy of myrtle and thick vines / And doves and swallows, companions and lovers / And roses and spices old and new / The soul shall indulge in all delicacy / on beautiful dishes and from overflowing jugs.[565]

And:

> I arrived at twelve springs / in No-Amon, and at seventy date palms / at a house of delicacy, of cinnamon and spice / and at an orchard of henna and nard.[566]

And more prosaically in a letter to Samuel ha-Nagid:

> He met me with grace, and delicate handiwork / with gifts and a house of repose, a sanctuary with a spacious alcove / a tabernacle and a domicile, a table and a candelabra, I indulged in the comforts he afforded me / I was surrounded by his exquisite foods [...] low beds, and strewn pillows, let us dine on delicacies, and become intoxicated in his pleasures.[567]

One should note that Judah ha-Levi extolls other hosts in his letters, men more honored and of greater stature than Ibn al-ʿAmmānī, such as Ḥalfon b. Nethanel and Samuel ha-Nagid;[568] though the detailed verses describing the pomp and

---

565 *Diwan*, 1, no. 33, ll. 1–15. See also Gil-Fleischer, *Yehuda ha-Levi*, 139, n. 137.
566 *Diwan*, 1, no. 36, ll. 3–6.
567 *Diwan*, 1, letter 2, ll. 23–30.
568 On Ḥalfon b. Nethanel as a host, see ibid., ll. 34–41. In these lines the poet particularly emphasizes Ḥalfon's role as a recommender (*melitz*) who connected him with Samuel ha-Nagid. On the latter as a host, see ibid., 54–59, in which he mentions "his dwelling-place" and "his table," but the description is much briefer than that of Ibn al-ʿAmmānī's home, and completely lacks the realistic details mentioned there. A comprehensive study on Ḥalfon and Judah ha-Levi was published as vol IV/A of the India Book series. See Mordechai A. Friedman, *Ḥalfon and Judah ha-Levi: The Lives of a Merchant Scholar and a Poet Laureate According to the*

splendor of his host are unique to Judah ha-Levi's visit with Ibn al-ʿAmmānī. One may, therefore, assume that these descriptions are not literary formulae, but are an accurate reflection of Ibn al-ʿAmmānī's lifestyle.[569] This flaunted wealth most likely reflected the way of life and conduct of the ruling elite in Alexandria at this time.[570] Al-Maqrīzī, the fourteenth-century historian of Egypt, dedicates many pages to a description of the life of luxury led by the Muslim qadi of Alexandria of that period, Makīn al-Dawla Ibn Ḥadīd, who was known for his opulent lifestyle. Al-Maqrīzī relates the following illustrative account:

> Makīn al-Dawla had a palace in Alexandria and in it there was an exquisite orchard. In the orchard there was a great fountain fashioned from the finest marble, and the waters therein would pool and burst forth like a great volcano. The owner used to brag about it to his fellows of that generation, until Badawiyya, Caliph al-Āmir's concubine, heard of it, and coveted it. The qadi granted it to her. The fountain was brought to Cairo and was reconstructed in the Orchard of the Palanquin (*al-hawdaj*) that the caliph had built for his beloved Rawḍa Island. The qadi was greatly saddened and never stopped sending Badawiyya gifts, until she acquiesced and had the fountain returned to him.[571]

Aaron Ibn al-ʿAmmānī, the court physician, the man of lofty position, adopted this ostentatious lifestyle with all its refinements, and turned it into one of the hallmarks of his leadership.

4 His Position in the Community

Beginning in 1109 we find Aaron Ibn al-ʿAmmānī's signature on court documents. Two documents from al-Maḥalla, one dated 1109 and the other dated 1114, are written in his handwriting and signed by him as the guarantor of the deed in Alexandria.[572] His signature appears on a deed of purchase for a building

---

Cairo Geniza Documents (India Book IV/A) (Jerusalem: Ben-Zvi Institute and Rabbi David Moshe and Amalia Rosen Foundation, 2013) [Hebrew].

569 This very house is described in a halakhic query presented to Maimonides in 1195, over 50 years later, Maimonides was asked about the validity of a leasing bill of a house in Alexandria known as the house (*dār*) of R. Aaron Ibn al-ʿAmmāni, or as the Judge's house (*dār al-dayyān*). The huge mansion was now divided between several heirs and parts of it were rented. Maimonides, *Responsa*, 1:2–3, no. 2.

570 See above, Part I, Chapter 2.10: Residential Buildings.

571 Shayyāl, *Aʿlām*, 74.

572 TS 10 J 162: a court document of 1109, with the signatures of Jacob ha-Kohen b. Muvḥar and Japheth ha-Levi b. Mevorakh, as well; INA D 55.7, a guardianship document from 1114, alongside the signature of Abraham b. Yeshūʿā and another unidentifiable signature.

in Alexandria from 1129.[573] He is a signatory and guarantor of a marriage contract from the 1140s[574] and his name also appears on a will from 1143.[575] His signature is always the same: "Aaron b. Yeshūʿā the Physician, may his memory be for a blessing." There is no indication that he served as a judge (*dayyan*) or as a fellow of the Yeshivah (*ḥaver*).[576] On all court documents his signature appears either first or second, which indicates that he did not serve as the chief justice, even at the time of Judah ha-Levi's historic visit to Alexandria.[577] This is somewhat surprising considering that Judah ha-Levi refers to him in some of his poems and letters as *ḥaver*, as *dayyan*, or even as *Rav*.[578] In the letter he sent Aaron Ibn al-ʿAmmānī the latter is addressed as "the honorable, great, holy, majestic, magnificent, grand, and glorious teacher, R. Aaron the splendid *ḥaver*, the marvelous judge, the dignified lord, the father of morality, the crown of scholarship,"[579] and in a letter to Samuel b. Hananyah the Nagid, he refers to Aaron Ibn al-ʿAmmānī as "the wonderful *ḥaver*, our teacher and *Rav*, Aaron the Judge."[580] Moreover, Aaron himself, in unofficial documents, appropriates the title *ḥaver*. In some of his poems the beginnings of verses are signed "Aaron the *ḥaver*" or "Aaron the *ḥaver*, the Mighty One of Zion."[581]

---

573 ENA 2806.2, alongside the signature of Isaac b. Joseph Yerushalmi and another unidentifiable signature.

574 TS 20.5, alongside the signatures of Shelah ha-Levi b. R. Moses the Teacher and Isaac b. Joseph Yerushalmi.

575 TS 18 J 1.15, alongside the signatures of Shelah ha-Levi b. R. Moses the Teacher and Nissim b. Mevorakh.

576 Neither in the signatures of his son, Judah, are there any hints of titles his father might have borne. He always signs "Judah the Teacher, son of R. Aaron the Physician Ibn al-ʿAmmānī." See also Mann, *Jews*, 2: 305–306, where he wonders why Judah does not note in his signature his father's offices as judge and *ḥaver*.

577 On the dating of the visit, see Shelomo D. Goitein, "The Biography of Rabbi Judah Ha-Levi in the Light of the Cairo Geniza Documents, *PAAJR*, 28 (1959): 41–56; idem, "The Last Phase of Rabbi Yehuda ha-Levi's Life in the Light of the Genizah Papers," *Tarbiẓ* 24 (1954): 21–47, 119 [Hebrew]; Joseph Yahalom, *Yehuda Halevi: Poetry and Pilgrimage* (Jerusalem: Magness Press, 2009), 162–163; Goitein, *Society*, 5: 458–462; Gil-Fleischer, *Yehuda ha-Levi*, 81–113.

578 *Diwan*, no. 70, l. 35: "Ask a *ḥaver*, ask a judge, ask a *Rav* who has spread for every wisdom wings / of the son of Zion / ask about matters of life and death." In another poem he even mentions Aaron's "court of law." See ibid., no. 2, l. 18: "Be silent, sea-roar, until/ a student kisses the *Rav*'s face/ the hand of R. Aaron, whose authority / has not vanished"; and no. 32, ll. 9–10: "In the house of a sage, the house of a *ḥaver*, the house of a *Rav* / in the house of justice, in the house of a just and pious man."

579 *Diwan*, no. 1, ll. 29–32.

580 Ibid., no. 2, l. 22.

581 See Schirmann, "Poets."

This discrepancy is accounted for in a number of Judah ha-Levi's poems and composition. In his poem "Where is God's glory," Judah ha-Levi states: "They named him *ḥaver* though he wasn't one / For he was *sui generis* in his generation and a veritable wonder."[582] In other words, because of his rare and wondrous attributes, there were those who referred to Aaron Ibn al-ʿAmmānī as "*ḥaver*," though he held no official title. It is apparent in Judah ha-Levi's statement that Ibn al-ʿAmmānī's rivals harassed him and sought to undermine the special position he maintained in the community: "And what shall one who is jealous do? For the God of your fathers / Bequeathed you a great treasure and the added advantage of great perspicacity";[583] and: "They are friends only **in name**, but if you search for them / All you find is southern storms and fierce gales / And those who know that his stalks are full and ripe / Will they indeed covet their own emaciated stalks?"[584]

In other words, Ibn al-ʿAmmānī is the beneficiary of natural attributes including his innate intelligence and great knowledge, a "full stalk." These attributes grant him an advantage over his rivals, and because of this everyone elevates him over his friends, who are the "emaciated stalks" – despite the fact that he is not a judge or a *ḥaver*.

Matters are further clarified in Judah ha-Levi's letter to Ibn al-ʿAmmānī, wherein he states the following about Samuel b. Hananyah the Nagid quite explicitly:

> And your majesty is valued greatly by him, and your well-being is precious to him, and he elevates and never denigrates, and he does not embarrass, nor undermine support, he does not separate one from the object of his love, nor disturb anyone in their repose, and does not disturb equanimity [...] And who among the elders of your age, compares to you, they may be judges by name , and powerbrokers, but they are the wells, and you are the source. Not every liquid is water, and not every canopy is sky , and not from every pregnancy is an Aaron born, and not every oak makes a flagpole. He is deserving of all majesty, and it is fitting that you be his second in command *(mishneh)*.[585]

A bitter struggle is being alluded to, a struggle for the position of the Nagid's second in command and representative in Alexandria. Ibn al-ʿAmmānī wished to fill this position, but it was contested by a serious rival, who was an official judge, and "bore the title," which was his main advantage. Judah ha-Levi offers a mes-

---

582 *Diwan*, no. 2, 304.
583 Ibid., no. 67 (Golden Bell and Pomegranate), ll. 20 – 21.
584 Ibid., no. 70 (Beautiful Voice), ll. 43 – 46. See also Gil-Fleischer, *Yehuda ha-Levi*, 139 – 140, esp. n. 148.
585 *Diwan*, no. 1, ll. 75 – 85.

sage of reassurance to Ibn al-ʿAmmānī, and promises him that despite his rival's attributes, the Nagid is on his side and values him, not because of any official titles but because of his personal attributes. These qualities are described employing imagery of creativity and resourcefulness (water and source) and of majesty and elevation (sky, flagpole). In a letter to Samuel ha-Nagid he names Ibn al-ʿAmmānī as "one who serves his Lordship in his official capacity."[586]

An echo of this struggle, from the side of Ibn al-ʿAmmānī's opponents, is found in a letter written by Abū al-ʿAlāʾ, a high-ranking dignitary in Fustat, and addressed perhaps to Samuel the Nagid himself. This is a secret letter, the conclusion of which is written in Arabic script: "Upon reading this burn immediately," no address is appended.[587] The central thrust of the letter is a blatant attempt to slander the good name of Aaron Ibn al-ʿAmmānī and present him and his faction as a group acting detrimentally against Judah ha-Levi and as provoking riots in Alexandria. Abū al-ʿAlāʾ accuses Ibn al-ʿAmmānī of two wrongs: The first is well-known – the accusation that Ibn al-ʿAmmānī recorded Judah ha-Levi's paeans in his honor, while the latter was his guest in Alexandria, and edited them in a way that would engender derision of the pilgrim poet:

> The judge took all these poems and put them in a compilation of poems (*dīwān*), and gave them titles: "This is what our teacher Judah said regarding the pool and the fountain, and this is what the judge answered, and this is what the honored Judah, may the Rock preserve him, said regarding chickens and this was his answer, and this what he said about this per-

---

586 Ibid., letter 2, l. 21.

587 TS 13 J 24.8: Goitein, "Letters About R. Judah ha-Levi's Stay in Alexandria and the Collection of His Poems," *Tarbiẓ* 28 (1959): 352–354 and his translation on 356–358 [Hebrew]; Gil-Fleischer, *Yehuda ha-Levi*, 48; Frenkel, *"The Compassionate and Benevolent"* [Hebrew], no. 76. In Goitein's opinion (ibid., 343, n. 3), the lack of an address is evidence of correspondence between people of the same rank, connected by ties of intimate friendship; but I think that the reason is the letter's character as a top secret one, intended to be passed discreetly from hand to hand. Goitein also stated that the addressee is Judah ha-Levi himself, based mainly on the section in which Abū al-ʿAlāʾ promises to organize for the addressee place on a ship sailing "to the east or the west." See ibid., 346, and his translation of 1, ll. 13–18. My opinion is different: this section speaks of trade and goods, rather than of organizing a sea voyage; see my translation in the appendix to Frenkel, *"The Compassionate and Benevolent"* [Hebrew]. Gil and Fleischer republished the letter; they follow Goitein and assume that the letter was meant for Judah ha-Levi. They published another letter (Gil-Fleischer, *Yehuda ha-Levi*, 49), that Abū al-ʿAlāʾ wrote to Ḥalfon b. Nethanel, in which he apologizes for this letter, but the additional letter does not indicate that the first one was written to Judah ha-Levi, either. There it is written *wa-qad gharānī al-jahl ʿalā katb kitāb ilayhi wa-farraṭa dhālika minnī* (stupidity caused me to write a letter to him and this came out of me). While *ilayhi* in the masculine does not refer to Ḥalfon b. Nethanel, since Abū al-ʿAlāʾconsistently uses the feminine to address him (ibid., n. 3), there is no hint that this refers to Judah ha-Levi, either.

> son, and that person, and the other person, and what he said about the dream," in a way that if one reads these poems and does not read the others, one will say the pilgrim who said these things is a little muddled in his mind.[588]

The second allegation was only a rumor and Abū al-ʿAlāʾ had no corroboration for it. It is connected to things that "someone from the judge's faction" said:

> And it is he who said: "The most honored dignitaries offered him [Judah ha-Levi] in his home in Spain food to eat and he did not consume it, and here he does not stop eating and writing paeans about us." And a hubbub ensued amongst the people who thought the reference was to them. Upon your life, I gave every one of them an appropriate answer, despite the fact that I was not happy with that individual from the judge's faction who was the cause of this, for they provoked these people.[589]

In other words, Abū al-ʿAlāʾ accused the members of Ibn al-ʿAmmānī's faction of two things: The first, that they were maligning Judah ha-Levi's good name, by relating to him as a person who lives at the expense of the community, even though he could have easily made a living and earned sufficient money (= eat bread) in his own home in Spain. The second was that this faction's statements were provocative and were intended to disturb people and cause disquiet in the community. Abū al-ʿAlāʾ described himself as a mediator and one who brought calm, and adopted a neutral position. He castigates both sides, though he knows full well who is responsible for the brouhaha. It is thus reasonable to assume that the man to whom he is writing the letter is a figure of authority in Fustat who saw himself as responsible for maintaining calm in Alexandria as well, almost certainly Samuel the Nagid himself. This assumption is corroborated in the poems and letters of Judah ha-Levi, who intimated that there were those who would slander Ibn al-ʿAmmānī in the Nagid's hearing.[590]

---

588 TS 13 J 24.8, 1, l. 25 – 2, l. 6: Frenkel, *"The Compassionate and Benevolent"* [Hebrew], no. 76. See also Baneth's translation, cited by Yahalom, "Poetry and Society," 297, n. 45; also: Gil-Fleischer, *Yehuda ha-Levi*, 465, n. 11 and 220, n. 180. For the identification of the poems in Judah ha-Levi's *dīwān*, see Goitein, "Letters About R. Judah ha-Levi's Stay in Alexandria," 347, nn. 17 – 19; Gil-Fleischer, *Yehuda ha-Levi*, 218 – 219. Part of a pamphlet that contained the *dīwān* edited by Ibn al-ʿAmmānī is found, apparently, in a Genizah fragment: TS K 16.19. See Schirmann, "Poets."

589 TS 13 J 24.8, 2, ll. 10 – 16: Frenkel, *"The Compassionate and Benevolent"* [Hebrew], no. 76. My translation differs from those of Goitein and of Gil and Fleischer, who followed him. See Gil-Fleischer, *Yehuda ha-Levi*, 217 – 465 and in the appendix to Frenkel, *"The Compassionate and Benevolent"* [Hebrew].

590 See above, nn. 588 – 589.

5 Conclusion

Aaron Ibn al-ʿAmmānī was an important, even dominant figure in the Alexandrian community. Aside from serving as a regular member of the court in Alexandria for many years, it is almost certain that he held no official position or title. His aspiration of serving as Samuel the Nagid's representative in Alexandria was met with fierce resistance from his opponents in the community, who were part of the official leadership. Nevertheless, with the help of Judah ha-Levi, who served as his forceful advocate,[591] Ibn al-ʿAmmānī succeeded in propagating a new spirit in the community, which placed the Land of Israel and its holiness in the center. This focus on the importance of the Holy Land contributed to the legitimacy of Ibn al-ʿAmmānī and his family as leaders of the community, since he saw his family's pedigree as having special missionary significance, ultimately bringing them from the Land of Israel to lead the community in Alexandria.[592] This underlying spirit is apparent in many poems that Judah ha-Levi wrote in his honor. These paeans were written in accordance with Ibn al-ʿAmmānī's expectations, and perhaps even at his request and commission.

In light of this, one understands the full significance of recording these poems in writing in a separate compilation (*dīwān*) and the fierce opposition that this move provoked amongst Ibn al-ʿAmmānī's enemies. Ibn al-ʿAmmānī's activities mark an attempt to reinforce and perpetuate a novel world view, aimed at legitimating his family's rule over the community – more than just boasting about his relationship with a famous poet.

Aaron Ibn al-ʿAmmānī burst forth on to the political landscape of Alexandria as a new ascending force. In some ways he resembled his predecessors. Like them he was active in the local judiciary, and his skills as a liturgical poet and as a physician are comparable to theirs. This being said, as far as we

---

591 The letter of the Alexandrian, Abū Naṣr b. Abraham, testifies to the way Ibn al-ʿAmmānī managed to become Judah ha-Levi's exclusive host and to overcome the other eminent Alexandrians who wished to host him. See TS 13 J 19.17, 1, ll. 1–11: Goitein, "Letters about R. Judah ha-Levi's stay in Alexandria," 354–355; Frenkel, "*The Compassionate and Benevolent*" [Hebrew], no. 69. Judah ha-Levi himself writes, in his letter to Samuel the Nagid: "I intended to make of Alexandria a short cut, and I did not allow the steps of the chariot to delay [me], until I met one who was stronger than I." See *Diwan*, 1, letter 2, ll. 19–21. For more on Judah ha-Levi's embarrassment at the insistence on hosting him, see ENA NS 18.33 (Gil-Fleischer, *Yehuda ha-Levi*, 41).

592 It is very possible that this new focus was integrated with, or even part of, the new emphasis in the Jewish world at this time on the centrality of the Land of Israel, in response to the Crusader conquest. See Elchanan Reiner, "Overt Falsehood and Covert Truth: Christians, Jews and Holy Places in Twelfth-Century Palestine," *Zion* 63.2 (1998): 157–188, esp. 158–149. [Hebrew].

know his activities in the mercantile sphere were limited in comparison with his predecessors. In contrast to them, his ties and relationship to the Muslim rulers and the Muslim elite were much stronger than his fellows of the Jewish elite. He had to struggle and strive for his position and prestige and to create for himself a powerbase *ex nihilo*. He occasionally resorted to the traditional ways of securing power, such as procuring titles and establishing a personal relationship with the Nagid. At the same time, Ibn al-ʿAmmānī employed hitherto unknown methods to bolster his position, such as using his wealth as an ostentatious display of power and acquiring ideological legitimation for his rule on the basis of his family's origins in the Land of Israel, which he tied to the new religious trends of his time and place.

Chapter 6 Abū Naṣr b. Abraham

Abū Naṣr b. Abraham left behind many documents in the Cairo Genizah, but unfortunately they were all written in a very short span of time, during the seven years between 1134–1141. This prevents us from sketching a portrait of his life, except in the most general way. This being said, the relatively ample documentation from this seven-year span allows us to analyze the power dynamics and take note of the influential figures in the community at this time. It seems to be worthwhile, then, to sketch, even if only some general lines, the activities of this man, who lived at the nexus of power in Alexandria and who maintained relationships with the most important figures of his time and place.

1 Initial Forays into the Business World

Abū Naṣr was first and foremost a merchant, and his correspondence indicates business ventures of many different types.[593] He began as a merchant on the India route. A letter from 1134 describes his first ventures. Abū Zikrī ha-Kohen, the representative of the merchants of Fustat asked Ḥalfon b. Nethanel—an experienced businessman in the India trade, and one who would become in the fullness of time Abū Naṣr's patron—to help Abū Naṣr on one of his first voyages to India.[594] At the same time, Abū Naṣr dealt in the sale of grain between Alexandria and Fustat. In a letter from this time period Abū Naṣr, a novice in this type of commerce, apologizes that he did not buy the wheat when it was still cheap; though ultimately someone came along and "saved" him, by purchasing the wheat on his behalf. This was none other than Abū Isḥāq, the *nāʾib* or tax collector, who would eventually become his main business partner.[595] All this occurred at the very beginning of Abū Naṣr's career as a merchant when he was still trying out different types of commerce, and when he began forging the personal relationships that would be the basis of his future ventures.

---

593 ENA NS 21.14: Frenkel, *"The Compassionate and Benevolent"* [Hebrew], no. 17, cloths from the Maghreb; TS 8 J 21.7: ibid., no. 44, cloth from Sicily; ULC Or 1080 J 258: ibid., no. 99, silk; TS 13 J 22.31: ibid., no.74, wheat; TS 12.290, ibid., no. 22: medicines, perfumes gold, pearls and books.

594 Bodl MS Heb c 28 (Cat. 2876), fol. 22, upper margins, ll. 5–6: Gil-Fleischer, *Yehuda ha-Levi*, no. 25. See also Goitein, *Society*, 5: 280, n. 35.

595 TS 13 J 19.17r, ll. 15–19: Goitein, "Letters About R. Judah ha-Levi's Stay in Alexandria"; Gil-Fleischer, *Yehuda ha-Levi*, no. 42.

https://doi.org/10.1515/9783110713619-011

2 At the Nexus of Information and Relationships

It seems that Abū Naṣr did not undertake many business trips after these initial forays. In a letter from 1137 we find him in his store in Alexandria overseeing his business from there. It is apparent that he was primarily a broker or intermediary. The main business deal mentioned in this letter is the placement of a large order of prayer shawls and clothes for members of the elite in Fustat. Abū Naṣr's job was to coordinate between the seller of the fabric, the weaver, and the buyer. He does inquire in this letter about the Kārim convoy, but it seems that he himself did not embark on business trips at this time.[596] In another letter he is mentioned as an intermediary in the selling of fabric, various clothes, headgear,[597] and other types of merchandise.[598] His store was not only a venue for buying and selling, but also a nexus for the dissemination of letters and the safekeeping of merchandise.[599] Even Judah ha-Levi left an expensive turban at Abū Naṣr's store before his departure for the Land of Israel and asked that it be given to his grandson Judah b. Ezra, who was supposed to follow him to Egypt. Indeed,

596 ENA NS 21.14: Frenkel, *"The Compassionate and Benevolent"* [Hebrew], no. 17. The Kārim was a powerful commercial guild that took control of the India trade at the beginning of the thirteenth century, but began to be active already in the Fatimid period. See *Encyclopedia of Islam*, 2nd edition, *s.v.* Subhi Labib Y., "Kārimī"; Shelomo D. Goitein, "The Beginning of the Kārim Merchants and the Character of Their Organization," in *Studies in Islamic History and Institutions* (Leiden: Brill, 1966), 351–364; idem, "New Light on the Beginnings of the Kārim Merchants," *JESHO* 1 (1958): 175–84; Gaston Wiet, "Les marchands d'épices sous les sultans mamlouks," *Cahiers d'Histoire Egyptienne* 7 (1955): 81–147; Walter J. Fischel, "The Spice Trade in Mamluk Egypt," *JESHO* 1 (1958): 157–174; Subhi Labib Y., "Egyptian Commercial Policy in the Middle Ages," in *Studies in the Economic History of the Middle East*, ed. Michael A. Cook (London: Oxford University Press, 1970), 63–77; Eliyahu Ashtor, "The Kārimī Merchants," *JRAS* 1.2 (1956): 45–56; Roxani E. Margariti, "Mercantile Networks, Port Cities, and 'Pirate' States: Conflict and Competition in the Indian Ocean World of Trade before the Sixteenth Century," *JESHO* 51.4 (2008): 543–577; Muḥammad ʿAbd al-Ghanī al-Ashqar, *Tujjār al-tawābil fī miṣr fī al-ʿaṣr al-mamlūkī* (Cairo: al-Hay'a a-Miṣriyya al-ʿĀmma lil-Kitāb, 1999); Sato Tsugitaka, "Slave Traders and Kārimī Merchants during the Mamluk Period: A Comparative Study," *Mamluk Studies Review* 10.1 (2006): 141–232; idem, *Sugar in the Social Life of Medieval Islam* (Leiden: Brill, 2014), 76–90.

597 TS 8 J 21.7: Frenkel, *"The Compassionate and Benevolent"* [Hebrew], no. 44.

598 See above, Part II, Chapter 6.1: Initial Forays into the Business World.

599 TS 13 J 14.1, 1, ll. 1–7: Frenkel, *"The Compassionate and Benevolent"* [Hebrew], no. 62 – the courier from Almería brings letters to his shop for Judah ha-Levi, Isaac b. Ezra and Ḥalfon b. Nethanel; TS 10 J 24.4, 1, right margins, ll. 5–6: Frenkel, *"The Compassionate and Benevolent"* [Hebrew], no. 56 – a courier from Spain brings letters to his shop for Judah ha-Levi, and Abū Naṣr brings them to the poet when he was already on board the ship.

Abū Naṣr was a very trustworthy custodian and he kept this hat for Judah ha-Levi's grandson even after the poet had passed away.[600]

Abū Naṣr's store also served as clearinghouse for transmitting information. People arriving at the port would come to his store in order to keep abreast of the local news and tell Abū Naṣr what was happening in the rest of the Jewish world:

> A ship arrived from al-Mahdiyya, upon which Abraham b. Muqillah's nephew of Almería had been a passenger for seven months. He recounted that Joseph Ben al-Shāmī had passed away in the month of Nissan and our master Joseph Ben Migash passed away in the month of Sivan. Alas for the three dignitaries who died within five months of each other. May God forget the day of your esteemed lordship's death."[601]

The support that Ḥalfon b. Nethanel lent Abū Naṣr at the beginning of his forays into the business world eventually developed into a permanent liaison, and Abū Naṣr became Ḥalfon's representative in Alexandria. Most of the letters written by Abū Naṣr are addressed to Ḥalfon, and include information beyond the usual business reports, especially the local "news." Thus, for example, Abū Naṣr reported to Ḥalfon, who was very involved in Judah ha-Levi's pilgrimage to the Land of Israel, about the rifts in the community that were caused by the latter's visit to Egypt,[602] about the case of Judah ha-Levi and Ibn al-Baṣrī the apostate,[603]

600 TS 10 J 24.4, 1, right margins, l. 5–2, l. 7: Frenkel, *"The Compassionate and Benevolent"* [Hebrew], no. 56. See also Goitein, "Rabbi Judah ha-Levi in Spain in Light of the Geniza Papers," *Tarbiẓ* 24 (1955): 134–149 [Hebrew]; Ezra Fleischer, "Yehuda Halevi—Remarks Concerning His Life and Poetical Oeuvre," in Reuven Tzur and Tova Rosen (eds.), *Israel Levin Jubilee Volume,* I (Tel Aviv: Katz Institute for Hebrew Literature, 1994), 264 ff.; and Gil-Fleischer, *Yehuda ha-Levi*, 245–251, who disagree as to the identity of Judah b. Ezra.

601 TS 10 J 24.4, 2, ll. 7–12: Frenkel, *"The Compassionate and Benevolent"* [Hebrew], no. 56. For Joseph Ben al-Shāmī, a poet and halakhic jurisprudent, see Shelomo D. Goitein, "Did Yehuda ha-Levi Arrive in the Holy Land?," *Tarbiẓ* 46 (1977): 245–250 [Hebrew]; Schirmann, "Poets," 243. For Joseph Ben Migash, the spiritual leader of Spanish Jewry, the pupil and successor of R. Isaac Alfasi (the Rīf) as the head of the Lucena yeshivah, and his ties to Judah ha-Levi, see Hayyim Schirmann, *Hebrew Poetry in Spain and Provence* (Jerusalem: Mossad Bialik, 1959), 435–436 [Hebrew]. The third person who died is probably Judah ha-Levi himself. See also Gil-Fleischer, *Yehuda ha-Levi*, 253, n. 283.

602 TS 13 J 19.7: Frenkel, *"The Compassionate and Benevolent"* [Hebrew], no. 69; Goitein, "Letters About R. Judah ha-Levi's Stay in Alexandria"; Gil-Fleischer, *Yehuda ha-Levi*, no. 42.

603 TS 13 J 14.1: Frenkel, *"The Compassionate and Benevolent"* [Hebrew], no. 62; Goitein, "Rabbi Judah ha-Levi in Spain," 136–138. He reports on this affair, which caused heated controversy, also to his partner, the *nā'ib* Abū Isḥāq. See ULC Or 1080 J 258v: Frenkel, *"The Compassionate and Benevolent"* [Hebrew], no. 99.

about the riots against the Jews in Alexandria, and about the general anarchy that had spread in the community.[604]

3 Commerce as a Conduit to Advocacy

With Ḥalfon b. Nethanel the experienced merchant as an intermediary, Abū Naṣr forged ties with the Muslim authorities. His most frequent and closest contact was Rayḥān, who was one of the more influential servants of the caliph and did business on behalf of the royal court. We hear of letters that Abū Naṣr sent him and the large order of silk that Rayḥān bought from Abū Naṣr for the court.[605] Abū Naṣr tried to exploit this relationship to ameliorate the political situation of the community. In the same letter, he mentions that Rayḥān promised to get an edict signed by the caliph himself, which would prevent any rise of the *jizya* tax collected from Jews and Christians. He asks Ḥalfon to meet with Rayḥān and remind him of this promise.[606] In another letter, Abū Naṣr asks his frequent companion Abū Zikrī ha-Kohen b. Judah to take advantage of his connections and procure a series of reference letters from the authorities and from the religious leaders in Cairo to the governor (*wālī*) of Alexandria. This move was an attempt to roll back the onerous financial demands that the *wālī* had laid upon the Jewish community and to get involved in quieting the riots against the Jews in the city.[607] Abū Naṣr was the puppeteer in the background. His stature was not elevated enough to engage the authorities directly, but he knew exactly what was necessary and who to go to, and gave his associates who acted in his name precise instructions:

> Can you perhaps send frequent letters to "the judge," and let whoever is there take them. I know that you have no one but the most honored and revered Shaykh Abū al-Makārim, may God sustain his magnificence, and he is a man of stature. The Jews would not have been

604 TS 12.290v, ll. 15–16: Frenkel, *"The Compassionate and Benevolent"* [Hebrew], no. 22. It is possible that it was the Judah ha-Levi-Ibn al-Baṣrī affair that was the root cause of the anti-Jewish riots that broke out in 1141, the *sin'ūt* in Alexandria. See above, Part I, Chapter 1.2 (h): Days of Hatred (*sin'ūt*) (1140–1150). On the Ibn al-Baṣrī affair, see above, n. 595.
605 ULC Or 1080 J 258r, ll. 6–9: Frenkel, *"The Compassionate and Benevolent"* [Hebrew], no. 99. See also Goitein, *Society*, 1:147, n. 113; ibid., 2:387, n. 29. The Muslim authorities used to confiscate great quantities of the silk inventory of Alexandria, against the will of the merchants themselves (see ibid., 268).
606 ULC Or 1080 J 258r, ll. 22–26: Frenkel, *"The Compassionate and Benevolent"* [Hebrew], no. 99.
607 TS 12.290v, ll. 5–13: Frenkel, *"The Compassionate and Benevolent"* [Hebrew], no. 22.

> released from the *jizya* and its collection without him. And so it will be with regard to this crisis, with God's help. And among the letters there should be also one from the Shaykh al-Amīn to the *faqīh* Ibn ʿAwf, for it may be very useful. If the *wālī* of Alexandria is still in power, there should be letters to him as well, and if there is a new *wālī*, the reference letter should be addressed to him from there, as is proper.[608]

On another occasion he actually tells Ḥalfon exactly what to say to Rayḥān: "If his enduring eminence meets with Rayḥān, he should be induced in this way and tell him that if this is something that he succeeds in doing himself, he may be able to overcome the other servants of the court."[609]

Abū Naṣr's familiarity with the proper modes of advocacy and his intimate acquaintance with key figures at the royal court and with their mindsets, show that these were not the only occasions that he took action. It is evident that his position at the nexus of power made him an effective advocate vis-à-vis the Muslim authorities.

4 Activity within the Community

Abū Naṣr employed the same behind-the-scenes tactics in order to preserve quiet and equilibrium within the Jewish community as well. When there was disagreement regarding Judah ha-Levi's visit in Alexandria and his sojourn in the city, Abū Naṣr wrote to Ḥalfon b. Nethanel and urged him to calm the spirits of those involved employing his typical subtle way, all the while complimenting Ḥalfon's attributes and skill: "This disagreement must now end. His eminence has sufficient wisdom and ability to govern and solve great problems, so this issue should be fairly simple."[610]

When, however, the affair of Judah ha-Levi and Ibn al-Baṣrī the apostate erupted, Abū Naṣr did not hesitate to adopt a tone that could be construed as a rebuke towards Ḥalfon:

> And I was surprised at his eminence. How could this notorious figure, known as a trouble-maker and as one who abuses people in Damietta and elsewhere, and people of little intellect came and made trouble for strangers because of this fearmonger and you did not

608 On these Muslim men of religion, see above, Part I, chapter 2.8 (a): Madrasas, the Muslim Schools for Religious Learning.

609 ULC Or 1080 J 258r, ll. 26–28: Frenkel, "*The Compassionate and Benevolent*" [Hebrew], no. 99; Gil-Fleischer, *Yehuda ha-Levi*, no. 51.

610 TS 13 J 19.17r, ll. 26–28: Frenkel, "*The Compassionate and Benevolent*" [Hebrew], no. 69.

> stop them, until matters reached this state. May God not grant any goodness to whoever was the instigator of all of this.[611]

This implies that in the symbiotic and complex relationship between Abū Naṣr and Ḥalfon b. Nethanel there was an underlying assumption that Ḥalfon would employ his authority and his skills to preserve equilibrium and keep the peace in Alexandria. Abū Naṣr did not hesitate to demand that Ḥalfon and his other associates involve themselves in community matters if there was cause, and he did this by means of his skills as an intermediary. Abū Naṣr's letters provide us with a good opportunity to understand the techniques of persuasion and advocacy that he had honed into a profession. When it came to Abū Zikrī, his mercantile patron,[612] Abū Naṣr employed the same tactics he had previously used to secure the help of Rayḥān; in other words, allusion to political expedience. He hints that in due time the public official would be able to take credit for helping: "In these matters whoever invests reaps the benefits, and gains a good name. For this is a matter for a patient and prudent man."[613] Exploiting his understanding of Abū Zikrī's psyche, he added a further inducement, namely the religious reward promised to him in the world to come: "Perhaps, if you help with this, this will be considered a great merit in days to come."[614]

It thus seems that Abū Naṣr considered himself responsible for peace and order within the community and deemed it proper to take advantage of his particular talents and relationships in furtherance of this objective – all of this without holding any formal office in the community.

611 TS 13 J 14.1r, margins, ll. 29–32: Frenkel, *"The Compassionate and Benevolent"* [Hebrew], no. 62.

612 See above, Part II, Chapter 6.1: Initial Forays into the Business World.

613 TS 12.290v, ll. 4–5: Frenkel, *"The Compassionate and Benevolent"* [Hebrew], no. 22. Cf. above, Part II, Chapter 6.3: Commerce as a Conduit to Advocacy, n. 607.

614 TS 12.290v, ll. 4–5: Frenkel, *"The Compassionate and Benevolent"* [Hebrew], no. 22. The expectation for reward in the world to come for good deeds in this one was at the foundation of the thinking of people of that time. See Goitein, *Society*, 5: 412. Despite this, I am not familiar with similar formulas that accompany other requests for help, and therefore I assumed that this is a personal and deliberate plea, intended to pluck at Abū Zikrī's heartstrings. See Mark R. Cohen, *Poverty and Charity in the Jewish Community of Medieval Egypt* (Princeton, NJ: Princeton University Press, 2005); idem, *The Voice of the Poor in the Middle Ages: An Anthology of Documents from the Cairo Geniza* (Princeton, NJ: Princeton University Press, 2005); idem, "Four Judaeo-Arabic Petitions of the Poor from the Cairo Geniza," *JSAI* 24 (2000): 446–471; Elinoar Bareket, "Begging for Help in Letters from the Genizah," *Te'uda* 16–17 (2002): 359–389. [Hebrew]

Abū Naṣr's community activism intertwined public work and private interests in a way that made it virtually impossible to distinguish between them. During the anti-Jewish riots in Alexandria, for example, he himself was under house arrest by the authorities (*tarsīm*) for taxes owing from previous years, specifically *jizya* payments. Hence, he had a vested interest in canceling the harsh decrees, and indeed devoted considerable effort to enlisting Abū Zikrī ha-Kohen b. Judah to help him with these matters.[615]

Aside from his direct interest in matters such as these, Abū Naṣr's public work enabled him to engage in joint projects with his patron and other associates and afforded him opportunities to strengthen and deepen his ties with them. These ties, as we saw above, helped him consolidate his position as a merchant, but he also employed them to advance the careers of younger family members. Thus, for example, in one of his letters, he asks Abū Zikrī ha-Kohen b. Judah to look out for his younger brother Abū ʿUmar, who underwent a period of mercantile apprenticeship with him, just like Abū Naṣr himself at the beginning of his career.[616] In another letter he asks Ḥalfon b. Nethanel to help his young nephew, who was just beginning his career in the mercantile sphere, just as he himself had benefited from Ḥalfon's help as he took his first steps in commerce.[617]

In his letters, Abū Naṣr b. Abraham discloses a dense network of unofficial relationships, which sustained and nurtured an elite group. It was likely that members of this group, like Abū Naṣr himself, would wish to maintain the *status quo*. The prime imperative of maintaining equilibrium and social order and the fear of any social change are articulated in Abū Naṣr's description of the riots in Alexandria. Ibn al-Baṣrī the apostate is depicted as a professional villain who attacks decent people (*nās*) and brings about social malaise,[618] and the riots themselves are comprehended as a provocation of the *hoi polloi* (ʿ*awwām*) against the nobles: "every pipsqueak and petty upstart besmirches the dignified people."[619] Hence, Abū Naṣr's voluntary communal work turns out to be anchored in the vested interests of a defined elite group.

---

615 TS 12.290v, ll. 4–5: Frenkel, "*The Compassionate and Benevolent*" [Hebrew], no. 22.

616 TS 12.290v, right margin, ll. 4–6: Frenkel, "*The Compassionate and Benevolent*" [Hebrew], no. 22.

617 ENA Misc. 13r, l. 13: Frenkel, "*The Compassionate and Benevolent*" [Hebrew], no. 13.

618 See above, nn. 613, 614.

619 See above, n. 319. Goitein (*Society*, 2: 280) believes that the term *nās* indicates Jews and that the reference is to anti-Semitic riots. However, comparison to other places where Abū Naṣr uses this term shows that he means respectable and decent people – in contrast to the ʿ*awwām*.

5 Personal Profile

(a) Secrecy

Abū Naṣr b. Abraham acted in the shadows. He never sought to put himself forward, and was satisfied with working in the background, pulling unseen strings and directing other protagonists. He was quite adept at managing the players, using a system of pressure and inducement, a derivative of his profound understanding of psycho-political dynamics and close relationship with the people with whom he interacted. His work was always conducted in intimate environments, though it is readily apparent that he had a good idea of the broader picture, as is evident in his descriptions of the community.[620] It seems likely that this pattern of behavior was more a matter of personal proclivity than of any deliberate tactic. Abū Naṣr's tendency to be secretive was reflected in other spheres of his life, and is most evident in his rather odd behavior during Judah ha-Levi's visit to Alexandria. Abū Naṣr was very eager to meet the famous poet and was even asked by Ḥalfon b. Nathanel's nephew to offer Judah ha-Levi accommodation in his house. But when intrigue was bubbling in the community and every person of status vied for the privilege of hosting Judah ha-Levi, Abū Naṣr sequestered himself at home under the pretext of an eye infection. He did not dare to meet the illustrious guest, but rather sneaked to the poet's abode at night to listen to him speak. The presence of Ḥalfon was required to facilitate a meeting between Abū Naṣr and Judah ha-Levi, and Abū Naṣr urged him to make haste and come to Alexandria for this purpose, among others:

> I am sequestered at home because of the eye infection with which I am afflicted. God will grant me healing. And I am embarrassed before his lordship, your nephew the illustrious Shaykh Abū al-Munā, may heaven be his abode, for reasons that you know. For until this time no one has come to my house, and I, when I wished to meet our teacher and master Judah ha-Levi, may his God preserve him, I overcame my night blindness and went to him[...] and I look forward to his everlasting eminence's arrival and count the minutes, and perhaps the meeting with him will take place in your presence.[621]

620 See above, Part II, Chapter 6.2: At the Nexus of Information and Relationships.
621 TS 13 J 19.17r, ll. 14–25: Frenkel, *"The Compassionate and Benevolent"* [Hebrew], no. 69. Ḥalfon b. Nethanel's sister's son is Abū al-Majd b. Abū al-Munā b. al-Dimyāṭī, mentioned in TS K 6.49 and TS Ar. 41.140.

(b) Admiration for Poets

In all likelihood, Abū Naṣr's yearning to meet Judah ha-Levi was completely genuine. As many people of his generation and milieu, Abū Naṣr valued intellectuals and showed them respect. At a certain point he considered collecting Judah ha-Levi's compositions himself. It is not at all surprising that this, too, he wished to do in secret. In a letter to Ḥalfon b. Nethanel, Abū Naṣr expresses his great consternation at Judah ha-Levi's departure and reveals to him: "I have decided, that beyond my apology to you, I wish to please you by collecting his worthy verses. And I ask that you hide this and thus grant a boon to your servant."[622]

When the news about the death of the poets Joseph Ben al-Shāmī and Joseph Ben Migash of Spain spread, immediately after the passing of Judah ha-Levi, Abū Naṣr was overcome with grief: "See how these three dignitaries passed away within five months of each other."[623]

(c) Trustworthiness and Moral Fortitude

Other noteworthy aspects of Abū Naṣr b. Abraham's character are his trustworthiness and moral fortitude, attributes that were manifested in the case of Judah ha-Levi's turban.[624] These traits enabled him to act as mediator, whether as a commercial middleman, or as a trusted source for letters and information delivered orally, or as an intermediary in interactions between individuals.

6 Summary

Abū Naṣr b. Abraham was a merchant with an intellectual pedigree, a public figure in Alexandria, and the representative of the merchant prince Ḥalfon b. Nethanel in Alexandria. His multiple spheres of activity were synergistically intertwined: His communal work helped him with his commercial undertakings, and his business ventures helped him create leverage for his public activities and his advocacy. He was the man behind the scenes, who stood at the nexus of a web of relationships. This position gave him a great deal of covert power, through which

622 TS 12.287.
623 See above, Part II, Chapter 6.2: At the Nexus of Information and Relationships.
624 Ibid.

he was able to guide major figures in the community and to influence events in Alexandria and beyond.

Chapter 7 Meir b. Hillel b. Ṣadoq

1 Origins and Background

Meir b. Hillel b. Ṣadoq was the scion of one of the most prominent Palestinian families. His grandfather Ṣadoq b. Josiah the third was the chief justice of the Palestinian Yeshivah in the days of Evyatar Gaon and was one of Evyatar's most prominent supporters in his struggle against David b. Daniel the Nagid.[625] His father Hillel b. Ṣadoq was a senior official in Egypt in the days of Samuel b. Hananyah the Nagid. The Nagid refers to him in his letters as: "our lord (*sar*) and master R. Hillel the Great Lord, son of Ṣadoq the righteous, the chief justice of all of Israel." The title *sar* appended to his name likely alludes to the station he held in the Muslim court.[626]

As the scion of an aristocratic family, Meir b. Hillel was trained appropriately. His elegant and confident handwriting indicates great aptitude, and it is quite likely that he was a professional writer and copyist. A number of booklists written in his hand were found in the Cairo Genizah.[627] The lists are in effect catalogues of various texts in order of subject: Talmud, lexica of Mishnaic words, responsa of Geonim and their legal monographs. Some of the books are catalogued by their incipits, which indicates that they constituted part of his private library, which served him for purposes of reading and study rather than commerce. Had Meir b. Hillel dealt in books, he would have certainly identified them in other ways, such as their size, the type of binding, or their monetary value. His intellectual curiosity and great love of books is also expressed in a letter he writes to Maimonides:

> Allow me to also inform his eminence that I have sent him [letters] in which I ask him a variety of questions. May he answer me as he is wont according to his great intellect. I also asked his eminence if he would write us something in the science of astronomy, that he would guide us in our understanding of various sayings of our sages that we find in the Talmud or in the responsa of the Geonim and in the composition he wrote on the six hundred and thirteen [commandments] [...] and afterwards he may complete the rest of it with the help of Heaven. And the scribe will be reimbursed from my pocket.[628]

625 See Gil, *History of Palestine*, §915.

626 TS 13 J 18.25: Mann, *Jews*, 2: 287.

627 Nehemya Allony, *The Jewish Library in the Middle Ages: Book Lists from the Cairo Genizah* (Jerusalem: Ben-Zvi Institute, 2006), lists 37–39. [Hebrew].

628 TS 8 J 15.17: Shelomo D. Goitein, "A Letter to Maimonides and New Sourcesregarding the Negidim of this Family," *Tarbiẓ* 34 (1965): 235–236. The translation follows Goitein.

https://doi.org/10.1515/9783110713619-012

Study and intellectual pursuits were a large part of Meir b. Hillel's life and he prioritized them as a religious commandment. In a letter to his son he advises the following:

> I advise you that you should strive [to be at one with your] Creator[...]what is my opinion – that you should read so long as you are able to do so[...]. O my son, cleave to the Torah in joy[...] and do not be too proud to learn[...] and al-Ṣayrafī should be your companion in learning.[629]

In another letter to three family members, either nephews or step-brothers, he counsels them following the marriage of one of their number:

> It is imperative that you and your brother al-Baḥīr set regular times to study with the judge al-Fāḍil al-Maskīl, may the Guardian of Israel preserve him. This is more of a priority than marriage, dinars, or dirhams [...] my advice to you is to cleave to the Torah and to read, and you shall be rewarded in this world and in the world to come, and you shall become cleansed through the commandments.[630]

Meir b. Hillel was evidently a member of the intellectual and pedigreed elite. He was the scion of one of the ruling families of the Palestinian Yeshivah, that had settled in Egypt at the end of the eleventh century, and were integrated among the elite in their new country of residence.[631] He was also a genuine intellectual in his great aptitude for learning, in the way he perceived himself and in his world view, in which the acquisition of knowledge was of paramount importance.

2 Judge in Alexandria

(a) Nethanel ha-Levi Gaon's Policy of Appointments

The appointment of Meir b. Hillel as judge in Alexandria is strongly related to Nethanel ha-Levi Gaon's idiosyncratic policies, and a few lines to delineate his traits as leader are due, since not enough has been written about this Gaon.

---

629 TS NS J 171r, ll. 19–20; v, ll. 1–2, 6: Frenkel, *"The Compassionate and Benevolent"* [Hebrew], no. 91.
630 Moss. L28 (VII)-200r, ll. 6–8, 10–11: Frenkel, *"The Compassionate and Benevolent"* [Hebrew], no. 20.
631 See Cohen, *Self-Government*, 87–90.

In 1160, the twenty-year tenure of the Nagid Samuel b. Hananyah came to an end.[632] His place as the head of the Egyptian community was filled by the dominant figure of Nethanel b. Moses ha-Levi the Sixth. Nethanel held two titles, "Gaon of the Palestinian Yeshivah" as well as "Gaon of the Babylonian Yeshivah" (the "Yeshivah of the Diaspora"), but in practice he functioned as the overall leader of the Jewish communities in Egypt.[633] In a paean composed in his honor he is referred to as "Nagid and champion among the wise."[634] Benjamin of Tudela referred to him as "lord of lords" (*sar ha-sarim*), a title habitually employed by Nagids, and ascribed to his leadership the traditional attributes and activities typical of previous Nagids – the headship of all the communities of Egypt, shored up by his close contact with the Muslim court: "And he is the head of all the communities in Egypt; he appoints Rabbis and cantors, and serves the great King, who lives in the palace in the city of Fustat (Tzoʿan)."[635]

Indeed, the legal documents that survive from that period indicate that his authority encompassed all the Jewish courts in Egypt.[636] Moreover, immediately after the passing of Samuel b. Hananyah, Nethanel ha-Levi removed all the local community leaders in Egypt who had served under his predecessors, and replaced them with his own associates. His deep involvement in new appointments is plainly reflected in Benjamin of Tudela's description.[637]

---

632 See Mann, *Jews*, 1: 233–234; Gil-Fleischer, *Yehuda ha-Levi*, 142–143, 231 n. 221.

633 Following the Yeshivah's migration from Syria to Egypt in the 1120s, family members of the Palestinian Gaons began to fulfil leadership roles in Egypt and even bore the title of "Head of the Jews." See Goitein, *Society*, 2: 15–19; Menahem Ben-Sasson, "Egyptian Jewry in the Tenth-Twelfth Centuries: From Periphery to Center," *Bulletin of the Israeli Academic Center in Cairo* 8 (1987): 14–16; Menahem Ben-Sasson, "Maimonides in Egypt. The First Stage," *Maimonidean Studies* 2 (1991): 17. On Moses, the father of Nethanel, see Gil-Fleischer, *Yehuda ha-Levi*, 52 nn. 142, 230–231.

634 Gil-Fleischer, *Yehuda ha-Levi*, 293 n. 3.

635 Benjamin of Tudela, *Itinerary*, 71. My translation differs from that of Adler.

636 For example, ENA 4011.51, ll. 11–13. This is a will from al-Maḥalla al-Kubrā from 1166, which ends with the words: "in the city of al-Maḥalla al-Kubrā, under the leadership of our lord and gaon, the unique one of the generation, the Lion of Torah, Nethanel ha-Levi, the head of the Yeshivah in the Diaspora, 'Israel's chariots and horsemen' [Kings II 2:12], let his name continue forever"; TS 18 J 1.26: Frenkel, *"The Compassionate and Benevolent"* [Hebrew], no. 82 – a witness document from al-Maḥalla dated 1160, that begins with the words "in the city of al-Maḥalla near Fustat of Egypt, that is on the small river, under the leadership of our lord Nethanel ha-Levi, let his name continue forever."

637 See above, n. 637: "he appoints Rabbis and cantors."

(b) Meir b. Hillel's Appointment

This was the case in Alexandria as well. In his first year in office in 1160, Nethanel ha-Levi compelled Meir b. Hillel b. Ṣadoq to leave his house and his family in Fustat and relocate to Alexandria to serve as judge, replacing R. Jacob. An account of these events is recorded in Meir b. Hillel's own words in a letter to his friend Nethanel b. Ḥalfon ha-Talmīd:

> Additionally, when I came before our master [= Nethanel ha-Levi Gaon] he commanded me: "You will leave for Alexandria and in remuneration I will transfer the wages of R. Jacob the Judge to you." I said to him: "Is it not better that I remain in a place that [...]." He said to me: "No! Moreover [if you remain here] you shall pay twelve dinars a year for it [for the domicile]."[638]

In other words, Nethanel Gaon appointed Meir b. Hillel without his consent as a judge in Alexandria in place of R. Jacob the local judge.[639] Meir b. Hillel preferred to remain in Fustat, but Nethanel the Head of the Academy refused to let him do this, and made his life difficult so that he would accept. He stated that if Meir was obstinate and wished to remain in his home in Fustat, a home which was almost certainly the property of the community, he would have to pay an exorbitant fee in rent.[640]

---

638 TS NS J 193, ll. 6–9: Frenkel, *"The Compassionate and Benevolent"* [Hebrew], no. 92. On the term *jārī* for the regular wages paid to government officials, see Goitein, *Society*, 2: 605, nn. 14, 15. Of R. Jacob, Meir b. Hillel's predecessor, we know nothing. Goitein surmised that he was identical to "our rabbi Jacob," mentioned in Meir b. Hillel's letter to Maimonides as someone who signed, together with R. Ḥiyya, the document appointing R. Isaiah responsible for endowments, in the days of Samuel b. Hananyah ha-Nagid; see Goitein, "A Letter to Maimonides," 233. It is more likely, however, that the reference is to R. Jacob ha-Kohen, "the Great Rav," who was a permanent member of the Nagid Samuel b. Hananyah's court of law in Fustat, not in Alexandria, and who signed several court documents in Fustat. On him, see Mann, *Jews*, 1: 222, where his name is listed among the members of the Nagid Samuel b. Hananyah's court, esp. ibid., n. 1; see also ibid., 2: 293.

639 The very mention of the wages that Meir b. Hillel is going to receive indicates his great reluctance to accept the proposed appointment. Only very seldom, and almost always in negative contexts, are wages for public office mentioned or discussed in this period. See Goitein, *Society*, 2: 358–457. It is possible that the issue of this appointment is the first harbinger of the future policy of Sar-Shalom ha-Levi, Nethanel's brother, who appointed paid judges. See Ben-Sasson, "Maimonides in Egypt," 11–12.

640 On the free accommodation provided for bearers of public office in the community, see Goitein, *Society*, 2: 123–124 and appendix 149 A. The price that Nethanel Gaon threatened to demand is truly astronomical, and there is no doubt that his intention was to deter Meir b. Hillel from refusing the appointment. The sum of a dinar per month is more or less the same as the

Meir b. Hillel was thus compelled to accept the appointment, but even while serving in Alexandria he continued to look for ways to free himself of his duties and return to Fustat. In a letter he wrote to Nethanel Gaon, shortly after his arrival, he recounts that the people of Alexandria suspected that he was trying to flee, and had forced him to swear that he wouldn't leave the city: "So much so that they compelled me to swear that I would not leave the port city in the direction of [...]"[641]

In the same letter, Meir b. Hillel tries to convince the Gaon Nethanel that there is a local leader in Alexandria that the members of the community respect, who is adept at governing the community and its tax liabilities, and that, moreover, his (i.e., the local leader's) loyalty to the Gaon is not in doubt: "And the Creator, blessed be His Name, had already taken note of this miserable nation [...] and in the port city [= Alexandria], R. Eleazar is loyal to my master [the Gaon] as much as I am [...] and he has ensured that there is respect in their hearts for him [...] honor and service to the community [...] in leadership and with regard to taxation."[642]

Later in the letter Meir elaborates upon his hopes for leaving Alexandria: "I shall leave with him and my notebooks and my clothes and some provisions."[643] He tries to convince the Gaon in various ways that his appointment is not an auspicious one. He emphasizes, among other things, his feelings of loneliness and his great distance from his family: "And if his eminence thinks that this appointment is justification enough to leave my sons. And I, were it not for what has already occurred[...]."[644] He even says that he wishes to be close to the Gaon himself: "If it is decided [...] in the port city [= Alexandria], far away, and with no possibility to see his eminence, there is no need to [...]."[645]

Indeed, in the earlier letters addressed to his family in Fustat, Meir b. Hillel's feelings of loneliness and isolation are readily apparent, as is his deep frustration. The frustration was due to his feeling that he is extraneous in his new

average *annual* rent at that time. See Goitein, *Society*, 5: 93–95; cf. the sum of twelve dirhams paid by another public official for lodging in one of the community's endowed houses, Goitein, *Society*, 2:433, no. 168. Goitein understood and interpreted this document differently; his reconstruction of Meir b. Hillel's biography is also at variance with mine – see Goitein, "A Letter to Maimonides," 232–233.

641 Moss. A VII-154.2 (L222), r, l. 3: Frenkel, "*The Compassionate and Benevolent*" [Hebrew], no. 19.

642 Ibid., r, ll. 8–14 (the text is very broken, but the gist can be understood).

643 Ibid., r, 1–2.

644 Ibid., v, ll. 1–2.

645 Ibid., r, ll. 16–17.

home and that he cannot subsist there but in penury. The following is excerpted from a letter to his son in Fustat:

> Abū al- [...] does not support me, and my son is not with me [...] I sit all day in the synagogue like all the beggars [...] he is their leader and one may get something from him only grudgingly, and how my father may his memory be for a blessing [...] showed him favor. [...] All of this is only twenty dirhams and he, as you know, [...] I have not seen even one penny of it [...] my soul is overwhelmed with yearning [...] I sit there with nothing to do and they arranged a pledge (*pesīqā*) for me [...] and I cry and am greatly saddened.[646]

In another letter to his three sons he greets each member of the family individually and asks: "Tell me of the welfare of all our family members. It seems as though you are in a well. I hear nothing from you."[647] Meir b. Hillel thus felt that his residence in Alexandria was punitive. He was far from his natural environment and from his family and he was isolated from the power centers and from the Gaon. He did not earn enough money; the little that was given to him, was given to him as charity, as though he were a beggar. He thought that there was no benefit to his presence, and that others could fill the position better than him.

3 Tenure in Alexandria

(a) A Personal Aide to the Gaon

There is very limited documentation available regarding Meir b. Hillel's sojourn in Alexandria. It is difficult to ascertain what exactly the nature of the position that Nethanel Gaon had in mind for him was, but one may surmise that he wished to give him power of attorney over his affairs and wanted him to be his liaison in Alexandria. This, in any case, is how Meir b. Hillel understood his position. In a letter to the Gaon, in which he tries to free himself of his responsibilities and leave them in the hands of R. Eleazar, Meir b. Hillel emphasizes the abiding loyalty and love of R. Eleazar for the new leader. "R. Eleazar loves my Lord [= the

646 TS NS J 171r, ll. 6–10, 12, 14, 16: Frenkel, *"The Compassionate and Benevolent"* [Hebrew], no. 91. The *pesīqā* was the contribution to the public chest of a certain sum of money for a certain purpose. In this case it was intended to remunerate Meir b. Hillel for his services to the community. Goitein, *Society*, 2:106; Cohen, *Poverty and Charity*.
647 Moss. L268 (VII)-200r, ll. 14–15: Frenkel, *"The Compassionate and Benevolent"* [Hebrew], no. 20.

Gaon] as I do," in order to convince the Gaon that the other is as worthy as he is to be the Gaon's representative in Alexandria.[648]

Meir b. Hillel's family background, being the grandson of a chief justice of the Palestinian Yeshivah, his father's friendship with Nethanel Gaon,[649] his own association with the Gaon, and his intellectual aptitudes made him the right type of person to be a close confidant of the Gaon and serve as his representative. It is possible that Meir served as an aide or as a secretary to the Gaon before his appointment in Alexandria and then again upon his return. Corroborating evidence is a list of books in Meir's handwriting entitled: "An Index to the Notebooks of the Head of the Academy." In this list there is an organized index of the opening phrases of all the notebooks in which there are legal responsa which likely belonged to the Gaon's family.[650] This list may indicate that Meir b. Hillel may have served as a personal aide to the Gaon at his residence.

In a letter that Meir wrote to Nethanel b. Ḥalfon following his return to Fustat, he responds to him in the Gaon's name: "Our Lord, may God grant him a long life, is a man of honor. When he is asked for something he grants it. Regarding your request, he has not been unconscientious, and it has been taken care of."[651] This message indicates that Meir was also in charge of the Gaon's correspondence. It is thus not surprising that the Gaon chose his aide and close associate to serve as his trusted representative in Alexandria.

(b) Judicial Activities

Only three documents have survived that relate to Meir b. Hillel's sojourn in Alexandria. Two of them are legal documents, which are connected to the philanthropic and loan business of the banker Samuel b. Judah b. Asad, who did business in Alexandria and al-Maḥalla.[652] The first is a loan bill from 1160 from al-Maḥalla, in which Samuel b. Judah loans ten dinars to a man by the name of

648 See above, Part II, Chapter 7.2 (b): Meir b. Hillel's Appointment.

649 See, for example, TS NS J 171r, ll. 8–9: Frenkel, *"The Compassionate and Benevolent"* [Hebrew], no. 91 – a letter from Meir b. Hillel to his son, in which he reminisces "how much good my late father did him [=Nethanel]."

650 TS Ar. 51.79, ll. 11–20: Allony, *Jewish Library*, list 38.

651 TS 8 J 22.21r, ll. 15–17: Frenkel, *"The Compassionate and Benevolent"* [Hebrew], no. 47.

652 Abū al-Maʿālī Samuel b. Judah b. Asad, "lord of those with understanding," was a banker and merchant, devoted to charity and served as trustee of the court in al-Maḥalla and in Alexandria. Among other things, he owned a house in Alexandria. The documents connected to him are dated 1133–1167. See Goitein, *Society*, 3: 296–297, 5: 268–269, 356–357.

She'erit b. Shemaryah b. Hillel is a signatory on the document. The signing of this document almost certainly took place in Alexandria, and Meir b. Hillel was one of three signatories.[653] Another document is an affidavit from 1161, which states that a widow in Fustat is to receive ten dinars from Samuel b. Judah b. Asad, who appears as a signatory on this document as well, along with Isaac b. Mevorakh. Though the document was signed in Fustat, it is connected to the philanthropic activities of Samuel b. Judah, a resident of Alexandria; he came to Fustat solely for the purpose of dealing with this case.[654] The third document is an engagement contract from al-Maḥalla from 1160, written in Meir b. Hillel's handwriting. This suggests that he served not only as a judge, but also as the scribe of the court.[655]

4 His Relationship with the Community

Though Meir b. Hillel was clearly reluctant to serve as a judge in Alexandria, it seems that the residents saw him in a favorable light. As was mentioned above, they were afraid that he would try to flee, and took steps to prevent this.[656] Moreover, they supported him and granted him room and board through a pledge (*pesīqā*) [657] and even after he had left Alexandria and returned to Fustat, they tried to enlist him to continue to help them with various problems in the community. Thus, for example, his successor sent him a letter in which he asked Meir b. Hillel to intervene on their behalf with the Gaon regarding the rental of a certain property in Alexandria. The inhabitants of Alexandria saw it as an advantage to have a figure with such a close relationship to the Gaon in their city, and they tried to maintain this advantage as has been shown above.[658] Meir b. Hillel responded to their requests very grudgingly, which was characteristic of his tenure in Alexandria in general, and after a failed attempt at helping, he states that he is unable to do more: "I am not to blame that I was asked to do something that I have no ability to do."[659] In a tone of clear impatience and aloofness, he directs

653 On the ties between al-Maḥalla and Alexandria, see TS 18 J 1.26: Frenkel, "*The Compassionate and Benevolent*" [Hebrew], no. 82.
654 Bodl MS Heb d 66, f. 78: Frenkel, "*The Compassionate and Benevolent*" [Hebrew], no. 4.
655 TS 8 J 5.21: Frenkel, "*The Compassionate and Benevolent*" [Hebrew], no. 19.
656 See above, Part II, Chapter 7.2 (b): Meir b. Hillel's Appointment.
657 TS NS J 171r, l. 14: Frenkel, "*The Compassionate and Benevolent*" [Hebrew], no. 91. On *pesīqā*, see above, n. 347.
658 TS 8 J 22.21: Frenkel, "*The Compassionate and Benevolent*" [Hebrew], no. 47.
659 Ibid., r, ll. 10 – 11.

the new leader to consult with members of the Bilbays community: "I am assuming that I write a letter to a man who is not a dullard and thus you should learn from the people of Bilbays [...] and 'the wise have eyes in their heads' and 'instruct the wise and they will be wiser still'."[660]

5 Summary

Meir b. Hillel, an intellectual of a distinguished lineage, was a typical scion of the Palestinian elite, which led the Yeshivah and following its dissolution migrated with it to Syria, finally arriving in Egypt at the beginning of the twelfth century. This account of Meir b. Hillel's life reveals a new epoch of local leadership in Alexandria. The Nagids, Nethanel Gaon's predecessors as leaders of Egyptian Jewry, nurtured a system of close relationships with homegrown local leaders, who were validated by the community and who wished to lead. Nethanel Gaon, however, attempted to impose his leadership on peripheral communities through the forced appointment of his representatives, who were his personal associates – but were outside transplants to the community, and completely disconnected from it. In many cases, such as Meir b. Hillel's, they had no desire to serve in this capacity. The desire of the community nonetheless to accept the appointed leader and thus maintain a channel to the Gaon who lived in Fustat, brings this pattern into greater focus, namely a pattern of greater centralization and the decline of the peripheral communities.

---

660 Ibid., r, ll. 12–15. Ecclesiastes 2:14; Proverbs 9:9.

Chapter 8: Eleazar ha-Kohen b. Judah, Sa'd al-Mulk

1 Background and Origin

Eleazar ha-Kohen was the scion of an Alexandrian family, the members of which served in official capacity in the royal court. His father Judah was the royal scribe and his official title was 'Amīd al-Dawla (chief of the dynasty). Eleazar's title was Sa'd al-Mulk (support of the crown), and his son was given the nickname Zayn al-Kuttāb (the most splendid of scribes) – a sobriquet that reflected his social milieu and the expectations of his family.[661]

In a letter written by Manasseh the Teacher, the private tutor of Eleazar's young son, he proudly reports to the father of his son's progress:

> I have already sent a letter to your eminence, Master Sa'd al-Mulk, may God grant him a long life, regarding Zayn al-Kuttāb, and his progress in reading, may God grant that he ascends to greater heights, and give you joy. And he has already read five Torah portions and today he is reading the portion beginning in Leviticus 16. His grandfather, Lord al-'Amīd, returned from his journey, and the boy read before him and he was filled with joy. May God continue to grant him this pleasure.[662]

These lines demonstrate how important scholarly skills, such as reading and writing fluently, were for Eleazar's family throughout the generations in their social and professional milieu.

2 Judge and Leader

(a) His Appointment

We do not know when and under what circumstances R. Eleazar was appointed as judge in Alexandria. Above, we noted that he was the *de facto* leader of the community at the time of Meir b. Hillel's appointment. According to Meir b. Hillel, R. Eleazar filled every leadership position in the community: He represented

661 TS 12.425: Goitein, *Jewish Education*, 49–50, where his full name with all titles is mentioned, "Sa'd al-Mulk Eleazar ha-Kohen b. 'Amīd al-Dawla Judah ha-Kohen, the royal scribe," as well as his son's name.
662 Ibid.

https://doi.org/10.1515/9783110713619-013

the community in interactions with the Muslim authorities (*taqdima*), served the community (*khidma*), functioned as the taxation officer (*rusūm*), and was endorsed by community members, who accepted him as leader.[663] It is not clear that he held any official position, and his presentation as the accepted leader is suspect and reflects Meir b. Hillel's immediate considerations.[664] One may surmise, however, that already at this time R. Eleazar was the dominant figure in the community, and he was appointed officially as judge immediately after Meir b. Hillel's return to Fustat, following his short tenure in Alexandria.

(b) Judicial Activities

As a judge, R. Eleazar was in charge of routine judicial activities such as the writing of bills and court deeds. A letter to Maimonides states: "Regarding a fifteen year old boy, who came to the synagogue [i.e to the court], and another man came with a bill concerning this young man, which has been written in front of our teacher and master, Eleazar the Judge, may his righteous memory be for a blessing."[665]

Like all Jewish judges, he was dependent upon the Muslim authorities to execute any punitive actions. A letter from a leader of another community, who sought the arrest of a fugitive from a serious crime who had fled to Alexandria, states: "And his servant requests that you grant him this boon and do this favor for him, that you ask R. Eleazar that he should check with the inspector (*nāẓir*) regarding his arrest."[666] In other words, R. Eleazar acted as an intermediary vis-à-vis the Muslim authorities, who had the actual power to detain people.

(c) Public Activity

R. Eleazar was an active philanthropist and dedicated himself to the ransoming of captives. These activities involved a great deal of personal involvement, in which private as well as communal funds were used without distinction, as

663 See above, Part II, Chapter 6.2 (b): Meir b. Hillel's Appointment.
664 Ibid.
665 Maimonides, *Responsa*, 317, §173.
666 ULC Or 1080 J 112, 1, ll. 14–16: Frenkel, "*The Compassionate and Benevolent*" [Hebrew], no. 98. On the *nāẓir*, the inspector of the *dīwān* under the Fatimids, see: Al-Imad, *The Fatimid Vizierate*, 20.

had been the custom of his predecessors. Thus, for example, in order that the treasurer be allowed to use the money from an estate without inheritors to finance the redemption of a captive who was in danger of losing his life, R. Eleazar gave Joseph al-Maqdisī, who was in charge of this estate, a personal guarantee.[667]

(d) Religious Leader

R. Eleazar intended that his leadership extend to the religious realm as well, and he actually succeeded in shifting the liturgical traditions of the community at least for a short period. This is evident in a question posed to Maimonides:

> May our master teach us regarding the tradition in Alexandria, whereby the Torah reader, when he gets to the thirteen attributes in the Torah portion of Exodus 30:11–34:35, he remains silent until the community reads it out loud as a quorum. And (previously) they would begin chanting: "The Lord! The Lord! A God compassionate and gracious, etc.[...]" [Exodus 34:6]. This came to the attention of R. Eleazar who said that it is not appropriate to read from the beginning, but rather from the second iteration of the divine name, thusly: "The Lord! A God compassionate and gracious, etc.[...]" [The reason for R. Eleazar's disapproval] was that a pause exists between the two names and one must not elide them under any circumstance, since it may lead to a wrong belief. And we have kept this tradition since his time.[668]

This emendation, which R. Eleazar succeeded in implementing in the local prayer traditions, which were usually sacrosanct and difficult to change, point to the great level of authority wielded by him. This emendation was made in order to protect the community from false beliefs, as is evident from the question to Maimonides. In other words, pronouncing God's name twice in succession as part of the liturgy may detract from the belief in His uniqueness. The care taken by R. Eleazar indicates a severe and orthodox monotheist way of thinking.

---

667 Maimonides, *Responsa*, 733–734, §542 – a question sent from Alexandria in 1190. Maimonides' ruling was unequivocal: the sum can be demanded back from the guarantor only when the rightful heir comes to demand his inheritance.
668 Maimonides, *Responsa*, 505–506, §267.

(e) Commercial Ties

Like others before him, R. Eleazar tried to bolster his position by means of personal ties with powerbrokers from outside of the community. These ties were based to a great extent upon mercantile activity. Thus, for example, R. Eleazar himself was the agent for a big order of reed mats, a product which the Alexandrian community excelled at manufacturing. He performed this service on behalf of Solomon, one of the exilarchs from Mosul, who had arrived in Fustat.[669]

3 The Leadership Crisis and Its Resolution

R. Eleazar's tenure as leader was not uneventful. Members of the community searched for a new leader, and found the figure they sought when R. Ephraim arrived in Alexandria. R. Ephraim was a charismatic preacher from foreign lands, who arrived incognito and became the leader of the community. The unfolding of events that led to his appointment are credibly described in great detail by a member of the community who witnessed the rise of this leader first hand. In the following letter he relates to the circumstances surrounding the preacher's arrival in Alexandria:

> He chose a house for himself and lived in it. And we did not know of him until he began living in the house he had chosen for himself. And he did not burden the community with any request that someone come and greet him. We came, all of us, the entire community, and we greeted him as is appropriate for someone of his station. And nothing has come to light about him from the time of his arrival until now, that would indicate that he was anything but good and humble, and that he feared God, and was truthful and modest and a good and an able leader. And he gave a sermon on *Shabbat Shuvah* [the Sabbath between the New Year holiday and the Day of Atonement] and it was well-delivered. And there were many people in the two synagogues. And he enchanted everyone and everyone was exceedingly happy with him after he respectfully said the prayer for the head of the community [...]. And people followed him to a man. And a number of members of the community gave him ten golden dinars and one dinar for provisions. And he accepted this and was grateful. Afterwards the community asked if he would deliver the sermon on the Day of Atonement, but he was unable to do so. And they asked him if he would deliver the sermon on the Sabbath in the middle of the festival of Tabernacles at the Babylonian synagogue. And both communities attended. And he said the prayer for the head of the community as

669 TS 20.175, 1, ll. 4–8: Frenkel, "*The Compassionate and Benevolent*" [Hebrew], no. 36.

> is proper and he gave a sermon regarding the meaning of the verse "And this is the blessing" [Deuteronomy 33: 1] and the letter with which the verse begins.[670]

The actual rousing sermon, which captivated the entire congregation was never found, but according to the content of the Torah portion with which it dealt (Deuteronomy 33–34) one may surmise that the message he delivered was one of consolation and encouragement.[671] R. Ephraim's inclination to pietism was probably inherent in his family, as can be surmised from the first lines of the letter, in which his genealogy is given. These lines are almost completely illegible, but one may clearly discern the last link of the chain, who is named "the knowledgeable and wise, may God preserve him, Ben Azaryah, who was a devout pious person (*ḥasid*), may he rest in honor."[672]

The great draw of this preacher, who delivered sermons of consolation and encouragement, was so apparent that R. Eleazar came out against him immediately and vociferously, in order to protect his position which was now in jeopardy:

> R. Eleazar the Judge, may the Merciful One preserve him, interrupted him during his sermon. He [R. Ephraim] said to him: "Please wait with your question until I am finished." But he once again spoke up and bothered him, and disrupted the proceedings and seized his [R. Ephraim's] clothes and went outside and spoke coarsely in a way that does not accord with basic etiquette. Afterwards he said: "These words are fitting for [...] the brave." Our R. Ephraim said: "You, members of the community, speak up against him!" The judge said to the community: "Come out with me." The community yelled back at him: "No! No! No!" a number of times and only less than ten people left with him. And he [R. Ephraim] remained on the pulpit and finished his sermon. People reassured him and promised him good things and surrounded the judge and chastised him harshly. And there was

670 TS 16.149, ll. 3–16: Frenkel, *"The Compassionate and Benevolent"* [Hebrew], no. 28. Goitein (Shelomo D. Goitein, "The Renewal of the Controversy over the Prayer for the Head of the Community at Abraham Maimuni's Time," *Ignace Goldziher Memorial Volume, II* [Jerusalem: Reuven Mass, 1958], 53–54) thought that this was a document from the time of the Nagid Mevorakh (1094–1111), but already Mark Cohen showed that this date is not reasonable: see Cohen, *Self-Government*, 268–269, n. 200.

671 Midrashim based on letters are known from the earliest periods. See for example, William Brinner (ed.), *An Elegant Composition Concerning Relief after Adversity by Nissim ben Jacob Ben Nissim Ibn Shāhīn* (New Haven: Yale University Press, 1977). ch. 30; Meir Havatzelet and Uri Melamed, "Commentaries on Alphabets in Psalms," *Pe'amim* 88 (2001): 4–20 [Hebrew].

672 TS 16.149, ll. 2–3: Frenkel, *"The Compassionate and Benevolent"* [Hebrew], no. 28. It is not clear whether the term *ḥasīd* here indicates a formal adherence to institutionalized pietistic groups of the kind we encounter in the thirteenth century, or is just a term indicating Ben Azaryah's personal religious devotion and piety.

great conflict between members of the community and they called for help against the judge.[673]

Following these tumultuous events, the community asked R. Ephraim to be their *muqaddam*, but R. Eleazar once again attempted to forestall the move by demanding that R. Ephraim present a letter of appointment from the *ra'īs*. R. Ephraim claimed that he had such a document in his possession though he avoided presenting it.[674] The end of the letter is truncated, but a later letter written by R. Ephraim indicates how the situation was ultimately resolved. This later letter was written when R. Ephraim was already a judge in Alexandria, and in it he relates to an unknown addressee about the harassment he had been subjected to by various members of the community and the Muslim authorities. Among other things, he alludes to the "partnership" between himself and R. Eleazar.[675] One may surmise, therefore, that in the end R. Ephraim was appointed as judge and served together with R. Eleazar in a partnership. R. Ephraim's letter is replete with allusions to conflict within the community. He frequently speaks of a "rejection of peace," and complains that members of the community "devote themselves to disagreement."[676] One may thus assume that this "partnership" did not necessarily lead to calm in the community, but instead exacerbated existing tensions. Moreover, R. Ephraim himself hints to a lack of direction when in a certain case he was forced to adopt a particularly lenient position so as to appease one of the litigants, and his rivals used this as ammunition to attack him and "made a big deal of it."[677] One may deduce that two rival judges serving at the same time prevented the flexibility needed for a well-run court: The fear of one judge vis-à-vis his rival caused the system to stall, and in R. Ephraim's words: "to cease functioning completely."[678] R. Ephraim summarizes the situation in the following way: "I do not know how to resolve my position in this 'partnership,' except by the help of God and you."[679] With this statement he indicates how complicated, even chaotic, the situation in the community was during the period of transition between the Fatimid and Ayyubid regimes.

---

673 Ibid., ll. 16–24.
674 Ibid., lll. 25–34.
675 TS 16.272v, l. 25: Frenkel, *"The Compassionate and Benevolent"* [Hebrew], no. 30.
676 Ibid., v, lower margins.
677 Ibid., v, lower margins, l. 15.
678 Ibid., v, l. 25.
679 Ibid., v, upper margins, ll. 17–18.

4 Conclusion

R. Eleazar was a scholar of the old type, one who held fast to orthodox positions. He was a member of the traditional elite intelligentsia, which had coalesced in no small part due to the positions it occupied in the Fatimid court. The sources of R. Eleazar's authority and power were based, like his predecessors', upon his personal and commercial relationships with power centers outside of the community. This type of leader no longer met the community's needs. R. Eleazar's tenure as leader was during a period of crisis and great upheaval in all of Egypt. The decline of the Fatimid regime and the consolidation of Ṣalāḥ al-Dīn position, as a completely different type of leader, heralded the beginning of a revolution.[680] At this time of great change and general uncertainty, the community was no longer satisfied with the rigid lackluster leadership of R. Eleazar and searched for a leader of a different type: A charismatic leader who could offer it reassurance and security. This type of leader presented itself in Alexandria with the arrival of the foreign preacher, R. Ephraim, whose charisma swept through the community like wildfire, and the community seized hold of him as to a life preserver. The installment of R. Ephraim as co-leader was spontaneous and responded to a real need for change. From the moment that the leader was found, the Gaon's approval was only required for official purposes. This being said, this was a genuine period of transition, in which the old and the new served together: The conservative voices in the community used the Gaon's approval or lack thereof as an attempt to prevent the change, and in the end the situation stabilized and the "partnership" compromise was settled upon. This attempt to preserve both styles of leadership in tandem, however, was ultimately revealed to be a failure.

680 See above, Part I, Chapter 1.2 (i): The Twilight Era (1150 – 1171).

Chapter 9 R. Ephraim

1 Background and Origin

R. Ephraim arrived in Alexandria as a visiting preacher of some fame. In a letter that documents his arrival, one detects an apologetic note that the community did not greet him properly: "And he did not burden the community with a demand that someone should come to greet him, and we went, the entire community, and we greeted him as is appropriate for one of his stature."[681]

R. Ephraim was a scion of a family, some of whose members were known for their great pietism, and the sermon he delivered indicates that he himself may have had such tendencies.[682]

R. Ephraim was foreign to Alexandria and apparently to Egypt in general. The label of "stranger" with which he was saddled was perhaps part of the secret of his early success, but was also part of his persona after he became a judge.[683] After he attempted – as a judge – to raise funds for the redemption of prisoners, a member of the community was skeptical of his efforts: "Why does one of these strangers request a dinar [...] if he cannot dwell in the city without being supported by special pledges?"[684] In other words, the person attempted to deny R. Ephraim the right to raise funds, which was one of the central powers that leaders had at their disposal, claiming that as a stranger he himself was dependent upon the community for his livelihood.

2 A Controversial Leader

Only one letter documents R. Ephraim's tenure as leader. This letter, written by R. Ephraim himself, focuses almost exclusively on the harassment he endured from a group opposing his leadership within the community. Though biased and limited in scope, this document may sketch some of the contours of R. Ephraim's leadership.

681 See above, Part II, Chapter 8.3: The Leadership Crisis and Its Resolution.
682 Ibid.
683 The most famous sociological analysis of the status of the "stranger" as an individual who settles down, but forms only weak and short-term connections, is Georg Simmel, "The Stranger," in Kurt H. Wolf (ed.), *The Sociology of Georg Simmel* (Glencoe IL: Free Press, 1959), 402–408.
684 TS 16.272v, ll. 9–10: Frenkel, *"The Compassionate and Benevolent"* [Hebrew], no. 30.

https://doi.org/10.1515/9783110713619-014

R. Ephraim's rivals presented him as a fifth column, a disruptive figure who attempted to raise a peripheral group of people to positions of leadership over their betters: "Abū al-Riḍā said: 'Master, this judge has swayed these people, painters, collectors of seashells, and the rabble, and referred to them as "the fellows of the Yeshivah (*ḥaverim*)," and granted them authority over the notables'."[685] R. Ephraim, however, is revealed as a mediator, who sought to prevent disagreements and fighting at any cost. The opening of the letter outlines the beginning of the disagreement between him and Abū al-Riḍā b. al-Maghribiyya, one of the local community leaders. The first lines of the letter are preserved only in fragmentary form, but the little that is preserved indicates actions whose purpose is reconciliation:

> [...] And I urged him and I sat at the gate, just outside the gate [...] for he and Abū al-Riḍā b. al-Maghribiyya were at home [...] and the first person I greeted, conveyed [...] my response was that I had no leader (*ra'īs*) except for him and there was no [...][686]

When the disagreement in the community escalated to outright violence and came close to bloodshed, in R. Ephraim's words, he undertook a policy of active reconciliation:

> And it came to the point of bloodshed, and there was nothing for me to do except to go to their houses and to try to draw the hatred from their heart. I left the people who conveyed messages between us behind and I took with me most of the members of the community who had separated themselves and I brought them to his house, and they promised each other, may God live, that [...] would no longer be heard [...] regarding the people between whom the disagreement took place and I appeased them on his behalf.[687]

At a different stage of the conflict, when Ibn al-Tallāj, one of his most vocal opponents, harmed him in a very explicit and direct way, R. Ephraim wished to excommunicate him, but even that was attempted in a conciliatory and hesitant fashion: "And I swore to myself and said: 'I shall be cursed' if what was said about me is true. And regarding the person who said this to besmirch my honor, he is excommunicated anyhow, I have no need to excommunicate him."[688]

This *modus operandi* of quiet at any cost was adopted by R. Ephraim as a judge as well. When a woman appeared before him, who was afraid that her bri-

685 Ibid., r, ll. 23–24.
686 Ibid., r, ll. 3–6.
687 Ibid., r, ll. 35–36 – right margins, l. 19.
688 Ibid., v, ll. 12–13.

dal money would be squandered, he confirmed her claim over part of the bridal property, "so that the woman who was owed this bridal price would have peace of mind," and thus earned a scathing rebuke from his opponents.[689]

3 Summary: A Jannus-Faced Leader?

How can one reconcile the *prima facie* contradiction between the charismatic preacher, who swayed the entire community, who put fear into the heart of the veteran local leader, who gathered to himself groups on the periphery to challenge the local leadership – and the moderate and hesitant mediator?

The charge against R. Ephraim that he was attempting to incite the *hoi polloi* and to overthrow the existing leadership and replace it with the rabble, is a typical allegation, which reappears as a mantra whenever there is an attempt to undermine the legitimacy of the existing leader.[690] Underlying this claim is the accusation that the person who is being attacked is trying to change the *status quo*, and replace the elite, who are leaders by right and by birth, with the local rabble, undermining the natural order of things. This motivation was thus seen as a challenge to the very laws of nature and therefore quite serious. It is, thus, not at all surprising that the opposition to R. Ephraim accused him of this in the context of their struggle against him, and we should not accept these accusations at face value. One may thus view R. Ephraim as an accomplished rhetorician who arrived in Alexandria at a time of crisis, at a time when members of the community were searching for a different type of leader, which explains his meteoric rise.

It is apparent that charismatic oration and messages of consolation and reconciliation are insufficient to stabilize a community. The only letter that have survived from the period of R. Ephraim's leadership points to an increase of tension and strife. The time he served as leader was very short indeed. In the end, he did not leave any distinct impression in the collective memory of the community. Only a few years after he was judge, when an individual wished to ask Maimonides a legal question regarding a case that arose at that time, he referred to the case in the following way: "May our master teach us regarding the case in which a man passed away at the time of our master, R. Eleazar, may his righteous memory be for a blessing, and left an orphan maiden behind."[691] In other words, the

689 Ibid., v, upper margins, ll. 1–17.
690 See, e.g, TS 18 J 3.5, ll. 37–38: Gil, *Palestine* [Hebrew], no. 599. About a century earlier, Ibn al-Qāsh was accused of the same thing, almost verbatim.
691 Maimonides, *Responsa*, 102, §64.

short span in which he served was still remembered as part of the period of R. Eleazar's tenure, and the memory of R. Ephraim, who was R. Eleazar's partner in leadership, was completely obliterated.

Chapter 10 R. Pinḥas

The sources documenting R. Pinḥas' tenure as judge in Alexandria are predominantly the responsa and epistles he exchanged with Maimonides. Naturally, one learns more of the relationship between the two and less about his activity as a community leader. One may, however, outline at least some facets of his leadership and character.

1 Background and Origin

R. Pinḥas arrived in Alexandria from Europe. It is difficult to determine whether he originated in Île de France (in the north of France), known as Francia at that time, or from the city of Montpelier in Provence, an area which was distinct at that time, and was known as Provincia.[692] In an epistle that Maimonides wrote to R. Pinḥas, he confessed that one of the cases he was considering was mystifying to both him and his court – and he was forced to explain to them the particulars of the strange case and excuse its idiosyncratic nature: "Do not be surprised, these are from France (Francia), all the Jews residing in the towns of the uncircumcised, even the greatest sage among them, is not proficient in legal minutiae, since they are not accustomed to them, for the uncircumcised do not allow them freedom to practice the law, as the Ishmaelites allow us."[693]

This being said, at the end of his epistle to the community in Montpelier in Provence, he apologizes and says: "My lords, forgive me for the brevity of my response, the writing evinces the haste I took with it, I am very busy with the business of the gentiles. And the Lord knows, that if it were not for R. Pinḥas, may his Rock preserve him, sending an emissary, who persistently requested that I ad-

692 Norman Golb, "New Light on the Persecution of French Jews at the Time of the First Crusade," *PAAJR* 34 (1966): 5–7, n. 9; idem, *History and Culture of the Jews of Rouen in the Middle Ages* (Tel Aviv: Dvir, 1976), 4, n. 12 [Hebrew]. On the borders of the region of northern France and its politico-cultural cohesiveness, see Robert Chazan, *Medieval Jewry in Northern France: A Political and Social History* (Baltimore and London: Johns Hopkins University Press, 1973), 6–7. Emigration from Europe to the East occurred in this period in two separate waves: the first from Provence at the beginning of the thirteenth century, and only later – the immigration (*ʿaliyah*) of three hundred French rabbis. On the waves of immigrations, see Elchanan Reiner, "Pilgrims and Pilgrimage to Eretz Yisrael, 1099–1517" (unpublished Ph.D. diss., The Hebrew University of Jerusalem, 1988), 51–60; Alexandra Cuffel, "Call and Response: European Jewish Emigration to Egypt and Palestine in the Middle Ages," *JQR* 90 (1999): 61–102.
693 Shailat, *Letters*, 446, ll. 19–21.

https://doi.org/10.1515/9783110713619-015

dress this, and who did not leave until I had written it – I would not have answered, since I have no time."[694]

R. Pinḥas' monumental effort to procure a response from Maimonides on behalf of the community in Montpelier leads one to assume that this is where he originated – rather than Francia. Moreover, the epistle Maimonides sent to him regarding the obligation of one suffering nocturnal emission to wash prior to praying, he writes: "And this is a tradition only in the communities of Shinar and the West [= Spain and the Maghreb], but in all the cities of Rome and France and all the communities of Provincia [= Provence], the men in your cities, have never followed this tradition."[695]

It is quite clear that R. Pinḥas did not read or write Arabic. All the epistles he exchanged with Maimonides are written in Hebrew, and the court protocols he wrote had to be translated from Hebrew into Arabic: "Afterwards they wrote down a court deed which was the judge's words in the holy tongue, and then it was translated into Arabic by the Elder Abū Saʿīd ha-Talmīd, the cantor, may he be well."[696] The only sermon of R. Pinḥas which survives is apparently an Arabic translation of the original.[697]

2 His Appointment

Maimonides was apparently the central figure who pushed for and supported the appointment of R. Pinḥas in Alexandria. This is corroborated by the frequent correspondence between the two, in the form of responsa and epistles. Maimonides confesses that R. Pinḥas was one of his protégés: "And regarding that which you made me swear to you, that I wouldn't banish you from my presence, regarding this – God forbid, that I would uproot that which I planted, that I would destroy that which I built."[698]

3 Judge in Alexandria

The extant documents mostly consist of legal responsa and epistles, and by their nature shed the most light on R. Pinḥas's activities in the judicial sphere.

694 Ibid., 490.
695 Ibid., 437, ll. 17–19.
696 Maimonides, *Responsa*, 419, §233.
697 TS 13 J 19.7.
698 Shailat, *Letters*, 436, ll. 10–12.

(a) Legal Activity

R. Pinḥas' authority extended over a fairly broad geographical area. The community of Minyat Ziftā, in the Delta area between Alexandria and Fustat, for example, was under his jurisdiction.[699]

R. Pinḥas presided over marriage and divorce cases, such as the requirement of the father to provide for his elder daughter who was in the care of her mother and step-father,[700] the release of women who could not remarry (*'agunot*),[701] property disputes between couples in the process of divorce,[702] and the right of a woman in dire straits to sell her plot of land in the Muslim court.[703] R. Pinḥas was also involved in public cases, such as the promulgation of an edict forbidding a corrupt ritual slaughterer (*shoḥet*) from butchering on behalf of the public.[704]

(b) His Style as a Judge

R. Pinḥas' foreignness was perhaps the most prominent aspect of his judicial activities. In most of the cases over which he presided, it is evident that he understood the role of the judge differently than his peers and predecessors. He tended to rule from a place of deep personal and emotional involvement, rather than from an aloof and neutral viewpoint based on knowledge of the law, which was the way the role of the judge was normally understood. The most obvious example of this is the case in which a woman granted her husband a document relinquishing her claim over the rest of her dowry. R. Pinḥas certified the document, but confiscated it from the husband: "And the judge validated the signature but said: 'The document is legal, but this woman is a fool.' And he confiscated the document relinquishing her claim from her husband."[705] Maimonides angrily took him to task for this: "And it is difficult in my eyes that you are both judge and litigant, and that you enter into a conflict with him, and rip up the document, and all this is not proper."[706]

699 Maimonides, *Responsa*, 448–451, §246.
700 Ibid., 641–644, §367.
701 Ibid., 448–449, §246.
702 Ibid., 414–425, §243.
703 Ibid., 31–33, §21.
704 Ibid., 321–322, §173.
705 Ibid., 417.
706 Ibid., 424, §233.

R. Pinḥas' foreignness is also apparent in his ignorance of the routine of legal proceedings. Thus Maimonides was forced to comment regarding his arcane questions: "A sage such as yourself has no need to go into great detail and generalize beyond basic references."[707] On another occasion he comments about R. Pinḥas' tendency to resend the same question on more than one occasion. "And I did not find any question here beyond the same ones that I was occupied with a number of times, until I told you: 'I have told you my opinion on this matter, now do as you wish'."[708]

(c) His Proficiency

It is quite clear that R. Pinḥas was at a decided disadvantage in his knowledge of legal sources as compared with other judges in Egypt. Maimonides attributes this to his foreignness as well:

> The Jews residing in the towns of the uncircumcised, even the greatest sage among them, is not proficient in legal minutiae...and when a case is brought before them they take too long to pore over it, and they do not know what the proper ruling is until they look it up for a long time in the Talmud. [This is] just like us regarding sacrificial laws, which we no longer practice, but when we did practice them – everyone knew them, and no one had to ask or search, just as those who now dwell among the Ishmaelites know legal cases and even students are familiar with them.[709]

His deficient knowledge of the sources and his general lack of competency led R. Pinḥas to hand down bizarre rulings, which confounded the judges on his court and Maimonides himself.[710] Sometimes he would give different, even contradictory rulings on the same case, such as the case in which a man who had divorced his wife and refused to grant her child support unless she agreed to raise their daughter. R. Pinḥas ruled in favor of the father, but when the man's erstwhile wife remarried to an individual who had guaranteed to support her daughter, but in the end did not, the woman turned to the court again; this time he ruled in favor of the wife, and required the father to provide exclusive support for his daughter. R. Pinḥas, who eventually realized the contradiction between his two rulings, found an innovative way to present the case to Maimonides without admitting his ignorance: He described the two rulings as originating with dif-

707 Ibid., 643, §377.
708 Shailat, *Letters*, 447, §28.
709 Ibid., 446–447.
710 For example, ibid., 446, ll. 15–19.

ferent judges. Ultimately, though, he was forced to reveal the process in order to receive cogent advice:

> And I shall now reveal to you, our master, that the first judge and the second judge were both me. It is I who dictated this question to the scribe who transcribed it. And when I first ruled [...] this was my initial thinking regarding the case over which I had presided. After a long while, I remembered the legal sources, and realized that I had handed down an unjust ruling, and I said to myself, I will now go to the tent of meeting, where all who seek God's word come, so that I could understand the situation more fully.[711]

(d) His Relationship with Maimonides: Between Dependence and Rebellion

As we indicated above, Maimonides stood behind R. Pinḥas' appointment to the bench in Alexandria. This fact and the great difficulty R. Pinḥas had whilst deliberating over cases illustrate R. Pinḥas' great dependence upon Maimonides. This dependence is reflected in the great volume of legal queries R. Pinḥas addressed to Maimonides, and his heartrending plea that Maimonides shouldn't abandon him when the relationship between them reached a crisis point, as we find in Maimonides' own words: "And regarding that which you adjured me in your previous letter that I should not spurn you, and all the matter alluded to there – God forbid that I should do so.[712]

This being said, R. Pinḥas still saw himself as an independent judge, and tried to use his own faculties in coming to decisions. When he doubted Maimonides' rulings, he did not hesitate in dismissing them, as Maimonides himself reveals: "And regarding the question of the divorce document to that woman, which you said was invalid because of the emissary, and I wrote to you that it was valid, and then I proceeded to demonstrate the discrepancy between our views, yet you adamantly dismissed [my view]."[713] And when Maimonides ruled against R. Pinḥas, the latter ignored the ruling, and was slow to follow his instructions, as community members indicate in correspondence with Maimonides: "And his eminence sent his valuable letter regarding the proper conduct [in this matter], and none of it was implemented."[714] Moreover, when his rulings did not correspond with those of Maimonides, R. Pinḥas stood firm, and did not hesitate to turn to the Muslim authorities to decide which ruling would be adopted. This is evident from Maimonides' answer to R. Pinḥas' ques-

711 Maimonides, *Responsa*, 642, §377.
712 Shailat, *Letters*, 436, §28, ll. 10 – 11.
713 Ibid., 447, §28, 9 – 11
714 Maimonides, *Responsa*, 419, §233.

tion as to why he sent his response with the signatures of other members of the court, instead of signing it by himself alone. Maimonides answers him without any attempt at evasion:

> Indeed, it is true, and it is deficient on my part, but people wrote to me from Alexandria, that if I were to write it in my name only – the judge would tell the officials or the judiciary: "This man says one thing and I say another, and who is to determine [the way in which to proceed]? They would not decide, and if there are many signatories – then his opinion is the opinion of one against many." And when I realized that this is indeed the way they operate, I decided to swallow my pride, in order that a just verdict may be reached.[715]

In one instance, R. Pinḥas was even the leader of public opposition to Maimonides. This occurred when Maimonides' ruling in a particular case, which was contrary to local custom, angered the Alexandrian community. R. Pinḥas supported the members of his community, delivered a sympathetic sermon and even wrote an epistle to Maimonides protesting the ruling.[716] Maimonides' attempt to promulgate and to teach his *Code* [*Mishneh Torah*] was forcefully opposed by R. Pinḥas, and he even wrote a long and detailed epistle in which he explains his reservations and criticism of the book.[717]

R. Pinḥas' judicial activity was thus characterized on the one hand by his foreignness coupled with his position of weakness and great dependence upon Maimonides, and on the other hand – by his determination to fortify his own position and to act independently.

4 His Relationship with the Community

(a) The Rival

R. Pinḥas' determination to act independently is perhaps due to the presence of a second judge in the city, R. Daniel, who was a student and an associate of Maimonides. R. Daniel was not a resident of Alexandria and either stayed there temporarily or split his time between Fustat and Alexandria, as Maimonides himself states: "He fears God and is a public advocate here [in Fustat] and in Alexandria."[718] In Alexandria R. Daniel was seen as Maimonides' spokesman and rep-

715 Shailat, *Letters*, 447–448, §28, where the editor vowels *paqaḥim*, inspectors, but this should be read *piqeḥim*, intelligent men, referring here to the Islamic jurisprudents, the *fuqahā'*.
716 Ibid., 436–438.
717 Ibid., 438–445.
718 Ibid., 440, §28, ll. 6–8.

resentative, and Maimonides himself saw R. Daniel as his student and hoped to disseminate his magnum opus, *Mishneh Torah*, in the Alexandrian community with his help. As he relates to R. Pinḥas: "And if [R. Daniel] were to instruct you in the [intricacies of the] *Code* [= *Mishneh Torah*] – you would enlighten them [= the people of Alexandria] with it, and you would inform them of the general principles and the secrets therein. It is my hope that it be this way."[719]

R. Daniel's presence and activity in Alexandria was irksome to R. Pinḥas, who saw him as a rival. It seems that the strained relationship between the two was quite evident and well-known, since Maimonides speaks of it explicitly, when he refers to the "hatred between you and R. Daniel"[720] and "all the things that happened between you and R. Daniel."[721]

(b) The Case of the Nocturnal Emitter

As Maimonides' spokesman in Alexandria, R. Pinḥas drew to himself all the local resistance that Maimonides' rulings provoked. This opposition to Maimonides was expressed in a public protest against one of Maimonides' decisions: He allowed a nocturnal emitter to pray without bathing. This ruling went against local custom and was so vehemently opposed that a number of people threatened to go to the Muslim authorities and litigate the matter. R. Pinḥas attempted to use this opposition for personal gain in his struggle against R. Daniel. He positioned himself against Maimonides and R. Daniel and with the community. Thus, for example, he delivered a sermon against the ruling, and sent an angry epistle to Maimonides on the subject.[722] Maimonides astutely understood R. Pinḥas' hidden motives and rebuked him: "Love destroys order and so does hate, because of the hate between you and R. Daniel – you got angry, and were happy to join those who rose against him, and thus ignored the paths of justice."[723]

It is not unlikely that in addition to R. Pinḥas' short term motives, which Maimonides so ably discerned, other factors were at work, such as R. Pinḥas' great desire to integrate into the community and speak its language. The people of Alexandria coalesced with a great deal of fervor to safeguard the tradition that a nocturnal emitter must wash before praying, entering the synagogue, or reading from the Torah scroll. This tradition was unique to the Jewish communities in

719 Ibid., 440, ll. 8–10.
720 Ibid., 438, l. 6.
721 Ibid., 440, l. 6.
722 Ibid., 437.
723 Ibid., 438, ll. 5–7.

Muslim countries, one of their badges of identity, and distinguished them from the communities in Christian Europe. Maimonides himself states that in the Jewish communities in Christian Europe, this was not the practice:

> And this is only a tradition in the communities of Shinar and the West [= Spain and the Maghreb], but in all the cities of Rome and France and all the communities of Provincia [= Provence], the men of your cities, have never followed this tradition. And it frequently happens that great sages and rabbis from our cities to Spain, when they see us bathe after a nocturnal emission – they laugh at us and say: you learnt about cleanliness from the Ishmaelites.[724]

One must also note that it is not unlikely that this tradition, supported as it was by the early sages of the Land of Israel and practiced in Alexandria, was particularly important to members of the community, since Alexandria was a community that preserved ancient traditions of Palestinian origin.[725] R. Pinḥas' policy on this matter, whereby he made himself the central spokesman for the community defending this tradition, which was a distinct marker of identity for the community, may be seen as an attempt to divest himself of his "French" origins and to lead the community as one of its own.

5 Conclusion

It is difficult to know whether R. Pinḥas' attempt to integrate into the community was successful. On the one hand, when R. Pinḥas attempted to change the local prayer tradition, the community refused to accept his ruling, and even went over his head to Maimonides to ask about his proposals.[726] Moreover, we hear from Maimonides that members of the community harassed R. Pinḥas to such an extent that in desperation he attempted to leave and return to his homeland: "And I have heard that you wish to return to Romaniah [= Christian Europe] due to the anguish the people cause you."[727]

---

724 Ibid., 437, ll. 18–21.

725 On Alexandria as a preserver of ancient Palestinian custom, see Goitein, *Society*, 5: 157. The Talmudic discussion of the ritual purification of one who suffers from nocturnal emission is in the Babylonian Talmud,. Berākhōt 21b-22a, and see Daniel Boyarin, *Carnal Israel: Reading Sex in Talmudic Culture* (Berkeley: University of California Press, 1993).

726 Maimonides, *Responsa*, 505–507, §267; see also Mann, *Jews*, 2: 316.

727 Shailat, *Letters*, 440, l. 11. Romaniah here is a general name for Christian lands; see ibid., n. 23.

On the other hand, a copy of one his sermons translated into Arabic survives in the Genizah. The sermon, explicitly attributed to R. Pinḥas, focuses on the verse from the Song of Songs 4:12: "A garden locked is my own, my bride, a fountain locked, a sealed-up spring." And the attribution: "We heard this interpretation of the verse from the mouth of R. Pinḥas, may Heaven be his abode, when our young men [= the young men of Alexandria] would walk in the gardens and vineyards during the holidays."[728] It is evident that members of the community in Alexandria would transcribe the sermons they heard from R. Pinḥas, and afterwards they would translate them and copy them. They continued to copy and preserve his sermons even after his death, which we know since the copyist appended the blessing for the dead to R. Pinḥas' name. This may indicate that in the end the foreign judge was accepted and valued in the community which he had joined.

728 TS 13 J 19.7.

Chapter 11 Anatoly b. R. Joseph

1 Background and Origin

(a) Judge in Sicily

Anatoly b. Joseph arrived in Alexandria from one of the countries of Christian Europe. In a legal query addressed to Maimonides from 1199, right before his arrival in Alexandria, he asks:

> May our master be so gracious as to answer this question I was asked by the community of Siraqusta [= Syracuse] on the island of Siqillia [= Sicily] [...] And let your answer be expressed clearly, and I shall send it to them with the help of Heaven, since they do not know the Torah well enough to understand, unless it is written clearly."[729]

One may surmise (based on the excerpt above) that prior to coming to Alexandria, Anatoly did not live in Syracuse, on the eastern tip of Sicily, but was within travelling distance of it, since he had to send his answers there. His residence was probably close enough to Syracuse that Anatoly was familiar with the intellectual prowess of the inhabitants, but far enough away and disconnected enough from his experience that he related to the community in the third person in his epistle.[730] Confirmation of this hypothesis may be found in a collection of R. Anatoly's poems: The titles of the poems indicate that Anatoly lived in Palermo, except for a one-time journey to Messina. On the eve of his journey to Messina he dedicates a number of poems to his exodus from Palermo and to his return. One poem is prefaced in the following way: "R. Samuel al-Nafūsī sent these verses to R. Anatoly, may his memory be for a blessing, when he journeyed to Messina." Another poem is prefaced with the following: "And R. Samuel al-Nafūsī wrote to him when he arrived in Palermo."[731] Upon his return to Palermo,

---

729 Maimomides, *Letters*, 472, ll. 7–10. Regarding the dating, see ibid., 471.

730 R. Joseph Sambari counted R. Anatoly among the learned men of Lunel in Provence. See Adolf Neubauer, *Mediaeval Jewish Chronicles and Chronological Notes* (Oxford: Clarendon Press, 1887), 1: 133, but his report is full of mistakes and misunderstandings, and it is difficult to rely on it. Thus, for example, he mentions R. Joseph, Anatoly's father, as "R. Joseph ʿAmshi, not realizing that *ʿ.m.sh.y* is an acronym for *ʿal mishkavo yanuʾaḥ*, may he rest in peace. See Mann, *Jews*, 2: 325, n. 7. For a summary of the scholarly debate about his exact origin in Europe, see Mordechai A. Friedman, "Maimonides Appoints R. Anatoly *Muqaddam* of Alexandria," *Tarbiẓ* 83 (2015): 149, n. 57 [Hebrew].

731 Mann, *Texts*, 1: 412–413. *Al-Madīna*, "the city," is the conventional epithet for the city of Palermo. See, for example, Ben-Sasson, *Jews of Sicily*, nos. 8 a 55, 9 a 13, and many more. In con-

https://doi.org/10.1515/9783110713619-016

R. Elyakim also composed a number of verses on his behalf, prefaced in the following way: "Theses verses were sent by R. Elyakim to R. Anatoly when he came to Palermo."[732]

One may deduce from this that before coming to Alexandria, he served as a judge for all the communities of Sicily, whose members would send him their legal queries. His residence was, as far as may be ascertained, in Palermo, the capital of Sicily, on the western shores of the island.

(b) Arrival in Alexandria

R. Anatoly arrived in Alexandria very shortly after sending the legal queries from Sicily. If these letters were indeed written when he was still in Sicily, in 1199, or perhaps a little before that – as we surmise – then Anatoly arrived in the same year, and began to serve the community in Alexandria in legal matters after a short while. A bill of consent from 1199 written in Alexandria already bears his signature as a witness.[733] In another document from 1201, also from Alexandria, he appears as a signatory attesting to the document's validity.[734] Indeed, according to Anatoly, he was appointed as an official and full-time judge in Alexandria immediately upon his arrival.[735] In any event, while Maimonides still

trast, Alexandria was never called *al-madīna*; its medieval epithet is *al-thaghr*, "the port city." Therefore, Mann's hypothesis (ibid.), that the poem as composed in honor of R. Anatoly's arrival in Alexandria, is groundless.

732 Mann, *Texts*, 1: 413.

733 Abraham Maimuni, *Responsa*, 161–167, §102, esp. 161–162, 164–165, 167. Friedman claims that Anatoly sent the queries to Maimonides, accompanied by a very elaborate personal epistle in which he sought Maimonides' protection, when he was already in Alexandria, but it seems more plausible to assume that the epistle was intended to pave Anatoly's way for migration to Egypt. Indeed, Anatoly apologizes for sending an epistle and not coming to meet Maimonides personally, saying that "the elders in my place prevented me from doing so," which can only be understood to be the notables of Palermo, where he served in the crucial position of judge, and could not permit himself to leave his people.

734 TS 16.126. This is a bill of sale of a house in Alexandria.

735 Abraham Maimuni, *Responsa*, 169, §103. This is Anatoly's response to R. Abraham's ruling given above in §102. The matter concerns a group of guardians put in charge of an orphaned boy already in 1191, but who brought the certificate of guardianship to be approved only eight years later, in 1199. The confession confirming the guardianship was signed by Anatoly as a witness. A few years later, when the child reached his majority and wished to take control of his money, the guardians gave back the remainder of the money after deducting their expenses for the orphan since 1191, but Anatoly demanded that they deduct those expenses only from 1199, the year that the certificate of guardianship was formally approved in court. Since Anatoly was a witness to

lived, in other words before 1205, he was already referred to as *Beit dīn* (the court). It was during these first years in Alexandria that Anatoly married, probably into a local family. This was a typical strategy of immigrants, pursued also by Maimonides upon his arrival to Egypt, aspiring to integrate with local elite families.[736]

2 An Intellectual Portrait

When Anatoly arrived in Alexandria he was already a renowned judge, and his reputation as a scholarly polymath preceded him. In a rhymed epistle that Maimonides composed in his honor upon his arrival in Egypt, he heaps praises upon him:

> A great lord in Israel, a man "who performed great deeds, from Kabzeel" [2 Sam. 23:20], nurtured in the tents of the wise, he has shunned all evil conduct, he is mighty among sages, and is unerring in his battles for the sake of Torah [...] And when upon the path of judges he trod, and arrayed himself with his knowledge of Talmud – may your blessing be his [...] R. Anatoly, may the Rock protect him, the judicial adept, the brilliant instructor of law, a shining light to all who understand, beloved of sages, preeminent among officials [...] You are a wise man, and have acquired voluminous knowledge of Talmud, and have gained subtlety in the Hebrew language, and are gifted with eloquent speech.[737]

R. Anatoly was also known as a poet. We noted above that he actively composed and exchanged verses with his associates.[738] The collection of his poems, under the title *Dīwān Anatoly*, is included in a list of books from the beginning of the thirteenth century, indicating that it was not unpopular even while he lived.[739] Moreover, his literary compositions passed the test of time and are considered

---

the confession bill, he could not serve as judge in this case. To this Anatoly responded that already in the year that he signed the confession as a witness, he was serving as a permanent judge: "and I wonder at those who say, 'we have become witnesses.' How shall we have become witnesses when we are permanent [judges]?"

736 Abraham Maimuni, *Responsa*, 151, §196: "and the court—that is, our rabbi Anatoly the wise and wonderful—found him guilty." Anatoly's marriage is mentioned in TS 20.133v, a letter from Abraham b. Eleazar to Moses ha-Kohen Ibn Ghulayb written between 1195–1200. Friedman, "Maimonides Appoints," 141–142.

737 Maimonides, *Letters*, §31, 468, l. 19–469, l. 2; 470, ll. 1–2, 6–8.

738 See above, Part II, Chapter 11.1 (a): Judge in Sicily.

739 Allony, *Jewish Library*, list 98, l. 67. On Anatoli's poetry, see: Samuel M. Stern, "A Twelfth-Century Circle of Hebrew Poets in Sicily," *Journal of Jewish Studies* 5 (1954): 60–79, 110–113; Schirmann, *Hebrew Poetry in Spain and Provence*, 440–452; Elisheva Hacohen, "The Poetry of R. Anatoly Bar Joseph," M.A. thesis (The Hebrew University of Jerusalem, 1996) [Hebrew].

to be part of the medieval Jewish bookshelf. A Firkovitch manuscript includes poems and epistles written by him, with prefaces indicating that he had passed away (*z"l* – of blessed memory),[740] alongside other liturgical poems with prefaces which refer to him with the blessing for the dead.[741] This indicates that Anatoly's literary compositions were copied and still of interest even after the author's death. In a list of books from the thirteenth century, a composition in Anatoly's handwriting is mentioned, evidence that he, like many intellectuals of his generation engaged in copying books.[742]

3 Judge in Alexandria

(a) Centralization

R. Anatoly's tenure as judge was characterized by greater centralization than his predecessors. In a letter that Joseph (Yehosef) b. Samuel ha-Bavli sent him, the author refuses under any circumstances to release a deposit in his possession, since the receipt that was given to him was not signed by R. Anatoly the Judge:

> I have come to inform you in short with all the confidence and goodwill of your grace, that I have put my trust in your honor, and when I see your signature upon the line I will hand over what I have in my possession to the owner of the deposit. For R. Abraham ha-Kohen ha-Ma'aravi came to me with a receipt and your signature was not upon it, and as I indicated previously when I see the signature of our master, I will hand over the object to whomever he commands. And until I see it explicitly validated, despite the importance of the messenger in my eyes, I must adhere to what is proper.[743]

In a letter from 1216, Judah the Teacher Ibn al-ʿAmmānī complains quite explicitly about Anatoly's tendency to centralize: "But he sits on the bench, and the court always meets at his house. He does not rule decisively and takes it hard when things in the city are done without consulting him."[744]

---

740 Mann, *Texts*, 1: 412–413.
741 Mann, *Jews*, 2: 326.
742 Bodl Ms Heb d 76, fol. 5: Mann, *Jews*, 2:326.
743 Mann, *Jews*, 2: 325, ll. 8–16.
744 TS 10 J 25.3r, ll. 15–17: Frenkel, *"The Compassionate and Benevolent"* [Hebrew], no. 57.

(b) A Different Interpretation of Law

As a judge Anatoly enacted a new and stricter interpretation of the law than was previously the norm in Alexandria. He implemented his new policy highhandedly, confident that his way was better and preferable to the local custom. The court was dumbfounded when he compelled a widow, who was attempting to secure her dowry, to swear that she had ritually immersed after her menstrual cycle as is prescribed. When she refused, "the judge did not want to sign over the money to support her orphans until she agreed to take the oath. The people standing there said to him that this had never been heard of, nor had it been previously enacted in Alexandria […] The judge answered that he wanted her to fear so that she would not transgress the law […] he said that the women of Egypt are suspect regarding this issue."[745]

(c) Communal Activities

R. Anatoly dealt with routine legal matters such as signing documents, mediating settlements, and hearing cases.[746] He also undertook the transcription of proceedings on behalf of the court and was paid for the composition of documents. Judah Ibn al-ʿAmmānī describes in his letter how Anatoly argued with his uncle, the cantor Ṣadoq Ibn al-ʿAmmānī, and demanded payment for the transcriptions of documents that he had made. "I cannot adequately describe what happened between him [= Anatoly] and my uncle [= Ṣadoq Ibn al-ʿAmmānī, the Cantor]. There was a big 'meeting' (*moshav*) at his house, and the judge demanded from my uncle his part of [the payment for] the transcription of documents, and they argued with one another."[747]

It is quite likely that R. Anatoly also ruled on legal questions, and responded to queries. We know that he did this when he was judge in Sicily.[748] A truncated opening of a legal query addressed to him has survived in the Genizah: "What says our precious eminence, our crown, the honored teacher and master Anatoly the Judge, the great and impregnable fortress, the bright light, the shining star,

745 Abraham Maimuni, *Responsa*, 648, § 371. The laws of ritual purity were a central bone of contention between European immigrants and local Jews in the thirteenth century, see Cuffel, "Call and Response," 78–80.

746 See above, Part II, Chapter 11.1 (b): Arrival in Alexandria.

747 TS 10 J 25.3r, ll. 17–18: Frenkel, *"The Compassionate and Benevolent"* [Hebrew], no. 57.

748 See above, Part II, Chapter 11.1 (a): Judge in Sicily.

may his God preserve him, and may his splendor be magnified and he rise in stature, amen [...] regarding the case of Simeon and his bill."[749]

It is impossible to know for certain whether this query was sent to him while in Alexandria, or whether its origins are from his days as a judge in Sicily.[750] If, indeed, he was accustomed to answering legal questions while he was in Egypt, a number of questions arise: How was he able to serve as a legal authority when he was in such close proximity to the luminaries of the age, Maimonides, and afterwards his son Abraham? Why did people turn to him and not to the greatest legal minds of the generation? If he did issue rulings, did he rule independently, or inquire with them? All these questions, as interesting as they may be, cannot be answered at this time.

4 Community Leader

Anatoly's activities encompassed more than just presiding over the local court. He acted as the leader of the community both internally and vis-à-vis other communities.

(a) Charitable Work

Anatoly was involved in public charity and in fundraising. In 1208 he signed a letter of reference on behalf of a man from Sicily who went blind following an operation on his eyes in Alexandria and who sought financial aid.[751] He raised funds for other communities as well. Thus, for example, R. Menahem urged him to send the donation that the Alexandrian community had promised in order to fix the roof of a synagogue in another town which had collapsed:

> Many letters have arrived from Elijah and his associates, and they complain about the delay in the arrival of the donation promised by the community of our master, for the refuge they

749 TS NS J 32.

750 The language of the query being Arabic is of no help here, since at this time the Jews of Sicily spoke and wrote in Arabic.

751 TS 16.267, l. 32: *wa-fī al-kitāb khaṭṭ al-dayyān*, "and on the letter is the judge's signature." See Eliyahu Ashtor, *The History of the Jews in Egypt and Syria under Mamluk Rule* (Jerusalem: Mossad Harav Kook, 1944–1951), 3: 101–105 [Hebrew].

had in the synagogue is lost to them, and all mourn for it, and the synagogue is left without a roof, and they fear the rain.[752]

(b) The Struggle over His Position

Anatoly's position as the community leader was not a foregone conclusion. His foreign origins and his attempt to accrue more authority led to resistance, and he had to wage a difficult campaign to protect his position.

The very nomination of a foreign immigrant for *muqaddam* encountered fierce opposition from the very beginning. In 1199, upon Anatoly's arrival in Alexandria, when the first rumors about Maimonides' intention to nominate him as the *muqaddam* of Alexandria probably started to spread, a group of local "rebels" (*al-mordīn*) wrote an ordinance according to which there would be no *muqaddam* in Alexandria who was not a native Egyptian. They sent it to Maimonides and demanded that he appoint to the position either R. Isaac b. Sasson the *ḥasīd* or R. Samuel b. Saʿadyah ha-Maskīl, both native Alexandrians.[753] This initiative did not succeed , and Anatoly was eventually nominated as *muqaddam* by Maimonides, but opposition to his rule continued.

Anatoly's primary rival in Alexandria was the cantor Ṣadoq Ibn al-ʿAmmānī, a scion of the powerful and entrenched al-ʿAmmānī family.[754] People of that period saw this rivalry as a financial matter,[755] but it almost certainly reflected a deeper struggle – between the old elite and the new immigrants who replaced them at the head of the community and brought with them a new style of adjudication and leadership.

Ṣadoq managed to acquire an edict signed by some of the community elders, which certified the appointment of his son Mufaḍḍal as judge. This appointment led to an uproar in the community. According to Judah Ibn a-ʿAmmānī, who relates to this imbroglio in a letter, most of the community preferred to be led by an older person rather than a young man with little experience: "And the majority of the community thought that it would be better if an elder led them rather than a youth."[756] And elsewhere: "...has served the community up until now. His

752 TS 13 J 9.9: Mann, Jews, 2: 324, ll. 5–12. A letter from R. Menahem is mentioned also in Judah Ibn al-ʿAmmānī to R. Abraham Maimuni, TS 16.305v, ll. 37–42: Frenkel, *"The Compassionate and Benevolent"* [Hebrew], no. 32.

753 ENA2744.2+ENA2740.4, published by Friedman, "Maimonides Appoints," 156–161.

754 On this family and its status, see Part II, Chapter 5 and Chapter 14.

755 See above, Part II, Chapter 11.3 (c): Communal Activities.

756 TS 10 J 25.3r, ll. 19–20: Frenkel, *"The Compassionate and Benevolent"* [Hebrew], no. 57.

beard has not come in and he has not married. It would have been better had [...] and the majority of the community think that only an older person should lead them."[757]

Additional complaints and accusations against Anatoly were made during the years he served as the *muqaddam* of Alexandria. In one letter he is accused of not paying for books he had ordered to be copied and bound for him, in another he is blamed for informing on someone to the Muslim authority (*masrūt*) and is described as a furious and impatient person. In yet another letter, he is portrayed as a tough man.[758]

It is apparent that Anatoly himself did not rest on his laurels and was very active in promoting himself and his position within the community. One of his tactics, among others, was the violent removal of any potential rival. In a long and detailed letter, Judah the Teacher Ibn al-ʿAmmānī relates the woeful tale of Joseph al-Baghdādī, a sage who was banished from Alexandria in shame and destitution since Anatoly considered him to be a threat to his position:

> Allow me to tell my brother about an unfortunate incident that took place here in Alexandria. It relates to what happened a little while ago to R. Joseph al-Baghdādī. "Deeds that ought not to be done" [Genesis 20:9] were done to him, may the Lord repay those responsible in kind. Such things that had never been heard of in Alexandria, and had never happened here before [took place]. "No such deed has been done or seen" [Judges 19:30]. And the root of all the troubles was that Anatoly, that judge, could not under any circumstances countenance a[nother] scholar in his vicinity. He did not cease in spurning him. Not once, not twice, not thrice, he never stopped.[759]

In this letter Judah Ibn al-ʿAmmānī tells the sordid tale of harassment in which the Muslim authorities were "informed," and in which larceny and bribery were employed by Anatoly in order to eliminate his rival. Anatoly was not alone in this, but had the help of "elders who loved the judge" as allies.[760] All of this indicates a power struggle within the community, in which Anatoly was able to enlist members of the community to support him and to act on his behalf.

---

757 Ibid., v, ll. 10–11.

758 Not paying for a purchase of books: BL Or, 5542.32; informing: Mosseri V.339; tough: TS NS J 380. After Friedman, "Maimonides Appoints," 155, n. 80.

759 TS 24.67r, ll. 49–56: Frenkel, *"The Compassionate and Benevolent"* [Hebrew], no. 40. It is possible that this Joseph al-Baghdādī is Joseph (Yehosef) b. Samuel ha-Bavli, whose letter to R. Anatoly is mentioned above.

760 TS 24.67v, l. 12: Frenkel, *"The Compassionate and Benevolent"* [Hebrew], no. 40.

5 Conclusion

In the end, how successful was Anatoly in his quest to consolidate the leadership in his hands and act as the only legitimate ruler of the community? One may gain some insight into this in a letter that was written shortly after his death. Barakāt, a man of Alexandria, writes to Elijah b. Zechariah in Fustat: "Anatoly passed away on Wednesday the 15th of Av, and the city was bereft, and there was no one to manage its affairs."[761]

It is interesting that such a feeling of helplessness and loss took hold of the community despite the fact that Anatoly made sure that a successor was in place before his death. In the same letter Barakāt elaborates upon the choice of R. Samuel as leader, who "had been active as a legal authority in the community for the past three years."[762] It is difficult to assume that Anatoly, who eliminated any threat to his leadership so successfully, would let anyone manage the affairs of the community, if he had not approved of him. Anatoly chose Samuel, another *Rūmī* (i.e., European) immigrant like himself. Not only was he successful in his quest to consolidate the leadership in his hands and to manage the affairs of the community high-handedly, he was also able to have a measure of influence upon the character of the community's leadership in subsequent generations.

761 TS 18 J 3.15r, ll. 20–21: Frenkel, *"The Compassionate and Benevolent"* [Hebrew], no. 83. According to Friedman, the year of his demise as mentioned here is 1221, but he does not explain why the year 1228 suggested by Goitein (*Society*, 2: 71) is not correct. Later on in his article he admits, however, that Anatoly "apparently died in 1221, or later." (Friedman, "Maimonides Appoints," 139, n. 9, 152, n. 70.)
762 TS 18 J 3.15r, l. 31.

Chapter 12 R. Samuel b. Jacob

1 Acclimatization

Samuel b. Jacob was an immigrant from Christian Europe, probably from Marseille.[763] In 1214 he was already living in Alexandria, which we know from a letter of reference written by Judah Ibn al-ʿAmmānī on his behalf, in which he attempts to help him with his financial troubles and obtain money for him from the community in Fustat.[764] One may surmise that it was around this time that he had arrived in Egypt, since Judah explained in his letter that Samuel b. Jacob could not support himself since he knew no Arabic at all: "Any help that the community may grant, will not be forgotten before God. He does not know how to speak Arabic, and how will he survive at all?"[765]

When Samuel arrived in Alexandria he was already recognized as a legal and religious authority, and Judah Ibn al-ʿAmmānī refers to him as "my teacher and master."[766] Thus it comes as no surprise that in 1220 his signature appears on a document from Alexandria, together with R. Anatoly, Berākhōt b. Ḥalfon, and Ratzon b. Fityān.[767] One may thus surmise that in the course of those six years Samuel had successfully integrated into the community's judiciary. It was noted above that R. Anatoly handpicked him as his successor, and indeed he served the community with a great deal of distinction in R. Anatoly's final

---

763 Mordechai A. Friedman, "The Nagid, the Nasi and the French Rabbis: A Threat to Abraham Maimonides' Leadership," *Zion* 92 (2017): 230, n. 210.

764 TS 13 J 27.11v, ll. 18–19: Goitein, *Jewish Education*, 102; Frenkel, *"The Compassionate and Benevolent"* [Hebrew], no. 79.

765 Ibid., ll. 18–20. Goitein's interpretation of these lines differs from mine, and therefore his translation is different: "And any help [or: salary] that he will receive from the community will not harm you, since in any case he does not know to speak Arabic, so how can he succeed [in leading the community]?" In contrast to Goitein's interpretation, I do not believe that at this stage, R. Samuel could have been any kind of threat to Meir b. Yakhin, the person to whom the request for help was addressed, especially given that Meir lived in Fustat while R. Samuel was in Alexandria. The expression *mā yuḍīʿ* is an abbreviation for *mā yūḍīʿ laka bayna yaday Allāh*, "it will not be lacking for you before God," that usually accompanies requests for donations to the needy, and it is very common in letters by Judah Ibn al-ʿAmmānī the Teacher; see, e.g., TS 16.287, l. 30 (Ashtor, *History of the Jews*, 3: 101–105) – a letter by Judah Ibn al-ʿAmmānī asking for donations for a blind immigrant in Alexandria.

766 TS 13 J 27.11v, l. 17.

767 TS 12.698: Frenkel, *"The Compassionate and Benevolent"* [Hebrew], no. 26.

https://doi.org/10.1515/9783110713619-017

years.[768] A letter from 1227 to the judge of Fustat, towards the end of R. Anatoly's life, is indicative of the scope of his judicial activities before his appointment as the official *muqaddam* of Alexandria. The letter deals with a difficult case of a convert whose husband had abandoned her. R. Samuel offers his opinion in this case, with its legal and social ramifications, and wields his eminence in order to convince the judge that her cause is just. Despite his sickness at the time, he was apparently quite active in his pursuit of this case: After deliberating with both sides, he formulates a clear position and a plan to execute it:

> And I, in my sickness, at death's very door, I, Samuel b. Jacob of blessed memory, prostrate myself before you, and beg that you not make common cause with the criminals. Do not let her husband do as he wishes, for his evil mother suborned him to act in this way, for he had no desire to leave his daughters and his wife. The snake tempted him against his better judgement and this is what he said to me: It is better that he goes [...] so that they do not say: "We have descended from greater holiness to lesser holiness." And only God knows the suspicions I harbor against the mother and the son. Peace.[769]

Though the letter is written in Hebrew, it is clear that R. Samuel already spoke and understood Arabic. When people wished to have him appointed as the *muqaddam* after Anatoly's death, there were those who objected to the appointment on the grounds that one could not appoint foreigners to the position. After examining the edict closely, however, it was apparent that this caveat specifically prohibited those who did not speak Arabic and required a translator. Since R. Samuel already spoke and understood Arabic, he was deemed qualified for the position: "The elders said, this R. Samuel speaks Arabic fluently and when he presides over the court he does not require a translator."[770]

R. Samuel spent fourteen years in Alexandria before his appointment as the city's *muqaddam*. In these years he managed to integrate himself successfully in the community, to learn the language and to become a prominent judicial and religious authority, serving the community actively.

---

768 See above, Part II, Chapter 11.5: Conclusion. TS 18 J 3.15, l. 31: Frenkel, "*The Compassionate and Benevolent*" [Hebrew], no. 83.

769 TS 12.575v, margins, ll. 1–23, 210: Friedman, *Jewish Polygyny*, 210.

770 TS 18 J 3.15r, ll. 26–27: Frenkel, "*The Compassionate and Benevolent*" [Hebrew], no. 83.

2 The Appointment Affair: A Rearguard Battle against the European Immigrants

The opposition to R. Samuel's appointment as the *muqaddam* of Alexandria was based on his foreignness. The locals attempted to prevent the immigrants from Europe, who were arriving in Egypt in great numbers at that time, from insinuating themselves into leadership positions.[771] The edict by which the opposition wished to prevent the appointment of R. Samuel was understood as an explicit prohibition against appointing anyone from Europe to the position of *muqaddam:* "There were those among them who said: We have an edict that forbids the appointment of a leader of *Ifranjī* [=Byzantine or French] origin."[772] Their ultimate goal seems to have been exactly this.

The opposition to R. Samuel's appointment and to the infiltration of European immigrants to the ranks of leadership was almost certainly a lot broader and deeper than is initially apparent. One notes the repeated emphasis by the authors of the abovementioned epistle regarding the unanimity of the decision. Their claim that no one objected to it and that all members of the community were satisfied is evidence that there was an attempt to present a united front of validation so as to marginalize dissenting voices. Thus the writer highlights time after time: "All the elders united together to appoint R. Samuel as the leader";[773] "and all agreed that this edict should be annulled";[774] "and all the elders of the community from the greatest one among them to the least of them wrote in it [=in the new edict that was composed following the appointment of R. Samuel] that they were satisfied with his appointment as *muqaddam.*"[775] If there was no objection to the appointment, there would have been no reason to repeatedly allude to the unanimity of the decision.

The author's request to receive official recognition for the appointment from the Nagid indicates that there was need to ensure the latter's approval in an official and authoritative document, so as to overcome those who objected to the appointment: "I request from his grace, that when he goes up [to Fustat] that he take with him letters from us regarding R. Samuel so as to support us, for they

---

771 See Joshua Prawer, "Chapters in the History of the Jewish Community in the Latin Kingdom of Jerusalem," *Shalem* 2 (1971): 103–112 [Hebrew]; Benjamin Z. Kedar, "The Jewish Community of Jerusalem in the Thirteenth Century," *Tarbiẓ* 41 (1971): 82–94 [Hebrew]; Goitein, *Palestinian Jewry*, 338–343; Chazan, *Medieval Jewry in Northern France*, 86–87.

772 TS 18 J 3.15v, ll. 22–23: Frenkel, *"The Compassionate and Benevolent"* [Hebrew], no. 83.

773 TS 18 J 3.15r, ll. 21–22.

774 Ibid., ll. 27–28.

775 Ibid., l. 30.

[...] do nothing without the approval of the lord, the great minister, and most elevated prince."[776]

The great wave of immigration from Europe to Alexandria at that time significantly altered the social fabric of the community, and especially the ranks of its leaders. This aborted attempt to prevent R. Samuel's appointment as *muqaddam* was an attempt to halt the demographic and social changes that were taking place in Alexandria at that time.

3 "The Beloved Judge"

In the end, R. Samuel was appointed as the *muqaddam* of Alexandria and was recognized as such by the entire community. Members of the community would refers to him in their missives as "Our Lord the Beloved Judge, our R. Samuel."[777] And later, at a time of grave crisis in the community due to hunger and a lack of food, people wished for the return of R. Samuel, who was absent from the community at that stage, so that "greatness could return."[778]

R. Samuel's position was based upon his close association with the Nagid Abraham Maimuni, Maimonides' son. Members of the community would request his intercession in order to secure the Nagid's involvement when they encountered difficulties. In one of the missives addressed to him, R. Samuel is requested to involve the Nagid in the difficult case of an abandoned wife. And indeed, attached to the original missive one finds R. Samuel's request that the Nagid intercede.[779]

These close relations deteriorated significantly when R. Samuel took the lead in the struggle to annul the ban declared by the *Nasi* Hodayah b. Jesse,[780] on whoever helped or cooperated with a European (*Rūmī* or *Ifranjī*) immigrant. R. Samuel sought the assistance of the Nagid Abraham Maimuni and was deeply

---

776 Ibid., ll. 32–35.

777 TS NS 320.20: Friedman, *Jewish Polygyny*, 213–216. Friedman believes that the reference is to the fourteenth-century R. Samuel ha-Kohen the Judge, who was active in the period of the Nagid Joshua b. Abraham Maimuni (1310–1355), but in my opinion we may safely assume that this is our R. Samuel, especially given that he is called *sayyidnā al-dayyān al-jalīl* in other documents, such as TS 10 J 16.6r, margins, l. 3 (Frenkel, *"The Compassionate and Benevolent"* [Hebrew], no. 54). Friedman (ibid.) reads *al-g[ado]l* but the reading *al-jalīl* is quite clear.

778 TS 10 J 16.6r, margins, ll. 3–4: Frenkel, *"The Compassionate and Benevolent"* [Hebrew], no. 54.

779 TS NS 320.20: Friedman, *Jewish Polygyny*, 214–216.

780 See about him: Arnold E. Franklin, *This Noble House*, 198–199, no. 53; Gil, *Kingdom*, 442–443.

disappointed when he did not receive it. It seems that R. Abraham preferred to leave the decision to the people of Alexandria themselves and refused to use his authority in order to cancel the ban. The Nagid's policy aroused R. Samuel's anger which he expressed in several impudent letters against the Nagid, and against the people who opposed the ban's annulment. These letters aroused R. Abraham Maimuni's anger in turn, and there were rumors that he reacted by declaring a ban on R. Samuel and his followers and on whoever appointed a foreigner as *muqaddam*. As suggested by Friedman, it is doubtful whether the Nagid actually declared such bans and the information spread about it should rather be understood as part of the propaganda used by R. Samuel's supporters during this dispute. One of R. Samuel's main opponents was R. Elijah b. Zechariah, who was not only very active in the struggle to keep the ban, but also strove to replace R. Samuel as chief judge of Alexandria.[781]

In spite of the rivalries and the stormy disputes that R. Samuel was involved in, his active and self-confident policies reflect a deep degree of integration into the Jewish society of Egypt. The struggle he conducted against the ban on foreigners during which he confronted the *Nagid* himself without hesitation, was daring and even presumptuous. Despite his strong opponents, he succeeded in consolidating around him devoted supporters who assisted him and fought for him. Elijah b. Zechariah's attempt to replace him eventually failed, and R. Samuel remained in his position till his death.

In the letter apprising people of his death, the author employs formulaic expressions of grief common in eulogies of leaders, with no reservations regarding his appointment: "I wish to inform you that when R. Samuel of blessed memory passed away, the community grieved over him [...] and with regard to the community, it is deteriorating into oblivion and the reason for this is that there is no one to manage its affairs."[782] It is precisely this fairly routine expression of grief said habitually over almost any leader who passes away, that may serve as a good indication of R. Samuel's successful integration into the community.

---

781 These disputes and events were minutely described by Friedman upon discovering new Genizah documents from this period, which shed new light on the politics and power relations during the last years of R. Abraham Maimuni's Nagidate. See Friedman, "The Nasi."

782 TS 13 J 21.30r, ll. 6–7, 9–10: Frenkel, *"The Compassionate and Benevolent"* [Hebrew], no. 72.

4 Conclusion

In the documents at our disposal R. Samuel comes across as a success story. He arrived in Alexandria as a destitute immigrant in need of support, but by the end of his life he had transformed himself into a community leader, upon whom the community depended for good management. His power and authority was based upon on his reputation as a legal scholar and upon his energetic activity on behalf of the community, and especially on behalf of the growing segment of European immigrants within it. In the first years he depended upon the support of the Nagid, but when he refused to back him in his fight for the cause of the new comers, R. Samuel did not hesitate to turn against him and confront him openly.

R. Samuel arrived in Alexandria at a time of growing tension between local Jews and new immigrants from Europe, but when the demographic changes caused by these massive waves of migration were already an unchangeable reality. The fierce struggle waged against the newcomers during his rule was, among other reasons, a response to these changes, a rearguard battle taken against the new social circumstances. The stout and determined fight he conducted for the sake of the immigrants from a position of leadership reflects, to a great extent, the new social fabric and new constellation of power created in Egypt following the ongoing process of incorporation of the European immigrants into the community.

Chapter 13 Isaac the Judge b. Ḥalfon

1 Origin and Background

Isaac b. Ḥalfon was the scion of an old Alexandrian family of local dignitaries. His father, who held the title of *sar* (lord), probably served as an official in the Sultan's court. Isaac was well-educated in Jewish sources, and R. Abraham Maimuni the Nagid refers to him as the "esteemed master" and praises his knowledge and his understanding of the law: "What the great judge and esteemed master R. Isaac ruled [...] he ruled justly in this matter [...] and this demonstrates the breadth of his wisdom and the veracity of his learning."[783]

2 Events Leading up to his Appointment

Isaac b. Ḥalfon served as a judge while his predecessor R. Samuel was still alive and there was overlap in their tenures. At a time of great crisis in the community, when there was a famine and a serious lack of food in the city, R. Samuel was actually absent from Alexandria and R. Isaac served in his place. The overseer in charge of the distribution of bread, in his report of the crisis states that the actions of the "fellow" (*ḥaver*), who gave out bread in secret, were done without the knowledge of "the Judge our master Isaac, may his Rock preserve him," and contrary to his explicit instructions,[784] which indicates that R. Isaac was serving in R. Samuel's place. Isaac did not serve with any particular distinction at this juncture. His instructions were not heeded and he did not succeed in preventing the fracas that the overseer refers to. His ineptitude is so apparent, that the author of the letter is explicit in his hope that R. Samuel will return expeditiously to bring back order and calm.[785]

Indeed, when R. Samuel died, the elders of the community did not consider R. Isaac the Judge for the position. The letter from Alexandria announcing R. Samuel's death reflects great consternation and general helplessness as they contended with his death. The elders offered the leadership to a number of unlikely candidates. Abū ʿAlī b. Ḥanikh was suggested, for example, though it was evident that he was an eminently unsuitable candidate for the position. Immediately, an alternative proposal was floated: to appoint Elijah b. Zechariah, who was a

783 Abraham Maimuni, *Responsa*, 187, §106.
784 TS 10 J 16.6r, ll. 4, 15: Frenkel, *"The Compassionate and Benevolent"* [Hebrew], no. 54.
785 Ibid., margins, l. 4.

https://doi.org/10.1515/9783110713619-018

judge in Fustat at that time, to serve jointly with Abū ʿAlī. According to this complicated compromise, Elijah would be the named judge in Alexandria, serve in this capacity, and be paid a full salary: "He would be a partner both in title and in practice and all the salary shall be Elijah's."[786] The straw candidate Abū ʿAlī b. Ḥanikh accepted the proposal with alacrity and offered a further concession: "He who is entitled shall serve as judge, and I shall serve as his deputy."[787]

In the end, these proposals were not implemented and R. Isaac b. Ḥalfon was seen as the most fitting successor to lead the community in lieu of R. Samuel. The great consternation and drifting that preceded his appointment leave the impression that his appointment was more of a default measure than any indication that he was qualified. Had there been any other appropriate figure, it is almost certain that the elders of the community would have preferred him over R. Isaac.

3 Leadership with no Authority

Isaac b. Ḥalfon served as the official judge, the *muqaddam* of the community, and the head of a seminary (*Beit midrash*) that he supported in Alexandria. His leadership, however, continued to be overshadowed by a lack of authoritativeness. Most of his activities were tinged by the constant suspicion that the people would not listen to him and would not follow his instructions. The case of Sitt al-Nasab illustrates this pattern most explicitly:

Sitt al-Nasab was married to Surūr b. Sālim. Shortly after her husband divorced her, he had second thoughts and wished to marry her a second time. This complicated case came before Isaac b. Ḥalfon's court, and Isaac explicitly forbade Surūr to remarry his ex-wife. In order to ensure that his instructions were followed, he declared that anyone who officiated at their marriage ceremony would be summarily excommunicated, and he instituted a general penalty of excommunication upon anyone who performed a marriage without approval

786 TS 13 J 21.30r, ll. 17–18: Joseph Braslawsky, "Genizah Fragments from the 11th-13th centuries concerning Rabbath ʿAmmōn and Māʿān," *Eretz-Yisrael 3: Cassuto Book* (Jerusalem: Israel Exploration Society, 1954), 208 [Hebrew]; Frenkel, *"The Compassionate and Benevolent"* [Hebrew], no. 72.

787 TS 13 J 21.30r, l. 14. Braslawsky (ibid.) for some reason translates the word *ghulām* as butcher or purger. On Elijah's deep involvement in the dispute around the ban declared by the *Nasi* Hodayah on the new immigrants and on his attempts to undermine R. Samuel's position in Alexandria and replace him, see Friedman, "The Nagid," 230–242.

from the *muqaddam*. This policy was put in place because the aforementioned judge "feared that someone would officiate at their marriage without his knowledge," according to a question sent to R. Abraham Maimuni.[788] His fear was well-founded since "sometime afterwards it became known that the young woman remarried without the court's knowledge, and that a marriage contract was composed on her behalf."[789] Moreover, the excommunication seems to have had little effect, and the members of the community seem to have ignored it. This is evident from R. Abraham's great consternation at the rash behavior of the community, as seen in the following letter:

And when we had heard that this had occurred [=that members of the community had ignored the excommunication order] we were greatly chagrined, and afterwards they told us that it never happened. And in our eyes it is more likely that the second rumor is true, for the *hoi polloi* would not dare to do this, and a sage who is accustomed to considering matters would never be vulgar enough to do this.[790]

One should not take R. Abraham Maimuni's statement that this refusal to follow R. Isaac's edict was a baseless rumor at face value. His apparent refusal to believe was merely a rhetorical device to express the depth of his consternation at this behavior, which he considered should never have come to pass. The reference to the sages in Alexandria who "would never have been vulgar enough to do this," is actually a sophisticated didactic mechanism intended to point an accusatory finger toward those who, in his eyes, bore the greatest responsibility for disobeying the excommunication injunction, and to scold them.

R. Isaac b. Ḥalfon ran a seminary in Alexandria. A letter from that time, of which only the address survives, lists "the seminary of our master Isaac, may the Merciful One preserve him" as the intended recipient.[791] This being said, even his own students did not hesitate to challenge his rulings. Indeed, this is what occurred after he called for the aforementioned excommunication: Isaac was asked to convene a special panel that would look into the case of Sitt al-Nasab's marriage one more time. The entire panel was composed of R. Isaac's so called "pupils" – most likely students of his seminary – but they did not confirm their teacher's ruling and disagreed amongst themselves. A number of them even offered their own ruling which was diametrically opposed:

788 Abraham Maimuni, *Responsa*, 182, §106.
789 Ibid., 184.
790 Ibid., 191.
791 ENA 2727.11: Frenkel, *"The Compassionate and Benevolent"* [Hebrew], no. 8.

> Afterwards they urged the aforementioned judge to convene a panel that would look into this matter once again. And they convened the panel and a group of pupils gathered together and looked into it. And some of them said: "The first *get* [divorce bill] is valid and even if he once again had relations with her" [...] and the panel adjourned and they still disagreed amongst themselves.[792]

R. Abraham Maimuni castigated the students for the way they conducted themselves in this matter:

> There is no fault when there is disagreement amongst jurists with regard to difficult case, especially when there are beginners among them who are not yet known for their wisdom. One should, however, excoriate any rivalry [in these matters], or pursuit of anything but the truth [...] abandoning religious norms which then leads to a correlation between legal rumination and the insolence of those of little knowledge directed at those who are greater than them, and from those who bear no official religious position vis-à-vis those who are officially responsible for religious matters.[793]

And regarding a question these same students posed:

> And we do not denounce you regarding the question that you were discussing or the disagreement and dialogue amongst yourselves. What we do denounce on logical and religious grounds – is the impudence of those who went ahead and officiated at the marriage of this divorcée and wrote a marriage contract for her and appointed witnesses, for they are deserving of what my natural benevolence, and the moderation that we are commanded, prevent me from doing and publicly enforcing.[794]

In other words, R. Abraham Maimuni had to come to R. Isaac's aid and confirm his ruling in the face of his students' rebellion.

Another letter, which is very fragmentary, alludes to a further edict issued by R. Isaac forbidding the adoption of gentile laws, but the community disregarded this very publicly: "The community became angry, and annulled it, and did not take heed."[795] The author of the letter requests that R. Isaac enforce his ruling: "And I ask from his eminence to inform our master Isaac, may the Merciful One preserve him, that he should act in this matter as is required according to the law, and the fence that he created in Alexandria should not be overrun, and no one should adopt the laws of the gentiles."[796] As in other cases, wherein

792 Abraham Maimuni, *Responsa*, 183–184.
793 Ibid., 184.
794 Ibid., 191.
795 ENA NS 16.32, ll. 5–7: Frenkel, *"The Compassionate and Benevolent"* [Hebrew], no. 15.
796 Abraham Maimuni, *Responsa*, 191, ll. 7–10.

much is unclear, one thing is entirely evident – the lack of authority which characterized the tenure of Isaac b. Ḥalfon.

4 The Triumvirate

In the final years of R. Isaac b. Ḥalfon's term as judge, the anarchy in Alexandria had become so problematic that R. Abraham Maimuni saw the need to become involved more actively. In a drastic and unprecedented step, he appointed two additional judges to serve together with R. Isaac.[797] The two judges were recognized authorities imported from outside of Alexandria. The first, Elijah b. Zechariah, had previously served as a judge in Fustat.[798] R. Elijah was well-liked and acceptable to the Alexandrian community, perhaps because he originated in the city, and some of his family still lived there.[799] Indeed, as we mentioned above, members of the community were the first to suggest his appointment.[800] Elijah himself was interested in the appointment, and even asked his son Abū Zikrī, who lived in Alexandria, to investigate his chances of being accepted. Abū Zikrī confirmed the community's enthusiasm for Elijah's candidacy: "When I told al-Ṣafī [=one of the senior doctors in Alexandria] what my lord suggested regarding potentially serving the community, he said: 'If he came he would save Israel from this great misfortune.' [...] and if you turn to them, they will accept you and will not turn you away."[801]

The second judge appointed by R. Abraham Maimuni was R. Joseph b. Gershom of France, who was one of a number of French rabbis who had immigrated to Egypt in that period. It is unclear where R. Joseph resided prior to Alexandria, but we do know that he was chosen by R. Abraham Maimuni to come serve there as a judge. He attests to this in a letter: "You have sent for me and I come at your command."[802]

---

797 See a different interpretation of this nomination in Friedman, "The Nagid," 243–244, who suggests that the third judge in the triumvirate was R. Samuel b. Jacob, and not R. Isaac b. Ḥalfon.
798 On this judge, see Aryeh L. Motzkin, "The Arabic Correspondence of Judge Elijah and his Family (Papers from the Cairo Geniza): A Chapter in the Social History of Thirteenth Century Egypt," unpublished Ph.D. diss. (Philadelphia: University of Pennsylvania, 1965), 12–31. For some reason, Motzkin ignores the Alexandrian chapter of Elijah's life.
799 Ibid., 13.
800 See above, Part II, Chapter 13.2: Events Leading up to his Appointment.
801 TS NS J 29v, ll. 3–5, 9–10: Frenkel, *"The Compassionate and Benevolent"* [Hebrew], no. 89.
802 TS 10 J 24.8r, ll. 17–18: Mann, *Jews*, 2: 372, which mistakenly has TS 13 J 34.2.

The three judges were supposed to cooperate. All activities that they undertook had to be approved by the three of them, as R. Joseph attests:

> Whoever transgresses the law [...] would tell me: you are only one of the judges, I shall not accept this [ruling] from you until you all agree [...] I was afraid that I would be reported on to the deputy or to the judge[803] and that they would say: this man transgressed against the Nagid's order, since the Nagid did not allow him to do anything without the agreement of all three.[804]

Moreover, all activities of the court had to be reported and approved by the Nagid: "And I must report to him everything that I do, whenever I preside over a monetary case or a felony or taking the Lord's name in vain, and I am supposed to fulfill this commandment or not to say anything."[805]

The move to appoint two new judges did not please R. Isaac b. Ḥalfon and he made every effort to undermine the position of the other two judges. His natural target was the weakest of the two, namely R. Joseph b. Gershon, who was unknown in Alexandria. His struggle against them was not undertaken publicly, but rather in private, as R. Joseph b. Gershon himself attests: "And I know the evil of this man who prefers to spread rumors [...] and if he doesn't say it to my face, he says it behind my back and will swear that he didn't."[806] Despite this, as one may surmise from the aggrieved tone of the letter, it was apparent that R. Isaac did in fact succeed in undermining R. Joseph so much that the third judge, Elijah b. Zechariah, saw fit to rebuke him and even complained of this problem in a letter to the Nagid: "For he reprimanded him a number of times so that he would walk on an upright path and would not behave shamefully, and the words of the proverb 'a rebuke impresses a discerning person' [Prov. 17:10] were applicable, but he who rebuked him was tired out too and nothing was left, and he mentioned some of this in a letter to the great Nagid."[807]

This triumvirate did not last for very long, quickly morphing into a partnership of two. Joseph b. Gershon left Alexandria in great wrath after a very short time.[808] Isaac b. Ḥalfon and Elijah b. Zechariah continued to serve together as

803 Probably the *wazīr* and the chief qadi are meant here.
804 TS 10 J 24.8v, ll. 1–6.
805 Ibid., ll. 9–10.
806 Ibid., ll. 6–8.
807 Ibid., ll. 19–22.
808 R. Joseph b. Gershon spent less than a year in Alexandria. He travelled to Acre and hoped to reach Babylonia from there – he seems to have died *en route*. See Mann, *Jews*, 2:370–371. On the period he spent in Acre, see Joshua Prawer, *The History of the Jews in the Latin Kingdom of Jer-*

judges for an extended period of time. Their signatures appear side by side on a document composed by the court in Alexandria in 1241.[809]

5 R. Isaac and R. Abraham Maimuni

Above I noted that in stark contrast to the disdain and hostility directed at Isaac b. Ḥalfon by the community, R. Abraham Maimuni himself valued the depth of his knowledge and offered him his full support.[810] He confirmed R. Isaac's ruling regarding the divorce of Sitt al-Nasab and backed the excommunication edict he had issued. He then proceeded to compare it to the edict issued by his father Maimonides, and thus lent R. Isaac some of his authority:

And the answer according to the second view is that the excommunication edict issued by the illustrious judge R. Isaac, may God grant him aid, against the man who would officiate at a marriage in Alexandria without the permission of the overseer, is binding since it fortifies the lineages of Israel and preserves the good order of their laws and prevents anarchy in marriage ceremonies which leads to the destabilization of families and it is similar to the excommunication edict that was agreed upon and was implemented by my father and teacher and the sages of his generation, may their memory be for a blessing. And whomsoever transgresses against this edict and officiates at a marriage or a divorce without the permission of the overseer, this man has sinned and the excommunication is to be applied to him, and he shall be cursed and shunned from [the community of] Israel.[811]

6 Conclusion

The obvious disdain of the community for R. Ḥalfon, in contrast with the unmitigated support of the Nagid, leads one to assume that the appointment of R. Isaac was proposed by R. Abraham Maimuni himself. Perhaps one may also infer that

usalem (Jerusalem: Yad Ben-Zvi, 2001), 262–264 [Hebrew]. He stayed in Alexandria around the year 1234–1235. See Abraham Maimuni, *Responsa*, 193, n. 13.

809 TS 1.620: Nadia Zeldes and Michael Frenkel, "The Sicilian Trade: Jewish Merchants in the Mediterranean in the 12th and 13th Centuries," *Michael* 14 (1997): 134–135 [Hebrew]. This is a bill confirming the *kashruth* (fitness according to Jewish dietary laws) of cheese imported from Sicily.

810 See above, Part II, Chapter 13.1: Origin and Background, and 13.3: Leadership with no Authority.

811 Abraham Maimuni, *Responsa*, 189.

Isaac b. Ḥalfon was one of the pietistic coterie of students loyal to R. Abraham Maimuni, and that he was sent to Alexandria to disseminate the latter's mystical-pietist views, and to establish a local group of followers.[812] Indeed, R. Abraham Maimuni refers to the judge as "R. Isaac the Wise, the *ḥasid*."[813] At the present time there is no further information regarding R. Isaac b. Ḥalfon's worldviews that may corroborate this hypothesis. It should be mentioned though, since it is in line with what we know of the pietist groups of R. Abraham Maimuni's students, who were active in Alexandria, and may benefit a future line of inquiry.[814]

812 On Abraham Maimuni's pietist thought and his circles of disciples, see Shelomo D. Goitein, "Abraham Maimonides and His Pietist Circle," in Alexander Altmann (ed.), *Jewish Medieval and Renaissance Studies* (Cambridge, MA: Harvard University Press, 1967), 145–164; Elisha Russ-Fishbane, *Judaism, Sufism, and the Pietists of Medieval Egypt* (Oxford: Oxford University Press, 2015); Nathan Hofer, *The Popularisation of Sufism in Ayyubid and Mamluk Egypt, 1173–1325* (Edinburgh: Edinburgh University Press, 2015).
813 Abraham Maimuni, *Responsa*, 192.
814 See Goitein, "Abraham Maimonides," 148–150.

Chapter 14 Judah the Teacher b. Aaron the Physician Ibn Al-ʿAmmānī

1 The Family

Judah was a scion of the Ibn al-ʿAmmānī family, one of the most influential and notable families in Alexandria. He was the great-grandson of Aaron b. Yeshūʿā Ibn al-ʿAmmānī, who was active in the community in the 1140s.[815] At the beginning of the thirteenth century the family continued to occupy key positions in the community. They were members of the Alexandrian elite, bound together by social and family ties, who ran the community for all intents and purposes. Judah the Teacher was neither judge nor *muqaddam* in Alexandria and did not hold office in the community. Nevertheless, a portrait of his character can serve as a typical example of a local dignitary, well-integrated into the densely interconnected networks of ruling.

2 Social Milieu and Family Ties

(a) Correspondence

Judah was a frequent correspondent with many of the central figures in Alexandria, Fustat, and Cairo. He corresponded with R. Abraham Maimuni and regularly reported to him about the comings and goings in the community.[816] R. Menahem, the judge in Cairo, would also send him letters.[817]

Four letters that Judah wrote to Meir b. Yakhin (Thābit), the cantor of Fustat, have survived, which probably represent only a miniscule portion of a vast regular correspondence.[818] Aside from serving as a cantor of great renown, Meir also

815 See above, Chapter 5; Mazor and Lev, "Dynasties," 240 – 246 on the Ibn al-ʿAmmānī dynasty.
816 TS 16.305: Frenkel, *"The Compassionate and Benevolent"* [Hebrew], no. 32.
817 TS 16.305v, ll. 37 – 41: "and the letter of our master Menahem, may he be remembered in a thousand torrents of greetings, has already reached me."
818 The letters are TS 13 J 21.25: Frenkel, *"The Compassionate and Benevolent"* [Hebrew], no. 71; TS 13 J 27.11: Frenkel, *"The Compassionate and Benevolent"* [Hebrew], no. 79; TS 12.299: Goitein, *Palestinian Jewry*, 340 – 341.

https://doi.org/10.1515/9783110713619-019

served as the scribe for the court and the treasurer of the Fustat community.[819] The family of Meir the Cantor lived in Alexandria, and in the letters Judah sent he was careful to report to Meir regarding their welfare. From his reports it is evident that he knew them well and met with them frequently, and that they were part of his social circle: "Your mother is well. She has received the five dirhams, may the Lord ensure that you are always one to be thanked. Your brother Saʿīd has quarreled with his wife, he left, and no one know where to. The ceiling fell on his wife, she was not hurt and was saved from death. All your household is healthy."[820]

(b) Matrimonial Ties

Judah was related by marriage to central figures both within the community and outside of it. Ṣadoq the Cantor Ibn al-ʿAmmānī was his uncle through his father. Ṣadoq served as the cantor of Alexandria, a prestigious position that came with a lot of power. The relationship between the two was fairly fraught and continually gravitated between crisis and reconciliation,[821] though Judah clearly benefited greatly from his close association with Ṣadoq, who was a multi-talented person.[822]

Yeshūʿā the Physician b. Aaron, his cousin, was a court physician in Cairo. Judah was a beneficiary of these ties, and with Yeshūʿā's aid attempted to help his nephew secure a permit to practice medicine.[823]

The family ties with other elite families were deliberately reinforced and expanded. Thus, for example, we hear of the marriage of Judah's son Hibat Allāh with the cousin of Solomon b. Elijah the Judge, a member of one of the most influential families of the time.[824] From a description of the wedding celebration, it

819 See Goitein, *Society*, 2: 420 – 421; Moshe Gil, *Documents of the Jewish Pious Foundations from the Cairo Geniza* (Leiden: Brill, 1976), 416 ff.
820 TS 12.299v, margins: Goitein, *Palestinian Jewry*, 340 – 341. The translation follows Goitein.
821 See, for example, TS 16.305: Frenkel, "*The Compassionate and Benevolent*" [Hebrew], no. 32 – a letter by Judah to R. Abraham Maimuni, in which he thanks him for the reconciliation (*ṣulḥa*) he made between him and his cousin. On the intricate family relations between them, see also: Friedman, "Maimonides Appoints," 145 – 146.
822 See below, Part II, Chapter 14.3 (a): Teacher.
823 TS 24.67: Frenkel, "*The Compassionate and Benevolent*" [Hebrew], no. 40, Judah's letter to this cousin, that deals almost entirely with his attempts to help his brother to acclimate in Cairo and to receive further education as a doctor there.
824 ULC Add 3343 (Cat. 867), verso, right margins. On Elijah b. Zechariah the Judge, see Motzkin, "Arabic Correspondence."

is evident that the occasion was a significant social event, and that everyone who was anyone within the ruling elite attended. Moreover, the social significance of these marital ties was clear to everyone:

> The honorable shaykh and bridegroom Hibat Allāh Ibn al-ʿAmmānī, may his Rock preserve him, sent a letter to my brother the *raʾīs* Abū Zikrī, may his Rock preserve him, and in it he boasted that he had married my cousin, may God grant her success, and that the *Nasi* had attended, and that it was a haughty affair and beautiful marriage. Say to him, oh Abū al-Barakāt my brother, that she is not the one who is honored by him, but rather it was he who is elevated in [his association] with her and the rest of her pure and noble family on her maternal grandfather's side, may the exalted Lord grant them mercy. And had he looked into all the distinguished families he would not have found the like [of her family] in all the world.[825]

3 Sources of Income

(a) Teacher

Judah's sobriquet, *melamed* or teacher, indicates that his income derived mostly from teaching young boys. Indeed, in a letter to Meir the Cantor b. Yakhin, wherein he recounts the effort he put into copying liturgical poems on his behalf, he says explicitly: "By the name of Israel's religion, I even cancelled the classes with the young boys, so that I could write them [=the liturgical poems] since I love you, and they are attached to this letter. My lord, I cannot afford food to sustain me without these little ones. And may God help."[826] This job involved constant competition with other teachers, who endangered his source of income, and this included relatives. His uncle Ṣadoq founded a rival school for boys in Alexandria, which led to much hand wringing:

> He attempts to take me away from everything like one would extract a hair out of dough. He opened a school for boys and his father and mother helped him, and began to suborn the

825 ULC Add 3343 (Cat. 867), recto, margins; 2, ll. 1–3. The prince mentioned here is Hodayah b. Jesse, of the princely dynasty of Damascus, who was sojourning in Alexandria at this time. Hibat Allāh, Judah Ibn al-ʿAmmānī's son, also signed a bill of cancellation of a betrothal from Alexandria in 1234, quoted in the question that R. Abraham Maimuni is asked. There he signs using his Hebrew name: "Nethanel b. R. Judah the Teacher." Hibat Allāh, "God's gift," is an Arabic translation of the Hebrew Nethanel. See Abraham Maimuni, *Responsa*, 180, §106.
826 TS 13 J 27.11v, ll. 8–10: Goitein, *Jewish Education*, 101; Frenkel, *"The Compassionate and Benevolent"* [Hebrew], no. 79.

> fathers of the boys against me in my presence. I ignored him. And I, at this point, do not know how the matter will end.[827]

(b) Locating and Transcribing Liturgical Poems

Another source of Judah's income was locating liturgical poems and copying them out for cantors, mainly for Meir b. Yakhin of Fustat. He describes his method in the following letter to Meir:

> Moreover, I was happy that the lamentation entitled "And we know not etc..." has arrived. And regarding the other lamentation, I have already confessed to you the reason for the delay, and I am greatly chagrined over it. I listened closely to my uncle when he recited it at the first watch and I discerned that it opened with the words: "They shall tell of your rectitude." Perhaps you will meet again with Ibn al-Sadīd and attempt to get it from him. By your good life, I inquired as far as Marseille to find it. My Lord, if it were sung on weekdays I would copy it out, but he sings it only on the Night of the Binding or on Sabbath eve when one cannot transcribe it at all.[828]

In another letter he asks the cantor: "Please, when you ask for a liturgical poem from me, or a lamentation, or jeremiad, please write down their beginnings and I will quickly copy them and send them to you. If, however, you ask for something unknown and new, I am at a loss of what to write and my enthusiasm is dampened. I say this to my lord, and let a hint be enough for a discerning person."[829]

These labors of obtaining liturgical material for cantors and its transcription was remunerated. Evidence of this is Judah's delicate allusion to Meir the Cantor in the above letter, that the great labor he invested in acquiring a specific liturgical poem was detrimental to his steady income as a teacher. The implication therein is that he should be paid commensurately.[830] This being said, there was definitely reciprocity at the base of the exchange: Meir the Cantor sent other scholarly documents to Judah, mostly legal (halakhic) responsa. Thus, for instance, the request Judah makes in his letter to Meir the Cantor: "the other halakhic response, the one which remained with you [...] that which I took together with the Nagid's response, do me a favor and send it to me."[831]

827 TS 10 J 25.3r, margins, l. 16; 2, l. 3: Frenkel, *"The Compassionate and Benevolent"* [Hebrew], no. 57.
828 TS 13 J 27.11r, ll. 24–33: Goitein, Jewish Education, 101; Frenkel, *"The Compassionate and Benevolent"* [Hebrew], no. 79.
829 TS 13 J 21.25r, ll. 13–17: Frenkel, *"The Compassionate and Benevolent"* [Hebrew], no. 71.
830 See above, Part II, Chapter 14.3 (a): Teacher.
831 TS J 21.25r, ll. 20–22: Frenkel, *"The Compassionate and Benevolent"* [Hebrew], no. 71.

In another letter he confirms: "I sent you the halakhic response together with your letters."[832]

In other words, despite the monetary reimbursement that was inherent to this association, this was not an employer-employee relationship, but rather a complex system of mutual interchange involving favors and services. This relationship is very reminiscent of the *muʿāmala* relationship that existed in the world of commerce. Indeed, Judah the Teacher's letters to Meir the Cantor are signed with the conventional *muʿāmala* formula: "And any service or requirement my master, may God preserve him, has, he should let his servant know of it," which is identical to the way in which merchants would sign their business letters to their *muʿāmil* partner.[833] Just like a *muʿāmala* relationship, the ties between Judah and Meir involved a regular correspondence and exchange of information and intelligence, and was based on a social and familial association. Indeed, Judah the Teacher's letters to Meir the Cantor are replete with information and community news, especially when it involved people of their social circles. Judah was quite intimate with Meir the Cantor's family who lived in Alexandria and maintained a close relationship with them. He shared their stories with Meir in great detail as is evident from the following excerpt: "And your brother the shaykh Hilāl, may God preserve him, is ill. A nail got stuck in his foot a few months ago and he still has not recovered fully. And matters are very difficult for him. And your mother is ill, her situation is grave."[834]

4 Education and Skills

Judah the Teacher's activities depended upon his education and professional skills, and he indeed valued them greatly and would routinely allude to them.

(a) Professional Writing

Judah the Teacher's professional writing skills included knowledge of the etiquette of correspondence. He rebukes Meir the Cantor more than once in their letters in a tone of unveiled condescension, for not observing these rules:

832 TS 10 J 25.3, ll. 22–23: Frenkel, *"The Compassionate and Benevolent"* [Hebrew], no. 57.
833 TS 13 J 21.25, ll. 22–23: Frenkel, *"The Compassionate and Benevolent"* [Hebrew], no. 71.
834 TS 13 J 27.11r, ll. 15–18: Goitein, *Jewish Education*, 101; Frenkel, *"The Compassionate and Benevolent"* [Hebrew], no. 79.

> My dear sir, I have no choice but to take up a serious matter with you. I have asked numerous times that when you write a letter, you include a date. Two letters have just arrived without a date. Regarding these letters, I know you were travelling, but regarding the rest of the letters, there is no way to tell whether they are old or new.[835]

In another place he notes that Meir should include the opening lines of the liturgical poems he requested for sake of clarity.[836]

(b) Medicine

Judah the Teacher had some knowledge of medicine. Whatever it was, he saw himself as sufficiently qualified to offer an opinion and give medical advice: "That which you had written that your ill health is primarily caused by the consumption of wine is a pithy observation. I adjure you to drink no more, and instruct you [that if you do drink] to drink only modest amounts."[837] This advice was offered to Meir the Cantor in a letter. Judah was, however, most adept at navigating the intricacies of the medical establishment, with which he was very familiar. When his brother wished to study medicine in Cairo, he provided him with an impressive array of letters to key figures and with very practical advice, which indicate an insider's knowledge of the system:

> I sent [...] a letter and in the letter is a list of some of the things he will need to do when he arrives in Cairo. I advised him to deliver letters to the governor and to the qadi and to Muwaffaq and to Ben Tammām and to Ben Ṣedaqah, which will serve him well, since Ben Tamām is the overseer right now. And everyone who comes to study with them says that the studies are in Fustat and their license is from Fustat. Do not focus on anything except obtaining a license. If you have laid your hands on a license, you have accomplished everything [...] and I wrote [...] to a man who is known as the overseer of hospitals, that he should make an effort on behalf of my brother and that he should be with him and help him as much as he is able.[838]

---

835 TS 13 J 27.11v, ll. 1–5.
836 See above, Part II, Chapter 14.3 (b): Locating and Transcribing Liturgical Poems.
837 TS 13 J 27.11r, ll. 22–24: Goitein, *Jewish Education*, 101; Frenkel, "*The Compassionate and Benevolent*" [Hebrew], no. 79.
838 TS 24.67r, ll. 5–11, 18–21: Frenkel, "*The Compassionate and Benevolent*" [Hebrew], no. 40. The introduction to this document there should be corrected. The letter is addressed to two family members in Cairo, with whom his brother probably resided, since he transmits advice to the brother through these two family members. See also Goitein, Society, 2:249–50, who provides a different interpretation; Mazor and Lev, "Dynasties," 244–245.

It is quite likely that Judah's broad education and various skills were gained in the framework of his family. He learnt from close family members, and considering the large number of cantors and physicians in the Ibn al-ʿAmmānī family, one may reasonably assume that these professions were passed down in the family from father to son.[839]

5 Leading the Community

Judah the Teacher held no official position in the community, but his manifold talents led him to occupy unofficial positions in the community apparatus and to take an active part in local politics.

(a) Judicial Activity

We saw above that Judah the Teacher displayed much interest in the legal responsa collected and transcribed on his behalf by Meir the Cantor, and indeed he was fairly active in Alexandria's local Jewish court. His signature appears upon legal documents originating in the court of Alexandria, such as a contract from 1219;[840] an engagement contract from 1191, quoted in full in a question addressed to R. Abraham Maimuni by members of the community;[841] a sale bill of a house in Alexandria from 1204;[842] and kosher certification for cheese imported from Sicily in 1244.[843]

Judah Ibn al-ʿAmmānī also served as a scribe for the court in Alexandria and an affidavit from 1207 in his handwriting has survived.[844]

---

839 On the Ibn al-ʿAmmānī family, see Goitein, *Society*, 2: 245, n. 21; Mann, *Jews*, 2: 305; Schirmann, "Poets."

840 TS NS J 346. The document is severely damaged, but it is possible to read the date ("4879 *anno mundi* in No [Amon]") and signature ("Judah the Teacher, son of R. Aaron the Physician, may he rest in Eden") clearly.

841 Abraham Maimuni, *Responsa*, 140 – 143, §88. Judah signs there alongside two additional witnesses, both of them teachers like himself: Abraham the Teacher, son of R. Japheth, may he rest in Eden; and Joseph the Teacher, son of R. Michael, may he rest in Eden.

842 TS 16.126. Next to his name appear that of Japheth b. Moses.

843 TS 13 J 4.8: Zeldes and Frenkel, "The Sicilian trade," 136 – 137. This is the latest evidence for his activity.

844 TS 24.81, part of a court register. The affidavit concerned Sitt al-Nasab's inheritance dispute.

(b) Social Activity

Judah the Teacher was quite active in philanthropic projects in Alexandria and was especially involved in fundraising. Above we saw how he exploited his close ties with Meir the Cantor to get help through him for R. Samuel.[845] Beyond his personal interest in R. Samuel's welfare, to whom he refers as "my teacher and master," this solicitation was also a corollary of his fundraising activities. In the same letter Judah refers to other activities related to fundraising: He asks Meir the Cantor not to delay the donation to the Jerusalem synagogue, and organizes a fundraising event for "the rabbis."[846]

The industry of donations was bilateral. Judah directed recommendations and letters of reference for charitable causes, and also received such letters. There was a regular exchange between him and Meir the Cantor of such letters, but they both evidently served only as intermediaries. Meir the Cantor would merely hand letters over to the Nagid, R. Abraham Maimuni, and the latter would decide which solicitations to accept and which to reject.[847] The same was true of Judah the Teacher. On one occasion, for instance, Meir the Cantor asked him to pass along a letter of reference from Abū al-Ḥasan the Teacher on behalf of a refugee from Baghdad to the judge of Alexandria.[848] It is thus evident that the two were merely two links in a chain of intermediaries, who operated within the sophisticated apparatus of a vast charity network, which enabled its members to preserve and buttress the personal channels of communication among them.[849]

Another example of this network is the letter written on behalf of Rachel the Convert of Byzantium. Her husband had abandoned her and she was destitute, and now he wished to marry another woman. In her letter, written in Judah Ibn al-ʿAmmānī's handwriting, she addresses Elijah b. Zechariah, the judge of Fustat, and pleads for his help in preventing her husband's second marriage. Judah appends a personal letter to the judge with a special request to help the woman. The letter is written in a familiar register. Judah sends his regards to

---

845 See above, Part II, 12.1: Acclimatization.

846 TS 13 J 27.11v, ll. 11–13: Frenkel, *"The Compassionate and Benevolent"* [Hebrew], no. 79. He must surely be referring to the French rabbis who arrived in Alexandria at this time. See above, Part II, Chapter 12.

847 See Goitein, *Palestinian Jewry*, 338, n. 2.

848 TS 12.299r, margins; 2, l. 2: Goitein, *Palestinian Jewry*, 338–343.

849 Miriam Frenkel, "Charity in Jewish Society of the Medieval Mediterranean World," in Miriam Frenkel and Yaacov Lev (eds.), *Charity and Giving in Monotheistic Religions* (Berlin-NY: Walter de Gruyter, 2009), 343–363.

the children and to the family of the judge, and emphasizes his personal relationship with him:

> I would like to extend my personal and sincere regards to his eminence and our master, the lord judge, and to his exceptional and most lordly progeny. My most special regard. And to all who rest in his shade both great and small, the best salutations. And I, the man who writes these words, Judah the Teacher, who serves his lordship, and asks about him and feels desolate at his absence, prays to He who spoke and the world came into being, that there should be many people like you in Israel.[850]

While taking advantage of his personal ties to the judge in order to help this convert, Judah the Teacher could at the same time buttress his own relationship with the man. Charity, which is a very frequent topic in Judah the Teacher's correspondence, constituted a shared interest and a joint activity of Judah and other members of the elite, thus enabling open and frequent channels of communication among them.

(c) Political Involvement

Judah the Teacher's letters are replete with allusions to political affairs. Since his letters are addressed to men immersed in local politics, he often employs a shorthand, foregoing explicitness – which does not help us reconstruct the chain of events. It is quite evident that Judah was very involved in what was happening in the community. He alludes to the "problem regarding the disagreement I had with the judge."[851] One may only surmise that the reference is to R. Anatoly. In another letter he complains that Anatoly convenes the court at his private house.[852] Judah was very angry with his uncle, Ṣadoq the Cantor Ibn al-ʿAmmānī, who tried to appoint his juvenile son as the *muqaddam*, despite the preference of most of the community for a leader whose "beard had already come in."[853] He felt that the burdens of the community were upon his shoulders, remarking to R. Abraham Maimuni: "It is I who bear the burdens of the community."[854] In another letter, to Meir the Cantor, he explains that only he can bring

850 TS 12.575v, ll. 1–5: Friedman, *Jewish Polygyny*, 212. The translation follows Friedman.
851 TS 13 J 21.25r, ll. 20–21: Frenkel, "*The Compassionate and Benevolent*" [Hebrew], no. 71.
852 TS 10 J 25.3r, ll. 15–17: Frenkel, "*The Compassionate and Benevolent*" [Hebrew], no. 57.
853 Ibid., ll. 19–20; 2, ll. 10–11. About adolescence and youth in this society, see: Miriam Frenkel, "Adolescence in Jewish Medieval Society under Islam," *Continuity and Change* 16 (2001): 263–281.
854 TS 16.305v, ll. 44–45: Frenkel, "*The Compassionate and Benevolent*" [Hebrew], no. 32.

peace to a fitful community: "Were it not for me, 'disagreement' would be rampant every single day."[855]

6 Conclusion

Though he did not serve in any official capacity, Judah took upon himself certain positions as a matter of course, in the fields of law and social services, and saw himself responsible for the preservation of the reigning *status quo*. Judah the Teacher was a fourth-generation descendant of a family that had succeeded in preserving its elite position in the community.[856] His education and his professional training; his social networks, which included other members of the elite in Alexandria and in the corridors of power in Fustat and Cairo; his ties to the Muslim authorities and members of the ruling regime; all of these contributed to his standing as a typical member of the elite which had governed Alexandria for many generations. In his writing, he presented his public work as selfless sacrifice and as bearing the burden and being at one with the community. This is the way he most likely understood it as well. Judah the Teacher and his circle, however, were first and foremost preserving and protecting the interests of their class.

A parenthetical and seemingly trivial statement in one of Judah's letters reflects his basic social perceptions, and that of his social milieu. Regarding a disease that had spread in town, he remarks: "There is no one in the city who is healthy. Neither the leaders, nor the dignitaries, nor the commoners."[857] This division into three stations is at the basis of the social worldview of Judah the Teacher and his circle: At the top are the leaders (*muqaddamūn*), and the dignitaries (*shuyūkh*), Judah's relatives and acquaintances with whom we are quite familiar through his letters, and at the bottom of the hierarchy are the broad and amorphous *ʿāmma* or commoners.

855 TS 10 J 25.3v, ll. 16–17: Frenkel, *"The Compassionate and Benevolent"* [Hebrew], no. 57.
856 There was very likely also a fifth generation. See above, Part II, Chapter 14.2 (b): Matrimonial Ties, concerning his son Hibat Allāh Nethanel.
857 TS 10 J 25.3, ll. 6–7: Frenkel, *"The Compassionate and Benevolent"* [Hebrew], no. 57.

Part III Towards a Characterization of the Jewish Leadership in Alexandria

Chapter 1 Sources of Power

1 Introduction

This chapter examines how the ruling elite of Alexandria survived and succeeded in maintaining its position of leadership. It is prudent to introduce this chapter with a clarification of some of the basic assumptions connected to the concept of power, which I will be employing in this chapter.

Power is an instrument evident in all association between rulers and subjects,[858] and as such is an integral element of all relationships that exist in a society. Power is not necessarily negative and manifests in a large variety of ways.[859] Scholars often distinguish between four types of power:[860]

a. Coercion – this type of power is dependent upon punitive sanctions; coercion employs external tools to influence the behavior of human beings and its basis is fear of punishment and reward for obedience.
b. Authority – a type of power which is deemed acceptable by society. The basis of "authority" is the right a society grants certain individuals to act as leaders of others. Authority is always legitimate. Max Weber distinguished between three types of authority: traditional authority – authority which is recognized as part of the way things were always done; rational authority – authority inherent to a system of rules and laws and which is defined and limited to certain domains or for a certain time period; charismatic authority – this type of authority depends upon the belief that the leader embodies power beyond the normal forces, and thus has greater validity than those forces.[861]
c. Influence – this power depends on persuasion, or in other words, the ability to maneuver social relationships to one's advantage.
d. Dominance – power that is a derivative of control over resources and what society values. This type of power does not necessarily entail active involve-

858 Cohen, *Two-Dimensional Man*, xi.
859 See, for example, Amitai Etzioni's comment: "The notion that evil is imposed by power while goodness flies on its own wings assumes an optimistic view of human nature and societal institutions that has little evidence to support it" (Amitai Etzioni, *The Active Society: A Theory of Societal and Political Processes* [NY: The Free Press, 1968], 321).
860 Martin N. Marger, *Elites and Masses: An Introduction to Political Sociology* (Berkeley: University of California Press, 1987), 54 ff.
861 Eliezer Goldman, "Authority and Autonomy," in Avi Sagi and Zeev Safrai (eds.), *Between Authority and Autonomy in Jewish Tradition* (Tel Aviv: Hakibbutz Hameuchad, 1997), 32–39 [Hebrew]; Roderick Martin, *The Sociology of Power* (Oxford: Routledge & Kegan Paul, 1977), 75 ff.

https://doi.org/10.1515/9783110713619-020

ment in decision-making but is rather due to the very fact of controlling power centers.

In order to survive and thrive, all kinds of power require sources. Sources of power are many and vary greatly: Supporters, money, sex, social prestige, expertise, control over sources of information, the ability to offer remuneration – these are only a small sample of a long list of the sources of power. If it is to be effectively employed, power must always be connected to the motives of the people the leader wishes to lead, and to accord to the particular social context in which he acts.[862] Power is, thus, dependent upon societal circumstances, and the sources of power a leader uses may tell us a great deal about the society in its entirety.

Power is not a constant nor is it inherent. It is a dynamic variable which shifts with the circumstances of societies, and in turn leads to a set of outcomes in those societies. One must present it, therefore, within a temporal framework. In this chapter, the sources of power will be examined along a temporal axis, whose periodization combines external and internal-Jewish criteria.

The Yeshivah period (1030–1070) is marked by the dominance of the Palestinian Yeshivah. It begins in the 1030s, from which the earliest Cairo Genizah documents originate. Without this constraint, we would have surely begun this period earlier. It ends in the last third of the eleventh century, with the collapse of the Yeshivah.

The Nagidate period (1070–1130) begins at the end of the eleventh century with the rise of the Nagidate in Egypt, which brought with it an important shift in the power dynamics of the community. It ends in the 1130s.

The period of transition (1130–1170) – Beginning in the 1130s, a new period commences, which is marked by the transition from the Fatimid empire to the Ayyubid regime. The protracted dissolution of the Fatimid empire affected the Jewish community and brought about significant changes in its power dynamics.

The Ayyubid period (1170–1250) begins in the 1170s with the ascent of the Ayyubid dynasty. It was marked by the change of government in Egypt, shifting demographics, and the rise of Maimonidean dynasty. This period may be subdivided into two: a period of searching for new paths (1170–1200); and a time of new leaders, recently arrived from Europe.

862 Marger, *Elites and Masses*, ibid.

2 The Yeshivah Period

(a) Normative Approaches

Fatimid Political Theory

The Fatimids apprehended their sovereignty as cosmic and holistic. According to their political theory, the caliph was God's representative upon the earth, from whose primary vessel a chain of authority radiated downwards – until the least of his subjects.[863] This chain of power included not only the various Muslim denominations, but also members of other religions in the caliphate, who were an inseparable part of this cosmic world view. The Fatimid *Weltanschauung* was manifested in ritually organized processions, in which all official functionaries in the caliphate would march according to a constructed hierarchy. At the far end of the parade the Christian Patriarch and his officials marched, and following him, at the very end of the parade – the Head of the Jews (*ra'īs al-Yahūd*) with his cortege .[864]

According to this world view, the leaders of the Jewish communities were seen as an organic, albeit inferior, component of the ruling system. The Gaon was the "Head of the Jews," whose authority was drawn from the official appointment granted by the caliph. He was entitled to delegate this authority downwards and to appoint local community leaders.[865] In accordance with

863 On the Fatimid bureaucratic machine, constructed on the model of the Ismāʿīlī *daʿwa*, see Al-Imad, *The Fatimid Vizierate*, ch. 4, esp. 161–162. See also Sanders, *Ritual, Politics and the City*, showing how the Fatimid concept of rule was expressed in public ceremonies in Cairo.

864 For a description of the ceremony, see Ibn Muyassar, *Akhbār miṣr*, 61–62, cited in Goitein, *Society*, 2: 374. For the Ismāʿīliyya's metahistorical conception that locates other religions within a universal sacred history, see Nanji, "Portraits of Self and Others."

865 Goitein, *Palestinian Jewry*, 57–60, 77–78. Goitein published there two documents from which it appears that the Gaon – and also the judge of Alexandria – needed to have their appointments renewed when a new caliph ascended the throne. This means that the caliph was understood as the primary source of their authority, just as he was the primary source of authority for all other holders of public office in the Fatimid kingdom. See also Gil, *History of Palestine*, §746, n. 746; Shulamit Sela and Elinoar Bareket have published a series of articles aimed at proving that the Gaon of the Palestinian Yeshivah did not have governmental authority but religious authority alone, and that only over the Rabbanites, while the title *ra'īs al-Yahūd* was held by another official, who had close ties to the Fatimid court and who had authority over all three Jewish denominations (Rabbanites, Karaites and Samaritans). This debate is beyond the scope of the present study; in any case, it does not change the fact, clearly expressed in the letters of appointment, that according to the Fatimid worldview, the Gaon and the local community leaders derived their authority from the supreme source of such, the Fatimid caliph. See Shulamit Sela, "The Head of the Rabbanite, Karaite and Samaritan Jews: On the History of a Title," *BSOAS*

this perception, the Fatimid caliphs supported the Palestinian Yeshivah and the leaders of local communities financially.[866]

Jewish Perceptions of Local Leadership

In previous chapters we noted that during this period a dynasty of sorts ruled in Alexandria and leadership passed from father to son for at least three generations.[867] Nevertheless, leadership was not seen as inherently passing from father to son, and as was related above, Yeshūʿā b. Joseph, who succeeded his forefathers, had to invest considerable efforts in suppressing rebellion and preserving his status as leader. In this period, the idea of a biological dynastic right to leadership was never raised as an argument, neither by the leaders themselves nor by the populace. Moreover, as we saw, the leader had to undergo a prolonged training period before the community considered him worthy of a leadership position, and at no time was he able to depend solely upon his biological advantage to secure his appointment.

The source of a leader's authority, according to the Jews of the Fatimid empire in general and the Jews of Alexandria in particular, was the members of the community in and of themselves. This perception is well-expressed in Solomon b. Judah Gaon's pointed words to the community of Alexandria, who complain about Yeshūʿā's failed leadership: "He is your son and it is through your mouths that he sustains himself."[868] Solomon b. Judah reverses the conventional imagery: the leader is usually imagined as a father, authoritative or benevolent, tyrannical or loving while the community members are seen as his children who are at his mercy. In the image sketched by the Gaon, the leader is a nursing child, who is sustained by, and entirely dependent upon, the members of the community. There is, however, also an allusion to the symbiotic relationship between the two: Since the members of the community are understood as parents, they have responsibility for, indeed a vested interest in, supporting and nurturing

57 (1994): 255–257; idem, "The Headship of the Jews in the Fatimid Empire in Karaite Hands," in Ezra Fleischer, Mordechai A. Friedman and Joel L. Kraemer (eds.), *Mas'at Moshe: Studies in Jewish and Islamic Culture Presented to Moshe Gil* (Jerusalem: Mossad Bialik, 1998), 256–281 [Hebrew]; Bareket, "Abraham ha-Kohen."

866 Mann, *Jews*, 1: 38–39, 71–72; Cohen, *Jewish Self-Government*, 53–54; Gil, *History of Palestine*, 550–551.

867 It is interesting to note that in this period, the office of Chief Qadi of Egypt was also held by the al-Nuʿmān family. See Lev, *State and Society*, 134.

868 See above, Part II, Chapter 1.3 (c): Sources of Support, in the section: The Geonim, the Heads of the Palestinian Yeshivah.

the leader-son who has sprouted among them. On another occasion the Gaon explicitly states that the crucial reason for granting Yeshūʿā the title of *ḥaver* was the support he had received from the community:

> It has become apparent to them [= to the heads of the Palestinian Yeshivah] that he is worthy and upright and that nothing bad had ever been heard of him from among all of you that have been in our midst, and from among your communities and from among the sojourners that arrive [to your community]. All valorize him unanimously [...] and it is upon their words that the leaders of the Yeshivah relied when they conferred upon him the title *ḥaver* [...] And it has already been said that many of you favor him.[869]

(b) Sources of Power

The main source of power that was at a communal leader's disposal was in key positions he could manage to occupy within the dense and prolific networks of relationships, which encompassed a good deal of the Jewish world and connected its central loci of power, as shall be elaborated below.

The Yeshivah Connection

The leaders of Alexandria at this time were connected to the Palestinian Yeshivah and to the Gaon at its helm in a number of ways. Joseph b. Yeshūʿā, although never granted an official title from the Yeshivah, signed official Yeshivah documents, along with Solomon b. Judah Gaon and his son Abraham,[870] which shows that he was an active participant in the Yeshivah's activities. His son Yeshūʿā b. Joseph was already an official fellow (*ḥaver)* of the Yeshivah.

These relationships between the Yeshivah and the local community leaders proved to be critical. They offered the local leader a powerbase, not by virtue of the Gaon's authority, but rather because he was one of many players among others in a vast network. Having the right connections in this network was the key to any position of power. The official authority granted to the Gaon to appoint a local community leader was restricted, and was ultimately of secondary impor-

869 Ibid.
870 ENA 2804.20: Mann, *Jews*, 2: 115 (there mistakenly as ENA 2804 fol. 1). This is the end of a letter of which only the signatures are extant. The order of the signatures is evidence for the signatories' importance: the last signatory has the highest rank. In this letter, Yeshūʿā b. Joseph's signature appears in the third place, before those of "Solomon the Younger, the Head of the Yeshiva, son of R. Judah, may he rest in Eden" and the latter's son, "Abraham the Fellow, son of R. Solomon Gaon of the Palestinian Yeshivah."

tance. In contrast with the Fatimid theory of governance, the Gaon himself did not hold authority which radiated downwards to the local leader. Appointments were rather made by the Yeshivah, as a collective institution, as Solomon b. Judah Gaon explains: "This view is shared by me as well as by the Chief Justice of the Court, may the Rock preserve him, and by everyone else. This is the accepted custom: to offer prayers in unanimity on behalf of he who bears the title *ḥaver.*"[871] This dependence upon the other fellows of the Yeshivah diminished the Gaon's power as a source of authority. Moreover, the appointment and the granting of the title by the Yeshivah did not come to pass except as a *post facto* validation of the community's will: "It is upon their word [that of the community] that the fellowship members granted him the title *ḥaver*,"[872] Solomon b. Judah continues, as he describes the circumstances under which Yeshūʿā was granted the title.

This being said, the ties between the local leader and the Gaon were important and even central to both the leader and the Gaon – not as the source of authority and its recipient, but rather as figures occupying key positions in the same network. We have already seen how the Gaon's support, reflected in the conferral of a title, tilted the balance in favor of Yeshūʿā and buttressed his position as the leader of the community, and how he earned the support of another Gaon, Daniel b. Azaryah, due to his connection to another central figure in the network, Abraham Ibn al-Furāt.[873] The clinching argument that the Gaon was not the sole source of authority , but rather one of a number of players, is found in the way the community leaders related to the heads of the Yeshivah. They did not hesitate to conduct themselves in a very manipulative way toward the Geonim. Yeshūʿā b. Joseph was publicly derisive of the title granted to him by Solomon b. Judah Gaon. On another occasion, he plotted behind the back of Daniel b. Azaryah and was implicated in a series of clandestine and fake letters.[874] This type of relationship indicates that the local leaders viewed the Gaon as a central leadership figure – but only one individual in a dense social network, which they had to belong to in order to preserve their status.

---

871 See above, Part II, Chapter 1.3 (c): Sources of Support, in the section: The Geonim, the Heads of the Palestinian Yeshivah.

872 Ibid.

873 Ibid., in the section: The Fustat Leaders.

874 Ibid., in the section: The Geonim, the Heads of the Palestinian Yeshivah.

The Fustat Connection

Although there was no official obligatory tie between the Alexandrian community and the Fustat community, the leaders of Fustat felt justified in taking a very active role in the politics in Alexandria. Above we referred to the close connection between Yeshūʿā's position in Alexandria and the internal politics of the Fustat community. This was a derivative of the central position held by the Alexandrian leader in the political arena, whose contours stretched all over the Fatimid empire and beyond. An allied and cooperative leader in Alexandria was beneficial to the leaders in Fustat, and the latter's support for the leader in Alexandria or their withholding of support from him could often be of critical importance to his status.

Independent Loci of Power

Aside from the two centers delineated above, relationships between local leaders and influential figures unconnected to either of the centers could also be of great import. These figures constituted independent loci of power in and of themselves and were active in the highest echelons of the political arena that encompassed the entire Jewish world. These figures included persons like Abraham ha-Kohen Ibn al-Furāt, whose proximity to the Muslim authorities and great wealth made him a person who attracted others to him and who was deeply involved in all Jewish centers of the time. Above we noted the great importance of the special relationship Yeshūʿā had with him.

3 The Nagidate Period (1070 – 1130)

(a) The Turn Over

In the last third of the eleventh century, the infighting within the Yeshivah converged with external political factors and led to the decline of the Palestinian Yeshivah. At the beginning of the twelfth century the Palestinian Yeshivah ceased being a significant factor in international Jewish politics.[875] The dissolution of this important Jewish center naturally affected the leadership in Alexandria. The Nagidate largely replaced the Gaon and the "fellowship" of the Palestinian Yeshivah (*ḥavurah*).[876] The Nagidate brought with it a new type of

875 For a succinct description of this process, see Cohen, *Jewish Self-Government*, 79 – 84.
876 Cohen, *Jewish Self-Government*, 79 – 101.

leadership. Unlike the Gaon, the Nagid was not the representative of any institution. His personal *hayba*, this unfathomable ability to engender fear and awe in his subjects, was the main source of his authority.[877] In a number of instances, the *hayba* was transformed into a veritable cult of personality, which included symptoms of saint veneration. Here, for example, is how the arrival of a letter from the Nagid is described:

> And on Monday, the ninth day of the month of Kislev, groups of people would pass by and say that they had a letter from our master the lord of lords, may his honor be exalted [= Mevorakh b. Saʿadyah the Nagid] and they would congregate together and wave (*yumandilu*) the letter...and caw in the marketplaces and in the houses.[878]

Āraḥ b. Nathan described the occasion in a letter to his brother Abraham employing the quadrilateral root *m.n.d.l* .This verb is not found in the dictionaries. It may be a denominative verb derived from the noun *mandil*, which denotes a large piece of fabric used as clothing or as a cover for household furniture;[879] and thus the meaning of the verb would be "to wave," as in waving a kerchief. There is, however, another possibility, that the verb is derived from the word *mandal* which in Egyptian Arabic refers to the magical act of conjuring up the dead.[880] If this is the case, then not only did the people of Alexandria display disrespect and misuse of the Nagid's letter, but actually treated it as a magical ritual object. The attribution of magical power to an object that originated with the Nagid indicates a real shift in understanding the leader's source of authority. Henceforth, it is no longer consigned to a sacred institution, but rather is found in individuals and their charisma.

(b) Understanding the Ties between the Local Leader and the Nagid

The shift described above was clearly manifested in the local leadership of Alexandria. The main source of authority following the establishment of the Nagidate, and most clearly following Mevorakh b. Saʿadyah's rise, was the personal

877 Goitein, *Society*, 2: 35; Cohen, *Jewish Self-Government*, 248–250.
878 TS NS J 24r, ll. 23–26: Frenkel, *"The Compassionate and Benevolent"* [Hebrew], no. 88.
879 Goitein, *Society*, 4: 132, 191, 167.
880 See El-Said Badawi and Martin Hinds, *A Dictionary of Egyptian Arabic, Arabic-English* (Beirut: Librairie du Liban, 1986); Socrates Spiro, *Arabic-English Dictionary of the Colloquial Arabic of Egypt* (Beirut: Librairie du Liban, 1973); Sarah Stroumsa, *The Beginnings of the Maimonidean Controversy in the East* (Jerusalem: Ben-Zvi Institute, 1999), 112–113, 146–147, 152–153 [Hebrew].

and intimate relationship one had with the Nagid. This was not a gradual process; but a far-reaching change that took place within a very short time span. The rapidity of this change is clearly evident in the biography of Shelah b. Mubashshir. At the beginning of his tenure this leader depended upon the traditional sources of power, namely the support of the powerful Ben Nahum family and mainly his stature in the Palestinian Yeshivah as the "Sixth" amongst seven leading fellows. In these first years he did not hesitate to push back again the centralized leadership of Mevorakh in the name of the local powers in Alexandria. In the final years of his term, he morphed into an advocate of the Nagid and his mouthpiece and was dependent on his personal relationship with Mevorakh as his primary source of authority.[881] The relationship with the Nagid did have some formalized contractual element to it, since it was he who was officially responsible to appoint community leaders,[882] but more than anything the relationship was characterized by personal intimacy. The fate of this relationship was entirely dependent upon the Nagid's motivations and whims. The local leader was forever apprehensive that the Nagid might withdraw his support and that his term would come to an ignominious end.[883] Shelah's relationship with the Nagid, in which the personal and the public were inseparable, was a mélange of commercial, family and social ones. .[884]

(c) The *Niyāba* System in Its Jewish Version

The shift of authority from an institution to an individual changed the perception of local leadership. For the first time the community leader was a *nā'ib*, the Nagid's personal representative in Alexandria. The term *nā'ib* was likely drawn from the Fatimid bureaucracy, which had developed the *niyāba* into a complex system. ʿAlī Ibn al-Nuʿmān, the first Ismāʿīlī qadi of the Fatimid kingdom, appointed his brother Muḥammad as his *nā'ib* and as the qadi of the coastal cities of Farāma, Tinnīs and Damietta. Muḥammad in turn continued to live in Cairo and appointed local *nā'ib*s, who acted in his name in the abovementioned cit-

881 See above, Part II, Chapter. 2.5 (b): Shelah's Ties with the Nagid Mevorakh b. Saʿadyah.
882 See Cohen, *Jewish Self-Government*, 176, 234, 246.
883 See above, Part II, Chapter 3: Relationship with Mevorakh b. Saʿadyah Nagid, concerning the affair of al-Darʿī and Nathan b. Judah.
884 See above, Part II, Chapter 2.5 (b), on Mevorakh's second term as Nagid.

ies.[885] Beginning in the second third of the eleventh century the system was expanded to other areas: Not only the qadi could appoint *nāʾib*s but also the head missionary (*dāʿī al-duʿāt*) of the caliphate was permitted to do so.[886] Even the overseer of markets (*muḥtasib*) began to send his *nāʾib* to survey the markets, while he remained ensconced in the central mosque or in his office (*majlis al-ḥisba).*[887]

Even so, there was a critical difference between the Fatimid *nāʾib* and the Jewish one. The Fatimid *nāʾib* governed as a replica in miniature of the qadi himself. He had all the power of the chief qadi and he was given full authority to act independently. His authority was drawn from the chief qadi, and this was the sole meaning of functioning as the qadi's representative.[888] The Jewish *nāʾib*, however, represented the interests of the Nagid in the local community and acted as his spokesman and advocate, as well as having to report back to the Nagid regarding everything he did.[889] The Nagid was his only source of power and his dependence upon him was absolute.[890] Using Fatimid terminology, one may characterize the Fatimid *nāʾib* as an independent local leader with power of attorney (*tafwīḍ*) from the chief qadi, whereas the Jewish *nāʾib* was an executive representative (*tanfīdh*) and acted upon the Nagid's requests.[891]

---

885 Aḥmad b. ʿAlī Ibn Ḥajar al-ʿAsqalānī, *Rafʿ al-aṣr ʿan quḍāt miṣr* (Leiden: Brill, 1912), 590; Al-Imad, *Fatimid Vizierate*, 21; Richard J. Gottheil, "A Distinguished Family of Fatimide Cadis," *JAOS* 27 (1906): 230.

886 Heinz Halm, "The Isma'ili Oath of Alliance and the Sessions of Wisdom," in Farhad Daftary (ed.), *Medieval Isma'ili History and Thought* (Cambridge: Cambridge Uiversity Press, 1996), 104–105, cites Ibn al-Ṭuwayr on this matter; Samuel M. Stern, "Cairo as the Center of the Ismaʿili Movement," *Colloque international sur l'histoire du Caire* (Cairo: al-Hay'a al-Miṣriyya al-ʿĀmma lil-Kitāb, 1972), 437–450, provides an eleventh-century letter of appointment in which the *dāʿī al-duʿāt* is given permission to appoint *nuwwāb* for himself.

887 Bianquis, "Une crise frumêntaire," 85, quoting Maqrīzī, *Ittiʿāẓ*, and al-Qalqashandī, *Ṣubḥ al-aʿshā*.

888 See, e. g. the papyrus containing the letter of appointment for the qadi of Ashmunayn from 1068. According to this, the *nāʾib* was responsible for "justice and prayer and sermons and jurisprudence and correcting injustices in the town of Ashmunayn and its hinterland." See Adolf Grohmann, *Arabic Papyri in the Egyptian Library* (Cairo: Egyptian Library Press, 1934), 1: 102, no. 45; cited in Lev, *State and Society*, 136, n. 11.

889 See above, Part II, Chapter 3.3: Relationship with Mevorakh b. Saʿadyah Nagid.

890 See Abraham al-Darʿī's desperate response when he thought he had lost the Nagid's favor, ibid.

891 On this differentiation in the Fatimid theory of governance between *wizārat tafwīḍ* and *wizārat tanfīdh*, see Daftary, *The Ismaʿilis*, 223; Al-Imad, *Fatimid Vizierate*, 62–68.

(d) The *Nā'ib* as a Sectorial Leader

Another corollary of this shift was the division of the office. We saw that the Nagid Mevorakh b. Saʿadyah was careful to employ a number of representatives at the same time. In order to prevent the centralization of power in the hands of local leaders, the Nagid created as many competing loci of power as he could. At least four people served as his representatives in Alexandria during his tenure, and each of them saw himself, and even referred to himself, as the Nagid's *nāʾib*. Not only did these rivals fight bitterly among themselves in a no-holds-barred struggle,[892] but each served as spokesman and representative for a different sector of the community. Shelah b. Mubashshir was the representative of the indigenous inhabitants; Mariut ha-Kohen was the representatives of the "Shāmīs," the refugees from the Land of Israel and the fellows of the Palestinian Yeshivah who found refuge in Alexandria following the dissolution of the Yeshivah at the end of the eleventh century; Abraham al-Darʿī was the representative of the Maghribi sector, a large and powerful element in the community; regarding Nathan b. Judah, the fourth of these representatives, very little is known, and it is unclear who he represented.

(e) Drama in the Community: A Reflection of the Turn Over

The rapid shift of authority of the local leadership is best reflected in the social drama that took place in Alexandria. Shelah b. Mubashshir refers to it in a letter he wrote to the Nagid Mevorakh b. Saʿadyah (the beginning of the document is missing):

> [...] the synagogue [regarding the] "disagreement." And I will lead the community and govern it. Until he aimed his arrows at me and greeted me with profanity. I ignored him and said: "Perhaps he will retract what he said." He belongs to the Barqa clan. – I said: "Times are difficult and I do not wish to involve our lord, may he live forever [= Mevorakh the Nagid], for I know how busy he is at this time." Then this man focused his malice upon a young orphan, who was educated by his mother and taught Torah by her. He suborned him and corrupted his good qualities and said to him: "I will support you against your mother." And he turned one against the other. And he served as the boy's guarantor in a purchase of grapes. The youth went to his mother and stole the Torah book from her and sold it on his behalf and the widow complained vociferously and she brought him before the community and I applied my *hayba* and recovered the Torah book and gave it to Abra-

892 The most salient case is the assassination attempt of Abraham al-Darʿī on the part of his rival Nathan b. Judah. See above, nn. 531, 532.

ham al-Darʿī , may God preserve him, for safekeeping. And he did not veer from his evil ways and he suborned the youth to go to the qadi and sue her [his mother] in order to gain his father's inheritance. Once again I brought him before the community, and I said to him: "O so-and-so, God does not permit you to do these things. You are trying to corrupt the relationship between the youth and his mother." He said: "I shall not veer from my path, but I will support his suit before the Muslim authorities." We said to him, I and the elders: "The woman is a widow, no one should sue her. Moreover, she raised her children from the time they were babies until they were grown and taught them Torah. You really should not harass her in this way." He did not accept our direction. [It continued in this way] until a male member of her family helped her and said to him: "You do not accept the ruling of a Jewish court. You will have to accept the ruling of the Muslim authorities." He went with him to the authorities and they attacked one another and there was a great struggle because of what occurred between them. The elders issued a detailed edict regarding the events and sent it with Dawūd al-Rūmī, and we heard that they had left, he and his father, and the son of an associate. May God grant them according to their deeds. And may our lord, may he live forever, be appraised of their deeds from the mouth of one who is to be trusted. The sons of Barqa dissociate themselves from him because of his wild behavior. In the name of all that is precious to me, I disturb our lord's mind during these times. And peace unto his eminence our lord, may he live forever, and peace unto his son, may he live an everlasting life. The servant and all the community pray that peace [may be granted] to his lordship.[893]

The drama that Shelah describes in his letter accurately reflects the crisis of the local leadership in Alexandria. A lawless individual scorns all authority and breaks every taboo, both social and religious, creates a hubbub in the synagogue, curses the judge (Shelah himself) and suborns a youth against his widowed mother, causing him to steal a Torah book. He is not satisfied with this and continues to encourage him to sue her for his father's inheritance in the Muslim courts. The presence of this type of provocateur constitutes a real test of the strength and resolve of the leadership. At first Shelah turns to the traditional authorities: Initially he deploys his usual arsenal of tools and attempts to "lead the community and govern it." Here he fails abjectly: The scion of the Barqa family does not turn away from his evil ways, and goes a step further. From the moment Shelah gets personally involved, he becomes a new target for the criminal. This reprobate aims his arrows at the leader himself, and curses him personally. Shelah, aghast and at a loss, does not do anything, swallows his pride and waits. According to him, he had already considered involving the Nagid, but it seems that this is only to justify his actions post factum as he explains them to the Nagid, and he was likely in shock and paralyzed.

893 TS 13 J 16.3: Frenkel, *"The Compassionate and Benevolent"* [Hebrew], no. 66.

This passive response, which broadcast subservience and weakness, was exploited further by this Barqī, and he continued to provoke the Alexandrian leadership. He suborned a young orphan to steal a Torah book from his mother in order to finance a shady purchase of grapes, probably in order to manufacture wine. This scion of the Barqa family thus transgressed against every possible social and religious norm: He abused the weak members of the community (an orphan and a widow). He undermined the sanctity of the family unit by setting the son against the mother. He caused a Torah book to be stolen – symbolizing the mother's dedication, since she had made a great effort to teach her children Torah by herself – and suborned the youth to desecrate the Torah scroll by making cynical use of it to finance an operation promoting drunkenness.[894] This time Shelah was forced to act, since the widow herself came to him and loudly protested this behavior before the entire community at the synagogue in an accepted procedure known as "delay of prayer." Shelah proceeds to brag that he succeeded in returning the stolen Torah book with the help of his *hayba*, but it stands to reason that this occurred by virtue of the "delaying prayer" procedure, which brought the full force of the moral authority of the community and the holiness of the place to bear.[895] The authority of the community and the holiness of the synagogue were only good for a very short while. The reprobate continued on his evil path and further suborned the youth. It thus follows that neither the community, nor tradition, nor religious praxis were an absolute source of authority in this time of transition. Shelah's attempts to bring this member of the Barqa family before the community once again and his castigation of him, whether religious ("God doesn't allow this"), moral (the seeds of discord that he sows between mother and son), and legal ("the case of a widow in the house of her widowhood") – were all destined to fail, since they no longer held any great authority.

The members of the community who understood this turned to an external source of authority, the Muslim court system, as did a relative of the widow's. At the same time, Shelah attempted to persuade a group with which the criminal had familial ties, the Barqa clan. One may assume that in other cases his family may have been able to use their authority over him and control him, but in this

894 On the phenomenon of drunkenness among young people in Alexandria in this period, see Frenkel, "Adolescence."

895 On "appeal to the congregation" in Islamic lands, see Menahem Ben-Sasson, "Appeal to the Congregation in Islamic Countries in the Early Middle Ages," in Shulamit Elitzur et al. (eds.), *Knesset Ezra: Literature and Life in the Synagogue* (Jerusalem: Ben-Zvi Institute, 1994), 327–350 [Hebrew]. On the expression "complaining vociferously" as part of the conventional descriptions of these events, see ibid., 343–344.

extreme case they disavowed him and refused to involve themselves. Only at this point did Shelah understand that he must turn to the real source of authority, the Nagid. The Nagid received two missives regarding this case. One – a formal missive from the elders, in their capacity as representatives of the community, which was scrupulously recorded in a memorandum (*maḥḍar*), and the second – Shelah's letter. As opposed to the *maḥḍar*, Shelah's letter was entirely personal: It was written in the first person, Shelah gives his regards to the Nagid's son, and the main signatory on the document is Shelah himself. In other words, a communal leader's personal association and closeness with the Nagid were the principal source of authority at that time.

(f) The Enduring Powerbase

In addition to a personal relationship with the Nagid, membership in the network of elite cosmopolitan Jews continued, as in the past, to serve as an important powerbase for the communal leader, as testified by the enduring ties which overrode allegedly political rivalries, as manifested by Āraḥ b. Nathan's public activities, [896] by Shelah b. Mubashshir's ongoing relationship with Nahray b. Nissim or with "the Rav" Judah ha-Kohen,[897] as well as by Shelah's family's intimate mercantile ties with Maghribi merchants.[898]

4 Interlude (1130 – 1170)

Personal association with the Nagid as a central source of authority for the leaders of the Alexandrian community continued to be the norm of internal communal politics at least until the end of the Ayyubid regime. Nevertheless, during the 1130s and 1140s, at the time of the Nagid Samuel b. Hananyah, one may discern a short intermediary period during which the dependence of the local leader upon the Nagid was somewhat lessened. This was accompanied by cautious attempts at creating an independent local powerbase in Alexandria.

---

896 See above, Part II, Chapter 4.

897 See above, Part II, Chapter 2.5 (c): Shelah and "the Rav," and (d): Shelah and Nahray b. Nissim.

898 See above, Part II, Chapter 2.4 (a): Shelah and "the Maghribis" (*al-Maghāriba*).

(a) In the Footsteps of the Fatimid Model

The dominant figure in Alexandria at this time was Aaron Ibn al-ʿAmmānī. There were other rival figures who claimed the position,[899] but it was he who endeavored to reimagine community leadership and transform it into an independent stronghold. Aaron Ibn al-ʿAmmānī attempted to craft his regime in the same dynastic paradigm as the qadis in Cairo and Alexandria, such as the family of Makīn al-Dawla,[900] by nurturing his five sons and promoting them as his successors.[901] The qadi Makīn al-Dawla Ibn Ḥadīd served as model for emulation. It was said of this qadi that anyone that the vizier al-Afḍal wished to nurture and promote would be sent with a letter to the qadi, and the qadi would lavish gifts upon him.[902] Likewise, Ibn al-ʿAmmānī tried to create his powerbase through an ostentatious lifestyle, the flaunting of his wealth and gracious hospitality.[903] Yet, he tried to base the legitimacy of his regime on his family's origins in the Holy Land and presented the family's arrival from Palestine to Alexandria in mythological terms as a divine mission.[904]

(b) The Nagid's Deputy.

The search for new sources of authority did not come at the expense of the Nagid's status as a central source of authority in Alexandria. The Nagid Samuel b. Hananyah controlled the entire Jewish judiciary in Egypt at that time, and the judges in the local courts, including in Alexandria, were seen as his deputies *(nuwwāb*, pl. of *nāʾib)*. For example: A *kashruth* certificate for cheese licensed by the court in Alexandria in the middle of the twelfth century was signed with the following formula: "We, who are signed below, the court of No Amon, the *nuwwāb* of the illustrious eminence, our lord, our teacher, and our master Samuel, the Great Nagid, the Nagid of Israel."[905]

---

899 See above, Part II, Chapter 5.4: His Position in the Community .
900 On this family of qadis, see Sālim, *Taʾrīkh madīnat al-iskandariyya*, 19 – 21; Goitein, *Society*, 2: 587, n. 22; Ibn Muyassar, *Akhbār miṣr*, 73, ll. 3 – 6. Qadis from this family are mentioned in several Genizah fragments, too, such as ULC Or 1080 J 258; TS 13 J 3.4; TS NS J 36; TS 13 J 22.23.
901 See above, Part II, Chapter 5.1: Origins and Family.
902 Maqrīzī, *Khiṭaṭ*, 2: 182.
903 See above, Part II, Chapter 5.3: Wealth as a Lifestyle.
904 See above, Part II, Chapter 5.5: Conclusion.
905 Christ Coll. Abrahams 10: Frenkel, *"The Compassionate and Benevolent"* [Hebrew], no. 5.

Aaron Ibn al-ʿAmmānī understood quite well that he could not consolidate his position without the support of the Nagid. He thus invested great effort in transforming himself into Samuel b. Hananyah's *nāʾib*.[906] This being said, one does discern parallel attempts of establishing alternative sources of authority. This process occurred at the same time as the almost complete dissolution of the Fatimid caliphate and vizierate, and consequently Egypt was transformed into a battlefield of disparate warring powers, who fought one another and attempted to establish independent powerbases.[907] One may, perhaps, better understand the ascendance of local families, such as the Ibn al-ʿAmmānī family in Alexandria, with these circumstances in mind.

5 The Ayyubid Period (1170–1250)

(a) Searching for a Path (1170–1200)

The last three decades of the twelfth century were a time of great trepidation and no clear direction. Following the fall of the Fatimid dynasty, which had ruled Egypt for two hundred years and the establishment of a new and different regime, the Ayyubid dynasty, a deep change took place throughout Egypt. The local Jewish leadership also changed. In those years the community vacillated between a number of different leadership models and searched for direction. The leadership positions in Alexandria were occupied variously by R. Eleazar, Meir b. Hillel who was the *nāʾib* appointed by the Gaon, and by R. Ephraim, the foreign preacher who swept the community with his magnetism. Not only the appointed *nāʾib*, but also the other leaders, who relied upon the goodwill of the community, remained dependent upon the Gaon – who at that time dwelt in Egypt proper – and required his official writ of appointment. We saw that in order to appoint R. Eleazar in his place, Meir b. Hillel tried to get the Gaon's approval;[908] and even R. Ephraim, who swept into his position by virtue of his charisma, required the official approval of the *raʾīs*.[909]

Yet, there was a persistent effort to find alternative fonts of authority. Each of the leaders of Alexandria at that time may be seen as a representative of a different source of authority: R. Eleazar was dependent upon the traditional commercial-social-intellectual network, which connected him to the Jewish and Muslim

906 See above, Part II, Chapter 5.4: His Position in the Community.
907 Lev, *State and Society*, 56–64.
908 See above, Part II, Chapter 8.2 (a): His Appointment.
909 See above, Part II, Chapter 8.3: The Leadership Crisis and Its Resolution.

political powerbases;[910] Meir b. Hillel relied upon his personal association with the Gaon and upon his intellectual prowess;[911] and R. Ephraim was dependent upon his personal charisma.[912] Charisma as a source of authority amongst local leaders was a new phenomenon, which is completely understandable considering the crisis Alexandria went through at the time.

Charismatic, or "[h]eroic leaders [...] usually arise in societies undergoing profound crisis [...]. Mass alienation and social atomization are rising. Intense psychological and material needs go unfulfilled... A variety of secondary leaders come to the fore to raise expectations and sharpen demands [...]. Then there appears a leader [...] equipped with rare gifts of compassion and competence [...] that rebels against authority and tradition" – this is how James Burns, an historian and political scientist, describes the backdrop to the emergence of a charismatic leader.[913] This description fits the arena of R. Ephraim's sudden and dramatic arrival in Alexandria very well: the multiple contenders for leadership and the desperate search for a figure of authority, when even Meir b. Hillel, the foreigner who turned down the office, is a sought after figure.[914] The answer offered by R. Ephraim for the woes of the Alexandrian community was symbolic, which created – through the rhetoric of consolation and blessing in his sermons – the mirage of a solution to the crisis. This is typical of a leadership based on charisma: "[...] people seek some release from their conflicts by projecting their fears, aggression, and aspirations onto some social objects which allow a symbolic solution."[915] Ultimately, the coronation of R. Ephraim was unsuccessful. The old elites were not eager to relinquish their advantages and to agree to a leadership that depended upon an authority which did not benefit them in any way. In the name of preserving "the natural order," in which leadership is under the purview of the elders and dignitaries, they waged a no-holds-barred campaign against R. Ephraim, and were ultimately victorious.[916] In the end, however, the vacuum that was created was filled by a different type of leader altogether.

910 See above, Part II, Chapter 8.1: Background and Origin.
911 See above, Part II, Chapter 7.
912 See above, Part II, Chapter 9.
913 James M. Burns, *Leadership* (NY: Harper, 1978), 244.
914 See above, Part II, Chapter 7.4: His Relationship with the Community.
915 Daniel Katz, "Patterns of Leadership," in Jeanne N. Knutson (ed.), *Handbook of Political Psychology* (San Francisco: Jossey-Bass, 1973), 216.
916 See above, Part II, Chapter 9.3: Summary; A Jannus-Faced Leader?

(b) The New Leaders (1200–1250)

Historical Background

Two external events greatly influenced the shift in local leadership in the last third of the twelfth century, a shift that ultimately led to a profound change in the composition of the ruling class in the course of the thirteenth. One event is related to the Crusades and the havoc they wreaked amongst European communities. The Crusades catalyzed a flow of immigrants from Christendom to Alexandria, amongst them great scholars who were referred to as "the rabbis."[917] These scholars became a critical component in the community, from both quantitative and qualitative perspectives, and succeeded in achieving positions of leadership. The second event was Maimonides' arrival in Egypt and the establishment of the position of "Head of the Jews" by him and his descendants.[918] The "rabbis" supplied the personnel for this new leadership, and Maimonides was the figure who catalyzed the process, though his path was not without its fair share of difficulties and impediments.

Dependence upon the Maimonidean Nagids

Being foreigners in Egypt, the immigrant rabbis, such as R. Pinḥas and R. Anatoly, did not have access to the dense network of ties that served the leadership in Alexandria so effectively. Their sole source of authority was drawn from the personal support of Maimonides. Maimonides saw R. Pinḥas as his protégé, guided him, and expected to disseminate his *Code* in Alexandria with his help.[919] Maimonides' guidance is apparent from the many and detailed responsa he sent R. Pinḥas. He tried to alleviate R. Pinḥas' difficulties with integration into the new community by elucidating the local codes of conduct for him,[920] and advocated on his behalf whenever he failed.[921] This is not meant to imply that their relation-

---

917 See Goitein, *Palestinian Jewry*, 338–343; Reiner, "Pilgrims and Pilgrimage," 55–60; Ephraim Kanarfogel, "The ʿAliyah of Three Hundred Rabbis' in 1211: Tosafist Attitudes Toward Settling in the Land of Israel," *JQR* 76 (1986): 191–215.

918 Menahem Ben-Sasson, "Maimondes in Egypt"; Shelomo D. Goitein, "Moses Maimonides, Man of Action: A Revision of the Master's Biography in the Light of Geniza Documents," in: Gérard Nahon andt Charles Touati (eds.), *Hommage à George Vajda; études d'histoire et de pensée juives* (Louvain: Peeters, 1980), 155–167.

919 See above, n. 717.

920 See above, Part II, Chapter 10.3 (b): His Style as a Judge.

921 See above, Part II, Chapter 10.3 (c): His Proficiency.

ship was without its tensions,[922] but it was certainly a relationship founded upon R. Pinḥas' dependence on Maimonides as the dispenser of authority. This is reflected quite clearly in the desperate plea that R. Pinḥas sends to Maimonides at a time of crisis, pleading with his mentor, that he should not cast him aside.[923] This type of relationship is also evident in the case of R. Anatoly. One of his first acts when he arrives in Alexandria was to send Maimonides an epistle introducing himself:

> And I came to No Amon and it is a great city founded with the blessing of the Most High[...] and upon their lips praise[...] A voice calling out in my ears, Moses received the Torah from Sinai[...] and had the elders of my community, may the Rock preserve them and grant them life, not prevented me, this letter would not have come to you, but I myself would have presented myself.[924]

This letter ostentatiously demonstrates Anatoly's intellectual proficiency and literary prowess, and its purpose was to secure Maimonides' approval and acceptance. Anatoly's anxious anticipation of Maimonides' response to the letter and his approval is attested to in Anatoly's own words:

> And I pray before your office, and beg our master that he not consider it a sin on the part of his servant. For I have come before his intellect with meager gifts, but I do not wear a layabout's garb. For I only wished to bring an appropriate gift, a portion of first grains, so as to permit the precedent, until I send two loaves to the temple, as is appropriate. Herein, I attempt to burnish my aptitude for pithy phrases, which has become rusty with disuse, but if I may at least try to polish it, and if it may be found pleasing to wise men, so that my associates and bosom friends shall not fear, that I misspeak, and I fear for my soul, lest it deceive me, "for the skin of Moses' face was radiant" [Exodus 34:30], "why, my clan is the humblest in Manasseh" [Judges 6: 15].[925]

It was evidently clear to R. Anatoly, as it was to the elders of Alexandria, that any appointment to the leadership of the community would not be successful without Maimonides' approval. And, indeed, Maimonides grants it, as is apparent from his response:

> For this I say to all my coreligionists, behold a field blessed by God. Let all rejoice in your arrival in our country, your appearance in our midst, and your presence at our windows. May the blessed Deity unerringly guide your footsteps in His castle so that you shall not

922 See above, Part II, Chapter 10.3 (d): His Relationship with Maimonides: Between Dependence and Rebellion.
923 See above, ibid., n. 698.
924 Maimonides, *Responsa*, ed. Abraham Lichtenberg (Leipzig: H.L. Schneuss, 1859), 2: 36b.
925 Ibid.

> stumble, and bequeath to you from the bounty promised to the faithful, and may you always be at one with His people. And now that He brought you here, let His grace flow to you as a river. Peace.[926]

Isaac b. Ḥalfon also depended upon his relationship with Abraham Maimuni, and actually served as the latter's contact with the community.[927]

Meritocracy

The "rabbis" lacked the supportive social network their predecessors had at their disposal, and thus had to depend not only upon Maimonides and his descendants, but also upon personal merit and upon their reputation. When R. Samuel arrived in Alexandria he was already known by the dignitaries of the community as a scholar of significant repute. Very soon after his arrival, R. Judah Ibn al-ʿAmmānī extended a helping hand and refers to him as *ustādhī* (my teacher and master).[928]

The letter of introduction that R. Anatoly sent Maimonides fulfilled its intended function, and with the help of the letter, Maimonides became familiar with Anatoly's virtues: "You are the chief of pundits, replete with grace, and good qualities."[929] R. Anatoly, who had come to Alexandria from Sicily, had a significant cultural advantage over the Ashkenazi rabbis, for the Jews of that island were still in tune with the culture of the Muslim regime that had previously ruled the island.[930] In contrast with R. Pinḥas, who was routinely flummoxed due to his cultural disconnect, and his inability to take an accurate pulse of the community and its expectations of him,[931] R. Anatoly found a common language with the locals and especially with Maimonides. Their correspondence reveals a vibrant dialogue and a common tongue, and it is clear that their cultural background was drawn from the same fount. An important element of this heritage was their ability to write elegantly and allusively: Anatoly's facility with pithy phrases, evident in his first missive, impressed Maimonides greatly, for as was made clear above, among his many qualities, R. Anatoly was also a famous poet.[932] Maimonides responded to the elegant poetic register of R. Anatoly's

926 Shailat, *Letters*, 470.
927 See above, Part II, Chapter 13.5: R. Isaac and R. Abraham Maimuni.
928 See above, Part II, Chapter 12, n. 766.
929 Shailat, *Letters*, 470.
930 Henri Bresc, *Un monde mediterranéen: économie et société en Sicile, 1300–1450* (Rome: École française de Rome, 1986), 2: 630.
931 See above, Part II, Chapter 10.3, 4, 5.
932 See above, Part II, Chapter 11.2: An Intellectual Portrait.

first missive with an equally elegant missive of his own, replete with metaphor and allusion. We present a short sample from his response, wherein Maimonides compares R. Anatoly's letter to a beautiful woman:

> And I remove the veil from her face so that I may play with her pearls, and behold she is first among all maidens, proficient at everything, well-arranged, an heir to royalty. Ornaments upon her neck, and choice garments, bracelets bound upon her arms, resplendent in gems, and upon her a dress befitting a queen, a golden breastplate upon her with choice gems, a jeweled belt encircles her, and a diadem upon her forehead.[933]

R. Anatoly's rare poetic ability was thus critically important to him as a channel of communication with Maimonides, who was to become his main source of authority. His literary abilities and cultural affinity to the inhabitants of Egypt paved the way for his easy integration into the local elite.[934] And indeed, in very short order R. Anatoly served as one of the local leaders and employed the traditional and acceptable channels of authority. Thus, for example, he created a powerbase among the elders of the community,[935] and collected donations – an activity that was one of the clearest mechanisms of accepted authority employed by the traditional elites.[936]

These advantages were not available to the Ashkenazi rabbis, who had great difficulty in reading the social and cultural map of the eastern communities. Their knowledge of law and their judicial experience was not always a good fit with their new home.[937] It does seem likely that one conduit of communication with the community was through the weekly sermons in the synagogue, that were translated, as far as we know, into Arabic. We have already seen that R. Pinḥas' weekly sermons were copied carefully and were preserved for generations to come.[938]

---

933 Shailat, *Letters*, 468. On Maimonides' particular weakness for flowery Hebrew, see Joseph Yahalom, "Maimonides and Hebrew Poetic Language," *Pe'amim* 81 (1999): 4 – 18 [Hebrew].

934 In Ashkenaz there was also great admiration for *piyyut* and *paytanim*, but the Italo-Ashkenazi school excelled rather in the simplicity of its language, and not in flowery language and decorative forms. See Ezra Fleischer, *Hebrew Liturgical Poetry in the Middle Ages* (Jerusalem: Keter, 1975), 433 [Hebrew]. On the art of writing elegant epistles in Islamic and Judaeo-Arabic culture, see Albert Arazi and Haggai Ben-Shammai, "Risāla," *Encyclopedia of Islam*, 2nd edition, 8: 532 – 539 esp. 535 – 536.

935 See above, Part II, Chapter 11.3 (a): Centralization.

936 See above, Part II, Chapter 11.4 (a): Charitable Work.

937 See above, n. 931.

938 See above, n. 728.

The New and the Old: The Powerbase that Survived

The ascendance of the European immigrants did not mean that that they completely took over the leadership of the community. Leaders born in Egypt continued to serve, such as Isaac b. Ḥalfon and Elijah b. Zechariah. Both, locals and new immigrants alike, were appointed by the Nagids of the Maimonidean dynasty, and relied mainly on their close association with these Nagids and on their support. One must add that the European leaders did not replace the ruling elite, but rather were integrated among them. In order to succeed as leaders, they had to earn the support of the old elite, learn to speak their language of authority, and adopt their channels of information and their conduits to power. Upon his arrival, R. Samuel took advantage of the support of Judah Ibn al-ʿAmmānī and their good relationship; R. Anatoly used the fundraising apparatus for the purpose of buttressing his position in the same way as his predecessors; and R. Pinḥas, who had difficulty understanding the political parlance of the locals, languished in his position. The closer a local leader was to the ruling elite in his cultural background and the common path of preparation for the position, the more successful he was. One may therefore conclude that despite the foundation of authority shifting over the years and epochs, reliance upon the local ruling elite and the imperative to integrate among them remained a constant.

Chapter 2 Methods of Governance: Tools and Strategies

1 Introduction

This chapter deals with the tools and the strategies employed by the community leaders to maintain their positions. I do not intend to list the executive privileges granted to these leaders by Muslim or Jewish law. Rather, I shall undertake a phenomenological examination of the *de facto* methods employed by these leaders, the ways in which they were employed, their efficacy and their limitations, as well as the willingness or hesitation of the leaders to employ these methods, and the frequency with which they ended up employing them. In other words, in this chapter I will analyze actual events, behaviors and modes of expression, rather than ideal paradigms of particular organizations as they were enshrined in written law codes. This empirical approach promises from the very beginning to lack organization and cohesion, since I am not analyzing a theoretical or official structure, but rather the chaotic ebb and flow of life.

Since this analysis focuses on one particular population group – the Jewish community of Alexandria – the descriptions and conclusions are only applicable to this group. That being said, one may surmise that at least some of the conclusions will have wider applicability.

2 Methods of Dissuasion, Punishment, and Execution

(a) Excommunication

One of the official and well-known punitive measures available to local leaders was excommunication of various types.[939] Throughout Jewish history this mea-

939 See Gideon Liebson, "*Gezerta* and *Ḥerem Setam* in the Gaonic in Early Medieval Periods," unpublished J.D diss. (The Hebrew University of Jerusalem, 1979) [Hebrew]; idem, "The Ban and Those under It: Tannaitic and Amoraic Perspectives," *Shenaton ha-Mishpat ha-Ivri: Annual of the Institute for Research in Jewish Law* 6–7 (1979): 177–202 [Hebrew]; idem, "Determining Factors in *Ḥerem* and *Nidui* (Ban and Excommunication) during the Tannaitic and Amoraic Periods," *Shenaton ha-Mishpat ha-Ivri: Annual of the Institute for Research in Jewish Law* 2 (1975): 292–342 [Hebrew].

https://doi.org/10.1515/9783110713619-021

sure shifted greatly as to its range and the way in which it was used.[940] Here I will examine what role excommunication played in Alexandria in the periods under question and how it served the leaders as a tool for exercising their authority.

Frequency of Use

The data we may glean from the Genizah documents reflect a certain hesitation on the part of leaders to employ this measure. Below we shall attempt to ascertain the reason for this careful policy. The official explanation on the part of the leaders was the constant fear that this serious punitive measure would cause people to convert to Islam. When Shelah b. Mubashshir was asked by members of the community to excommunicate a Spanish man who had fled to Alexandria, he explained his refusal in explicit terms in a letter to Maṣliaḥ, Head of the Yeshivah: "I am afraid to excommunicate him since he has threatened to convert."[941]

During the period of "disagreement" between the Maghribi immigrants to Alexandria and the locals,[942] great pressure was exerted upon Shelah b. Mubashshir from the native "inhabitants of the city" to declare the Maghribi leaders excommunicated. Shelah refused this time as well. In the end, two "inhabitants of the city" took it upon themselves to excommunicate the Maghribi leader, Benayah b. Mūsā. Benayah's vehement response to the excommunication sheds light upon the fears at the basis of Shelah's refusal to employ this to:

Upon God's life, I literally died from the intensity of emotion that overcame me. And once I almost left the community [= converted] so that my guilt and the guilt of my wife and children would fall upon he who sent us these bad people. I fasted for eight days and for three days I did not leave my house.[943]

Excommunication was a very potent measure: There were elements of physical deterrence, which were the product of social and economic alienation, as well as elements of magical deterrence, which played on the deep fears that

---

940 Jacob Katz, *Tradition and Crisis: Jewish Society at the End of the Middle Ages*, trans. Bernard D. Cooperman (NY: NY University Press, 1993), 85; Liebson, "Determining Factors."

941 TS 10 J 10.3r, ll. 13–14: Eliyahu Ashtor, "Documentos españoles de la Genizah," *Sefarad* 24 (1964): 41–80; Frenkel, *"The Compassionate and Benevolent"* [Hebrew], no. 49. The term used here is *pish'ut* (criminality), which signifies conversion from Judaism. See Goitein, *Society*, 2: 300.

942 See above, Part II, Chapter 2.4 (a): Shelah and "the Maghribis" (*al-Maghāriba*).

943 TS 13 J 23.3v, ll. 10–12: Gil, *Kingdom*, no. 605; Frenkel, *"The Compassionate and Benevolent"* [Hebrew], no. 75. My translation differs from Gil's.

the person who was excommunicated would lose his place in the world to come and his part in the Jewish people.[944]

As was the case with all deterrent measures, it could not be used frequently since it would cease being effective. The leaders feared the potency of this measure and the extreme reaction it could provoke among those who were excommunicated and ostracized, who could potentially take the ultimate countermeasure and convert. Excommunication and ostracism were thus a double-edged sword. The leaders of Alexandria were very careful about it, and generally chose not to use it. Another factor in the use of excommunication, beyond its judicious use as a deterrent, was the status and prestige of the leader who considered employing this measure.

There is evidence of excommunications that were not adhered to throughout the period under investigation. In 1080 the local judge tried to protect the property of a deceased man on behalf of his widow and orphans. To that end he declared that anyone who knew of evidence or proof that would help him with his case and did not deliver it to the court would be excommunicated. No one bothered to hand over any evidence or other proof, and the judge was forced, to his great chagrin, to announce this threat repeatedly:

> And he, from the time that the deceased passed away, excommunicates every Monday and Thursday whoever know of any testimony or read any notebook of his [the deceased] or [had anything from him] for safekeeping. And he didn't succeed in finding anything that would help him... and though he could excommunicate[...] one hundred times, that is forbidden.[945]

In 1235 Isaac b. Ḥalfon the judge excommunicated anyone who arranged marriages without the permission of the *muqaddam*. The measure was announced with great fanfare at the synagogue in the presence of all the elders and "the holy Torah scroll was opened" – but the community simply ignored this prohibition.[946]

At approximately the same time, the judge in Alexandria asked Abraham Maimuni what one should do regarding a tax collector who had abandoned his wife in Alexandria and fled with a Christian slave girl to al-Buḥayra. This "evil one," as the author of the letter refers to him, had already been excommu-

944 Katz, *Tradition and Crisis*, 84–86; Ben-Sasson, *Emergence*, 303–304.
945 TS 12.591r, ll. 6–9, 1–17: Frenkel, "*The Compassionate and Benevolent*" [Hebrew], no. 24. This excommunication is a *ḥerem setam*, a judicial procedure uses as a means for clarifying and locating the truth in court. On this, see Liebson, "*Gezerta* and *Ḥerem Setam*"; Ben-Sasson, *Emergence*, 72–73, 304–307; Goitein, *Society*, 2: 331–341, esp. 340.
946 See above, n. 790.

nicated a number of times but proceeded to ignore it.[947] Joseph b. R. Gershom, the French judge who served for a short period in Alexandria, understood the bind local leaders put themselves into, and how the authority to excommunicate and ostracize could in certain cases be completely ineffective:

> For whoever sins and I rebuke, the sinner remains silent and then says to me: you are just one of the judges and I will not accept your verdict until you all agree, and I cannot adequately respond to him, though the great dignitaries are with me and I have the power to ostracize them.[948]

In other words, the "power" to excommunicate could be completely useless if it was not accompanied by a modicum of authoritativeness on the part of the leaders, and thus most of them hesitated to use it.

The Severity of the Measure

The leaders were conscious of these constraints and employed the measure hesitantly.[949] R. Ephraim, who was subjected to a very serious attack by his detractors that included physical assault and personal insults, understood that the community expected him to respond by excommunicating the opposition. Despite this, he did not feel confident enough and did not feel he had sufficient support to take this step. He attempted to appease the community in a very convoluted way: he took an oath to respond to all the allegations that were hurled at him, but the responsibility for the excommunication of his main rival, Ibn al-Talāj, he redirected to the community's conscience – without attempting to excommunicate this man explicitly and refusing to stand behind the edict he had issued: "Whoever said these things about me in order to dishonor me, is hereby excommunicated. I do not need to excommunicate him [myself]."[950]

In contrast, Isaac b. Ḥalfon decided to employ this punitive measure because he was worried that if he did not do so, his instructions would not be heeded, and thus he was constrained to excommunicate anyone who arranged marriages without his approval. In order for people to heed him in this, he

947 ULC Or 1080 J 281, l. 25: Friedman, *Jewish Polygyny*, 326–330.
948 TS 10 J 24.8: Mann, *Jews*, 2: 372–373 (incorrect shelf mark there).
949 On the reluctance of the *Amoraim*)the Jewish scholars of the period from about 200 to 500 CE) in Palestine to use excommunication and banning, see Liebson, "The Ban and Those under It," 178–182.
950 TS 16.272v, l. 13: Frenkel, *"The Compassionate and Benevolent"* [Hebrew], no. 30.

had to get some validation for this act from above, and thus alludes to the excommunication edict that Maimonides had issued in a similar situation:

> Whoever arranges a marriage without the permission of the *muqaddam* of Alexandria, which is under the authority of... will be ostracized from the community and will be in the same category as those people [at the time of] our R. Moses, may his righteous memory be for a blessing, and our R. Isaac son of our R. Sasson, may his righteous memory be for a blessing, and all the judges of that time who excommunicated all the rural areas (*al-diyār*) who arranged marriages without the overseers who were appointed to this task by the Head of the Jews (*al-ra'īs*) of that period.[951]

Moreover, he further made use of a special communiqué written by R. Abraham Maimuni, which certified his excommunication.

> Regarding the excommunication that was issued by the eminent judge R. Isaac, may the Lord be with him, regarding those who arrange marriages in Alexandria without the permission of the *muqaddam*, it is a valid excommunication and strengthens the lineages of Israel and preserves the proper order of their Torah and prevents lawlessness with regard to marriage which undermines the pedigrees and it is similar to the excommunication agreed upon by my father and teacher, and the sages of his generation, may their memory be for a blessing, and they issued [the excommunication] and they ruled upon it and they erected a fence.[952]

The fear of the meaningless use of this tool – i.e., the congregation ignoring it – led to two different courses of action: On the one hand, a very curtailed use of the measure, so that it was barely perceptible, and an attempt to camouflage the authority enacting it; and on the other hand – the full-blown use of this measure, and the enlistment of prestigious individuals to support it.

The Extent of Use

Despite all of the above, there were certain leaders in this period who did not hesitate to wield the cudgel of excommunication, not necessarily as a method by which to govern the community, but as a symbolic display of strength, on the rare occasions where there was a definite threat against the status of the ruling elite.

The drama that took place in Alexandria in the final years of the eleventh century reflect this best. The account is recorded in a badly damaged letter, of

951 Abraham Maimuni, *Responsa*, 282–283, §106. Goitein (ibid.) translated *diyār* as "villages" and I changed this to "rural areas."
952 Ibid., 189.

which only the right half has survived. Nevertheless, one may reconstruct much of what took place from this part of the letter. The letter describes a major upheaval in the Alexandrian community: A group of people, who opposed the judge, Shelah b. Mubashshir, complained about him to the Nagid: "All the Alexandrian Jews came… to our eminent lord [= the Nagid] and complained about their situation."[953]

The activities of the opposition constituted a real threat against Shelah and the group of dignitaries who supported him. As always, when an existential threat arose against the ruling elite, the opposition was described as a fifth column intent upon overturning the *status quo*, placing those of lower status on high and diminising those of elevated status. The leader of the opposition, known only as *al-rajul* ("the man"), was accused of incitement and of enlisting "his friends the shoemakers" against the elites.[954] Shelah's response was decisive and was executed expeditiously:

> He went into the synagogue together with his shaykhs, there were five of them. And they removed the Torah scrolls and excommunicated everyone who had gathered there. Among them were three people: the Shaykh Abū… al-Faraj also known as Ibn al-Qāsh and…[955]

In other words, the leader and the group of dignitaries who supported him did not hesitate in this case to use the most extreme method at their disposal. In a dramatic move, they entered the synagogue in which the opposition had gathered. One may surmise that their arrival was unexpected, as the letter states: "They did not suspect anything until[…]"[956] Taking advantage of the surprise, the leader and his cadre performed a ceremony of mass excommunication: they took the Torah scrolls out of the Ark and excommunicated all who were present in the synagogue. It is entirely clear that some of the people that were excommunicated were eminent notables and members of the elite, such as the Ibn al-Qāsh family – and not just shoemakers from the fringes of society.[957] Unfortunately, we do not know how this matter was resolved. It is difficult to assume that the entire congregation who were present were excommunicated for any protracted period, and it stands to reason that the opposing sides came to

953 TS 20.170, ll. 11–12: Frenkel, *"The Compassionate and Benevolent"* [Hebrew], no. 35.
954 Ibid., l. 13.
955 Ibid., ll. 16–19.
956 Ibid., l. 15.
957 On the Ibn al-Qāsh family, See below, Part III, Chapter 2.7 (c), in the section: The Ibn Al-Qāsh Affair.

some sort of resolution. The act of excommunication was thus meant as an ostentatious demonstration of power, the function of which was to show to the entire community who was truly in control. It was undertaken as a decisive move in the power games amongst the leadership, not necessarily as a tool of ongoing sound governance.

Another example of how excommunication and ostracism were seen as an acceptable means in the personal power struggles among the leaders is the case of the rivalry between R. Joseph b. Gershom of France, who served as the judge of Alexandria in 1234 – 1235, and Hodayah b. Jesse the *Nasi*, who sojourned in Alexandria at that time. We learn of this case from a series of questions that R. Joseph b. Gershon addressed to R. Abraham Maimuni and the latter's answers[958] It seems that the community of Alexandria excommunicated themselves and afterwards wished to have this act reversed. Hodayah b. Jesse demanded ten dinars for the reversal of the excommunication, and the members of the community were unable to raise the funds. R. Joseph b. Gershom interfered and reversed the excommunication himself, so that "the name of Heaven would not be defiled because of a demand for money."[959] Hodayah was angry and excommunicated R. Joseph b. Gershon and announced that anyone who did business with inhabitants of the city originating in Byzantium or France would also be excommunicated: "And he excommunicated anyone who would derive benefit from his property, whether French or Byzantine."[960] R. Joseph responded that "a scholar who went bad is not [officially] ostracized in public,"[961] and for this reason he is judged "as someone who ostracized one who was not supposed to be ostracized, and he himself shall be ostracized, and the final ostracism of this scholar stands."[962] In other words, Hodayah himself is ostracized because he ostracized someone (R. Joseph) who did not deserve ostracism and it is R. Joseph's act of ostracism that stands. The rivalry and the personal jealousy that were at the basis of this ostracism war was aptly summarized by R. Abraham Maimuni in his response:

> And he complains to me that your honor has maligned him and you complain to me that he has maligned you and your forefathers and the sages of France [...] and each one of you has requested the privilege to excommunicate and ostracize whoever they want, and that all of Israel shall heed him alone [...] and the truth is that I know that he began by deriding you

958 Abraham Maimuni, *Responsa*, 13 – 24, §§4 – 8. Friedman, "The Nagid.'
959 Abraham Maimuni, *Responsa*, 15.
960 Ibid.
961 Ibid. and n. 1.
962 Ibid. and n. 3. See Palestinian Talmud, Mo'ed Qatan, 80:3 81:4; Babylonian Talmud, Mo'ed Qatan, 17:1.

> and all the people of France because you are French. His missives have come to me from No Amon regarding this from the time they agreed to appoint you as judge, and after having loved you and praised you, he became your enemy because you were appointed as the judge.[963]

As in the other case, here too excommunication and ostracism are ceremonial acts and part of the struggle for leadership. R. Joseph and Hodayah hurl excommunications at each other, as well as other forms of derision, curses, and malignant words.[964] Neither one of them is truly capable of bringing about his rival's excommunication, but the act of excommunication and ostracism constituted a ceremonial declaration of a state of enmity between the two opposing camps. In other words, the main reason for the unrestricted and frequent use of excommunication at this time was the narrow scope of the internal struggles for leadership of the community, and excommunication was primarily ceremonial.

(b) The Rebuke

Though the rebuke was very common in the Tannaitic period in Israel and was preferred to excommunication and ostracism,[965] there is only one allusion to the use of this punitive mechanism in Alexandria. In a letter sent by R. Joseph b. Gershon he complains of his inability to lead the community: "For whoever sins and I rebuke him, the sinner remains silent and then says to me: you are just one of the judges and I will not accept your verdict until you all agree, and I cannot adequately respond to him."[966]

The randomness of this data does not provide us with adequate information regarding the frequency and method of use of this punitive mechanism, but since parallel studies which describe the administrative and legal apparatuses in other communities under Muslim rule do not refer to this at all,[967] it is not unlikely that R. Joseph imported it from Europe.

---

963 Abraham Maimuni, *Responsa*, 18.

964 On the war of curses and name-callings that accompanied this struggle, see the remarks of R. Joseph b. Gershon (ibid., 15): "he called me a bastard and cursed my learned fathers after their death using the phrase damned son of the damned, and called all French Jewry heretics and infidels and anthropomorphizers of the Creator after the beds of scholars ... and if I abandoned him after he abandoned me, am I to blame? Even more so that I do not admit his claims at all."

965 See Liebson, "Determining Factors," 190.

966 TS 10 J 24.8: Mann, *Jews*, 2: 372.

967 Thus Goitein, *Society*, vol. 2; Ben-Sasson, *Emergence*; Cohen, *Jewish Self-Government*, Bareket, *Jewish Leadership*.

(c) Community Fines

There is one attestation regarding the levying of community fines by a local leader as a punitive measure and as a deterrent. In the course of the violent conflict that took place in Alexandria at the end of the final decade of the eleventh century between the Maghribi population and the city natives, Benayah b. Mūsā, the leader of the Maghribis, relates the following:

> They included in the plot a false allegation that I spoke against our master, the lord of lords, and they testified against me and submitted reports [...] and my property was confiscated and community fines were levied against me a number of times. But the Creator saved [me].[968]

This is a short and unique attestation and by its nature it offers more questions than answers: Was this a regularly levied tax that the inhabitants were required to pay in order to maintain the community apparatus, as implied by the term community tax? If so, this contradicts the layout of the communal system as sketched out by Goitein, according to which the community lacked a set budget, and was reliant on fundraisers and donations for specific functions and according to need.[969] Returning to the matter at hand, it is clear that the ruling elite in Alexandria could, when it wished, employ serious economic sanctions such as the confiscation of property and repeated fines. The dearth of information regarding such sanctions does not necessarily imply that they were used infrequently. The opposite may be true, the casual allusion to the concept "community fines" without further elaboration by Benayah b. Mūsā may imply that it was a fairly common punitive mechanism.

(d) Extradition to Muslim Authorities

Sentencing of Violent Offenders and Religious Sinners

The local leadership did not serve as an executive authority. Punishment of criminals, including corporal punishment and prison sentences, was retained by the Muslim authorities, and the local leader had to turn to them in such cases. In a letter from a small rural town, the local leader requests the detainment of a defendant in a serious case who had fled his city and found sanctuary in Alexandria. The author of the letter requests that the judge in Fustat direct his represen-

---

968 TS 13 J 23.3v, ll. 1–5: Gil, *Kingdom*, no. 605. Gil's translation is different.
969 Goitein, *Society*, 2: 91, 100–103.

tative in Alexandria, R. Eleazar, to ascertain on his behalf with the Muslim authorities whether it was possible to arrest the fugitive: "Your servant pleads with you that you grant him this boon and ask the master, our R. Eleazar, to check with the *nāẓir* regarding his arrest."[970]

In other words, the "master," R. Eleazar, who served both as judge and as leader at this time, did not have the authority to detain this criminal, and was merely the intermediary vis-à-vis the Muslim authorities who had this executive power. But, even as an intermediary, the local leader did not have any exclusive privileges: Other dignitaries and public figures from within and from outside the community could also function in this capacity. In the same letter, a few lines after the aforementioned request, the author of the letter informs the addressee that in the end he decided to appoint someone else to deal with the arrest of this criminal, after realizing that R. Eleazar was neglecting to deal with the situation in a satisfactory manner: "I appointed the shaykh Abū Zikrī regarding this man's detainment, since the judge, your eminence's *nā'ib*, did not demand satisfaction from this man on my behalf."[971]

Many times the extradition of a criminal to Muslim authorities was a very difficult decision, due to the inability to monitor the type or the severity of the punishment which these authorities would execute upon the criminal. One may learn of the hesitation that often accompanied this decision from a letter written by Elijah b. Zechariah the Judge.[972] He describes a case in which a man made particularly heretical statements in public that led those who heard him to exact punishment upon him then and there: They beat him and forcibly dragged him out of the synagogue. As a judge, Elijah was of two minds on this matter and debated for a long time how this man should be punished:

When I considered punishing him by handing him to the authorities, I knew that this would ultimately be detrimental. All the more so, since I do not know the governor, or the Muslim *nā'ib*, or the head of the district. I left his presence and considered what I should do, and I came to the decision to punish him as is required by law and that I have the ability to do so. I wrote down in a note: "This anonymous slave kisses the ground..." but I did not know to whom it should be

970 ULC Or 1080 J 112r, ll. 14–16: Frenkel, *"The Compassionate and Benevolent"* [Hebrew], no. 98. On the *nāẓir*, the Fatimid overseer of the *dīwān*, see Al-Imad, *Fatimid Vizierate*, 20–21. It is unlikely that the reference is to a Jewish *nāẓir* who served as a judge in a lower court, and certainly not that he had authority to imprison anyone. See Ben-Sasson, *Emergence*, 325–326.

971 ULC Or 1080 J 112r, ll. 17–19: Frenkel, *"The Compassionate and Benevolent"* [Hebrew], no. 98.

972 See above, n. 798.

addressed. Should it be to the qadi or to the governor? It occurred to me to address it to the overseer of the markets (*muḥtasib*) and write to him that this man was guilty of slander and then his punishment would be light."[973]

In other words, the judge wished to be lenient and tried to locate and contact the more moderate representatives of the Muslim authorities. It was specifically the Muslim authorities who wished to hand down as harsh a sentence as possible: "The *wālī* sent me a letter saying: If this is what took place [=the man's heresy against religion], I would be harsh[...] and I have heard about your religion and that Jewish law require that you be harsh with him."[974]

From this case we learn that the authority to punish was given to the Muslim authorities. The extent of the judge's powers (*qudra*) as to punishment was his right to hand the criminal over to a representative of the Muslim authorities. The most a judge could do vis-à-vis the Muslim authorities was to exert some influence, in a letter or otherwise, regarding the severity of the punishment. In the case at hand, the judge was unsuccessful in this regard. In the end, the *muḥtasib*'s representatives handed the criminal over to another authority figure, to the governor (*wālī*), and he ultimately punished the criminal more severely than the judge would have:

> The representatives of the overseer of markets looked for him until they caught him and handed him over to him [= to the *wālī*] and the latter beat him. And people asked that he be placed in confinement and they paraded him all over the *al-Qamra* quarter and they publicly announced that he was under ban. And the messengers around him proclaiming that he spoke derisively about religion.[975]

The severity of the punishment embarrassed the judge, and later in the letter he is very apologetic about the matter. He explains that he did everything in his power to minimize the severity of the punishment, and even prevented the extradition of the criminal to more senior members of the Muslim authorities, who would have exacted an even harsher penalty:

> This being said, I swear that I did not go as of yet to Nūr al-Dīn, who I mentioned above, and he does not know my man. Regarding the overseer of the markets, I did not see him and I did not make him aware of the matter, for this is not a matter of which I am proud, and I would therefore not seek his counsel.[976]

---

973 TS 16.231r, ll. 7–14: Frenkel, "*The Compassionate and Benevolent*" [Hebrew], no. 29.
974 Ibid., ll. 23–25.
975 Ibid., ll. 19–23.
976 Ibid., ll. 27–31.

In other words, the untenable situation in which the judge had little authority to mete out punishment, and which allowed him only to hand over criminals to the Muslim authorities without any ability to control the type of punishment or its severity, basically hamstrung the leader. This was very frustrating for him, as is evident from the agonizing decision process reflected in Elijah b. Zechariah's letter.

Exacting Political Retribution

Involving the Muslim authorities in punishment was employed not infrequently as a weapon against opposition forces in the community. This possibility was also open to the opposition, of course, and they too employed it on occasion.

An analysis of the drama in Alexandria at the end of the eleventh century reflects this very clearly. Āraḥ b. Nathan of Alexandria describes the case in a letter to his brother, Abraham b. Nathan Av, in Fustat.[977] A ruckus involving young Jewish men on Sabbath eve led to their imprisonment. After the *muqaddam* interceded with the Amir, all of them were freed and they did not even have to pay a fine. As Āraḥ, who is effusive in his praise of the *muqaddam*, recounts:

> There was a great commotion and the *wālī* [= the Muslim governor of Alexandria or the chief of police] came. And were it not for the help of God Almighty and the *jāh* of that man [=the *muqaddam*], may God Almighty grant him long life, a great disaster may have occurred, since he spoke ill of the regime. If a different *muqaddam* had been in the city and not that one, he would have been unable to do what this *muqaddam* did. They took the gang and imprisoned them. He came and freed them and they did not lose a penny. May the Almighty Creator protect this one, since it is through his success that this congregation exists.[978]

It is tempting to see this version of events as a classic case of a local leader using his ties with the authorities to help members of the community in trouble. Those involved in the case tell a different story. According to them, the *muqaddam* was the one who alerted the authorities in the first place in order to put them in jail, since they had maligned his good name. This version is corroborated to some extent in Āraḥ b. Nathan's letter:

> And though he had only been good to them [=to the group of young men who had been arrested], they in turn asked for help against him [...] and everything that they did marks

977 TS NS J 24: Frenkel, *"The Compassionate and Benevolent"* [Hebrew], no. 88.
978 TS NS J 24r, ll. 13–16.

> them as defamers. And they were not detained by the authorities for anything but maligning his good name, and because they screamed [raucously] at night.[979]

It is, in fact, apparent from Āraḥ b. Nathan's letter that this group of young men were the first to involve the Muslim authorities in community affairs when they complained about the *muqaddam*'s conduct (as the letter states: they maligned his good name). The *muqaddam* chose to exact his revenge upon them and made sure that the authorities would arrest them on the pretext of drunken revelry and noise at night. In the end, he became their savior, though this did not prevent them from once again requesting protection from the authorities.

In another case, the extradition was accomplished more subtly, taking advantage of the Ayyubid authorities' zeal to arrest Jewish religious transgressors. Abū al-Riḍā b. al-Maghribiyya, who waged a no-holds-barred campaign against R. Ephraim's leadership – a campaign that R. Ephraim describes in great detail in a letter – attempted to malign him by alleging that he worshipped idols and made sure that these rumors reached the ears of the Muslim authorities.

He then started to denigrate me to all the gullible people of the town and to turn all hearts against me, until the Muslim judge and the *pelilim* [=Muslim legal authorities] became convinced that I worshipped idols and they began to watch for my missteps."[980]

Conclusion

The local leader of Alexandria at that time had no power to execute any corporal punishments or to detain people. It was the Muslim authorities which were in charge of enforcing the laws. The local leader was entitled to deliver criminals to the authorities, but was usually hesitant to do so. The documents we have indicate that the reason for this was the inability to determine the type of punishment or its severity. This being said, alerting the authorities was a fairly common political tool in the pitched battle for survival between leaders and their rivals. The leader had no advantage in this quarter, and this stratagem could be used by anyone who wished.

979 Ibid., ll. 17–19.
980 TS 16.272v, ll. 5–7: Frenkel, "*The Compassionate and Benevolent*" [Hebrew], no. 30.

3 Legal Tools: The Edict (*Taqqanah*) and the Restriction (*Seyag*)

(a) Introduction

The Jewish worldview, which sees the law as an eternal order originating with God, did not leave much room for the introduction of new legislation. Despite this, the Talmud gave the sages a number of tools by which to adapt to a changing reality. The heads of the Yeshivahs did not see themselves as legislators, either, and did not issue many edicts;[981] one would have expected that the judges and the local rulers, who were not viewed as legislators at all, would also be reluctant to enact new laws. The local rulers, however, did in fact employ the traditional mechanisms allowed by the Talmud regarding legal innovation on various occasions.

The permission to issue restrictions and edicts[982] was given first and foremost to legal scholars, but other legislation was added and enacted by the community and its leaders, and this was certified by the sages of the time, who granted it the full force of the law.[983] This communal legislation, which is sometimes referred to as "community edicts" or "the edicts of the elders," was not given solely to the chief justice or the leader of the community, but to a group of sages or to the community as a whole. It was a tool that was perforce an expression of communal will, and one could not issue an edict without a great number of signatories from among the dignitaries of the community.[984]

---

981 Yerachmiel Brody, "Were the Geonim Legislators?," *Shenaton ha-Mishpat ha-Ivri: Annual of the Institute for Research in Jewish Law* 11–12 (1984): 279–315 [Hebrew]; Chaim Tykocinski, *The Geonic Regulations* (Jerusalem: Sura, 1960), 10 [Hebrew].

982 See Menachem Elon, *Jewish Law: History, Sources, Principles (Ha-Mishpat Ha-Ivri)*, trans. Bernard Auerbach and Melvin J. Sykes (Philadelphia: JPS, 1994), 2: 490.

983 Elon, *Jewish Law*, 2: 538, 1: 587–591, 3:1531.

984 Goitein, *Society*, 2: 65–66. For an extensive study of the regulation or enactment (*taqqanah*) in Jewish law, see Elon, *Jewish Law*, 2: 477–493 (ch. 13), 2: 494–544 (ch. 14), 643–665 (ch. 17). On the community's central role and great influence of the legislation and implementation of regulations, see ibid., 491; Gerald J. Blidstein, "Traditional and Modern Discourse: More on Autonomy and Authority," in Nahem Ilan (ed.), *A Good Eye: Dialogue and Polemic in Jewish Culture* (Tel Aviv: Hakibbutz Hameuchad, 1999), 687–697 [Hebrew].

(b) Frequency of Use

There is no record in the Genizah of any restriction or edict from Alexandria throughout the long period under consideration, perhaps for the reason Goitein submits in his book: documents of this sort (edicts) were of enduring value, and thus were seen as too precious to place in the Genizah.[985] This being said, we have indirect evidence of a few edicts that were issued, though it is hard to ascertain how often this legislative mechanism was actually employed.

(c) Efficacy of the Legal Tools

Ab initio these tools were meant to answer a specific need of the community, but it is apparent that on occasion, the way edicts and restrictions were used reflected the insoluble tension between the wishes of the ruling class and the community's desire and willingness to submit. We learn of this from the following case: A Jewish merchant who dealt in precious stones found himself in a commercial dispute and was forced to present Muslim witnesses who would testify on his behalf, since the Jewish witnesses that he had produced were deemed unfit.[986] The irate merchant wished to rely on "the restriction that R. Isaac b. Ḥalfon had enacted against a Jew relying on 'the laws of the gentiles'";[987] R. Isaac's intention was to prevent Jews from going to Muslim courts,[988] but it seems that R. Isaac, who was a weak leader and lacked authority,[989] was unable to enforce the restriction that he had promulgated. This limitation enraged the members of the community, who refused to be dependent solely upon the Jewish court system, and thus they chose to ignore it.[990]

985 Goitein, *Society*, 2: 65–66.
986 On the Jewish court's need for gentile witnesses, see Ben-Sasson, *Emergence*, 313.
987 ENA NS 16.32, ll. 8–9: Frenkel, *"The Compassionate and Benevolent"* [Hebrew], no. 15. The phonetic adaption of the Hebrew word *seyag* (סי״ג) to Judeao-Arabic occurred, it would appear, against the background of its similarity to the Arabic word *sayyāj* (fence). This is a borderline case, between semantic expansion and transcription. See Joshua Blau, *A Grammar of Judeo-Arabic, Based Mainly on Unliterary Texts* (Jerusalem: Magness, 1961), 153–154 [Hebrew].
988 On the recourse to gentile lawcourts, see Asher Gulak, *The Elements of Jewish Law* (Tel-Aviv: Dvir, 1967), 4: 24–29 [Hebrew]; Elon, *Jewish Law*, 1: 13–18; Haim Z. Hirschberg, *History of the Jews in North Africa* (Jerusalem: Mossad Bialik, 1965), 1: 172–183 [Hebrew]; Ben-Sasson, *Emergence*, 308–316; Goitein, *Society*, 2: 400–401.
989 See above, Part II, Chapter 13.3: Leadership with no Authority.
990 Ibid., n. 795.

(d) Extent of Use

Above we presented a case in which a member of the community attempted to make use of a restriction intended to prevent the public from going to the Muslim courts, thus ensuring the independence of the Jewish court system. In this particular case, the restriction was intended to serve the institutional interest. In other cases, that we know of, these edicts were employed as a manipulative mechanism by the leadership and the elite in order to buttress their position.

In 1216 there was a clash between Anatoly the Judge and the cantor Ṣadoq Ibn al-ʿAmmānī. It is likely that the two were partners in a business venture involving the production and sale of books.[991] Ṣadoq withheld Anatoly's portion of the profits. In order to undermine the latter's position, Ṣadoq succeeded in appointing his son Mufaḍḍal as the leader (*raʾīs*) of the community. This new leader was still a youth. According to Judah Ibn al-ʿAmmānī, the author of the letter relating to this incident, the young man's beard had not come in and he was still a bachelor. This not only led to bitterness among community members, but was also a legal problem. In order to overcome the issue of his son's age, Ṣadoq circulated an edict that permitted the appointment of a youth to the position of *raʾīs*. He succeeded in gathering many signatures from among the dignitaries, and in order to bypass the need to have it certified by the judge, who was none other than Anatoly himself, Ṣadoq sent the edict directly to Abraham Maimuni, who went ahead and validated it.[992] In this way, using fairly obvious manipulations, the edict could be used by leaders and their rivals as a political tool to buttress their position against opponents, even when it was very clearly not in the public's interest and against the public's will.

A second instance of the use of an edict took place following the death of R. Anatoly. The death of such a dominant and centralizing figure such as Anatoly[993] left the community feeling bereft and unsure of how to proceed. Several competing interests vied against each other. Among other factors there was a pitched battle between those who opposed "the rabbis" and those who supported them.[994] The candidacy of R. Samuel, who was of European origin, led to the opposition of one faction in the community. They unearthed a local edict from many years before, which prohibited a Byzantine (*Rūmī*) or a French (*Ifranjī*) Jew from holding the position of *muqaddam*. The faction in favor of his appoint-

991 On the *warrāq*, see Frenkel, "Book Lists."

992 TS 10 J 25.3: Frenkel, *"The Compassionate and Benevolent"* [Hebrew], no. 57.

993 See above, Part II, Chapter 11.3: Judge in Alexandria, and 4: Community Leader.

994 On this, and on the entire affair, see above, Part II, Chapter 12.2: The Appointment Affair: A Rearguard Battle against the European Immigrants.

ment preferred to understand the edict differently: According to their interpretation it was not the origin of the candidate, from Europe or Byzantium, that determined his eligibility, but rather his knowledge or lack of knowledge of Arabic. Since R. Samuel understood Arabic very well, this edict was not an obstacle to his appointment. In order to prevent competing interpretations of this edict, the faction in favor ripped it to shreds and wrote a new edict confirming the appointment of R. Samuel. We know of this case from a frantic letter sent by one of R. Samuel's supporters to Elijah b. Zechariah the Judge, the gist of which was a request to secure the agreement of Abraham the Nagid to this appointment – and thus put a quick end to the case.[995] The letter was written in so much haste that the author concluded the missive with an apology for his sloppy handwriting, and even in this final line he missed a letter, attesting to how quickly he wanted to send the letter.[996] The purpose of this alacrity was to secure the Nagid's agreement posthaste, and thus bring the matter to a satisfactory conclusion from the perspective of R. Samuel's supporters – since as the author of the letter professes, "we do nothing without the approval of the *raʾīs* our master, the lord of lords, and Nagid among Nagids." The author of the letter makes a concerted effort to present a united front, as though the entire community stands behind the appointment of R. Samuel, though from a closer look at the letter it is readily apparent that there was a struggle against this so-called "unity," pushed by the author of the letter.[997]

The edict may thus be seen as a fairly flexible mechanism, which at times was an effective tool for consolidating the leadership of a particular group or leader. Its use was susceptible to various manipulations, such as ordering new edicts, creatively interpreting old edicts, and ripping up and destroying undesirable ones.

(e) Conclusion

Edicts and restrictions, which were originally intended to address the needs of the community, were mainly employed in this time period to further the goals of the leaders. When they were used in defense of an institutional interest, but against the desires of the community, they were sometimes found to be ineffec-

995 TS 18 J 3.15: Frenkel, *"The Compassionate and Benevolent"* [Hebrew], no. 83.
996 TS 18 J 3.15v, l. 37: *wa-ʿalā khaṭṭihi yuʿtadahu* (sic; for *yuʿtadharuhu*), "and for my handwriting, forgive me."
997 See above, Part II, Chapter 12.2: The Appointment Affair: A Rearguard Battle against the European Immigrants.

tive. Occasionally, however, they were quite effective tools in the hands of local leaders who used them in order to buttress their political positions.

4 Mechanisms of Coercion

(a) Physical Presence

In certain cases, the physical presence of the *muqaddam* served as a deterrent. A letter describes two especially violent brothers, "completely evil" according to Elijah b. Zechariah, the author of the letter, who wished to prevent Ben Wāfī from entering into an engagement with Bint (the daughter of) al-Ṣiqillī (the daughter of the Sicilian), who previously had been engaged to one of the brothers. As long as the judge was in the city, the brothers were satisfied with verbal threats. When he left the city for a short time (four days) to a town only two hours away from Alexandria, they felt sufficiently at liberty to intimidate Ben Wāfī. They presented false documents and succeeded in securing a promise from him that he would never marry the woman.[998]

(b) Public Castigation and Shaming

Delaying prayer and public castigation served as one of the more important mechanisms by which an individual could sue for justice.[999] By means of this mechanism, which involved revealing an injustice to the public, one could exert social pressure. Using the same mechanism, a leader could create social pressure upon divisive and errant elements in the community by publicly chastising and shaming them. This was accomplished either as an announcement in synagogue, or by means of a crier, who went around the markets and in other public places announcing the transgressions of the errant individual. Thus, for example, Shelah b. Mubashshir acted in this way during the disagreement that developed in Alexandria following the refusal of the new settlers and the Maghribis to pay the *jāliya* payment.[1000] The Maghribis were deeply offended, proving that this step was considered a severe blow against their sector of the community, as articulated by their leader Benayah b. Mūsā: "When our Maghribi

998 TS 16. 231v: Frenkel, "*The Compassionate and Benevolent*" [Hebrew], no. 29.
999 See Ben-Sasson, "Appeal to the Congregation."
1000 See above, Part II, Chapter 2.4(a): Shelah and "the Maghribis" (*al-Maghāriba*).

friends heard of this, it was very difficult for them."[1001] It seems, however, that this was not a particularly effective move, since it did not bring about the desired change in the Maghribis's conduct, but rather led to further entrenchment in their positions, and to an escalation of the conflict – as the letter states: "And they did not accept the measures he enacted at all. And a mêlée ensued, which would take a long time to describe."[1002] Public castigation was thus a powerful tool, which could inflict great damage, but because it was so potent, it was not always as effective. At times this tool brought about the opposite of what was desired, namely the perpetuation of a conflict or its escalation, as related above.

(c) Intrigues and Terrorism

The lack of executive and punitive authority on the part of the local leaders in Alexandria led some of them to employ clandestine channels of sowing dissent and terrorizing their opponents in order to secure their positions.

At the end of the twelfth century the community in Alexandria sent a letter of complaint against Shelah b. Mubashshir to Mevorakh b. Saʿadyah the Nagid regarding "the highhandedness and the lack of leadership."[1003] This is a general complaint and we do not know a great deal about what prompted it. The best and most detailed example of this type of conduct is the secret letter Judah Ibn al-ʿAmmānī of Alexandria sent to Yeshūʿā b. Aaron, who was in Cairo. The letter reveals a systematic campaign of harassment perpetrated by Anatoly the Judge against the scholar Joseph al-Baghdādī. Anatoly saw him as a threat to his position in the community, and was not content until he was banished from the city:

> They bribed the convert and said to him: "Go and report that: 'R. Joseph threw watermelon peels at me and urinated upon me.'" He performed this task in an obviously artificial way. He went [...]to the judge and he told him of the problem. He said to him: "Tomorrow go to the synagogue and tear your clothes." They entered the synagogue on Thursday the seventh of this month and he tore his clothes and rolled upon the floor in front of the Holy Ark. There were those who believed him, and others said: "It is a travesty that such a thing should happen." And R. Saʿadyah the Pious [...] the judge closed the door upon him and there was no way to ascertain what happened inside. And the shaykh Hilāl came. And they coordinated with him and with a number of the shaykhs who were friends with the

1001 Ibid., n. 467.
1002 Ibid.
1003 TS NS J 334r, l. 8: Frenkel, *"The Compassionate and Benevolent"* [Hebrew], no. 93.

> Judge regarding the matter of R. Sa'adyah. And they gave him such a rich bribe that he went to the Amir Ḥusām al-Dīn and said to him: "That one blasphemes against religion and he does not deserve to live this town, would you be so good as to remove him from our presence." And the Amir still did not have the full story. The Amir sent the black slave to him with his servant. And [at that time] when I was with him they came and yelled: "Where is this foreigner who curses people and profanes their fathers?" I was shocked and I said to them: "This man is a learned sage and humble. God forbid that [you should do] this." They left saying: "We will ask Ṭāhir al-Dimashqī, who brought us, if this is the man." He said to them: "His name is Joseph; he is the man [you are looking for]!" They came to him and asked: "What is your name?" He answered: "Joseph." They said to him: "You are akin to one who transgresses the command of the Sultan," and they took him away.[1004]

The harassment of R. Joseph al-Baghdādī, which ultimately led to his expulsion from the town, was part of a systematic policy on the part of Anatoly the Judge. He saw R. Joseph as a potential rival who put his own position in jeopardy. Judah Ibn al-ʿAmmānī who wrote the letter states this explicitly: "The root of all of this is that God forbid a scholar reside anywhere in the vicinity of this judge, R. Anatoly. He attacks [the scholar] incessantly. He did this not once, not twice and not even three times."[1005]

Anatoly's policy was not a public one, but instead was implemented clandestinely. Anatoly was careful not to be seen as the enemy of R. Joseph al-Baghdādī. The scholar even saw the judge as a man who could help him and told him of his difficulties. Anatoly presented himself as a supporter and suggested that he protest his mistreatment to the community in the synagogue. But when R. Joseph came to the synagogue, the judge locked the door and prevented people outside from knowing what took place. The harassment, in the form of slander, bribery, and extradition to the Muslim authorities, was undertaken by a group of dignitaries who were close to the judge: "the shaykhs who were friends with the judge" in the words of Judah Ibn al-ʿAmmānī, and not by Anatoly himself. This veil of secrecy was achieved through violent intimidation and the perpetuation of fear. This is apparent in the final lines of Judah Ibn al-ʿAmmānī's letter: "This is what happened. And upon God's life, brother of mine, do not tell any of this to anybody. For if you do I shall not tell you anything ever again. And if you were not dear to me I would not have told you any of this."[1006]

The violent expulsion, accompanied by beatings and other forms of ridicule, which Ibn al-ʿAmmānī relates in detail in the letter, was a warning to others as well. Any person might find himself accused in this way, and could be expelled.

1004 TS 24.67v, ll. 3–23: Frenkel, *"The Compassionate and Benevolent"* [Hebrew], no. 40.
1005 TS 24.67r, ll. 53–56.
1006 TS 24.67v, right margins.

Even Ibn al-ʿAmmānī himself was accused of disobedience to the Sultan when he wished to protect R. Joseph al-Baghdādī, and could have easily met the same fate.[1007] Fear and an atmosphere of intimidation were clearly the backdrop of the secrecy of this letter.

A further example of sowing dissent and terror as a deliberate tool is the case of Abraham al-Darʿī's poisoning by his political rival, Nathan b. Judah.[1008]

5 Reconciliation and Persuasion

Reconciliation and persuasion were one of the more common methods of overcoming opposition and conflict in the community. This took the form of an institutionalized ceremony performed publicly in the holy enclave of the synagogue sanctuary; it thus included both religious sanctions and social pressure. The best example of this is the case of the scofflaw from Barqa.[1009] In order to bring him into line, the leader Shelah b. Mubashshir invited him to the synagogue, and adjured him before the entire congregation to reconsider his shameless conduct. The elders of the congregation fulfilled an important function and together with the local leader participated in the attempts to persuade. The judge and the elders intervened through inducement even in matters of family relations. They did it by "having words" (*dibburim*) with the parties concerned: "The judge and the elders in any place have permission to have words (*dibburim*) with him," says Yeshūʿā b. Joseph regarding a levir who refused to release his brother's widow.[1010]

In tandem with these official ceremonies of reconciliation, unofficial and spontaneous attempts were undertaken to intercede and reconcile opposing groups. The most prominent of these mediators was R. Ephraim, who left no stone unturned in his attempt to arbitrate between two opposing factions in the community and to appease the separatist group. He himself went to the house of the leaders of the separatist faction, who had secluded themselves in their home, and lay in wait for them outside their door. When they emerged he compelled them to be attentive to his greeting and his conciliatory message. On another occasion, he undertook to organize a meeting between the two groups in the home of one of the leaders, and made the members swear to aban-

1007 Ibid., ll. 22–23.

1008 See above, Part II, Chapter 3.3: Relationship with Mevorakh b. Saʿadyah Nagid.

1009 See above, Part III, Chapter 1.3 (e): Drama in the Community: A Reflection of the Turn Over.

1010 See above, Part II, Chapter 1.3 (d): Spheres of Activity, in the section: Presiding as Judge.

don their divisive ways. In this way, he succeeded, at least for a time, to reconcile between the two opposing factions.[1011]

6 Control of Resources: Appointments

The appointment of cantors and overseers of pious foundations was one of the official privileges granted to the *muqaddam*, guaranteed by writ by the Fatimid regime.[1012] Unfortunately, we do not have any letters of appointment written in Alexandria as we do for other cities.[1013] One may surmise, however, that in Alexandria, like in other communities, the appointment of cantors, overseers of pious foundations, and other communal positions was under the purview of the local leader.

A number of factors eroded this right to appoint and minimized it greatly. Among these factors were the custom of inheritance, group advocacy, and the involvement of influential magnates in the appointments.

The custom of bequeathing such positions to one's child obviously limited the role of the *muqaddam* in the appointment.[1014]But, the local leader was also forced to consider the desires of the stronger and more vocal groups in the community. The case of the ritual slaughterer Ṣedaqah, which is delineated in a query to Maimonides from Alexandria, may serve as an example:

> And may he guide us regarding a man, who is publicly responsible for slaughtering and checking [animals]. And he conducts himself as a strongman in public, and he steals meat from the stores of the butchers, and people attest to this. Moreover, he refused to certify [animals with] blemishes that were regarded by the sages of the nation as permitted, and that had never been disqualified before by the community. And the butchers catch him all the time with the stolen meat in his possession, in the presence of Jews and in their absence. And it leads to the undermining [of the law] and is a great travesty, and sacrilegious. Is it permitted that he remains in charge of this public [office], or is it not? May our master guide us, and may his reward be redoubled.[1015]

1011 See above, Part II, Chapter 9.2: A Controversial Leader.

1012 See above, Part II, Chapter 1.2 (b): His Position.

1013 Goitein, *Society*, 2: 90, n. 123.

1014 Ibid., 90 – 91. And in Alexandria, the Ibn al-ʿAmmānīs are an example of a family of hereditary cantors. See above, Part II, n. 533. Similarly, a certain Muwahhab the Cantor, son of Aaron the Cantor, is mentioned: Bodl Ms Heb c 28.11 (Gil, *Kingdom*, no. 623); CUL Or 1080 5.14 (Gil, *Kingdom*, no. 844).

1015 Maimonides, *Responsa*, 321, §173.

It seems that a powerful group of butchers, who were cheated by this ritual slaughterer, supported by a number of religious sages, whose examination regarding whether an animal was kosher was disregarded by him, banded together in order to terminate this man from his position. This opposition was successful in procuring the signature of the judge and of other sages in support of their request, and a document attesting to this is appended to their legal query.[1016]

Another case is attested to in a letter from an Alexandrian slaughterer, who writes in 1115 about an opposition group in the community attempting to supplant him by defaming and discrediting him:

> And no one wishes me ill except for Ibn al-Qāsh. He has supporters from amongst the Alexandrian fishmongers and shell collectors. He has swayed them against me, for I have criticized their conduct, such as the drinking of beer in taverns and other matters. And he does nothing but spread tales, which have no basis in fact, until he seizes upon a story. And he spread the tale in all the slaughterhouses, and it is untrue, since the uncircumcised do not eat what we slaughter. And there never has been anyone who is more punctilious in is work than me, all my life in the service of Israel.[1017]

In another instance, when Abraham the son of R. Nathan Av arrived in Alexandria, he attempted to consolidate his position by pushing out the local slaughterer, Ben Elhanan.[1018]

Intervention of the dignitaries was another major factor that minimized the *muqaddam's* right of appointmrnt. Elements from outside of the community would frequently grant their support to various individuals and would sometimes get involved more actively in the appointments and removals of holders of public office in Alexandria. The position and the status of the slaughterer was dependent not only upon the good will of the local leader and the community, but also upon the patronage of rich magnates from Fustat or Palestine. The slaughterer who was threatened by Ibn al-Qāsh did not seek the help of the local leader; he requested help from "the Lord" Joseph b. Yaḥyā, a man of considerable wealth and good connections in Fustat. He asks of him: "May a letter be furnished that would stay the hand of every harasser, and would serve as a letter of reference on behalf of his servant, as you see fit."[1019] The slaughterer adds that his previous patron who helped him secure his position in the community, was not the local judge, but rather Evyatar ha-Kohen, the Head of the Palestinian Yes-

1016 Ibid., 322.

1017 TS 18 J 3.5r, ll. 40 – 33: Gil, *Palestine*, no. 599; Goitein, *Palestinian Jewry*, 304. My translation differs from those of Gil and Goitein.

1018 See Gil, *History of Palestine*, §911.

1019 TS 18 J 3.5, right margins: Gil, *Palestine*, no. 599; Goitein, *Palestinian Jewry*, 304.

hivah: "The man who used to support me was none other than our master, the head of the Yeshivah, may his righteous memory be for a blessing. On various occasions his letters to the community would arrive and they would include a letter of reference for his servant wherein he required the community to support me."[1020]

Abraham son of R. Nathan Av, who wished to remove the local slaughterer from his position did not turn to the local leader, but rather to Nahray b. Nissim of Fustat.

This dependence upon patrons from outside of the community is especially apparent when it comes to teachers. Their livelihood depended upon the rich Maecenas who funded their studies, and who often was their own teacher with whom they had apprenticed. Thus, for example, the Alexandrian Manasseh the Teacher asks his patron in Cairo, Judah ha-Kohen Abū al-Barakāt al-Kātib (i.e., the royal scribe) for financial aid on the occasion of his marriage and on occasion of the holidays: "I just got married, and now have the burden of the house upon me, and I need charity on the occasion of the holidays, as has been your custom: for clothing, and the purchase of flour, and a sheep, and other provisions that one may need for the holiday."[1021] He justifies his request with the following statement: "For I am one of your students whom you sponsored in your great munificence and mercy."[1022]

Alluding to the gift as customary, as well as the confident and complacent tone of the request point to a well-oiled structured system of lasting sponsorship. The fact that Manasseh was only one of al-Kātib's students indicates that this is not an extraordinary case, but rather a well-known and accepted phenomenon. The possibility teachers had of supporting themselves through regular sponsorship from outside of the community naturally minimized their dependence upon the local leadership.

Despite the limitations listed above, some local leaders were adept at employing their right to appoint as a tool of executive authority. A letter from the thirteenth century attests to this:

When the *ḥaver* went to Alexandria he said to me once or twice: "Didn't you tell me that you would come with me if God wishes that I be the judge of Alexandria. And now why do you delay coming?" And he swore to me: "If you come, I will issue an appropriate writ on your behalf and you will be very happy with it

1020 TS 18 J 3.5r, ll. 33–35.
1021 TS 24.7v, ll. 26–28: Frenkel, *"The Compassionate and Benevolent"* [Hebrew], no. 39.
1022 Ibid., l. 31.

and I will make you a teacher for most of the young men in Alexandria and you will benefit from many additional privileges, which I shall bestow upon you."[1023]

It is clear that the *ḥaver*, whose identity is unknown to us, came to Alexandria with the explicit plan of forming a cadre of clients who would be dependent upon him and grateful to him for the positions he would appoint them to, such as the position of teacher which he had promised to the author of the above letter.

It was not enough that the local leader granted appointments to his close associates, he also had to guarantee that they could make a living in this capacity. We thus find leaders who become very involved in the running of schools, as Manasseh the Teacher attests in a letter:

> You know that there is no one there, only those who are in his class. And even the judge [himself], for whose greatness and happiness we yearn [got involved]. [For] when a young man leaves him and comes to me, this teacher tempts him greatly, and the judge goes to the mother and pleads with her, and he removes him from me and brings him [the student] back to him.[1024]

When private parties needed the services of a cantor, and there was potential for profit and income,[1025] the judge would direct the individual to his protégé. Thus Japheth b. Manasseh Ibn al-Qaṭāʾif, in a letter to his brother Ḥalfon from the beginning of the twelfth century refers to a period of mourning in Alexandria: "And on Sabbath the *ḥaver*, my master, may the Rock preserve him sent the cantor Ben al-Jāzifīnī to that home and...they sang the well-known lamentations, those which stimulate sorrow."[1026]

At the same time, the local leader would sometimes prevent a particular appointee from rendering his services to certain individuals. An adulterous woman, who gave birth to a male child in Alexandria in the middle of the thirteenth century had a difficult time finding someone to circumcise her son. Ultimately, a group of Byzantine Jews agreed to perform the ceremony, but "there was no judge or cantor in attendance and they did not say a blessing upon him [the baby]."[1027]

1023 Phil 386, ll. 20–24: Mann, *Texts*, 461.
1024 TS 13 J 33.8v, ll. 13–17: Goitein, *Jewish Education*, 95.
1025 Most of the officials' livelihood was, in the end, due to such services that they provided to private families and individuals. As Goitein (*Society*, 2: 125) says: "The dayyānīm, cantors, and beadles had regular functions at weddings and funerals, family events on which they probably made more cash than they received from the community chest."
1026 TS NS J 419r, ll. 7–8: Frenkel, *"The Compassionate and Benevolent"* [Hebrew], no. 94.
1027 GW IXv, ll. 7–8: Frenkel, *"The Compassionate and Benevolent"* [Hebrew], no. 18.

The control that the local leader had over appointments in the community was not total. This being said, it was successfully employed as a means of forming a cadre of loyalists, who owed their livelihood to him.

7 Controlling Financial Resources

(a) Managing inheritances and pious foundations

Throughout the entire period in question the local community stubbornly fought to maintain control over the property of Jewish inhabitants who passed away. The Muslim rulers of the Fatimid and the Ayyubid regimes regularly attempted to wrest control of this property from the community.[1028] The struggle in Alexandria was especially fierce since as a port city, the community could lay claim to many estates of merchants who were lost at sea. The situation was especially tricky since the Muslim administrators of the city were very stringent. But the struggle was also a local one, each community waging a campaign to keep this right for themselves by procuring the appropriate *sijill* (edict from the rulers), as Isaac Nīsābūrī attests to in his letter:

> In the days of our master the Nagid, may his righteous memory be for a blessing [= Mevorakh b. Saʿadyah], a royal edict (*sijill)* was procured from the Lord of Lords al-Mālik al-Afḍal, may God preserve him and grant him a long life, that no man from amongst the Jews shall be involved in the [apportioning] of the property of one who had died, but rather the matter shall fall under the jurisdiction of their Muslim leaders. If they attempt to do so, they are lost. For the people here are not like those in Fustat. And if they try to do this they will ruin everything. You must, therefore meet with his prestigious eminence the *raʾīs* [=Moses b. Mevorakh] and my eminent lordship the Great Shaykh Abū al-Mufaḍḍal [=the chief justice of Cairo], may God magnify his honor, and take counsel with him on this matter. Perhaps you shall procure a new *sijill* which will override [the old one] on this matter and shall annul it... just recently a *sijill* involving Christians was issued commanding that they [= the regime] should not involve themselves in matters of this nature. And they also mentioned that *sijills* were issued and were sent to upper Egypt, Tinnīs and Damietta, which state that no one should be involved with the property of the deceased except for members of their community. Jewish affairs should be handled in this way as well.[1029]

1028 Goitein, *Society*, 2: 394–399.
1029 TS 18 J 4.6r, margins – 2, l. 17: Goitein, *Letters*, 253–254; Frenkel, "*The Compassionate and Benevolent*" [Hebrew], no. 84. It seems to me that Goitein's translation is incorrect, since it implies – at the beginning of the letter – that the writer objects to the Jews retaining control of their bequests, and later attempts to obtain a *sijill* that would confirm this control. My translation, therefore, differs. On the rigidity and cruelty of government officials in Alexandria, see Ibn Ju-

Control over the property of deceased members of the community afforded the leaders of Alexandria a variety of ruling strategies, starting from the option of presenting themselves as munificent leaders, protectors of orphans and widows, to the opportunity of confiscating the property and using it as they wished. The fate of a great deal of property was under their control, and they could use it to curry favor and reward whomever they wished. Most often, they looked out for widows and orphans,[1030] but we do hear of cases where precedence was given to the deceased's creditors. The latter preference is exposed in a letter written by Jalīla b. Abraham, whose husband, the flax merchant, Baruch b. Sasson, passed away during a business trip without leaving a will. The *ra'īs* Shelah b. Mubashshir and the creditors managed to bypass the widow and seize control of the entire property, and even refused to pay her the money she was entitled to according to her marriage contract (*me'uḥar*) : "And the *ra'īs* and other aforementioned litigants tricked me in ways unknown to me... and afterwards the *ra'īs* and his son Nissim, and the litigants said: 'We shall not take heed of this woman's desires, we shall sell the property and to each person we will give what he requested.' And they took all the gold and the flax that was recovered."[1031]

One is hard put to understand Shelah b. Mubashshir's motivations in this case unless he was very eager to appease the creditors. In less clear-cut cases as well, control over the money enabled the local leader to ensure that the funds and property that had been promised as bequests were delivered to their appropriate destinations: "We also requisitioned a share for the poor, ten dinars for the poor," writes Shelah b. Mubashshir to Mevorakh the Nagid in a letter wherein he describes in detail how he dealt with the money from the estate of a deceased person and how he divided up the money between the heirs, who were at odds with one another.[1032]

bayr's description, and above, Part I, Chapter 2.11: Alexandria: Gateway to the Magic of the Orient.

1030 See, e.g., ENA 2805, f. 2 A: Gil, *Kingdom*, no. 790, Shelah b. Mubashshir's letter to Nahray b. Nissim in which he details three cases in which he worked to ensure the transfer of monetary bequests to widows and orphans.

1031 TS 28.19r, ll. 16–17, 27–30: Frenkel, *"The Compassionate and Benevolent"* [Hebrew], no. 42.

1032 ENA 2740.3r, ll. 14–15: Frenkel, *"The Compassionate and Benevolent"* [Hebrew], no. 9.

(b) Fundraising Campaigns

All evidence indicates that the finances of the community were not governed by a set budget but was dependent upon regular and occasional fundraising campaigns.[1033] One of the leader's most significant responsibilities was organizing these fundraisers. In Alexandria, these campaigns had a particularly central role, because of the need to ransom the large number of captives who arrived at the port.[1034] Administering such a fundraising campaign was a clear signifier of authority, since the administrator had to be legitimized by members of the community in order for him to succeed. A successful fundraising campaign was a mark of acceptance and recognition by the community, and leaders who were not seen as legitimate were pushed aside and their requests for funds went unanswered. When R. Ephraim sought to undertake such a campaign, one of his detractors opposed him by saying: "Why does this foreigner ask for dinars... if he cannot even dwell with us without a permit?"[1035]

The announcement of a fundraiser was an excellent occasion for a public spectacle of leadership. It provided an opportunity for the leader to pose an honorable challenge to the community, and guide the community as a united and cohesive group to successfully meet this challenge. The effort and sacrifice required from all members of the community regardless of gender and origin created a feeling of unity and security. This atmosphere is reflected in Joseph b. Yeshūʿā's description of a fundraiser he organized in 1027 for the purpose of ransoming Jewish captives who had been brought to the city:

> A public fast was announced and we did not labor on that day[...] we announced[...] we shall collect [funds] for the purpose of ransoming this captive, and every person who was moved to do so brought gold and silver objects and the women as well, until eighteen gold coins were collected and from the Maghribis two gold coins, thus the total came to twenty.[1036]

The campaign was thus transformed into a public spectacle; the day upon which the funds were gathered was deemed a holiday, disconnected from daily routine following the leader's announcement regarding the cessation of labor and fasting. The appeal was made to all sectors of the community, with an emphasis upon the marginalized members of society (women) and the opposition (Magh-

---

1033 Goitein, *Society*, 2: 103–112.

1034 Frenkel, "'Proclaim Liberty to Captives and Freedom to Prisoners'."

1035 TS 16.272v, ll. 9–10: Frenkel, *"The Compassionate and Benevolent"* [Hebrew], no. 30. See above, Part II, Chapter 9.1: Background and Origin.

1036 TS 24.29r, ll. 22–26: Mann, *Texts*, 368.

ribis). The gradual pooling of money, "one gold coin after another" until the entire sum was collected, heightened the tension until the complete and total completion of the goal was reached, which symbolized the community's image – many elements mingling together into a harmonious whole.

On some occasions, the entire community was invited to hear the ceremonial recitation of a letter requesting funds for the ransom of captives, through the employment of an *akhrazah*.[1037] In an epistle calling the members of the Alexandrian community to donate for the ransom of captives from Ashkelon, the judge was asked to read the missive to the entire community: "And who is more worthy than you to read this letter aloud to your community following an *akhrazah* requesting the attendance of the congregation. For it will be entirely beneficial both to the donor and the recipient."[1038] The letter is replete with heartrending detail of the miserable lives and fate of the prisoners and their hopeless predicament.[1039] A public reading of this type of letter to the community made it possible for the leader to stir up communal empathy, which in turn heightened the feeling of shared experience to unparalleled peaks, and led to a willingness to donate.

This public reading of the letter was usually accompanied by an oral request, a sermon-like exhortation delivered by the leader to the community, with the purpose of prodding the community to donate money. An example of such a request is found in another letter written by Yeshūʿā b. Joseph and addressed to Ephraim b. Shemaryah, in which he asks him to read his letter to the Jerusalemite community in Fustat, and even provides him with a template for a sermon to be read together with the letter:

> May I remind you what is required of a man such as yourself in this situation. Also regarding your honor's question about reading this letter to the eminent community and directing them about generous giving, and demonstrating that they are obligated in this commandment and to them falls this privilege [...] and in any case every man among them must be attentive regarding their situation, for this commandment is not upon one man or one fam-

---

1037 On the *akhrazā* or *ikhrāz*, requiring a person to appear before the court, see Mann, *Texts*, 1: 554–557.

1038 TS 20.113v, 21–22: Goitein, *Palestinian Jewry*, 247.

1039 For example, TS 20.113r, ll. 8–11: "Reports do not stop arriving, one after the other, that a number of those redeemed from the Franks who remained in Ashkelon are going to die of hunger, naked and penniless. And people remain in captivity, some of whom have been killed before the eyes of others who were killed in their turn by means of all kinds of torture with which the enemies murdered them in order to express their rage at them" (after Goitein, *Palestinian Jewry*, 242); and also ibid., ll. 18–22, the touching story of the boy of good family who refused to convert to Christianity and was still waiting to be ransomed.

> ily, it is upon all of the people of Israel who heard the commandments and accepted them generation after worthy generation, whoever heard them must put the fear of God in his heart and contemplate [his] destiny and know that God gives each man their just due and grants His reward both in this world and in the world to come.[1040]

This message transforms the leader into a religious preacher and elevates the request for funds, turning it into a religious commandment. Accompanying his message praising the act of charity is an explicit threat of divine retribution against those who do not heed the call. The leader thus presents himself on these occasions as one who speaks in God's name.

These campaigns granted the leader the opportunity to strengthen feelings of communal unity and reinforce the positive self-image of the community. The authors of the letter from Ashkelon understood this completely:

> [...] all the more so considering that the great valor [of the Alexandrian community] and their compassion and famous generosity. They have always been quick to make use of such an opportunity, which has given them a great advantage over other communities, and earned them great acclaim. And regarding this, they are like a tribe that is seen as pursuing acts of charity and is quick to donate.[1041]

(c) Levying of Taxes

The levying of the *jāliyya* or the poll tax was as a rule the responsibility of the Muslim regime and its tax collectors and not of the local community.[1042] This being said, some documents at our disposal indicate that at certain times, in Alexandria the Muslim authorities would seek the advice of the local leaders regarding the financial wherewithal of the community and their estimate regarding the total amount of taxes to be levied from the community.[1043]

Opportunities and Dangers

This situation caused constant friction between the community leaders and new groups of settlers, including immigrants, temporary residents, and itinerant traders, who all agitated for exemptions. In contrast, the leaders themselves had a

1040 Bodl MS Heb a 3.28, ll. 53–58: Cowley, "Bodleian Geniza Fragments," 253.
1041 Ibid., v, ll. 3–7; Goitein, *Palestinian Jewry*, 246.
1042 Goitein, *Society*, 2: 389; Ben-Sasson, *Emergence*, 386–388.
1043 The cases mentioned by Goitein, too, are also only from Jerusalem and Alexandria. See Goitein, *Society*, 2: 67, 384–385, 387, 391.

vested interest in compelling as many people to pay their taxes, so as to minimize the burden on the community as a whole. *Prima facie* the local leader had some influence on the internal division of the tax burden, and this should have afforded him a good deal of leverage. In reality, however, a detailed analysis of the mechanism by which taxes were apportioned reveals that this authority gave him no recourse, and he was a prisoner of the conflicting desires and expectations of powerful elements in the community. In other words, he had no real ability to take advantage of this position of influence.

The Disagreement

The case which Benayah b. Mūsā refers to in a letter to Nahray b. Nissim, which in the fullness of days became known as "the disagreement," reflects this bind.[1044] In this instance the local leader, Shelah b. Mubashshir, was evidently under enormous pressure from militant groups within the community, who demanded that the new immigrants be included amongst the tax payers, and even requested that the newcomers pay more than what their proportion in the community would indicate. At the climax of the case, two members of the militant faction of "the inhabitants of the city," who were long-time residents, declared themselves the *de facto* leaders and excommunicated the foreigners who had refused to pay. This step, which significantly escalated the conflict, was a very explicit rebuke of Shelah who was seen as too accommodating. This move was meant to prod him to adopt a stringent and forceful taxation policy vis-à-vis the new residents. The recent immigrants struck back by ignoring the monetary demands of the Jewish community apparatus completely, and instead paying their share directly to the qadi. This constituted a rebellion against Shelah's leadership as well. Their preference to deal with the Muslim courts, and the writ they managed to obtain, which forbade the Jewish leadership to demand money from them, constituted a refusal to recognize the authority of the local Jewish leadership. The leader was thus caught between the two factions, and as the conflict escalated, his status was further eroded. The new residents, and especially the Maghribis, who in normal times cooperated with him to some extent,[1045] cut off all channels of communication and declared: "No foreigner is able to live with him in peace."[1046] They escalated this conflict over a

1044 TS 13 J 23.3: Gil, *Kingdom*, no. 605. And see above, Part II, Chapter 2.4 (a): Shelah and "the Maghribis" (*al-Maghāriba*); Part III, Chapter 2.2 (a): Excommunication.
1045 TS 13 J 23.3: Gil, *Kingdom*, no. 605.
1046 TS 13 J 23.3r, upper margins, ll. 7–8: Frenkel, *"The Compassionate and Benevolent"* [Hebrew], no. 75.

specific issue and transformed it into a fundamental antagonism: "Whoever loved you, will never hate you, and whoever hated you will never love you, and enmity is primal."[1047] The indigenous residents questioned Shelah's authority and he was revealed as a weak and ineffective leader, especially after the Muslim regime divorced themselves from him.[1048]

The Ibn Al-Qāsh Affair

A similar disagreement arose in the days of the Nagid Judah b. Saʿadyah (1064–1074), which is described by Yeshūʿā b. Joseph Ibn al-Qāsh, one of the most prominent representatives of the indigenous residents. The letter is very fragmentary and one may only grasp the general gist of the matter.[1049] This too was evidently a conflict over taxes: "The people who were exempt stood up... from the *jāliyya* taxes and ʿAmmār Ibn Ḥadīd..."[1050] Here as well, the local leader attempted to leverage his position of influence in order to set the course straight. The dispute was brought before the Nagid in Fustat, and the Nagid's letter settled the matter.[1051] The local leader was unable to use his position to influence the division of the levy to decide the matter and prove that he was effective. In the end, both sides in the conflict required the intervention of the Nagid and the status of the local leader was once again eroded.

Anger and Frustration

The anger and frustration that were the end result of the attempts to find an equitable way to divide the tax burden are described in ʿAwāḍ b. Hananel's letter, written in the 1060s in Alexandria to his uncle, Nahray b. Nissim, in Fustat:

> Following your departure from us, much has befallen me regarding the poll tax. There are many people who have made their residence in this city and were not treated in the way I was treated. Every day I am bullied. They appointed guards over me and said: "You must pay the poll tax in full." They want to write me down as a long-time resident. You know, however, that my father was a new immigrant. They take [money] from me and they deduct what I have paid from others who they did not succeed in including on their list of taxpayers. The identity of these people is not hidden from you. This is my reward for your reference letter on my behalf. The payment this year was almost two dinars. I tell you of this. If

1047 TS 13 J 23.3v, l. 6.
1048 TS 13 J 23.3r, upper margins – v, l. 1.
1049 TS 12.264: Frenkel, *"The Compassionate and Benevolent"* [Hebrew], no. 21.
1050 TS 12.264r, right margins, ll. 5–8.
1051 Ibid., ll. 15–20.

> others had to endure what I have had to endure, then I would be appeased. Those who levy taxes and the overseer of the poll tax have no part in this. This is all perpetrated by Jews, may God pay them in kind, them and their children.[1052]

Conclusion

The authority of the local leader to determine the level of the tax and the proportion of the burden upon members of the community ultimately contributed to the erosion of his position. It made him a captive of conflicting forces in the community and brought upon him the ire of all sides, who challenged the legitimacy of his leadership. His need to involve the Nagid as a mediator between the warring factions further undermined his position.

8 Control of Information

(a) Information as an Essential Need

The local leader's constant fear of potential competitors and detractors on the one hand, and his great dependence on the Jewish population centers on the other hand, made the control of information all the more critical. When Meir b. Hillel wished to leave his position as the *muqaddam* of Alexandria and offered it to R. Peraḥyah, he promised, as one of his central commitments, to reveal to him the "secrets" of the community: "Your servant wrote to R. Peraḥyah, may his Rock preserve him [...] and he will serve as the *muqaddam* of the city and I promised him that I would reveal all its secrets to him... for the sake of the Creator blessed be His name. And I have already gone ahead and promised him that."[1053]

One of the preconditions facilitating service as a local leader was the control of hidden information at the basis of community life. It is hard to know what exactly "the secrets" were that Meir b. Hillel wished to impart to his heir, but one may surmise that it had to do with the politics of the community: the power relations, the identity of the various factions and their leaders, the powerful families and the ties between them, the rivalries and the pacts. In other words, all the unofficial information that a leader would find useful in understanding the unseen aspects of community life.

1052 TS Misc 25.62r, l. 3; upper margins, l. 1: Gil, *Kingdom*, no. 572.

1053 Moss. VII 154.2 (L222), recto, ll. 7–5: Frenkel, "*The Compassionate and Benevolent*" [Hebrew], no. 19.

(b) The Private Archive

Leaders who also served as judges had a certain advantage when it came to information: people were accustomed to deposit documents with them for safekeeping, and thus they came to control a private archive of sorts with a great deal of sensitive information that was also immediately accessible. These documents were bequeathed to the heirs of these leaders, and it is clear that they too comprehended how useful they could be and were not eager to part with them. In 1150, brothers of the Ibn Ḥabīb family required the last will and testament that their father had deposited with Aaron Ibn al-ʿAmmānī.[1054] The brothers undertook a discreet and convoluted campaign to gain access to the document from the sons of Aaron Ibn al-ʿAmmānī, who had already passed away. This family venture sheds light upon the great importance that was attributed to this "archive." We learn of this from a letter written by one of the brothers to his two siblings in Alexandria:

> I wish to inform you... that I left you, as you know, and God helped me. I was worried about the matter until the very moment I concluded this letter, as you know. I arrived in Fustat, hale and healthy and I met with the children of the judge Ibn al-ʿAmmānī, may the Lord have mercy upon him. They greeted me graciously and they gave me documents for their brother, Abū al-Jīth BaMeir which instruct him to hand over the will that was kept on our behalf with their father. Afterwards I took the letter from our master the Nagid, which offers me assurances and certifies that I am allowed to gain access to the will. The letter is addressed to his *nāʾib* in Alexandria.[1055]

In other words, in order to gain access to the will from Abū al-Jīth, Aaron Ibn al-ʿAmmānī's son, the author of the letter had to travel to Fustat and receive permission from the other sons of the deceased judge. In order to make sure that he would indeed be able to lay his hands on the document, he had to get another letter from the Nagid himself. This entire campaign was shrouded in secrecy; the author of the letter uses many hints and is reluctant to state anything explicitly. Moreover, he takes very serious safety measures:

> Upon God's life, you should never ever speak of what I have written here [...] and the moment you read this letter, write me a response and let me know... because of a matter already known to you. I am very worried because of it... I have already bought four mules. If there is danger lurking, let me know. And if not I shall meet you in Sanhūr [= a small landlocked town near Alexandria], and we shall plan out our next steps and I shall deliver

1054 See above, Part II, Chapter 5: Aaron b. Yeshūʿā the Physician Ibn al-ʿAmmānī.
1055 ULC Or 1080 J 29r, ll. 4–12: Frenkel, *"The Compassionate and Benevolent"* [Hebrew], no. 97.

the letters to you. And peace. If danger does not lurk. And if it does not lurk, I will meet you. And peace.[1056]

(c) External Information

The local leader also required up-to-date information on the events in the wider Jewish and gentile world. Of special importance was news about the power centers of world Jewry. We have already discussed the clandestine semi-institutionalized channels of correspondence between Yeshūʿā b. Joseph, the leader of the community in the eleventh century and Judah Ibn Sighmār. Along these channels flowed a great deal of external data regarding events taking place in the Palestinian Yeshivah and information about other major figures in the Jewish world.[1057] One may assume that this pattern was not exceptional and that Yeshūʿā corresponded with others who supplied him with such information.

An attestation to the importance of the control over extra-communal information is the special status accorded to Abū Naṣr b. Abraham due to the wealth of data that he gathered at his store in the port. His store served as an active information center from both written and oral sources from everywhere in the Jewish world.[1058] The power that Abū Naṣr accrued indicates the local leader's great dependence on information from outside sources as well as from his own community.

9 Ties with the Muslim Regime

(a) Lobbying

The local leaders did not lobby the Muslim regime directly. Due to the centralization of power during both the Fatimid and Ayyubid regimes, it was not enough to cultivate a relationship with the Amir or local governor (*wālī*), one had to have the right connection to the actual royal house. For this reason, actual lobbying was undertaken indirectly, usually by associates of associates – in other words, by those who were close enough to Jews in Fustat and Cairo who had positions in the court or did business with the royal house.

1056 Ibid., ll. 12–18; upper margins, ll. 1–9.
1057 See above, Part II, Chapter 1.3 (c): Sources of Support, in the section: Abū Zikrī, Judah b. Moses Ibn Sighmār.
1058 Ibid., Chapter 6.2: At the Nexus of Information and Relationships.

Ārah̩ b. Nathan, the brother of Abraham b. Nathan the Seventh who had ties to the royal house and who was a scion of a family whose members occupied positions in the court,[1059] was asked to enlist his brother to lobby the qadi Makīn al-Dawla to stop the harassment of Jews in Alexandria and obtain "a letter of endorsement and protection."[1060] Abū Naṣr b. Abraham, who maintained commercial ties with the caliph's court attempted to enlist his fellow merchants to lobby on behalf of the Jews of Alexandria. He asked his business partner Judah Ibn Sighmār to speak at the court of the caliph in order to quell the riots against the community.[1061] Ibrāhīm b. Farāḥ of Alexandria enlisted the help of Nahray b. Nissim to lobby the regime regarding the situation in the port city.[1062] The local leaders of Alexandria requested the help of Jewish officials in Cairo who were associated with the royal house, such as the Tustarīs and David ha-Levi b. Isaac, in order to help them with the ransoming of captives.[1063]

The ties between the local leaders and the Muslim regime was thus indirect, and the lobbying was accomplished by intermediaries and associates. This meant that the limited ability to lobby the Muslim authorities was dependent upon the Alexandrians' positions in the intra-community communication network of the Jewish elites.

(b) Cementing of Ties

On the other hand, ties with the local Amir could help to advance private interests. Thus, for example Japheth b. Shelah received permission for an exemption from taxes for goods worth three hundred dinars, "and this was granted because of the *qā'id* Gharāt's fondness" for him, in his words.[1064] Such ties were not exploited for lobbying, but proved to be useful in cementing relationships with the leadership in Fustat. Thus, for example, Yeshūʿā b. Joseph was asked to serve as an intermediary in the lease of a vineyard in Alexandria, on behalf of Mevorakh

1059 See Cohen, *Jewish Self-Government*, 130 – 131. In n. 88 there, Cohen mentions a family pedigree in which the names of family members occur together with titles that indicate court positions.
1060 TS 13 J 22.23r, ll. 10 – 16: Frenkel, *"The Compassionate and Benevolent"* [Hebrew], no. 73; and see above, Part II, Chapter 4.4: Communal Work.
1061 See above, Part II, Chapter 6.3: Commerce as a Conduit to Advocacy.
1062 TS 8 J 18.10r, l. 14-right margins, l. 3: Gil, *Kingdom*, no. 549.
1063 ENA 2804.11: Frenkel, *"The Compassionate and Benevolent"* [Hebrew], no. 10.
1064 TS 16.344r, ll. 8 – 12.

b. Saʿadyah the Nagid.[1065] Vineyards in Fatimid Egypt were owned by the Amirs[1066] and Mevorakh the Nagid wished to persuade the Amir of Alexandria to lease him the vineyard with Yeshūʿā b. Joseph, the local leader, acting as an intermediary. In this case, the mediation failed and the venture was unsuccessful, but it is a good example of the way in which a local leader used his special ties with the Amir in order to buttress his status as the community leader. He took advantage of this association not because it would necessarily benefit the interests of the community, but because it would help secure his own position through cementing his ties with the leaders of the Jewish community in Fustat.

(c) Conclusion

The lobbying of the local leaders was limited and indirect. This being said, they did not hesitate to take advantage of their personal, unofficial, ties with the local Amir or *wālī* as part of a reciprocal system of service, which connected them with the intra-communal network of elites and enabled their position as leaders. One must remember, however, that this network of ties ultimately guaranteed not only their personal status, but also nurtured the overall extra-communal lobbying apparatus, which vouchsafed the very existence and the security of all Jewish communities. It is thus an instructive example of the enlistment of the extensive network of the Jewish elites for the welfare of Jewish society as a whole.

1065 Bodl MS Heb b 3.16v, ll. 4–12: Gil, *Kingdom*, no. 671; Frenkel, "*The Compassionate and Benevolent*" [Hebrew], no. 1.
1066 See Goitein, *Society*, 1: 123.

Chapter 3 The Normative Understanding of Governance

1 Introduction

This chapter attempts to uncover how the Jews of Alexandria conceived the notions of leaders and leadership. To accomplish this, we must attempt to discover the primary concepts, sometimes unconscious, which serve as the basic semantic reservoir of the worldview shared by members of this group. Images and conceptualization are not created in a vacuum, but are a corollary of certain life experiences in a given reality. At the same time, they also affect and shape reality and are therefore of historically importance.

A question naturally arises: How can one delve into a society's or an individual's consciousness in order to arrive at these profound concepts, especially if we take into consideration the great temporal divide between the culture at the crux of this project and the milieu of the modern researcher? In this study, I attempt to follow in the trailblazing footsteps of the medievalist Aaron Gurevitch, and avail myself of his methodological toolkit.[1067] Gurevitch observed that the imprint of these basic categories is usually apparent in semiotic systems such as art, poetry, literature, science, and religion, and thus the pertinent categories may be isolated and identified through analysis. This being said, since we do not have any literary compositions written by members of the Alexandrian community in these areas, nor do we possess any *objets d'art* produced by them, we must confine ourselves to one semiotic system, that of language. Consequently, I shall attempt to isolate recurring phrases, modes of expression, and statements in general, which seek to impart accepted general knowledge. An etymological analysis of terms referring to rulers and leadership will also be of help. One must remember, however, that we will never be able completely to overcome the temporal gap alluded to above, since concepts that were taken for granted in the medieval period have reached us devoid of the meanings and associations with which the people of the time imbued them. We will, therefore, be unable to trace the original meanings in full, and to some degree will infuse these terms with new meanings from our society and time period. One must attempt to minimize the leakage from our time period as much as possible.

1067 Aron J. Gurevitch, *Categories of Medieval Culture*, trans. G.L. Campbell (London: Routledge and Kegan Paul, 1985).

https://doi.org/10.1515/9783110713619-022

As I noted in the introduction to this book, our field of research is the Alexandrian community. It is incorrect to assume that in this limited field a unique worldview developed that was very different from other communities of the time; the narrow focus of this project was simply conducive to more focused and more lucid observation. This chapter has two parts: The first part will seek to identify the ideal of the good leader in the eyes of the residents of Alexandria of this period and the attributes the community expected him to possess; the second part will deal with their general view of leadership, its purpose, its goals, and the leaders' responsibilities.

2 The Portrait of an Ideal Leader

(a) A Resident of the City

A fair proportion of the leaders in Alexandria were not originally residents of the city. In spite of this, according to the normative understanding of the populace, the leader should ideally be a local. When members of the community complained about Yeshūʿā b. Joseph's leadership, Solomon b. Judah Gaon replied to them: "Is he not your son, is he not sustained by you?"[1068] Inherent to this statement is the assumption that a leader who is originally from Alexandria is the natural and most appropriate choice for leader, and as long as a person of this type occupies this position there is no room for complaint. In contrast, if a non-resident becomes leader this is seen as a flawed and unnatural state of affairs. The foreignness of a leader was used on a number of occasions to undermine and delegitimize his leadership. "Why does one of these foreigners ask for dinars?" was a question posed to R. Ephraim by one of his detractors when he wished to raise money on behalf of captives.[1069]

Aaron Ibn al-ʿAmmānī's effort to base his leadership upon the origin of his family in the Holy Land, rather than in Alexandria, was an anomaly in the community's history.[1070] The attempt to shift the ideal of local leadership to a new ideal of a leader coming to the city as part of a holy mission represents a departure from the existing norms. Aaron Ibn al-ʿAmmānī hoped to transform his origins in a different land, which according to the local ethos was detrimental, into

1068 See above, Part II, Chapter 1.3 (c): Sources of Support , in the section: The Geonim, the Heads of the Palestinian Yeshivah.
1069 See above, Part II, Chapter 9.1: Background and Origin.
1070 Ibid.

an advantage by fostering an ideology focused on the holiness of the Land of Israel and its centrality. His prodigious propaganda machine, which he ran with the help of Judah ha-Levi, successfully swayed a sizable segment of the community at the time,[1071] though ultimately his tenure was no more than an interlude. In the long run this ideology did not endure.

Eighty years later, in the second decade of the thirteenth century, the norm of a non-foreign leader was still so entrenched that the locals wished to express it in an official edict. And indeed, from that time forwards an edict existed in Alexandria forbidding a foreigner from serving as the *muqaddam* of the community.[1072] The background of this edict was an immense wave of refugees migrating from Europe, who overran the community. This wave led to great fear and concern, as expressed in Judah Ibn al-ʿAmmānī's letter from Alexandria:

> And on this night, my lord, when I write these lines to you, seven of the rabbis came to us, great scholars they were, and with them one hundred people, men, women, and children, asking for food, as though we ourselves have no beggars of our own. There are about forty [beggars]. Most of the community is under duress for lack of income. And now they are charged with such great expenditures. We shall see how matters shall develop.[1073]

The angst which is readily apparent in this letter only served to cement this worldview, which was formalized into a written edict. The world of imagery and metaphor burst forth and threatened to dictate reality. Later on, however, in the eternal give and take between the world of imagery and reality, reality once again reasserted itself: A short while after the formulation of this edict, the residents of the city themselves moderated it: They needed R. Samuel, who was a foreigner, to serve as the leader, and were forced to recalibrate the edict in order to facilitate his appointment as *muqaddam*.[1074]

The primary task of a good leader beyond his residency status was to look out for the interests of the city's inhabitants. This is how Shelah b. Mubashshir explained his task in response to a thank you letter that he received from Surūr b. Ḥayyim. Surūr's daughter was married in Alexandria, but her marriage ran into trouble. Shelah intervened and rescued the marriage, for which Surūr wrote him a thank you letter. According to Shelah, it was his duty (*farḍ*) as a

1071 Ibid. 9.5: conclusions.
1072 See above, Part II, Chapter 12.2: The Appointment Affair: A Rearguard Battle against the European Immigrants.
1073 TS 12.299v, l. 15 – margins, l. 2: Goitein, *Palestinian Jewry*, 340 (the translation follows Goitein).
1074 See above, Part II, Chapter 12.2: The Appointment Affair: A Rearguard Battle against the European Immigrants.

leader, since "caring for the inhabitants of our city is a duty with which I am charged."[1075]

Shelah goes on and explains why he acted as he did:

> Regarding the gratitude that you conveyed to me and my uncle for what I did on behalf of your daughter, may God be good to her and keep her with her husband, it is our duty for many reasons. The first reason is that she was alone and without anything. Furthermore, it is our duty to care for matters concerning the inhabitants of our town, and lastly, [we do this] out of respect for my lord.[1076]

Shelah thus presents his public mission as being motivated by three things:

1. Humanitarianism. He was obliged to care for the indigent population of the city because of their impecunious state and because of their vulnerability. In this way, his Jewish ethos of charity was expressed – helping the weak and the stranger.
2. Local solidarity. He was obliged to care for the residents of the city. In this way his duty to act as a leader vis-à-vis the local community was expressed.
3. Class solidarity. He was obliged to care for those who were members of the elite like him. In this case, Shelah took care of Surūr b. Ḥayyim's family. Surūr was a member of the ruling elite, and like Shelah, was subject to the same ethical norms, "his munificence is upon dignitaries and commoners [alike]."[1077] In other words, he was rich enough to be responsible for giving charity, he was Shelah's replacement at the court,[1078] and thus he was counted among the educated elite and was seen as part of the governing apparatus. So too were his family: His nephew Abū al-Faḍl was a senior elder, entitled "the glory of the elders." Shelah knew the members of the family and extends a detailed greeting to each one which includes their names and their titles.[1079] It is thus evident that they were part of the same social group. Finally, Surūr b. Ḥayyim was a member of the Sabrah family, who were the loyal allies of the Ben Nahum family of Fustat, as Shelah explicitly

1075 TS 13 J 17.5r, ll. 8–10: Frenkel, *"The Compassionate and Benevolent"* [Hebrew], no. 67. See Oded Zinger, "Social Embeddedness in the Legal Arena According to Geniza Letters," in *Writing Semitic: Scripts, Documents. Languages in Historical Context*, eds. Andreas Kaplony and Daniel Potthast (Leiden: Brill, forthcoming).
1076 TS 13 J 17.5r, ll. 6–11: Frenkel, *"The Compassionate and Benevolent"* [Hebrew], no. 67.
1077 Ibid., l. 12.
1078 Ibid., ll. 13–15.
1079 Ibid., margins, ll. 1–17.

indicates: "Upon the life of my father, I know that the sons of Nahum have no greater comrades and loving associates than the Sabrah family."[1080]

(b) Shunning Leadership

The good leader does not fulfill his duties because of his love of authority, or because of competitiveness, or because he enjoys exerting power. In a letter that the community in Alexandria sent to Samuel ha-Levi of Fustat, in which they protested the ordinance against chanting liturgical poetry in the synagogue, they complained in the following way regarding their leader: "And because of all our sins, since we feared the evil of the gentiles, He sent us the wickedness of this one, who craves power and competition."[1081] And later in the letter, in the same vein: "Our subjugator was motivated by love of power and authority."[1082]

In another instance, Daniel b. Azaryah Gaon advises Yeshūʿā b. Joseph: "That he should comport himself gracefully, and shift the prevailing negative opinion about him...for his custom is to sit in his great *majlis* and preen."[1083] In other words, his belligerent behavior, his love and his appetite for power, and his aloofness were attributes that relegated a leader to the ranks of "evildoers." The opposite of this is a "humble" leader: "The reports concerning him are that[...] he is humble," is Solomon b. Judah Gaon's defense of Yeshūʿā b. Joseph.[1084] This was also the precondition the Gaon stipulated as he granted Yeshūʿā his position: "If he walks among you in humility, this is good and well."[1085] Humility is not only a prerequisite for appointment as a leader, it, in and of itself, is the goal of his service as leader. The Gaon continues to clarify the purpose of Yeshūʿā's appointment. "It is upon their words that the members of the fellowship depended when they granted him the title of *ḥaver*, that he should be humble."[1086]

1080 Ibid., ll. 18–24.

1081 TS 8 J 21.12r, ll. 16–17: Friedman, "A Cry of Destruction," 139; Frenkel, *"The Compassionate and Benevolent"* [Hebrew], no. 45. On the hypothesis that this letter was written in Alexandria and not in Fustat, as Friedman suggests, or in a small provincial town, as Goitein (*Society*, 2:60) does, see Frenkel, *"The Compassionate and Benevolent"* [Hebrew], appendix.

1082 TS 8 J 21.12r, l. 28: Friedman, "A Cry of Destruction," 141.

1083 See above, Part II, Chapter 1.3 (b): The Opposition, in the section: "The Meek Shall Inherit the Earth."

1084 Ibid., Chapter 1.3 (c): Sources of Support, in the section: The Geonim, the Heads of the Palestinian Yeshivah.

1085 Ibid., n. 343.

1086 Ibid., n. 342.

(c) Godfearing

As was the norm amongst medieval people, the Jews of Alexandria expected a good leader to be motivated by "fear of God."[1087] In a letter of reference which Yeshūʿā b. Joseph forged, he was most eager to name himself god fearing.[1088] Two hundred years later, when members of the community complained that their leaders wished to cancel the chanting of liturgical poetry, they dismissed their leadership with the claim that "they abandoned the words of the prophet:[...]'Fear God my son' (Proverbs 24:21),"[1089] and their motives "were other than for the sake of heaven."[1090]

3 Responsibilities of the Leader

(a) A Ceremonial Figure

According to the official Fatimid letter of appointment,[1091] the *muqaddam* of Alexandria was seen as an administrative leader, who was in charge of the community apparatus and the courts, not as a spiritual/religious leader. Despite this, the community chose to see the *muqaddam* as a religious figure as well. His religious leadership was mainly reflected in his ceremonial role as a prayer-leader in the synagogue. For this reason, when the community wished to supplant a failed leader, they demonstrated their discontent in a ceremonial context and refused to follow his lead in prayer. At the beginning of the twelfth century Ārah̩ b. Nathan wrote to the Nagid regarding such a case: "Afterwards, when the community came together to bless the honorable Amir Fakhr al-Mulk in the presence of the *muqaddam*. The *muqaddam* gave a speech, and the community proclaimed: 'This one, we do not follow his [lead] in prayer'.'"[1092]

1087 On the comprehensive religious outlook of Jews of this period, see Goitein, *Society*, 5: 323 ff.

1088 See above, Part II, Chapter 1.3 (b): The Opposition, in the section: "The Meek Shall Inherit the Earth."

1089 TS 8 J 21.12r, l. 29: Friedman, "A Cry of Destruction," 141; Frenkel, "*The Compassionate and Benevolent*" [Hebrew], no. 45.

1090 TS 8 J 21.12v, l. 3: Friedman, "A Cry of Destruction," 142, and n. 78.

1091 TS NS 320.45: Goitein, *Palestinian Jewry*, 77–78.

1092 TS 24.21v, ll. 65–66: Frenkel, "*The Compassionate and Benevolent*" [Hebrew], no. 38.

In another letter, written by Nathan b. Judah, it becomes clear that the community expected the *muqaddam* to take an active role in communal prayer, and if he did not perform as expected, the community immediately complained:

> The cantor wrote [...] that the people plead for help with regard to his rulings, and that the *ḥaver* is not at the synagogue on Monday or Thursday, or on New Moons or on Hanukkah, and when he frees himself from removing the foreskins from the uncircumcised along with their blood, he makes a mockery of the laws of God. He comes at night, presides over the court for a long time, and most of the people leave without praying.[1093]

In other words, the participation of the *muqaddam* in prayer was seen as vastly more important than presiding over the court.

The religious role that the community designated for the *muqaddam* was completely ceremonial. Leaders who wished to wield power through their role as prayer leaders, and envisioned it as a sphere in which they could exert their influence discovered to their chagrin that it was an area in which it was exceedingly difficult to change anything.[1094] R. Eleazar attempted to change the traditions of reading from the Torah scroll in a very limited way, maintaining that saying God's name out loud twice in succession, may be seen as detrimental to His uniqueness, and may lead in his view to "false beliefs." The changes he instituted lasted for a very short time, and his successor, R. Pinḥas, was quick to reinstate the original custom, emphasizing the importance of the local tradition: "It is entirely appropriate that you read according to the traditions you were accustomed to."[1095]

Saʿadyah b. Berākhōt the Teacher alludes to the great difficulty in changing any aspect of the liturgy, in a question to Maimonides:

> What is his opinion in the matter, for we worked at it until the change in the liturgical practices was accepted, and we brought upon ourselves the ire of many people and they continued to despise us for a long time. Until it came to my attention that may people were following it [=the older tradition]. And because of this we have asked him for a ruling regarding proper way to pray in holiness.... and people tried to prevent this and we forced the ruling upon them. They remained dissatisfied for a while, until a long time had passed and

1093 TS 10 J 6.5r, ll. 28–31: Frenkel, *"The Compassionate and Benevolent"* [Hebrew], no. 48.
1094 On this, see Friedman, "A Cry of Destruction"; M.A. Friedman, "Controversy for the Sake of Heaven: Studies in the Prayer Controversy of R. Abraham Maimuni and His Generation," *Teʿudah* 10 (1996): 254–298 [Hebrew]; Friedman, "Objection to Prayer"; Ezra Fleischer, *Eretz-Israel Prayer and Prayer Rituals as Portrayed in the Genizah Documents* (Jerusalem: Magness, 1988) [Hebrew]; Paul Fenton (Yinon), "Prayer for the Authority and Permission to Pray: Genizah Fragments," *Mi-Mizraḥ u-mi-Maʿarav* 4 (1983): 17–22 [Hebrew].
1095 Maimonides, *Responsa*, §267.

> it became better… but at the great synagogue the cantor prevented it during the Additional Service (*mussaf*) on the holiday, as did the person who chants the sacrificial regimen on the Day of Atonement. And perhaps they shall accept a ruling from his eminence, those who rely upon his word without disagreement… for the scholars among them do as they do, intending to buttress the tradition, and if they hear a ruling from his eminence, they shall cease from this practice.[1096]

The leadership of the *muqaddam* was thus expressed ceremonially in the liturgical sphere – as an ongoing active participant in communal prayer, and as a prayer leader. Despite this, leaders who attempted to set the agenda by enacting changes in liturgical traditions quickly discovered that the public price they had to pay was usually too steep: it led to the enmity of "many people" and a stubborn refusal to change anything.

(b) Preserving the *Status Quo*

The accepted terms designating the leader were *raʾīs* ("head") and *muqaddam* ("he who stands at the front"). These two terms reflect a stable worldview in which the hierarchical structure of a community with one leader is static and lacks the dynamic element of "leading" (*hanhagah*) in the sense of actively guiding a community towards a common goal. Indeed, it seems that the main duty of the leader was perceived to be the preservation of the *status quo* and the prevention of any turmoil or revolution. The extant *status quo* was seen as the natural and preferable order. The form of the community was imagined as a three-tiered structure: At the front, as the visible representatives, were the leaders (*muqaddamūn*); behind them were the dignitaries (*al-shuyūkh*), and behind everyone were the hidden masses (*al-ʿāmma*). This portrait of the community is expressed as an afterthought in a letter by Judah Ibn al-ʿAmmānī, when he describes the plague that has spread throughout the town: "There is no one in the town who is healthy. Not its leaders, nor its dignitaries, nor the masses of people that are there."[1097]

Reflected in this statement is the degree of attachment attributed to each of the strata of the population. The leaders and the dignitaries belong to the city and are an inseparable part of it. Their ties are expressed in terms of ownership: "its leaders," "its dignitaries." The *hoi polloi* are not part of this fabric; they just happen "to be there."

1096 Ibid., 485–486, §249.
1097 TS 10 J 25.3v, ll. 6–7: Frenkel, *"The Compassionate and Benevolent"* [Hebrew], no. 57.

This structure is what is the most appropriate and right one: any attempt to change it is seen as a shift of the very foundations of the world, and as such is exceedingly grave. One of the most serious allegations that one may make against a leader is that he is attempting to shift the leadership away from the dignitaries and to empower the rabble. This is seen as completely absurd and not to be tolerated. An accusation that such a course is being pursued is very severe.[1098] One must preserve the cohesion and unity of the communal edifice and prevent its dissolution or division by any means available. Creating disagreements and divisiveness in the community are sins of the same magnitude as religious transgressions and are often mentioned in tandem: "We have not burdened anyone and we did not sow dissent in the community, nor did we commit a religious transgression,"[1099] Shelah b. Mubashshir declared in 1071, referring to a disagreement between him and the Nagid Mevorakh. It is apparent from this statement that he was defending himself against concrete allegations directed against him by Mevorakh.

In another letter Yeshūʿā Ibn al-Qāsh describes the successful resolution of a conflict in the community: "The people confessed their sins and returned to God... and because we frequently sowed dissent."[1100]

The transgression that requires penitence and a return to God is none other than sowing dissent, which is seen as a religious transgression for all intents and purposes. Indeed, one of the central responsibilities of the leader was maintaining peace in the community – as is reflected in Solomon b. Judah Gaon's letter regarding the appointment of Yeshūʿā b. Joseph as *ḥaver:* "And we bestowed upon him the title of *ḥaver*, so that he would be humble and bear the burden of settling disagreements."[1101]

(c) Reciprocity-Based Service

The terms *raʾīs* and *muqaddam*, which were the most common sobriquets for the leader, signify a position in space: either one who stands before, or one who stands in front. Not only are they devoid of active connotations pertaining to leadership, but they also lack any reference to ruling or coercion. In fact, the position of leader was viewed in terms of community service, and indeed one occa-

1098 Ibid.
1099 TS 13 J 17.5r, ll. 19–20: Frenkel, *"The Compassionate and Benevolent"* [Hebrew], no. 67.
1100 TS 12.264v, l. 9: Frenkel, *"The Compassionate and Benevolent"* [Hebrew], no. 21.
1101 See above, Part II, Chapter 1.3 (a): An Alexandrian "Prince".

sionally find the position of the leader referred to as *khidma*, which denotes service.[1102]

Likewise, the activities of the leader are delineated in terms of cooperation and reciprocity. The leader must always act in tandem with the dignitaries and must always consider their advice. When members of the community sought to reject the legitimacy of one of their *muqaddams*, they did not allow him to lead them in prayer and declared: "This one, we do not follow his lead in prayer and there is no cooperation (*muʿāmala*) between us."[1103] The term *muʿāmala* that the members of the community employed was usually used to refer to a type of unofficial business partnership, in which each of the partners felt bound to grant his fellow broad commercial services without any remuneration except for the expectation that he would receive the same consideration when he needed it himself. The use of the term *muʿāmala* in the very different context of the relationship between the community and the leader shows that this was not necessarily a commercial term only, but had much broader significance as a basic and well-regarded social paradigm based upon mutual trust and cooperation without coercion.[1104]

(d) The Internal Arena

One of the most common terms used to describe the executive activities of the leader is *tadbīr:* "Regarding the status of the community, it is devolving and on the brink of dissolution. The reason for this is that there is no one to oversee their activities (*man yudabbiruhum*),"[1105] writes Barakāt b. Abū al-Ḥasan of Alexandria, after the death of R. Samuel the Judge. The term *muqaddam* denotes the front, and is a derivative of *qadam*, which means the forward-stepping foot, while *tadbīr* is derived from *dabr*, which denotes the back, or the rear part, and refers to activities that are accomplished behind things. Sometimes it has to do with strategies and secret plots, but usually, as in the case here, it has to do with managing and organizing. It mostly refers to the inner workings of a domicile, in other words, activities that are not undertaken in the visible part of the house, but behind things, in internal and hidden spaces. Thus, one may assume, was the role of the leader when he is referred to as *mudabbir* –

1102 Ibid.

1103 TS 24.21v, l. 66: Frenkel, *"The Compassionate and Benevolent"* [Hebrew], no. 28.

1104 On the extraordinary polysemy that characterized medieval language, see Gurevitch, *Categories*, 20.

1105 TS 13 J 21.30r, ll. 10–11: Frenkel, *"The Compassionate and Benevolent"* [Hebrew], no. 72.

one who organizes and takes responsibility for the inner failings of the community and all its various factions, or one "who endures the burden of disagreement," in the words of Solomon b. Judah Gaon.

Another term that is used to designate the leader is *muʿāyana:* "The community is in great distress because of the lack of *muʿāyana*," writes Judah Ibn al-ʿAmmānī from Alexandria, when Samuel the Judge was absent.[1106] The term *muʿāyana* is also a derivative of a body part – the eye, and it denotes seeing someone face to face, checking out, testing. In the present context, it refers to someone who examines matters closely, is attentive and observant. This term resembles, in some ways, the previous designation for leader, *tadbīr*, discussed above, as it also is associated with activities that are undertaken in intimacy, or in a closeted and hidden away environment. One may thus surmise that the leader's field of operation was understood as revolving around the inner workings of the community.

The leader was thus understood as having dual responsibilities. On the one hand, he was imagined at the forefront of the field, as the visible representative of the community. On the other hand, he was also seen as the man responsible for preserving the *status quo* as well as the unity and cohesion of the community, which he accomplished by ironing out problems discreetly. He fulfilled his responsibilities, not as a leader foisted upon the community by the powers that be, but rather in cooperation and reciprocity with members of the community.

1106 TS 13 J 27.11v, ll. 20–21: Frenkel, *"The Compassionate and Benevolent"* [Hebrew], no. 79.

Part IV **A Ruling Elite**

Introduction

Nothing, it seems, could prove more erroneous than the expectation to find in the medieval Jewish community of Alexandria an innate pyramidal leadership with one single communal leader, who oversees and runs all local affairs, at its tip.

In the previous chapters we could in some instances find one recognized leader at the head of the community, but it was not rare for two or even three leaders to rule in tandem. Sometimes they cooperated amongst themselves, but in many cases they competed viciously with one another and their relationship was fraught with enmity. The leader of the community was sometimes the chief judge (*dayyan*), such as in the case of Shelah b. Mubashshir, but in other occasions the leader was someone else, such as in the case of Aaron Ibn al-ʿAmmānī. In some instances, the leader was also the figure referred to as the *muqaddam*, whereas in other cases the leader of the community bore the title of *raʾīs*, and at other times it was the *nāʾib* who led the community. Some of the leaders were locals and belonged to indigenous, firmly rooted families. Many others were new settlers in Alexandria, some of them even European immigrants. There were leaders who were accepted and endorsed by the community, but whose actual degree of control over the community was very slight. In contrast, there were figures without any official position, who governed the community high-handedly. Though the strategies of the rulers and the fonts from whence authority was drawn underwent transformation throughout the periods in question, the unchanging powerbase was, and remained, one's position in the socio-economic-intellectual network that spanned the Jewish world under Islam.

Power, it seems, was spread over a social web of people who belonged to a definite class, referred to in this book as the ruling elite. This ruling elite was part of a meta-communal network that extended throughout the Islamic world. The elite in Alexandria did not act as a local subsidiary of the whole network, but was, rather, an unalienable part of it, and its members wandered throughout the communities and centers of leadership.

The supposition that such an elite existed depends on a number of pre-suppositions.[1107]

1. First and foremost, we assume that there were advantages and interests shared by the group members, and that they had to band together in order to preserve and advance them.

1107 See above, Part II, Chapter 1.3 (a): An Alexandrian "Prince".

https://doi.org/10.1515/9783110713619-023

2. We assume that an apparatus existed for training, selection, and acceptance. Since elites often act in an unofficial capacity, this training would have included not only official vocational education, but also the nurturing of elite characteristics, which are part of a long process of socialization. In non-formal groups, socialization is achieved within unofficial frameworks, designed to nurture "excellence" in the form of a wide skillset, which is the prerequisite for acceptance into the group. This amorphous and idiosyncratic "excellence" is usually inaccessible to outsiders. Such an apparatus allows the group to define its uniqueness and to set its boundaries.
3. We expect to identify a common culture shared by the members of the group, justifying and rationalizing its existence. This culture may include symbolic formations, such as a common genealogy, ancestor worship, or the development of a particular belief system emphasizing designation and mission; it may include rituals which convey its special status, or a unique lifestyle. This lifestyle is usually comprised of esoteric customs, particular codes of behavior, norms, morals, and a unique value system, which almost never can be learnt or adopted by outsiders. All these symbolic apparatuses together constitute the unique culture of the group and allow it to maintain its boundaries and its distinction.
4. We assume the existence of an organizational apparatus, official or unofficial, which enables coordination and cooperation between the members of the group and ensures its long-term survival. Such an apparatus requires efficient communication channels between the various group members, gathering venues that enable frequent reciprocal contacts, and frameworks, both official and unofficial, of decision-making.[1108]

The chapter uses these pre-suppositions to test the book's main thesis concerning the actual existence of a ruling elite in the Jewish community of Alexandria in the Fatimid and Ayyubid eras.

1108 Pareto and Mosca had other criteria for identifying an elite, called "the three Cs": group consciousness, coherence and conspiracy. As Abner Cohen has shown, an elite can exist without needing to conspire and is capable of acting even without group consciousness on the part of its members, since people may promote the interests of their group by means of lifestyle and actions, without even being aware of this. See Cohen, *Two-Dimensional Man*, 65.

Chapter 1 Common Interests

1 Shared Mercantile Interests

All elite members had mercantile interests in some capacity and were connected to one another through business ties. These business associations operated in small circles, often of only two people, but each merchant belonged to more than one circle thus constituting a link between several other circles. In effect, each merchant formed the focus of a cluster of interlocking circles, together creating a broad and multi-branched network of mercantile ties.[1109] This network, which encompassed a large geographical area, controlled considerable amounts of money and merchandise.[1110] The existence and preservation of this network was an essential condition for the perpetuation of this mercantile machine, and therefore business interests of the group often superseded short-term political considerations and local rivalries.[1111]

1109 Shelomo D. Goitein, "Formal Friendship in the Medieval Near East," *Proceedings of the American Philosophical Society* 115 (1971): 484–489; Abraham L. Udovitch, "Formalism and Information in the Social and Economic Institutions of the Medieval Islamic World," in Amin Banani and Speros Vryonis (eds.), *Individualism and Conformity in Classical Islam* (Wiesbaden: Harrassovitz, 1977), 74–75; Goitein, *Society*, 1: 164–169. Avner Greif understands the organizing principle of the commercial network differently. He conceives of it to be a reputation-based coalition of Maghribi traders. But as far as can be deduced from Genizah documents, the network was not defined ethnically. It was a multi-ethnic network in which trade constituted only one aspect of cooperation, and while reputation certainly played a central role in it, one's position in the large network and degree of connectedness were the most critical givens determining one's status. In order to prove the existence of a distinct Maghribi trade group, a long awaited systematic and comprehensive prosopographical study is still needed. See Greif, *Institutions and the Path to the Modern Economy*, esp. 58–90; idem, "Reputation in Medieval Trade: Evidence on the Maghribi Traders," *Journal of Economic History* 49 (1989): 857–882. See critical approaches to his thesis in: Goldberg, *Trade*, especially 86, 200–211; Jeremy Edwards and Sheilagh Ogilvie, "Contract Enforcement, Institutions, and Social Capital: The Maghribi Traders Reappraised," *Economic History Review* 65 (2012): 421–444, and Greif's response to the critics, in: Greif, "The Maghribi Traders: A Reappraisal?."

1110 Goldberg, *Trade*, 211–218.

1111 In this manner we may understand the ostensibly inexplicable behavior of the Ben Nahum family, who were prominent as the outspoken opponents of the Maghāriba merchants, yet continued to trade closely with them. See above, Part II, Chapter 2.4 (a): Shelah and the Maghribis (al-*Maghāriba*).

https://doi.org/10.1515/9783110713619-024

2 Reciprocal Benefits

Beyond mercantile considerations, the network conferred upon its members many perks and privileges, which they granted to one another. The feeling of mutual accountability, which prevailed among the elite members, was perceived as an everlasting commitment.

Meir b. Hillel, in a letter to his son, complained of his treatment by one of the community heads: "One only gets the minimum from him. And [remember] how my father of blessed memory treated him so well."[1112] It is unclear what exactly Meir b. Hillel wished to accomplish, but it is clear that he connected the favor shown by his father to this individual to the expectations he now had of this person. When Shelah b. Mubashshir helped the daughter of Surūr b. Ḥayyim b. Sabrah, who was in a dire predicament, he does not deny that he acted "in honor of his lord," in other words in deference to the daughter's father, who was at one time his representative in the court of the Palestinian Yeshivah.[1113] Requests for help by the heads of the community on behalf of the needy were more likely to be heeded when the supplicants were "of good family" who had fallen on hard times. Joseph b. ʿAllān of Alexandria pleaded for help from R. Hananel b. Samuel the Judge in these words:

> And I would like to apprise you that I am of good lineage and my father was one of the travelers to India, and the Lord was good to us. And my lord your father knows my father and my brother Futūḥ, who journeyed recently to Yemen and died whilst onboard the ship [...] And I, your servant, ascended to our illustrious lord, may his eminence be magnified, and was accepted into his presence, and he even wrote a number of letters to the community on my behalf, so that I may perhaps be able to procure something to sustain my household of nine souls. I am now, generally speaking, starving and thirsty, naked and completely destitute and I ask from the Lord and from him, that you hide me in a garment so that I may enter the synagogue and hear "the holy and the blessed" for the sake of the Lord's treasured presence. And this after [I had previously worn] clothes of *niṣāfī*, *sābūrī*, and *mautakhkhat.*[1114]

1112 TS NS J 171r, ll. 8–9: Frenkel, *"The Compassionate and Benevolent"* [Hebrew], no. 91.
1113 TS 13 J 17.5: Frenkel, *"The Compassionate and Benevolent"* [Hebrew], no. 67.
1114 TS 10 J 17.4: Shelomo D. Goitein, "Chief Judge R. Hananel b. Samuel, In-Law of R. Moses Maimonides," *Tarbiẓ* 50 (1980): 378 [Hebrew]. *Mutakhkhat:* checked patterned garment, see Yedida Kalfon Stillman, The Arab Dress: A Short Story from the Dawn of Islam to Modern Times.ed. Norman A. Stillman (Leiden: Brill, 2000), 59–60, and n. 80. *Sābūrī:* knitwear, see: Dozy, *Supplement, s.v. Niṣafi:* cloth of silk and canvas, see Dozy, *Supplement*, *s.v.*; Robert B. Serjeant, *Islamic Textiles* (Beirut: Librairie du Liban, 1972), 202; Francis J. Steingass, *A Comprehensive Persian-English Dictionary* (London: Routledge and Kegan Paul, 1892), 14061: stuff, half silk and half cotton. Goitein thought that this term denotes a name of a garment or of a dressmaking pattern which

The supplicant thus puts his faith in his good connections and those of his family. Members of his family had been wealthy India merchants and thus were of the elite. This letter was primarily intended to convince R. Hananel that he and his family were part of the group. He alludes to the acquaintance between his father and his brother and the father of the judge, and goes as far as to note external marks of belonging to the group: the splendid clothes that he used to wear.

This reciprocal favoritism also included taking advantage of ties with the Muslim regime. Thus, for example, Mevorakh b. Saʿadyah asked Yeshūʿā b. Joseph to take advantage of his good relationship with the Amir ofa Alexandria and help him rent a vineyard in the region.[1115] Similarly, Abraham b. Nathan Av, upon arriving to Alexandria asked Nahray b. Nissim to acquire a writ from the ruler that would help him establish himself in the community.[1116] These channels, which served the organizational needs of the elite, were also employed in times of existential crisis to protect the safety of the entire community.

covers half (*niṣf)* of the body rather than a kind of fabric, but its mention here among other prestigious textiles proves he was wrong. Shelomo D. Goitein, "Wills from Egypt from the Genizah Period," *Sefunot* 8 (1964): 115, n. 42. [Hebrew].

1115 See above, Part III, Chapter 2.9 (b): Cementing of Ties.

1116 TS 10 J 13.11: Frenkel, "*The Compassionate and Benevolent*" [Hebrew], no. 50.

Chapter 2 Systems of Training and Sorting

1 Training Curricula

(a) Mercantile Apprenticeships

Membership in the mercantile network was not open to all; a merchant who wished to join had to have the right ties, which were developed and improved upon following a long period of apprenticeship and throughout one's career as a merchant. A promising "apprentice" who had the right connections received a great deal of instruction and support at the beginning of his journey, and there are many cases of this in the archive at our disposal. A typical example shall suffice: Abū Naṣr b. Abraham[1117] recounts in a letter how, when still a novice merchant, his partner tried to prevent rookie mistakes by delicately hinting at them, without undermining the independence of the junior merchant: "I did not heed his advice on a number of occasions... and this was done elegantly so that I would note my mistakes... and I did not realize."[1118] After a number of years, when Abū Naṣr himself was an established and well-known merchant, he took advantage of the ties he had managed to forge in order to request that one of his associates extend his patronage and direct his little brother, Abū ʿUmar, who was beginning his career as a merchant: "[And I remind you again] of the patronage [that I asked you to extend] to Abū ʿUmar and to help him. Our parents miss him greatly."[1119]

(b) Academic Excellence

This mercantile network at the same time also supported an intellectual elite, whose cultural code was the acquisition of knowledge, which was greatly valued and served as a criterion of acceptance and advancement through its ranks. Meir b. Hillel's words, wherein he sees studiousness and pursuit of knowledge as the preeminent values, reflect the general attitude of the group.[1120] Members of the

1117 On him and his mercantile dealings, see above, Part II, Chapter 6.
1118 TS 13 J 22.31r, ll. 4–5, 12–14: Frenkel, *"The Compassionate and Benevolent"* [Hebrew], no. 74.
1119 TS 12.290v, right margins, ll. 4–6: Frenkel, *"The Compassionate and Benevolent"* [Hebrew], no. 22.
1120 See above, Part II, Chapter 7.1: Origins and Background.

https://doi.org/10.1515/9783110713619-025

elite were aware of the great importance of study. Parents and grandparents were accustomed to hiring private tutors for their children and followed their children's progress closely. Manasseh the Teacher's detailed report delivered to the parents of Zayn al-Kuttāb regarding his progress is a clear example of the great importance attributed to the training of the next generation through diligent study. The school-children of the present were the repository from which the leaders of the future were chosen. In the years 1082–1094, after having been ousted from the position of "Head of the Jews" in Fustat, Mevorakh b. Sa'adyah spent time in Alexandria as an exile of sorts.[1121] Far from the bustling center of Fustat, Mevorakh spent his years in Alexandria preparing for his return there and his renewed ascension to the leadership, and he spent a lot of time and effort cultivating a future cadre of supporters, who would ultimately occupy official positions in his governing apparatus. It was natural for Mevorakh to look for his future aides amongst the students at the school in Alexandria:

> When the *ra'īs* Abū al-Faḍl [= Mevorakh b. Sa'adyah] arrived in Alexandria, after having concluded his day's work, he would come to our teacher and say to him: "Find for me from among your young men those who already know how to read Mishnah, and let him come and read before me." The teacher would tell me and another youth to come read before him. And when Mevorakh b. Sa'adyah achieved his present status [that of Nagid] and we had already left the teacher, and he had already returned to Fustat [...] he reminded me in a letter of the debt I owed him for the privilege of learning (*ḥaqq al-Torah*).[1122]

This channel of learning and inquiry was a further course of training for admission into the ranks of the elite, alongside the mercantile curriculum. The criterion of scholastic excellence – which *prima facie* was an objective criterion of talent – was actually another way of culling candidates, since good-quality training was found only in private frameworks, which were costly,[1123] and only accessible to members of the elite. The elite thus possessed the key to good education and employed it to train their future members.

1121 See Cohen, *Jewish Self-Government*, 214–217.

1122 TS 10 J 6.5r, ll. 7–11: Frenkel, *"The Compassionate and Benevolent"* [Hebrew], no. 48. "The privilege of learning" was eventually translated into political loyalty and the author of the letter, Judah b. Nathan, became the Nagid's *nā'ib* in Alexandria. See above, Part II, Chapter 3.3: Relationship with Mevorakh b. Sa'adyah Nagid.

1123 See Goitein, *Jewish Education*, 96–97.

2 Methods of Sorting and Culling

(a) Encouraging and Preferring Marriage within the Group

Members of the elite preferred to marry within the group. The business partnerships described above, which began during the period of apprenticeship, were cemented not infrequently through marriage. In the best-case scenario, the apprentice merchant would marry the daughter of his partner; this marked his full acceptance into the family, but more importantly, into the mercantile network. Less auspiciously, the apprentice could marry a servant, which still signaled his reception into the network: "And I said to him: Did they not give you the orphan girl who lived with them and served them, as a wife? And you made them into your in-laws!"[1124] With this disparaging statement, Ḥayyim b. ʿAmmār attempts to belittle Nissim b. Shemaryah, partner and agent of the Alexandrian merchant Abū Isḥāq, and make light of the relationship between him and his partner.

Marriage between scholarly families was expected and seen in a very positive light. The most common blessing for such a union was the Talmudic aphorism: "Grapes of one cluster amongst grapes of another cluster."[1125] When Meir b. Hillel learned of his brother's intention to marry his cousin, he responded with the following: "Regarding what my brother Abū al-Mufaḍḍal mentioned, that he intended to marry my cousin. May God have mercy upon him, *first of all*, this is the right course of action for she is a daughter of a good family."[1126] Though later in the letter, Meir b. Hillel advises his brother to refrain from marriage and focus on his studies,[1127] he articulates a basic social tenet: marriage to "a daughter of a good family" is both good and desirable. Above we saw how the marriage of Hibat Allāh, the son of Judah Ibn al-ʿAmmānī, to the daughter of Solomon b. Elijah the Judge, was perceived as a blessed union between two distinguished families.[1128]

These marriage preferences allowed the male members of the group to strengthen the bonds of personal friendship between them and firmly establish their identities and place in the ranks of the elite. One of the clearest upshots of these unions was the closeness and friendship between a groom and his father-

1124 TS 20.122v, ll. 11–12: Ben-Sasson, *Jews of Sicily*, no. 76; ibid., 342.
1125 See Goitein, *Society*, 3: 58–59, n. 42.
1126 Moss. L268 (VII) – 200r, ll. 3–4: Frenkel, *"The Compassionate and Benevolent"* [Hebrew], no. 20.
1127 See above, Part II, Chapter 7.1: Origins and Background.
1128 See above, Part II Chapter 14.2 (b): Matrimonial Ties.

in-law, as is reflected in many letters: "And do not deny me a letter from you, for I find companionship in it as though I were seeing you face to face, and despite this[…] on God's great life, sometimes I remember you at mealtimes and lose my appetite, because you ceased sending me letters."[1129] This was written by Mubārak b. Isaac of Alexandria, in an epistle replete with expressions of amity, to his "father who was precious to him beyond anything," who was, in point of fact, not his father, but, rather, his father-in-law Surūr b. Ḥayyim b. Sabrah. The letter is signed: "From his son who thanks his munificence, Mubārak the son of Isaac, may his soul rest."[1130]

In this way the elite replicated itself and kept itself distinct. The restriction of membership through endogamy created intersecting relationships between members of the group: they found themselves tied to one another through mercantile associations, family unions, and friendships. This contributed to the cohesion of the group, and served as an important element in diffusing conflicts within the group.

(b) Boundaries of the Mercantile Group

As indicated above, trade amongst the Jewish elite took place in interlocking clusters and not within the framework of one official group. These circles, however, generated an informal group, the borders of which were invisible but, nevertheless, impregnable.

The merchants of the group were supposed to trade only amongst one another. Whoever dared to trade with Jewish merchants who were not part of the network was bound to be castigated for endangering himself by association with an unknown stranger, for whom no support network or guarantors existed. "Your actions do not befit those of a merchant. You should have traced the merchandise you were sending, that is what you should have done. Instead you sent the merchandise with a *ṣaʿlūk* (lit.: outlaw), without paying the taxes and fees that are required. And does he have the wherewithal to pay from his own pocket?"[1131] – this rebuke was delivered by an Alexandrian merchant to a family member at the beginning of the twelfth century for not taking sufficient care

1129 ULC Or 1080 J 264r, upper margins, ll. 1–15 – v, l. 1: Frenkel, *"The Compassionate and Benevolent"* [Hebrew], no. 100.
1130 Ibid., the address.
1131 TS 12.434r, ll. 9–12: Frenkel, *"The Compassionate and Benevolent"* [Hebrew], no. 23.

in his business dealings.[1132] The term *ṣaʿlūk* in this context is the accepted idiom for a merchant who is not part of the elite's merchant network.[1133] It is apparent that the merchant was not bothered by this *ṣaʿlūk*'s lack of funds; what disturbed him was that there was no support network for this merchant, since he hastens to reassure the addressee promise him that "there is a group of merchants looking out for him. They paid your brother. And the man is trustworthy."[1134]

(c) Non-Formality

I have already sent my lord a number of letters, but I have not received an answer to any of them. I hope that you are busy with good things. I have learnt that bales of flax and a package of sugar have arrived for you. I was angry at my lord for this. For he does not honor me in taking care of his needs [...] My lord, my trust in your love is what sustains me. I know of your love and the sincerity of your belief, do not ever cease from being benevolent and empathetic. [For this reason] I relied upon God's generosity and I sent you through Ḥasūn b. Yaḥyā al-Mahdawī, a package [...] and I have made a firm decision to travel to Alexandria in the near future to see you and meet with you, and renew the covenant with you. Any need you may have, write to me, so that I may happily and joyously grant it.[1135]

Thus wrote Jacob Ben Nahum, a scion of one of the oldest and most powerful families in Alexandria to his partner Nahray b. Nissim, when he was apprehensive that Nahray was planning to discontinue his partnership with him. The phenomenon that is revealed most clearly in this excerpt, as well as in many other mercantile correspondences, is the frequent use that the author makes of personal expressions in the business context. Jacob Ben Nahum does not talk of a partnership, but rather of a "covenant," not of trustworthiness or rectitude, but of "love," "faith," and "benevolence." The commercial relationship is presented as a yearning to render service. Presenting it in those unofficial terms

1132 In the Middle Ages, the term *ṣaʿlūk* came to mean a destitute person and thus it appears in many Genizah documents (see Cohen, "Four Judaeo-Arabic petitions," 458, n. 35), but in a class and mercantile context it preserves some of its original sense from the Jāhiliyya, i.e. a person who is outside the tribal framework and lives apart from the tribe, living a life of dearth and violence. See Clifford E. Bosworth, *The Medieval Islamic Underworld. The Banū Sāsān in Arabic Society and Literature* (Leiden: Brill, 1976), 17, cited in Cohen, ibid.
1133 See Goitein, *Society*, 1: 79, who gives a slightly different meaning to the use of this term.
1134 TS 12.434r, ll. 21–22: Frenkel, *"The Compassionate and Benevolent"* [Hebrew], no. 23.
1135 TS 13 J 25.8r, ll. 5–7, 10–12, 28–30: Gil, *Kingdom*, no. 691.

is not coincidental to this exchange; it was the way in which the elite prevented the entrance of foreign elements into its ranks. When the criteria for admission and belonging are not objective or formal, but rather are dependent upon subjective feelings such as love and hate, it is very easy to sort and cull who belongs to the group.

The principle of non-formality is expressed most clearly in the position that bookkeeping and commercial logs were detrimental to trust between merchants:

> Upon God's life, great is His name, I do not keep a tally. Not with you, nor with anyone else of course, but I do wish to know how much I owe and what you sent. Write me how much it comes to without reviewing the tally. God knows that I am not doing this because you have become despicable to me. I only do this because of my own troubles, which I will recount to you, and what these [troubles] demand of me.[1136]

Thus writes Ismāʿīl b. Faraḥ, an Alexandrian merchant to one of his partners in an attempt to mollify him. Ismāʿīl hems and haws, apologizes, and even swears upon God's name in order to convince his partner that he requires a bill from him only because he is constrained to do so, and that it does not indicate that he has grown tired of the partnership. At the basis of this message is the assumption that mercantile relationships needed to be based on complete personal trust between the partners, and any attempt to present them as based upon official and neutral principles, such as bookkeeping, is seen as a breach of trust and as an insult.[1137] Framing trade as a personal and unofficial transaction is thus a hidden mechanism, the function of which is to sort and cull members of the elite and to define the borders of the group.

(d) Defining the "Other"

In order to facilitate the process of sorting and culling and to present clear borders, groups must define the other that is not to be included. It has already been noted that the "other" in the eyes of the mercantile group was the poor *ṣaʿlūk* merchant. Distinguishing themselves from the *ṣaʿlūk* was not only a business matter, but also a cultural imperative.

1136 TS 12.335v, ll. 1–3: Gil, *Kingdom*, no. 487.

1137 Of course, this does not mean that these merchants did not keep detailed and precise accounts, down to the last penny. However, at the normative level, trade was presented as being based on inter-personal relationships of trust alone, which ensured the control and surveillance of the composition of the group and of new members. See Goitein, *Society*, 1: 205–209, for the many different kinds of accounts used in trading.

Japheth b. Manasseh Ibn al-Qaṭā'if of Alexandria, in a letter to his brother Ḥalfon, describes a mourning ceremony which took place in Alexandria. He includes the following depiction: "I prepared a carpet, and it was expensive for me and I brought cantors and M[...] and I resembled the *ṣa'ālīk* and it was a big carpet."[1138] In other words, because of financial constraints Japheth had to give up on a number of the ostentatious elements of the mourning ceremony, which were the norm amongst his group. He felt embarrassed because of this and expressed his consternation by comparing himself to the "other."

The fear of resembling the "other" is also apparent in the words Makhlūf b. Mūsā al-Nafūsī chose to reprimand his prodigal good-for-nothing son: "Behold the children of the *ṣa'lūk* in Alexandria, you resemble them."[1139]

The "other" sometimes included practitioners of certain professions. When Abū al-Riḍā b. al-Maghribiyya mounted an attack against R. Ephraim, he accused the latter of suborning "the painters, the shell-collectors, and the *hoi polloi*" against the dignitaries and the elite.[1140] In another letter Ibn al-Qāsh was alleged to have gathered followers from amongst the "shell-collectors of Alexandria";[1141] on another occasion he was accused of agitating "his friends amongst the shoemakers."[1142]

Another term for the "other" was drawn from Muslim culture: *'āmma* (commoners) as opposed to *khāṣṣa* (the distinguished ones, the elite). In a query to Maimonides the inquirers use the expression *'āmmat al-qahal* (the commoners of the community) in their description of the commoners' practice of purchasing bread and other baked goods from gentile establishments during the holidays.[1143]

1138 TS NS J 419r, ll. 13–14: Frenkel, *"The Compassionate and Benevolent"* [Hebrew], no. 94.

1139 TS 24.78v, ll. 39–40: Shelomo D. Goitein, "The Tribulations of an Overseer of the Sultan's Ships: A Letter from the Cairo Geniza (written in Alexandria in 1131)," in George Makdisi (ed.), *Arabic and Islamic Studies in Honour of H.A.R. Gibb* (Leiden: Brill, 1965), 270–284.

1140 See above, Part II, Chapter 9.2: A Controversial Leader.

1141 TS 18 J 3.5, l. 37: Gil, *Palestine* [Hebrew], no. 599.

1142 Goitein also mentions cobblers, and see TS 20.170, l. 13: Goitein, *Palestinian Jewry*, 304; Frenkel, *"The Compassionate and Benevolent"* [Hebrew], no. 35. He translated the word *askhāf* thusly, but the sentence structure indicated that it should be in the plural, *asākhifa*, and therefore the intention is probably base and inferior people, a word from the secondary root *kh-f-f* in the tenth form. Cf. Joshua Blau, *Dictionary of Mediaeval Judaeo-Arabic Texts* (Jerusalem: Hebrew Language Academy, 2006), *s.v.* [Hebrew].

1143 Maimonides, *Responsa*, 1: 198–200, §115.

Chapter 3 A Common Culture

The organization of a non-formal group requires a foundation of common culture: values, beliefs, norms, myths, symbols, and lifestyle – all of these come together to make a comprehensive ideological scheme, which gives meaning to human existence and positions the group in the tapestry of the world as a whole. A group may develop its own culture or adopt the culture and ideology of the society in which it is active. The Jewish ethos, which subscribes to unity and common destiny, could not allow a separatist elite group to be outwardly active as such in the Jewish community. Consequently, the group adopted some of the norms of the greater society of which it was a part, and used these to develop an ideology that would morally justify its special status. The Jewish consciousness of the time and place under consideration did not recognize elite groups as such,[1144] and viewed this group solely in terms of a category of individuals with the right pedigree and aptitudes. This elite group thus attempted to obfuscate its very existence, shrouding it in a veil of secrecy, in order to make its existence obvious to its members but hidden from society in general. For that purpose, it developed its culture as an inseparable part of the ideology and culture of Jewish society in general. This culture was active on two fronts at the same time, the common interest and its own particular interests, and it included both general Jewish elements and elitist group elements. These elements existed side by side, sometimes in conflict, and other times complementing one another in mutual support.

This chapter endeavors to identify and isolate the distinctive cultural elements of the group within the general society, for the better understanding of their function in the service of the elite. This analysis is based upon the assumption that a culture is not only an insignificant corollary of the social dynamic nor a superstructure appended to the "true" societal forces, but a central element in and of itself, with an instrumental function in the struggle between the forces that shape society.

1144 Such an awareness does exist in other societies, for example in India, where the caste system causes each group to define itself as such.

https://doi.org/10.1515/9783110713619-026

1 Torah Study

Members of the elite saw Torah study tudying the as a value of supreme importance, as was noted above.[1145] It was not only a method of advancement, preparing one for acceptance into the ranks of the group,[1146] but also a critical element of an adult's daily life. People continued to study Torah their entire lives in group frameworks and individually, with study partners.[1147] This group was the intellectual elite, for whom study and bibliophilia were significant aspects of their *raison d'être*. Information regarding books that had been written, copied, borrowed, or sold is a prominent feature of the correspondence between the members of the group: "I already asked you to get me the commentary to Isaiah, may he rest in peace, from Abū Naṣr. If you would be so kind, please send it with Abū al-Faraj"[1148] – Amram b. Isaac of Alexandria asks Ḥalfon b. Nethanel. Amram b. Isaac was in his seventies when he wrote this message and was gravely sick and alone, caring for his terminally ill wife, as he attests to in the letter;[1149] despite all of this his desire to procure this book and read from it was overriding and decisive for him. When he received no answer the first time, Amram once again pleads with Ḥalfon b. Nethanel to bring him the book:

> I have already asked you a number of times to take the commentary on Isaiah from the Shaykh Abū Naṣr for this pitiful one [=Amram b. Isaac himself] so that he may browse through it "perhaps the Lord, the God of Hosts Will be gracious" [Amos 5:15] and allow it to "sustain my Sabbaths" and fill my days. I renew my request in this matter, and ask that you should sent it to me with whomever you see fit.[1150]

The great price of books, the lengthy process of copying them and manufacturing them, coupled with the emotional attachment to them, transformed them into a very sensitive commodity. Borrowing or entrusting a book to someone required a great deal of mutual trust. For this reason, lending books to one's associates was one of the main ways of expressing faith in a fellow group-member. The great trepidation over misplacing or losing a borrowed book as it is reflected

1145 See above, Chapter 2.1 (b): Academic Excellence.
1146 See above, Part III, Chapter 1.5 (b): The new Leaders (1200–1250).
1147 See Goitein, *Society*, 2: 192–195. See also Meir b. Hillel's letter to his son, in which he advises him to choose a *rafīq*, i. e. a study-partner. See above, Part II, Chapter 7.1: Origins and Background.
1148 ULC Or 1080 J 24v, ll. 23–25: Frenkel, *"The Compassionate and Benevolent"* [Hebrew], no. 96.
1149 Ibid.
1150 TS 13 J 19.23v, ll. 6–9: Frenkel, *"The Compassionate and Benevolent"* [Hebrew], no. 70.

in Ephraim b. Isaac of Alexandria's letter to Nahray b. Nissim is indicative of the deep significance inherent to this type of this transaction:

> Regarding "the Book of the Key,"' upon God's great life, it did not leave my possession and was not given to anyone. If, however, the reference is to "the Book of the Lock," I returned it. And it is possible. In other words, the person who my lord hinted to requested a book from me and I said to him: "I do not have it among all your codices. It may be that you deposited it with someone else." The only [books] that has left my possession until the morning I wrote this letter are the two books that I promised to my lord the *ḥaver* Abū al-Faḍl, may God extend His help to him, after thousands of epistles and rebukes and entreaties and repeated visits, and his oath that he only [wished to emend] a copy in his possession with the help of a number of these [manuscripts]. I took his signature for both of them. And not one of them will have access without "two acceptable witnesses." And if his eminence's letter had arrived on that morning, I would not have relinquished them ever. Since this is your book that you copied as dictated to you by the author. There is none to gainsay this. And there is no recourse. The two aforementioned books are responsa, one without a cover which includes eighteen quires and begins [with the words]: "As Rabbi Ezekiel taught," the second is bound and begins [with the words]: "[...] the city."[1151]

In another letter, Ephraim b. Nissim recounts: "al-Sijillat [= Mūsā b. Abī al-Ḥayy] gave me two codices of Talmud and a small codex and [Midrash] Sifra. I said to him: 'I shall not take them.' I said: 'I am travelling and I fear that they will be eaten by the mice.'"[1152] The respect for books is further exemplified by Nathan b. Nahray, in whose house in Alexandria a box of books was deposited for safekeeping by his uncle Nahray. Nathan dutifully reports to his uncle that he was planning to transfer them into a different storage space, since the room he had previously designated for storage was going to be used for a wedding, and he needed the space.[1153]

The production of books was a profession that required intellectual acumen. Members of the network often participated in the manufacturing process themselves. They would copy books for themselves and for their friends, they would edit, correct, and even bind books themselves.[1154] Ordering books and producing

1151 TS 13 J 23.2r, ll. 4–12: Gil, *Kingdom*, no. 710. The term *samāʿ* mentioned here is connected to the process of book-copying in the medieval Muslim East. The disciples of a teacher, who had heard a series of lessons spoken by him on a specific topic, received special license from him to turn the words they had heard into an approved book. The teacher's signature confirming the book's accuracy increased its value very much. See George Makdisi, *The Rise of Humanism in Classical Islam and the Christian* World (Edinburgh: Edinburgh University Press, 1990), 71, 77, 79. Gil translates this passage differently.
1152 ENA NS 33.21r, ll. 5–7: Gil, *Kingdom*, no. 712.
1153 TS 10 J 20.18r, l. 10: Gil, *Kingdom*, no. 422.
1154 See Frenkel, "Book Lists."

them was a central topic in the correspondence between members of the network. As with commerce, books were an axis around which relationships were forged and strengthened: "What you wrote to me regarding the codices, I read your letter before ʿAwāḍ and he said: 'The codices are prepared, but something happened to me that distracted me from eating and drinking and R. Abraham is not available right now to bind them. If you want them to arrive without the binding, they will come to you with God's help.'"[1155]

In this message, written by Yeshūʿā b. Ismāʿīl al-Makhmūrī of Alexandria and addressed to Nahray b. Nissim of Fustat, the group-building aspect of preparing a book is revealed. A simple business transaction between Nahray b. Nissim, who had ordered book from ʿAwāḍ b. Hananel was transformed into a complex project involving a number of individuals. Nahray wrote to Yeshūʿā b. Ismāʿīl and asked him to inquire with ʿAwāḍ regarding the order. Yeshūʿā read Nahray's letter to ʿAwāḍ, who went to the bookbinder R. Abraham, who in turn explained why the order was delayed. ʿAwāḍ then relayed this message to Ismāʿīl, who wrote to Nahray. The same complexity is apparent in another letter from Alexandria regarding the order of a Torah scroll: "If it so happens that you encounter the Shaykh Abū Yaʿqūb Isaac al-Nafūsī, relay my greetings to him and let him know that his servant [= the author of the letter] has just finished editing the Torah scroll today as he had promised."[1156] In this case as well, the author of the letter did not announce the completion of the job directly to the individual who had ordered the Torah, but delivers the message through an intermediary, thus increasing the number of people involved in the transaction and magnifying the importance of the job.

Relationships centering on books did not only revolve upon the Alexandria-Fustat axis, but extended over a wide territory. Thus, for example, when Moses Ibn Tibbon wished to translate Maimonides' *Book of Commandments* in the thirteenth century he undertook the following:

> And I begged a scholar of our country who was travelling to Alexandria that he should seek it [= *The Book of Commandments*] there. And if he would not be able to find it [I asked] that he send a plea in my name to the great Nagid, the son of the master who composed it [R. Abraham Maimuni] to command one of the scribes of his country to transcribe it and send it to me. And the distinguished Nagid, as benefaction for the envoy and because he remem-

1155 ENA 2805.12r, ll. 17–20: Gil, *Kingdom*, no. 308.
1156 Bodl MS Heb b 3.26, right margins, ll. 4–17: Gil, *Kingdom*, no. 794. Gil's translation is different. On *tarjama* in the sense of editing a text by adding a title, see Goitein, *Studies*, 2: 216–217.

bered the ancient bond of love, sent him the book so he could copy it. And he [the Nagid] apologized that he had not sent another more exact copy, but he did not have any other.[1157]

We have already seen above how intellectual pursuits formed bonds between the members of the group. Both interpersonal associations, such as the ones between Yeshūʿā b. Joseph and Nahray b. Nissim,[1158] and a reciprocal business relationship of the *muʿāmala* type, like those between Judah Ibn al-ʿAmmānī and Meir b. Yakhin – which involved the exchange of liturgical poetry and other compositions – were forged in this way.[1159]

Bibliophilia was not confined to Torah study alone. Aside from the Bible and biblical commentaries, the Talmud and its commentaries, books of responsa, and legal monographs by the Geonim,[1160] the elite were also interested in secular literature. Thus, for example, members of the elite ordered two volumes of "tales,"[1161] Ibn al-Nadīm's *Fihrist*[1162] and Dioscorides' book on medicine.[1163] The elite were also interested in scientific literature, such as al-Rāzī's medical encyclopedia, *al-Manṣūrī*.[1164] The rationale for this intellectual pursuit was nevertheless expressed in terms of Torah study: "O my son, joyfully cleave to the Torah [...] my advice to you is to dedicate yourself to Torah and read and thus you will reap your reward in this world and in the world to come,"[1165] in this way Meir b. Hillel encouraged his family members to pursue book-based knowledge. "And when I ask him something from the Torah, from the Mishnah, from the Talmud, or from external wisdom literature, I find him replete with knowl-

1157 Chaim Heller (ed.), "Introduction," *Maimonides' Sefer ha-Mitzvoth translated by Moses Ibn Tibbon* (Jerusalem: Mossad Harav Kook, 1960), 19 [Hebrew].
1158 See above, Part II, Chapter 1.3 (c): Sources of Support, in the section: Nahray b. Nissim.
1159 See above, Part II, Chapter 14.3 (b): Locating and Transcribing Liturgical Poems.
1160 Bibles: TS 10 J 19.3r, l. 6 (Gil, *Kingdom*, no. 555); ENA 4100.29r, ll. 21–22 (Gil, *Kingdom*, no. 311); TS 13 J 21.25 (Frenkel, *"The Compassionate and Benevolent"* [Hebrew], no. 71), mentioning the *Tāj*. Bible commentaries: TS 13 J 14.25, *tafsīr* on Ezekiel. The Talmud and its commentaries: TS NS J 371 (Gil, *Kingdom*, no. 842) – tractate Qiddushin with commentaries. Books of halakhah: TS 13 J 14.25 (*Halakhot Gedolot*); Bodl MS Heb c 28.40 (*Sefer ha-ʿIbur*); TS 12.379 (Gil, *Kingdom*, no. 276) – on fringes, ritual purity and impority. Prayer books: TS 8 J 20.8r, l. 6; TS 6 J 3.19v, l. 6 (Gil, *Kingdom*, no. 723).
1161 TS NS 327.1, right margins, l. 5: Gil, *Kingdom*, no. 716. I do not necessarily agree with Gil's statement that the reference is to *Kitāb al-faraj baʿd al-shidda* by R. Jacob b. Nissim of Qayrawān.
1162 TS 13 J 19.23v, l. 16: Frenkel, *"The Compassionate and Benevolent"* [Hebrew], no. 70.
1163 TS 13 J 14.25: Frenkel, *"The Compassionate and Benevolent"* [Hebrew], no. 65, the letter of Aaron Ibn al-ʿAmmānī.
1164 ULC Or. 1080 J24r, l. 33: Frenkel, *"The Compassionate and Benevolent"* [Hebrew], no. 96. Amram b. Isaac explains what his wife's illness is, and quotes from this book.
1165 See above, Part II, Chapter 7.1: Origins and Background.

edge,"[1166] this was the impression Yeshūʿā b. Joseph had of the Spanish intellectual Joseph Ibn Kaskīl. With this statement, he inadvertently revealed the hierarchy of values of the group to which he belonged. This hierarchy placed Torah at the top and secular wisdom on the bottom.

The centrality of Torah study is reflected in the special status accorded to Torah scholars who were seen by the group as a model for emulation. The inclusion of Torah scholars in the group's ranks justified the position the group occupied in society, and consequently they were nurtured and given preferential treatment. One may discern this from the letter R. Hananel sent to Moses the *ḥaver* in Alexandria, wherein he congratulates him on the arrival of his son "the distinguished scion, the eminent student, R. Joseph, may his Rock preserve him," and reports to him with great pride of the son's worthy exploits: "From the moment he arrived in Fustat, he is always in the house of study. He is also busy with his cousin, 'the eminent, the wise and the knowledgeable' R. Peraḥyah. I think he is very grateful to him for his great industriousness, and splendid intellect."[1167] A good example of this preferential treatment is the generous hospitality Yeshūʿā b. Joseph extended to the Spanish intellectual Joseph Ibn Kaskīl when he arrived in Alexandria. The motivation for this treatment is lucidly expressed in Yeshūʿā's message to Eli b. Amram: "And I said to him [= to Elī b. Amram] what has been revealed to me [= regarding Ibn Kaskīl's depth of knowledge] so that one may show him the proper respect, for it is his duty and my duty to honor scholars of the Torah, for it is upon these [men] that the *hoi polloi* gaze [in awe]."[1168]

In other words, scholars of Torah were reservoirs of eminence and honor, since they functioned as objects of reverence vis-à-vis the commoners. The Torah scholars, in their total focus on study, served as a symbol, a concentrated embodiment of the elite *in toto* for whom Torah study was the ideological basis of their group identity and the justification for the group's existence. Torah study was the façade the group presented to the commoners and which thus needed to be cultivated and burnished.

It was publicly acknowledged, for example, that Torah scholars were the preferred recipients of community aid. In letters of reference, the erudition of the supplicant was always emphasized, first and foremost whether he was knowledgeable in the study of the Torah, but also whether he possessed other intellectual attributes. These factors figured prominently in the decision to help the in-

1166 See above, Part II, Chapter 1.3 (d): Spheres of Activity, 1.3 (e): Other Activities.
1167 TS 16.293r, ll. 4, 20–24: Goitein, "Chief Judge"; Goitein, *Jewish Education*, 186–187.
1168 See above, Part II, Chapter 1.3 (d): Spheres of Activity.

dividual. Thus, for example, in a letter written by the Alexandrian community to Ephraim b. Shemaryah of Fustat, asking him for help in the emancipation of a group of Jewish prisoners, who had arrived in the port city, he mentioned that among them was a "likely lad, who had Torah in him."[1169] Judah Ibn al-ʿAmmānī mentions that a refugee had come to him with "a letter of reference for him to the judge, wherein it says that he knew the entire Torah translation by heart."[1170] Another letter from Yeshūʿā b. Joseph to Ephraim b. Shemaryah refers to a captive by the name of "R. Shabbetai b. Nethanel from the land of Anatolia," who "knows some liturgy."[1171]

One may also attribute the success of the Ashkenazi rabbis in integrating into the ranks of the leadership of the Alexandrian community, despite their foreignness and disconnection from the elite's network, due to their great aptitude as Torah scholars. And indeed, one of the first letters that announced their arrival describes them as "great scholars."[1172] The ideology of Torah study, that was at its basis a pan-Jewish national ideology, was adopted by this particularistic group in a way that accorded with their organizational needs and strengthened their social network. It is obvious that the preoccupation with Torah study and its cultivation greatly enriched the depth of Torah learning and Jewish culture in general.

2 Poetry

Hebrew poetry was the cultured idiom of the elite. Most of the members of the group composed poetry, loved poetry and valued poetry greatly. The great poets of the period were the true cultural heroes, and this is reflected in the words of Abū Naṣr b. Abraham regarding the death of three famous poets, which resonate with a feeling of deep loss: "He communicated [to us] that our master R. Joseph Ben al-Shāmī passed away in the month of Nissan and that our master R. Joseph Ben Migash died in the month of Sivan. One beholds how these three luminaries passed away within five months of each other."[1173] We have already described the adulation bordering on worship of Judah ha-

1169 ENA 32804.9, l. 15: Mann, *Jews*, 2: 88.
1170 TS 12.299v, ll. 1–2: Goitein, *Palestinian Jewry*, 340.
1171 TS 13 J 24.11, ll. 16, 20–21: Mann, *Jews*, 2: 91.
1172 This is Judah Ibn al-ʿAmmānī's letter to Meir b. Yakhin from 1212, TS 12.299v, l. 16: Goitein, *Palestinian Jewry*, 343.
1173 TS 10 J 24.4r, ll. 9–11: Frenkel, *"The Compassionate and Benevolent"* [Hebrew], no. 56. The third person referred to here is Judah ha-Levi.

Levi by the elite of Alexandria when he visited the city, as is expressed by Amram b. Isaac:

> I did not cease worrying until one of them told me that they [= Judah ha-Levi and his companions] stayed in Abiyār [= a city on the Rashid tributary of the Nile] on Sabbath. Had I known this I would have groveled at the feet of our teacher and master Judah [...] in this house. I would have dusted my face, with the same dust "upon which his feet had trod."[1174]

One of the standard ways of forging ties and strengthening bonds among members of the group was the exchange of poetry, and there are many examples of this. Thus, for example, the cantor from Alexandria wrote to his friend "and ally," Eli the Cantor, also known as Yedūthūn: "When I hear a pithy turn of phrase or an elegant poem, I write it out, as I did on that day. And I had already heard those verses and I sent them together with this letter."[1175] Amram b. Isaac reminds Ḥalfon b. Manasseh how he used to send him verses and lamentations he had composed: "The lamentations that I mentioned and the poems of mourning that I composed about our master R. Judah ha-Levi 'the holy righteous one.' One may compare them to the verses that I used to send to you."[1176]

In another letter, written in Arabic script, Abraham b. Sahlān wrote to his friend in Alexandria: "Fuḍayl arrived [....] and he mentioned that you told him something about sending an urgent letter. I have no doubt that it is regarding the *qaṣīda* and the liturgical poem. The other necessities (*ḥawā'ij*) can wait until we see each other face to face."[1177] In this way, the author of the letter expresses the centrality of poetry in his view of the world. He also inadvertently betrays the basic understanding of the instrumentality of poetry, by placing the *qaṣīda* and the liturgical poem in the same plane as the other "necessities" (*ḥawā'ij*). The term he employs – *ḥāja*, *ḥawā'ij* – was usually employed in the

1174 ULC Or. 1080 J 24r, ll. 16–19: Frenkel, *"The Compassionate and Benevolent"* [Hebrew], no. 96.

1175 TS 13 J 24.14v, ll. 31–24: Frenkel, *"The Compassionate and Benevolent"* [Hebrew], no.77. On Yedūthūn, Abū al-Ḥasan b. Abū Sahl who served as cantor and *payṭan* in the synagogue of the Palestinians in Fustat, see Goitein, *Society*, 2: 449, 5: 89, 531; Friedman, "Controversy," 274.

1176 TS 13 J 19.23r, ll. 18–19: Goitein, "Rabbi Judah ha-Levi," 34; Frenkel, *"The Compassionate and Benevolent"* [Hebrew], no. 70. Goitein (ibid.) translates *ukābiruhu* as referring to a *mukābara* (altercation, rivalry) and concludes that Amram b. Isaac used to participate in poetry competitions with Judah ha-Levi. I prefer to read *ukhābiruhu* from the verb *khābara*, "wrote to, exchanged letters or information with" someone, and the reference is to the elegies for Judah ha-Levi that Amram composed and sent to Nethanel b. Ḥalfon, as we have seen was the custom.

1177 ULC TS 16.6v, ll. 1, 2–3: Frenkel, *"The Compassionate and Benevolent"* [Hebrew], no. 95. The reference is to Abraham b. Sahlān, the grandson of the leader of the Palestinians in Fustat. The letter is from the 1090s.

very particular circumstances of mercantile service that local merchants granted one another when they were associated through a *muʿāmala* partnership. The accepted formula which appeared at the end of mercantile correspondence between merchants in this type of partnership was: *wa-kull ḥāja takun lahu yusharrifani bi-qaḍāahā* (and all the needs that he may have, he shall honor me with their fulfillment). The mutual exchange of poetry thus fulfilled the social function that the exchange of merchandise and services did: They allowed the members of the group to strengthen the exclusive personal ties between them and they offered a solution to the organizational difficulties facing the group. Put in another way, this was a ceremonial act with symbolic value that constituted one of the elements of the ideological groundwork, and at the same time could also offer an answer to the chronic organizational problems of this particularistic group. The central position of Hebrew poetry and its intensive cultivation brought about an unprecedented flowering of this genre[1178] and in this way the elite did its part to cultivate the national and public interest.

3 Charity

(a) Charity as a universal and Jewish value

Charitable giving on behalf of the needy is a core cultural value of many societies. Charity fulfills an important role in society, and at the same time it serves the individual as an act of symbolic value, wrapped as it is in strong feelings of existential angst and empathy. On the personal level, charity offers a moral answer to basic existential problems such as destiny, reward and punishment, and reciprocal responsibility between human beings. This was true in the case of the Jews of Alexandria in the period under consideration as well. Charity was viewed as a type of insurance policy or future investment stilling the fears of great upheavals: "Do not leave us, for you will be rewarded on our merit," Abraham b. Abī al-Ḥayy of Alexandria begs, in his attempt to persuade his brother to continue supporting him.[1179] He expresses this somewhat more explicitly in a second letter: "And now, brother of mine, God on High has given my livelihood into your hands, for if He had wised to severe me from you, he would have let Abū

1178 See, e.g., Ezra Fleischer, "The Contribution of the Genizah to the Study of Hebrew Liturgical Poetry," *Teʿuda* 1 (1980): 83–88 [Hebrew]; Schirmann, *Hebrew Poetry in Spain.*
1179 ULC Or. 1080 J 271, right margins, ll. 1–5: Gil, *Kingdom*, no. 470.

al-Ḥayy live and we would have existed as we had previously. But God will grant you a livelihood because of the merit due to you for supporting us."[1180]

When Judah Ibn al-ʿAmmānī asked the judge Elijah b. Zechariah to extend a helping hand to the convert whose husband had abandoned her, he employed the following language: "Whatever you do for this convert and her daughters, the Creator blessed be He shall not forget it. Your reward shall be very great and it will be counted as a just act before God."[1181] The dignitaries of Ashkelon as well, in their attempts to persuade the people of Alexandria to donate money in order to ransom the captives of Jerusalem from the Crusaders, used similar language: "For the benefit is total, both for he who gives and for he who receives."[1182]

(b) Charity in the Service of the Elite

Charity and the ransoming of captives are two of the values most important to the Jewish ethos.[1183] When it came to the elite, these Jewish and pan-human values also served other purposes. *Prima facie*, the philanthropic apparatus was depicted as a spontaneous undertaking to solve specific problems, an apparatus that was unofficial and was open to any personal or group initiative. This is the impression one gains, for example, from R. Ephraim's words: "Five prisoners arrived, for whom eight dinars [were needed], and there was no one who would collect donations. I stood up, I and the cantors and the elders, and collected [donations]."[1184]

In point of fact, however, this apparatus was totally controlled by the ruling elite. It was an extra-communal system in which dignitaries and powerbrokers of other communities were involved, especially those of Fustat and Jerusalem. Above we examined Yeshūʿā b. Joseph's prolific correspondence with Ephraim b. Shemaryah, Nahray b. Nissim and other wealthy benefactors such as Nethanel ha-Kohen and David ha-Levi b. Isaac regarding the ransoming of captives.[1185]

1180 Bodl MS Heb c 28.52r, ll. 16–19: Gil, *Kingdom*, no. 473.
1181 TS 12.575v, ll. 12–14: Friedman, *Jewish Polygyny*, 206.
1182 TS 20.113v, l. 21: Goitein, *Palestinian Jewry*, 247.
1183 See Judah Bergman, *Charity in Judaism* (Jerusalem: Tarshish, 1944), 5 ff. [Hebrew]; Eliezer Bashan, *Captivity and Ransom in Mediterranean Jewish Society (1391–1830)* (Ramat Gan: Bar-Ilan University Press, 1982) [Hebrew]; Goitein, *Society*, 1: 327–337, 2: 91–143.
1184 TS 16.272v, ll. 7–8: Frenkel, *"The Compassionate and Benevolent"* [Hebrew], no. 30.
1185 See above, Part II, Chapter 1.3 (d): Spheres of Activity, in the section: The Ransoming of Captives. See also Frenkel, "Charity"; Frenkel, "Proclaim Liberty."

Similarly, Shelah b. Mubashshir depended upon the generosity of Nahray b. Nissim and Mevorakh b. Saʿadyah.[1186] They were able to help with their money, but their more critical contribution was their ability to take advantage of the right ties, their prestige, and their organizational skills. An example of the way in which the network functioned is apparent in the *modus operandi* of Nethanel ha-Kohen b. Eleazar, one of the wealthiest members of the Alexandrian community, in his efforts to ransom the captives who had recently arrived at the port. He met with Yeshūʿā b. Joseph in order to find a way to free them, and offered the following:

> I need to come up with the money for one of them, thirty-three gold pieces in total. That leaves two hundred gold pieces. Please send two letters to the two Fellows and to the Rabbanite congregations in the two synagogues. Also [send] a letter to the Karaite congregation. I shall also include among these, letters to all the elders, who will manage this, and they will expand their hearts and open their hands to also send letters to Tinnīs and Damietta and Ṣahrajt, from the Karaites and the Rabbanites, to volunteer [their help] and to ransom them, and perhaps they shall add more gold pieces and send them money for their clothes and other needs.[1187]

The above communication suggests an extra-communal charity network,[1188] which at the same time could function as a useful conduit of information and coordination between the members of the elite. And thus, in tandem with the official community letters, which were to be read publicly in order to make people aware of the need to give,[1189] it seems that the logistics were mostly decided upon in private letters between members of the group. These letters included not only matters pertaining to charity and the ransoming of captives, but also mercantile matters, as well as general and personal information relevant to the correspondents. The supplicant made an appeal on the basis of the personal connection he had with the addressee; thus for example Yeshūʿā b. Joseph signed his letter, the focus of which was the ransoming of captives and aid for refugees, with the words: "Your beloved friend, Yeshūʿā ha-Kohen b. R. Joseph the Judge, and graciously extend greetings and blessings in my name to R. Joseph [...] your father-in-law."[1190]

1186 See above, Part II, Chapter 2.5 (b): Shelah's Ties with the Nagid Mevorakh b. Saʿadyah, and (d): Shelah and Nahray b. Nissim.
1187 Bodl MS Heb a 3.28, ll. 43–47: Cowley, "Bodleian Geniza Fragments," 253.
1188 On the universal character of the social aid apparatus, see also Goitein, *Society*, 2: 91–97.
1189 See, e.g., the letters published in Mann, *Jews*, 2: 87–92, and the letter published in Cowley, "Bodleian Geniza Fragments." On the ceremony of public reading of letters requesting aid, see above, Part III, Chapter 2.7 (b): Fundraising Campaigns.
1190 TS 13 J 24.11, ll. 26–28: Mann, *Jews*, 2: 91.

The captives, the poor, and the refugees themselves functioned as an efficient corporal means of communication. They often traversed significant distances in order to find relief for their distress. Communities who did not succeed in providing for them would customarily send them onwards with letters of reference to try their luck in other communities,[1191] and thus they often wandered for long periods of time from community to community. Members of the elite, who always needed channels of communication, knew how to exploit this quite well. The case of Samuel Baghdādī Kohen, likely a refugee from Baghdad, reflects this quite clearly; one learns of him from an offhand communication in a letter Judah Ibn al-ʿAmmānī sent to Meir b. Yakhin:

> And you mentioned that the *seliḥot* [= liturgical pleas for forgiveness] that you requested had not arrived [...] I sent you these *seliḥot* with a man by the name of Samuel Baghdādī Kohen, he is a thin dark-skinned man, the same person on whose behalf you had sent a reference letter to me from the elder Abū al-Ḥasan the Teacher to the judge in which it says that he knows the Bible's translation by heart. And I am very sad, not a little, that they [= the *seliḥot*] did not come to you on time for the New Year [=Rosh ha-Shannah], for I sent them more than twenty days before Rosh ha-Shannah, and as God is my witness, I wrote you that letter with weary eyes and I expended a great deal of energy, [I wrote] part of it when I was with pupils, and the rest at night when I was tired [in my desire] in haste, hoping that it would come to you on time and undamaged, but that did not work out at all [...] from the moment that he [= Samuel Baghdādī] said to me: "I am going to al-Maḥalla, I shall stay there for two days, and then I shall go up to Fustat. I shall not delay at all," I told him "be careful that the [*seliḥot*] should not go missing when you need them. For if they do, your effort and my effort will have come to nothing." I was afraid that he would not go to Fustat at all, but instead go to Cairo, gather some donations there, and then go to the countryside, going further afield until he reached his place in the land of Israel. Will you please inquire about him and take the letter from him, which includes the *seliḥot* in a small codex.[1192]

It was very convenient and efficient for these two elite members, Judah Ibn al-ʿAmmānī and Meir b. Yakhin, to send the Baghdadi refugee back and forth between Alexandria and Fustat. In this way they enhanced the channels of communication between them, and increased the frequency of their exchange.

Needy people of all types served not only as a conduit for the transfer of poetic and literary composition, but were also a useful channel for the delivery of goods and money. Above we described the convoy of prisoners that made its way from Alexandria to Fustat. Armed with letters of reference from Yeshūʿā b. Joseph and accompanied by his agent and business partner, the convoy travelled from

1191 See also Goitein, *Society*, 2: 95–96.
1192 TS 12.299r, ll. 5–6, margins – verso, l. 14: Goitein, *Palestinian Jewry*, 338–343.

community to community to gather donations. The funds were to be used to ransom the members of their group, but at the same time Yeshūʿā did not hide the fact that the money was also to be used to finance his private business ventures.[1193]

The elite's abiding interest in philanthropy contributed as a matter of course to the development and efficiency of the community's fundraising apparatus.[1194] In the absence of any official institution in charge of this matter, it stands to reason that it was the best and in fact only solution for this social problem. One cannot help but note that the vested interest the elite had in maintaining this network, which was so helpful for their own purposes, helped create an enduring class of itinerant poor, who were rejected by their communities and suffered chronic homelessness. One also notes the tendency of cutting off donations rather abruptly and the haste with which the poor were furnished with letters of reference and sent out to wander: Moses b. Khalīfa, for example, a man of Maghribi origin, who had arrived from Sicily in order to undergo an eye operation, fell on hard times while in Alexandria with his family. Judah Ibn al-ʿAmmānī refused to give him a donation, but was quick to send him onwards to try his luck in other communities and furnished him with a letter of reference in which he [Judah ibn al-ʿAmmānī] explained: "He has relatives in Alexandria, there is no way to help him."[1195]

This phenomenon was very widespread as indicated by the great number of letters of reference and requests for such letters. The necessity of this apparatus and the efficient use the elite made of it contributed a great deal to its institutionalization and permanence.

4 Lifestyle

The culture of the elite was not only apparent in their distinct values, norms, and beliefs, but also in a different lifestyle that included, among other things, a particular dress code. The clothes of the elite were of good quality and made from expensive fabric: "I ask of the Lord and from your eminence that you clothe me in some piece of clothing [...] and this after I used to wear garments such as *niṣafī*, *sābūrī*, and *mutakhkhat*." This plea was addressed to R. Hananel by Joseph b. ʿAllān, a scion of the elite of Alexandria who had fallen on hard times

1193 See above, Part II, Chapter 1.3 (d): Spheres of Activity, in the section: Rewarding the Benefactors.
1194 On this apparatus, see in great detail in Goitein, *Society*, 2: 91–143.
1195 TS 16.287r, margins: Ashtor, *History of the Jews*, 3: 102, no. 49.

and who wished to convince the former that he was a member of the group so as to receive financial aid.[1196]

Many public offices were connected to the synagogue. Members of the elite, and especially the cantors and the caretakers (*shammashim*)[1197] were careful to present themselves when they were in synagogue in proper and distinct attire, particularly on Sabbaths and at public ceremonies. In the Cairo Genizah we find orders for especially lavish prayer shawls woven from expensive fabrics in bold colors and with interwoven letters.[1198] The desire for ornateness was clearly quite strong; it is reflected, for example, in a query to Maimonides regarding a man who showed up in synagogue in an especially fancy prayer shawl which included embroidery in Hebrew letters.[1199] Despite Maimonides' clear-cut ruling banning Hebrew letters on profane objects such as prayer-shawls and headdresses, the desire for ornateness often won out – and the people of Alexandria continued to debate the question after Maimonides' death, as is apparent in R. Hananel b. Samuel's response to a similar query.[1200]

It is apparent that members of the elite also adopted special customs when it came to donning phylacteries, and would customarily walk around in them during the day. This custom is attested to in a letter relating to a crisis at the beginning of the thirteenth century in Alexandria, at a time of a great wheat-shortage. One of the members of the community seized control of the granary and began to dole grain out as he saw fit, without notifying any of the dignitaries. He also appointed a person whose job was to go to the synagogues and to malign the overseer in charge of dispensing bread as well as the dignitaries in charge of disbursement. This man "announced his actions in the two synagogues on the Sabbath. He cursed and profaned saying: 'Those who wear the leather strings of the monks,' meaning by this those who wore phylacteries."[1201]

1196 On the great awareness of the importance of dress in Fatimid Egypt, see Yedida Kalfon-Stillman, "Medieval Egyptian Dress," in Ezra Fleischer, Mordechai. A. Friedman, and Joel. L. Kraemer (eds.), *Mas'at Moshe* (Jerusalem and Tel-Aviv: Bialik Institute, 1998), 237–245 [Hebrew], and additional bibliography in ibid., n. 8. On these textiles see above, Part IV, Chapter 1, n. 8.
1197 On the status of the *shammashim*, see Goitein, *Society*, 2: 82–85.
1198 Ibid., 4: 196–198.
1199 Maimonides, *Responsa*, 3: 510–515.
1200 Goitein, *Society*, 4: 198–199; Goitein, "Chief Judge," 386–388.
1201 TS 10 J 16.6r, ll. 12–14: Frenkel, *"The Compassionate and Benevolent"* [Hebrew], no. 54. The prevalent popular belief was that phylacteries were intended only for the especially pious, and therefore there was a general neglect among the common people of putting on phylacteries which became, to a large extent, a marker of the elite. This phenomenon caused Maimonides to emphasize their great holiness. See Gerald J. Blidstein, *Prayer in Maimonides' Halakhic Thought* (Jerusalem: Mossad Bialik, 1994), 115–122 [Hebrew].

The distinct style of dress adopted by the elite is apparent in their particular customs of attiring themselves, which were seen as strange enough that they were scorned by the commoners. This style was distinguished by great ornateness and the use of expensive materials, which were beyond the means of those who did not belong to the elite, and thus added another layer to the distinct shared culture of this group.

Chapter 4 Organizational Apparatus and Means of Communication

Social groups need some kind of apparatus to maintain continual communication between its members, to make operational decisions and to prevent dissolution. Such an apparatus does not necessarily need to be public or official. Elite groups, such as the Jewish ruling elite of Alexandria, could successfully employ informal methods and frameworks of communication as well, as will be demonstrated in this chapter.

1 Correspondence

The central means of communication employed by the Jewish ruling elite was a steady stream of letters.[1202] Letters were not only used to transfer data, but also formed a means of maintaining uninterrupted connection between members of the group. A regular exchange of letters between members was a sign of continued membership in the group. The final lines of each letter were usually dedicated to listing the people with whom the author wishes to keep in touch. The following is just one of a multitude of examples: at the conclusion of a very informative business letter detailing strictly commercial issues, such as the losses caused by one of the partners in the consortium, the price of silk in Alexandria, and the shipment of flax from Tripoli, the author of the letter, Yeshūʿā b. Ismāʿīl al-Makhmūrī, adds at the very bottom of the sheet a few lines of crowded script, which are probably the main point. He extends a detailed greeting to all the leadership in Fustat: "And to all those under your protection, extend my greeting. And to our Rav, may God preserve him, extend the most sincere of greetings. To the judge, the most sincere of greetings. And to whoever asks about me, regards."[1203]

With one letter a whole network could be mobilized, as is apparent from another letter written by Yeshūʿā b. Ismāʿīl, to ʿAyyāsh b. Ṣedaqah in Alexandria:

1202 Gil and Fleischer also noticed this, even in regard to the limited corpus of letters connected to Judah ha-Levi. They write: "A central topic in merchants' letters from the Genizah is communication. The documents provide details about letters: how many were sent, to whom and when, and from whom they were received" (Gil-Fleischer, *Yehuda ha-Levi*, 261).
1203 ENA 2805.12, right margins, ll. 1–14: Gil, *Kingdom*, no. 308.

https://doi.org/10.1515/9783110713619-027

I have already sent my letter to you, may God make your days long and may he perpetuate your peaceful existence, your happiness, and his munificence towards you. I hope that it has arrived and that you have read its contents [...] I also ask you, my lord, to inquire with Sulaymān the son of Faraḥ, may Eden be his abode, of the al-Qābisī family, after giving my regards to him, whether he had met with my brother-in-law, R. Joseph, and whether he had heard from him whether he [R. Joseph] was intending to send me anything. And write to me about this as soon as possible by means of the courier who leaves during the holiday. Do not delay this, for my heart is apprehensive about this and it is through this that I will find relief. I ask you to fulfill my request. And if he has already found out that I am travelling and he is prevented from sending [it]. Do not hide anything from me. And all in haste, with God's help."[1204]

In short, Yeshūʿā wishes to procure merchandise from his brother-in-law, R. Joseph, but instead of writing to him directly, he writes to ʿAyyāsh b. Ṣedaqah, who is asked to meet Sulaymān b. Faraḥ, who in turn is requested to ascertain with his brother-in-law if the merchandise was already sent. The message will be delivered through the same chain on its way back to Yeshūʿā: The brother-in-law shall let Sulaymān know whether the merchandise was sent, he will tell ʿAyyāsh, who in turn will inform Yeshūʿā of what he intends to do with the merchandise. In this way members of the network met with one another, sent their regards and perpetuated the existence of the system. When such correspondence was interrupted, this was treated as a grave threat and was viewed with great trepidation:

Aside from this, letters arrived from the Shaykh Abū al-Faraj Ismāʿīl to a group of Alexandrians. And he did not write anything to me. And I do not know whether there is a reason for this. I have already written to him and the message to him is attached to this letter to you. I ask that my lord confer with him on my behalf and check on the matters which I wrote to him about. And he should send me his letter as soon as possible, for I am enormously concerned about this. And I already sent him a letter about it. That letter is with the camel driver and there is a letter with Yaḥyā the [...] may God grant him God health. May my lord not delay this.[1205]

The cessation of correspondence functioned as an agreed-upon code for the termination of friendship, which was understood as a pact (*ʿahd*) between the correspondents. This is apparent in the words of Berākhōt the Cantor to another cantor by the name of Eli, also known as Yedūthūn: "And if you would be so

1204 Moss. II 131a r, ll. 2–10: Gil, *Kingdom*, no. 320.
1205 TS 10 J 2017r, ll. 11–17: Gil, *Kingdom*, no. 419.

kind [...] just two words, to calm my heart, so that I should know that you are still in a pact with me."[1206]

When the addressee was a person of lofty status, the right to correspond with him was perceived as a social asset. People were willing to sacrifice a great deal to earn this privilege. Above, we described the tragedy that took place when Mevorakh the Nagid incited jealousy and competition regarding the right to exchange letters with him, which ended in the death of one of the rivals for his attention.[1207] The cessation of correspondence with a figure of such importance often led to humiliation, as is apparent in a letter by Judah Ibn al-ʿAmmānī:

> Lord Abū Naṣr al-Ṭabīb sat with us, who had been with our lord. He and his two sons were with him at a drinking establishment, and he said: "I correspond with the *ra'īs* and he writes back," and he said other things too. Those present sat down and laughed, saying: "The *ra'īs* does not wish to correspond with the shaykhs of Alexandria, there are many of them that he does not deign to notify."[1208]

The great importance of these letters is apparent in the ceremony that accompanied their receipt: "Letters arrived from my master the shaykh, may the Lord perpetuate his honor [...] and I kissed them before I read them and I was happy, 'God knows this,'"[1209] writes Judah Ibn al-ʿAmmānī from Alexandria to Meir b. Yakhin in Fustat. Berākhōt the Cantor further embellishes the ceremony, as is apparent in a letter he writes to Eli the Cantor (Yedūthūn), in Fustat: "I miss you so much that I take the letters that you sent me a long time ago, read them and kiss them, and raise them upon my head and say: 'May God grant that you and I meet before fate intervenes.'"[1210] Āraḥ b. Nathan describes in his letter that even the Amir Fakhr al-Mulk would kiss letters he received from Mevorakh the Nagid and place them on his eyes.[1211]

The expectation of receiving a letter was also clothed in ceremony. When a ship would arrive at the port, the merchants would descend upon it, in order to conduct a *taqaṣṣī* (debriefing) of the incoming passengers regarding the fate of fellow merchants, who were on trading expeditions over the sea, and to check whether letters had arrived for them. The *taqaṣṣī* was a ceremonial mode of tak-

1206 TS 13 J 24.14v, ll. 17–18: Frenkel, *"The Compassionate and Benevolent"* [Hebrew], no. 77.
1207 See above, Part II, Chapter 3.3: Relationship with Mevorakh b. Saʿadyah Nagid.
1208 TS 16.305v, right margins, ll. 1–17: Frenkel, *"The Compassionate and Benevolent"* [Hebrew], no. 32.
1209 TS 13 J 27.11r, ll. 2–5: Frenkel, *"The Compassionate and Benevolent"* [Hebrew], no. 79.
1210 TS 13 J 24.14r, ll. 11–15: Frenkel, *"The Compassionate and Benevolent"* [Hebrew], no. 77.
1211 See above, Part II, Chapter 4.5: A Matter of Class.

ing an interest and showing affection for the merchant who was asked about, confirming and buttressing the association between them. Associates of a merchant, who was in Aden, were almost offended when the person who asked about him was none other than the Muslim owner of the ship: "Upon the Lord's life, my brother, the Muslims ask about you more than we do, so much so that one day a man passed through here, a book merchant who is a friend of my father, and the Muslim owner of the ship debriefed him (*taqaṣṣā*) about you and brought us your letter."[1212]

When Amram b. Joseph of Alexandria was prevented from sending letters to Nahray b. Nissim, but wished to preserve the stream of letters from Nahray to him, he says:

> I always ask the Shaykh Abū al-Ḥasan ʿAllāl to extend his greetings to my lord, and that he should ask him, according to his good manner with me and with others, indeed with whomever he is able to help, that he should try to debrief (*yataqaṣṣā*) [recent arrivals] and find out on my behalf if any letter or news has arrived, and he should be so kind as to write to me, 'and he shall receive his just reward from Heaven.'[1213]

Not only the docking of ships at the port, but any movement of people from place to place was exploited for the purpose of sending letters. The pronounced tension that was part of waiting for letters is reflected in the following words of Berākhōt the Cantor to Eli the Cantor (Yedūthūn):

> The Shaykh Mufaḍḍal ha-Kohen al[...] and the Shaykh Abū Naṣr b. Saʿd and all our friends, elders and cantors, big and small, and the Shaykh Zikrī al-Kaʿkī and Munajjā b. Ghallāb and all the rest were invited to the house of the Shaykh Yaḥyā al-Munayyir and Abū Karīm al-Khayyāṭ as a reflection of his great love and devotion. O Shaykh Abū al-Ḥasan [= Yedūthūn, Eli the Cantor], all that time my focus was upon anyone who had arrived from Fustat, from among the residents of Fustat or the residents of Alexandria. I said to myself: "Perhaps God shall move their hearts on my behalf and they shall deign to write to me at least two lines, so that I may gain honor by them."[1214]

2 Unofficial Meetings

Unofficial, but nevertheless exclusive, meetings afforded the members of the group opportunities to foster strong reciprocal ties, which facilitated the flow

1212 GW IXv, ll. 34–35: Frenkel, *"The Compassionate and Benevolent"* [Hebrew], no. 18.
1213 TS 13 J 23.10r, ll. 8–11: Gil, *Kingdom*, no. 676.
1214 TS 13 J 24.14v, ll. 2–10: Frenkel, *"The Compassionate and Benevolent"* [Hebrew], no. 77.

of information between the members, and above all created a common culture. This culture was reflected in a particular lifestyle, as well as in an unofficial but binding code of conduct, a code that distinguished members of the group and blocked entrance into the group by strangers.

These meetings between members of the elite often took place in taverns serving alcohol, referred to in documents from that period as the *maqām*. These meeting often involved the imbibing of wine, which fostered an entire subculture of drinking. The ideal drinker, in these circles, was one who did not drink excessively, but nevertheless could ingest copious amounts of alcohol without becoming drunk: "If I sit at a wine-house, I drink no more than one-quarter of a goblet of wine, and even if I would drink like this for the entire day, I would not get drunk,"[1215] brags Judah Ibn al-ʿAmmānī in a letter to Abraham Maimuni.

At these venues pacts were forged, factions formed, and important internal decisions of the group were made. Thus for example a reconciliation (*ṣulḥa*) between Judah Ibn al-ʿAmmānī and his uncle Ṣadoq took place at one of these wine-houses, while drinking together:

> [...] myself and my uncle and his two children. My uncle said to me: "My friend, I hereby announce to you that the teacher Abū al-Futūḥ [= Judah Ibn al-ʿAmmānī] is the one who [...] and I hereby hand my son over to him and let him punish him [my son] as he sees fit." He stood and drank to me [...] and I gave him permission to do so. Then his son, al-ʿAmīd [...] the teacher, stood and toasted me, and said: "Not everyone saw us." And the young man stood and toasted me and groveled before me a number of times. And everyone who was there rejoiced, and the owner of the wine-house rejoiced that a reconciliation took place in his establishment.[1216]

As was recounted above, Abū Naṣr al-Ṭabīb, a member of the Alexandrian elite, was publicly humiliated in a *maqām ḥafl* (a drinking place) [1217] when he bragged about his close relationship with the Nagid. Joseph b. ʿAllān, a scion of a distinguished family who lost his fortune, confesses in a letter that his brother's will, in which he left him his property, was not written out properly "because both of them were drinking wine."[1218]

Banquets were also a great opportunity for gossip. Those present exchanged opinions and information regarding other members who were absent, and formed their opinions about them, for good or for ill. It was under these circumstances that the relative social status of the members of the group was deter-

1215 TS 16.305v, ll. 47–49: Frenkel, *"The Compassionate and Benevolent"* [Hebrew], no. 32.
1216 Ibid., ll. 1–12.
1217 Ibid., right margins.
1218 TS 10 J 17.4, l. 13: Goitein, "Chief Judge," 378.

mined to no small extent. Members of the group were aware of this, and thus the gossip at banquets was not infrequently used as a lever to gain favor of various sorts. Japheth the Cantor b. Amram Ibn al-Jāzifīnī asked Hillel Ibn ʿAwkal for financial aid in the form of a pledge (*pesīqā*). He justifies his claim for *pesīqā* by mentioning that at banquets he often lavishes praises upon Ibn ʿAwkal: "The Creator on High knows of my boundless love for my lord the Shaykh's honorable eminence and the expressions of gratitude and frequent praise I heap upon him during banquets (*maḥāfil*). My gratitude to him extends all the way to Fustat and into the ears of its dignitaries, sages, and rulers."[1219]

One such unofficial get-together is described in a letter by Berākhōt the Cantor, wherein he states that all the big names of Fustat and Alexandria were invited to the private house of one of the dignitaries. All invitees held public positions, and they included the cantors and the elders of the community, but the gathering was clearly unofficial. All of them belonged to the same social group: *min aṣḥābinā* (from amongst our friends), but they were not invited based on their position in the community, but rather based upon their degree of friendship and closeness with the host.[1220]

The arrival of a distinguished guest in the town was seen as an opportunity to organize this type of gathering more frequently. The evening parties that took place in honor of Judah ha-Levi's arrival in Alexandria[1221] were almost certainly of a similar nature to the meetings described above. The draw of poetry was mainly confined to the elite, since it constituted a shared language among them. Figures such as Judah ha-Levi were their cultural heroes. Judah ha-Levi was surrounded during his visit by great merchants and public figures for whom the occasion of his visit provided the opportunity to increase the frequency of these unofficial meetings and to perpetuate their common culture.

1219 TS 20.28r, ll. 38–40.

1220 TS 13 J 34.14: Frenkel, *"The Compassionate and Benevolent"* [Hebrew], no. 77.

1221 Goitein, "Rabbi Judah ha-Levi," 29.

Chapter 5

Conclusions

In this section of the book, the very existence of a ruling elite group in Alexandria with distinct economic and political interests was scrutinized. This group acted within the Jewish community with the intent of preserving itself as a select and impermeable entity and in order to protect its own unique interests. It employed the covert strategies of a non-official group, in order to preserve its invisibility in a society that proclaimed unity as one of its most central ethoses. Its organization included special training tracks or curricula in the mercantile sphere and in the field of Torah study, and systems of sorting and culling, which helped define the borders of the group and the "other," who was destined to remain outside it. We saw that this elite developed its own culture, manifested in a unique dressing code and lifestyle, and that it based itself upon an ideological system of symbols, values, and norms valued by Jewish society in general, such as Torah study and charity. Upon closer examination of this ideological structure, however, the special ways in which the elite used these particulars to favor its own needs and interests, were identified.

At the same time, the group had to contend with the contradiction inherent to its very existence: the tension between pan-societal needs and group needs, between its duty to serve the Jewish community as a whole and its efforts to sustain its own narrow sectarian interests, since every elite, by definition, sees and presents itself as a body essential for the common good of society. In order to cope with this this conflict effectively, the group had to organize itself in a way that would maintain its distinct existence. At the same time, it had to justify its claim to elevated status by accepting certain responsibilities vis-à-vis the community as a whole. The way the group organized itself was thus intended to facilitate simultaneously pan-societal objectives and narrow sectorial needs. The elite that stood at the head of the Alexandrian community was a ruling elite and its members served in various leadership roles. In this capacity, its unofficial organizational apparatus and network were harnessed to find solutions to national-communal problems. This was apparent in its social work such as charity and ransoming of captives and especially when it came to lobbying the Muslim regime. Through its broad network of ties, members of this group succeeded in gaining the attention of the authorities and influenced them on behalf of the entire Jewish community.

https://doi.org/10.1515/9783110713619-028

Bibliography

al-ʿAbdarī, Abū ʿAbdallah. *Riḥlat al-ʿabdarī al-musammāt al-riḥla al-maghribiyya*. Rabat: Jāmiʿat Muḥammad V, 1968.

Abū Shāma, Shihāb al-Dīn. *Kitāb al-rawḍatayn fī akhbār al-dawlatayn*. Cairo: Lajnat al-Taʾlīf wal-Tarjama wal-Nashr, 1956.

Abulafia, David. *Italy, Sicily, and the Mediterranean, 1100–1400*. London: Variorum, 1987.

Ackerman-Lieberman, Philip. *The Business of Identity: Jews, Muslims, and Economic Life in Medieval Egypt*. Stanford: Stanford University Press, 2014.

Al-Imad, Leila S. *The Fatimid Vizierate 969–1172*. Berlin: K. Schwarz, 1990.

Allony, Nehemya. *The Jewish Library in the Middle Ages: Book Lists from the Cairo Genizah*. Jerusalem: Ben-Zvi Institute, 2006 [Hebrew].

Arazi, Albert and Haggai Ben-Shammai. "Risāla." *Encyclopedia of Islam*, 2nd edition, 8: 532–539. Leiden: Brill, 1960–2005.

Aron, Raymond. "Social Structure and the Ruling Class." *British Journal of Sociology* 1 (1950): 1–16, 126–143.

al-Ashqar, Muḥammad ʿAbd al-Ghanī. *Tujjār al-tawābil fī miṣr fī al-ʿaṣr al-mamlūkī*. Cairo: al-Hayʾa al-Miṣriyya al-ʿĀmma lil-Kitāb, 1999.

Ashtor, Eliyahu. "Aspects of the Character of the Jewish Community in Medieval Egypt." *Zion* 30 (1965): 78–61 [Hebrew].

Ashtor, Eliyahu. "Documentos españoles de la Genizah." *Sefarad* 24 (1964): 41–80.

Ashtor, Eliyahu. "The Kārimī Merchants." *Journal of the Royal Asiatic Society of Great Britain and Ireland* 1.2 (1956): 45–56.

Ashtor, Eliyahu. *A Social and Economic History of the Near East in the Middle Ages*. Berkeley: University of California Press, 1976.

Ashtor, Eliyahu. *The History of the Jews in Egypt and Syria under Mamluk Rule*. Jerusalem: Mossad Harav Kook, 1944–1951 [Hebrew].

Asín-Palacios, Miguel "Una descripción nueva del Faro de Alejandría," *al-Andalus* 1 (1933): 241–300.

Ayalon, David. *Gunpowder and Firearms in the Mamluk Kingdom: A Challenge to a Mediaeval Society*, 2nd edition. London: Frank Cass, 1978.

Badawi, El-Said and Martin Hinds. *A Dictionary of Egyptian Arabic, Arabic-English*. Beirut: Librairie du Liban, 1986.

al-Baghdādī, ʿAbd al-Laṭīf. *Kitāb al-ifādah wal-iʿtibār fī umūr al-mushāhada wal-ḥawādith al-muʿāyana bi-arḍ miṣr*. Cairo: Maṭbaʿat Wādī al-Nīl, 1870.

Baltzell, E. Digby. *Philadelphia Gentlemen*. NY: Transaction, 1989.

Baltzell, E. Digby. *Puritan Boston and Quaker Philadelphia*. NY: Transaction, 1996.

Baltzell, E. Digby. *Sporting Gentlemen: Men's Tennis from the Age of Honor to the Cult of the Superstar*. NY: Free Press, 1995.

Baltzell, E. Digby. *The Protestant Establishment: Aristocracy and Caste in America*. New Haven: Yale University Press, 1987.

Bareket, Elinoar. "Abraham ha-Kohen the Physician Ben Isaac." *Hebrew Union College Annual* 71 (2001): 1–19 [Hebrew].

Bareket, Elinoar. "Begging for Help in Letters from the Geniza." *Te'uda* 16–17 (2002): 359–389 [Hebrew].

https://doi.org/10.1515/9783110713619-029

Bareket, Elinoar. *The Jewish Leadership in Fustat in the First Half of the Eleventh Century.* Tel-Aviv: The Diaspora Research Institute, Tel Aviv University, 1995 [Hebrew].
Bareket, Elinoar. *The Jews of Egypt, 1007–1055.* Jerusalem: Ben-Zvi Institute, 1995 [Hebrew].
Bartels, Larry M. *Unequal Democracy: The Political Economy of the Gilded Age.* Princeton, NJ: Princeton University Press, 2008.
Bashan, Eliezer. *Captivity and Ransom in Mediterranean Jewish Society (1391–1830).* Ramat Gan: Bar-Ilan University Press, 1982 [Hebrew].
Beckert, Sven. *Monied Metropolis.* NY: Cambridge University Press, 2003.
Ben-Sasson, Menahem. "Appeal to the Congregation in Islamic Countries in the Early Middle Ages." In *Knesset Ezra: Literature and Life in the Synagogue*, edited by Shulamit Elitzur et al., 327–350. Jerusalem: Ben-Zvi Institute, 1994 [Hebrew].
Ben-Sasson, Menahem. "Egyptian Jewry in the Tenth-Twelfth Centuries: From Periphery to Center." *Bulletin of the Israeli Academic Center in Cairo* 8 (1987): 14–16.
Ben-Sasson, Menahem, ed. *The Jews of Sicily 825–1068: Documents and Sources.* Jerusalem: Ben-Zvi Institute, 1991 [Hebrew].
Ben-Sasson, Menahem. "Maimonides in Egypt. The First Stage." *Maimonidean Studies* 2 (1991): 3–30.
Ben-Sasson, Menahem. "The Ties of the Maghrebis to the Land of Israel, 9th-11th centuries." *Shalem* 5 (1987): 31–82.
Ben-Sasson, Menahem. *The Emergence of the Local Jewish Community in the Muslim World; Qairawan, 800–1057.* Jerusalem: Magness Press, 1996 [Hebrew].
Ben-Sasson, Menahem. *The Ties of the Maghrebis to the Land of Israel, 9th-11th Centuries.* Jerusalem: Academon, 1981 [Hebrew].
Bendix, Reinhard. *Max Weber: An Intellectual Portrait.* London: Heinemann, 1960.
Benjamin of Tudela, *The Itinerary of Benjamin of Tudela.* Edited and translated by Marcus N. Adler. London: Frowde, 1907.
Bergman, Judah. *Charity in Judaism.* Jerusalem: Tarshish, 1944. [Hebrew].
Best, Heinrich, György Lengyel, and Luca Verzichelli, eds. *The Europe of Elites: A Study into the Europeanness of Europe's Political and Economic Elites.* Oxford: Oxford University Press, 2012.
Bianquis, Thierry. "Une crise frumentaire dans l'Egypt fatimide." *Journal of the Economic and Social History of the Orient* 23 (1980): 67–101.
Blau, Joshua. *A Grammar of Judeo-Arabic, Based Mainly on Unliterary Texts.* Jerusalem: Magness, 1961 [Hebrew].
Blau, Joshua. *Dictionary of Mediaeval Judaeo-Arabic Texts.* Jerusalem: Hebrew Language Academy, 2006 [Hebrew].
Blidstein, Gerlad J. "Traditional and Modern Discourse: More on Autonomy and Authority." In *A Good Eye: Dialogue and Polemic in Jewish Culture*, edited by Nahem Ilan, 687–697. Tel Aviv: Hakibbutz Hameuchad, 1999 [Hebrew].
Blidstein, Gerald J. *Prayer in Maimonides' Halakhic Thought.* Jerusalem: Mossad Bialik, 1994 [Hebrew].
Bosworth, Clifford E. *The Medieval Islamic Underworld. The Banū Sāsān in Arabic Society and Literature.* Leiden: Brill, 1976.
Bourdieu, Pierre. *Distinction.* Cambridge, MA: Harvard University Press, 1984.
Bourdieu, Pierre. *Homo Academicus.* Stanford, CA: Stanford University Press, 1990.
Bourdieu, Pierre. *State Nobility.* Stanford: Stanford University Press, 1998.

Bourdieu, Pierre. *The Field of Capital Production.* NY: Columbia University Press, 1993.

Boyarin, Daniel. *Carnal Israel: Reading Sex in Talmudic Culture.* Berkeley: University of California Press, 1993.

Braslawsky, Joseph. "Geniza Fragments from the 11th-13th Centuries Concerning Rabbath ʿAmmōn and Māʿān." *Eretz-Yisrael 3: Cassuto Book,* 207–209. Jerusalem: Israel Exploration Society, 1954 [Hebrew].

Bresc, Henri. *Un monde mediterranéen: économie et société en Sicile, 1300–1450.* Rome: École française de Rome, 1986. 2 vols.

Brett, Michael. *The Rise of the Fatimids: The World of the Mediterranean and the Middle-East in the Tenth Century CE.* Leiden: Brill, 2001.

Brinner, William, ed. *An Elegant Composition Concerning Relief after Adversity by Nissim ben Jacob ben Nissim Ibn Shāhīn.* New Haven: Yale University Press, 1977.

Brody, Hayyim, ed. *Dīwān des Abū-l-Ḥasan Jehuda ha-Levi.* Berlin: Mekitze Nirdamim, 1894–1930 [Hebrew].

Brody, Yerachmiel. "Were the Geonim Legislators?" *Shenaton ha-Mishpat ha-Ivri: Annual of the Institute for Research in Jewish Law* 11–12 (1984): 279–315 [Hebrew].

Burns, James M. *Leadership.* NY: Harper, 1978.

Cahen, Claude. "La chronique des Ayyubides d'al-Makin b. al-Amid." *Bulletin d'Études Orientales* 15 (1955–57): 109–184.

Cahen, Claude. *Makhzūmiyyāt: Études sur l'histoire economique et financiere de l'Égypte medieval.* Leiden: Brill, 1977.

Chastagnol, André. "La Prosopographie, méthode de recherché sur l'histoire du Bas-Empire." *Annales. Economies, Societés, Civilisations,* 25.2 (1970): 1229–1235.

Chazan, Robert. *Medieval Jewry in Northern France: A Political and Social History.* Baltimore and London: Johns Hopkins University Press, 1973.

Cohen, Abner. *The Politics of Elite Culture: Explorations in the Dramaturgy of Power in a Modern African Society.* Berkeley: University of California Press, 1981.

Cohen, Abner. *Two-Dimensional Man: An Essay in the Anthropology of Power and Symbolism in Complex Societies.* London: Routledge, 1974.

Cohen, Mark R. *Jewish Self-Government in Medieval Egypt.* Princeton, NJ: Princeton University Press, 1980.

Cohen, Mark R. *Poverty and Charity in the Jewish Community of Medieval Egypt.* Princeton, NJ: Princeton University Press, 2005.

Cohen, Mark R. *The Voice of the Poor in the Middle Ages: An Anthology of Documents from the Cairo Geniza.* Princeton, NJ: Princeton University Press, 2005.

Cohen, Mark R. *Under Crescent and Cross: The Jews in the Middle Ages.* Princeton, NJ: Princeton University Press, 2008.

Cohen, Mark. "Four Judaeo-Arabic petitions of the Poor from the Cairo Geniza." *Jerusalem Studies in Arabic and Islam* 24 (2000): 446–471.

Cowley, Arthur. "Bodleian Geniza Fragments." *Jewish Quarterly Review Old Series* 18 (1906), 250–254.

Cuffel, Alexandra. "Call and Response: European Jewish Emigration to Egypt and Palestine in the Middle Ages." *Jewish Quarterly Review* 90 (1999): 61–102.

Daftary, Farhad. *The Ismāʿīlīs; Their History and Doctrines.* Cambridge: Cambridge University Press, 2007.

Derrida, Jacques. *De la grammatologie.* Paris: Les Éditions de Minuit, 1967.

al-Dhahabī, Abū ʿAbdallā b. ʿUthmān. *Al-ʿIbar fī ḥabar man ghabar.* Kuwait: Dāʾirāt al-Maṭbūʿāt wal-Nashr, 1960.

Dozy, R.P.A. *Supplément aux dictionnaires arabes.* Leiden: Brill, 1881.

Drory, Joseph. *Ibn al-ʿArabī of Seville: A Journey in the Land of Israel (1092–1095).* Ramat Gan: Bar-Ilan University, 1993 [Hebrew].

Dunand, Françoise. "Pratiques et croyances funéraires en Egypt romaine." In *Aufstieg und Niedergang de roemischen Welt, II*, edited by Wolfgang Haase, 18.5: 3216–3315. Berlin: De Gruyter, 1995

Eddé, Anne-Marie and Jane Marie Todd. *Saladin.* Cambridge, MA: Belknap Press, 2011.

Edwards, Jeremy and Sheilagh Ogilvie. "Contract Enforcement, Institutions, and Social Capital: The Maghribi Traders Reappraised." *Economic History Review* 65.1 (2012): 421–444.

Ehrenkreutz, Andrew S. *Saladin.* Albany, NY: SUNY Press, 1972.

Elbeheiry, Salah. "Les institutions de l'Egypte au temps des Ayyubides." M.A. thesis, Universitè de Paris IV-Lille, 1972.

Elon, Menachem. *Jewish Law: History, Sources, Principles (Ha-Mishpat Ha-Ivri).* Translated by Bernard Auerbach and Melvin J. Sykes. Philadelphia: Jewish Publication Society, 1994.

Etzioni, A. *The Active Society: A Theory of Societal and Political Processes.* NY: The Free Press, 1968.

Eyal, Gil, Ivan Szelenyi, and Eleanor R. Townsley. *Making Capitalism Without Capitalists: The New Ruling Elites in Eastern Europe.* London: Verso, 2001.

Femia, Joseph V. *Gramsci's Political Thought: Hegemony, Consciousness and the Revolutionary Process.* Oxford: Clarendon Press, 1981.

Fenton (Yinon), Paul. "Prayer for the Authority and Permission to Pray: Genizah Fragments." *Mi-Mizraḥ u-mi-Maʿarav* 4 (1983): 7–27 [Hebrew].

Fierro, Maria Isabel. "La polémique à propos de *rafʿ al-yadayn fī l-ṣalāt dans al-Andalus.*" *Studia Islamica* 65 (1987): 69–90.

Finer, Samuel E. *Vilfredo Pareto: Sociological Writings.* London: Pall Mall Press, 1966.

Firth, Raymond. "Introduction to Factions in Indian and Overseas Indian Society." *British Journal of Sociology* 8 (1958): 291–295.

Fischel, Walter J. "The Spice Trade in Mamluk Egypt." *Journal of the Economic and Social History of the Orient* 1 (1958): 157–174.

Fleischer, Ezra. "The Contribution of the Geniza to the Study of Hebrew Liturgical Poetry." *Teʿuda* 1 (1980): 83–88 [Hebrew].

Fleischer, Ezra. "Yehuda ha-Levi—Remarks Concerning His Life and Poetical Oeuvre." In *Israel Levin Jubilee Volume, I*, edited by Reuven Tzur and Tova Rosen, 241–276. Tel Aviv: Katz Institute for Hebrew Literature, 1994 [Hebrew].

Fleischer, Ezra. *Eretz-Israel Prayer and Prayer Rituals as Portrayed in the Geniza Documents.* Jerusalem: Magness, 1988 [Hebrew].

Fleischer, Ezra. *Hebrew Liturgical Poetry in the Middle Ages.* Jerusalem: Keter, 1975 [Hebrew].

Fleming, Crystal M. and Lorraine E. Roses. "Black Cultural Capitalists: African-American Elites and the Organization of the Arts in Early Twentieth Century Boston." *Poetics* 35 (2007): 368–387.

Frank, R. Richistan: *A Journey Through the American Wealth Boom and the Lives of the New Rich.* NY: Crown, 2007.

Franklin, Arnold. *This Noble House: Jewish Descendants of King David in the Medieval Islamic World.* Philadelphia: University of Pennsylvania, 2013.

Frenkel, Miriam. "Adolescence in Jewish Medieval Society under Islam." *Continuity and Change* 16 (2001): 263 – 281.

Frenkel, Miriam. "Book Lists from the Geniza as a Source for the Cultural and Social History of the Jews in Mediterranean Society." *Te'uda* 15 (1999): 333 – 349 [Hebrew].

Frenkel, Miriam. "Charity in Jewish Society of the Medieval Mediterranean World." In *Charity and Giving in Monotheistic Religions*, edited by Miriam Frenkel and Yaacov Lev, 343 – 363. Berlin-NY: Walter de Gruyter, 2009.

Frenkel, Miriam. "Genizah Documents as Literary Products." In *"From A Sacred Source": Genizah Studies in Honour of Professor Stefan C. Reif*, edited by Ben Outhwaite and Siam Bhayro, 139 – 155. Leiden: Brill, 2010.

Frenkel, Miriam. "Medieval Alexandria—Life in a Port City." *Al-Masāq* 26.1 (2014): 5 – 35.

Frenkel, Miriam. "'Proclaim Liberty to Captives and Freedom to Prisoners': The Ransoming of Captives by Medieval Jewish Communities in Islamic Countries." In *Gefangenenloskauf im Mittelmeerraum: Ein intereligiöser Vergleich*, edited by Heike Grieser and Nicole Priesching, 83 – 97. Hildesheim, Zurich and NY: Georg Olms Verlag, 2015.

Frenkel, Miriam. *"The Compassionate and Benevolent": The Leading Elite in the Jewish Community of Alexandria in the Middle Ages.* Jerusalem: Ben-Zvi Institute, 2006 [Hebrew].

Frenkel, Yehoshua. "Political and Social Aspects of Islamic Endowments (*awqāf*): Saladin in Cairo (1169 – 73) and Jerusalem (1187 – 93)." *Bulletin of the School of Oriental and African Studies* 62 (1999): 20 – 30.

Friedman, Mordechai A. "A Cry of Destruction about the Cancellation of the Saying of Piyyutim: A Request to Address the Sultan," *Pe'amim: Studies in Oriental Jewry* 78 (1999): 128 – 147 [Hebrew].

Friedman, Mordechai A. "Controversy for the Sake of Heaven: Studies in the Prayer Controversy of R. Abraham Maimuni and his Generation." *Te'udah* 10 (1996): 254 – 298 [Hebrew].

Friedman, Mordechai A. "Maimonides Appoints R. Anatoly *Muqaddam* of Alexandria." *Tarbiẓ* 83 (2015): 135 – 161 [Hebrew].

Friedman, Mordechai A. "Objections to Prayer and Prayer Customs of the Land of Israel as Reflected in the Responsa Found in the Geniza (Responsa of R. Yosef Rosh Ha-Seder)." In *Knesset Ezra; Literature and Life in the Synagogue*, edited by Shulamit Elitzur et al., 102–69. Jerusalem: Ben Zvi Institute, 1990 [Hebrew].

Friedman, Mordechai A. "The Commandment of Pulling off the Sandal Takes Precedence over the Commandment of Levirate." *Teudah* 13 (1997): 35 – 66 [Hebrew].

Friedman, Mordechai A. "The Nagid, the Nasi and the French Rabbis: A Threat to Abraham Maimonides' Leadership." *Zion* 92 (2017): 193 – 266 [Hebrew].

Friedman, Mordechai A. *Ḥalfon and Judah ha-Levi: The Lives of a Merchant Scholar and a Poet Laureate According to the Cairo Geniza Documents* (India Book IV/A). Jerusalem: Ben-Zvi Institute and Rabbi David Moshe and Amalia Rosen Foundation, 2013 [Hebrew].

Friedman, Mordechai A. *Jewish Polygyny in the Middle Ages: New Documents from the Cairo Geniza.* Jerusalem: Mossad Bialik, 1986 [Hebrew].

Gabrieli, Francesco. "Adab." *Encyclopedia of Islam*, 2nd edition, 1: 175 – 176. Leiden: Brill, 1960 – 2005.

Geertz, Clifford. *The Interpretation of Cultures*. NY: Basic Books, 1973.

Giddens, Anthony. *The Class Structure of the Advanced Societies*. London: Hutchinson, 1973.

Gil, Moshe, and Ezra Fleischer. *Yehuda Ha-levi and his Circle*. Jerusalem: Magness Press, 2001 [Hebrew].

Gil, Moshe. *A History of Palestine, 634–1099*. Translated by Ethel Broido. Cambridge: Cambridge University Press, 1992.

Gil, Moshe. *Documents of the Jewish Pious Foundations from the Cairo Geniza*. Leiden: Brill, 1976.

Gil, Moshe. *In the Kingdom of Ishmael; Studies in Jewish History in Islamic Lands in the Early Middle Ages*. Tel Aviv: Tel Aviv University Press, 1997 [Hebrew].

Gil, Moshe. *Jews in Islamic Countries in the Middle Ages*. Translated by David Strassler. Leiden: Brill, 2004.

Gil, Moshe. *Palestine during the First Muslim Period (634–1099)*. Tel Aviv: Tel Aviv University and the Ministry of Defense Publishing House, 1983 [Hebrew].

Goitein, Shelomo D. "Early Testimonies from the Geniza about the Jewish Community of Salonica," *Sefunot: Studies and Sources on the History of the Jewish Communities in the East* 11 (1971) = *The Book of Greek Jewry*, 1: 9–33 [Hebrew].

Goitein, Shelomo D. "Formal Friendship in the Medieval Near East." *Proceedings of the American Philosophical Society* 115 (1971): 484–489.

Goitein, Shelomo D. "New Light on the Beginnings of the Kārim Merchants." *Journal of the Economic and Social History of the Orient* 1 (1958): 175–184.

Goitein, Shelomo D. "The Beginning of the Kārim Merchants and the Character of Their Organization." In *Studies in Islamic History and Institutions*, 351–360. Leiden: Brill, 1966.

Goitein, Shelomo D. "Wills from Egypt from the Genizah Period." *Sefunot* 8 (1964): 105–126 [Hebrew].

Goitein, Shelomo D. *A Mediterranean Society: The Jewish Communities of the Arab World as Portrayed in the Documents of Cairo Geniza*. Berkeley, Los Angeles, and London: University of California Press, 1967–1994. 6 vols.

Goitein, Shelomo D. *Letters of Medieval Jewish Traders*. Princeton, NJ: Princeton University Press, 1973.

Goitein, Shelomo D. *Palestinian Jewry in Early Islamic and Crusader Times in the Light of the Geniza Documents*. Jerusalem: Yad Ben-Zvi, 1980 [Hebrew].

Goitein, Shelomo D. "A Letter to Maimonides and New Sources regarding the Negidim of this Family." *Tarbiẓ* 34 (1965): 232–256 [Hebrew].

Goitein, Shelomo D. "A Plea for the Periodization of Islamic History." *Journal of the American Oriental Society* 88.2 (1968): 224–228.

Goitein, Shelomo D. "Abraham Maimonides and His Pietist Circle." In *Jewish Medieval and Renaissance Studies*, edited by Alexander Altmann, 145–164. Cambridge, MA: Harvard University Press, 1967.

Goitein, Shelomo D. "Chief Judge R. Hananel b. Samuel, In-Law of R. Moses Maimonides." *Tarbiẓ* 50 (1980): 371–395 [Hebrew].

Goitein, Shelomo D. "Did Yehuda ha-Levi Arrive in the Holy Land?." *Tarbiẓ* 46 (1977): 245–250 [Hebrew].

Goitein, Shelomo D. "HaRav: An Obscure Chapter in the History of the Palestinian Gaonate, with an Appendix: A Letter by 'the Daughter of the Head of the Yeshiva'." *Tarbiẓ* 45 (1987): 64–75 [Hebrew].

Goitein, Shelomo D. "Letters About R. Judah ha-Levi's Stay in Alexandria and the Collection of His Poems." *Tarbiẓ* 28 (1958): 343–361 [Hebrew].

Goitein, Shelomo D. "Moses Maimonides, Man of Action: A Revision of the Master's Biography in the Light of Geniza Documents." In *Hommage à George Vajda; études d'histoire et de pensée juives,* edited by Gérard Nahon and Charles Touati, 155–167. Louvain: Peeters, 1980.

Goitein, Shelomo D. "Rabbi Judah ha-Levi in Spain in Light of the Geniza Papers." *Tarbiẓ* 24 (1955): 134–149 [Hebrew].

Goitein, Shelomo D. "The Biography of Rabbi Judah Ha-Levi in the Light of the Cairo Geniza Documents." *Proceedings of the American Academy for Jewish Research* 28 (1959): 41–56.

Goitein, Shelomo. "The Last Phase of Rabbi Yehuda ha-Levi's Life in the Light of the Genizah Papers." *Tarbiẓ* 24 (1954): 21–47, 119 [Hebrew].

Goitein, Shelomo D. "The Local Jewish Community in the Light of the Cairo Geniza Records." *Journal of Jewish Studies* 12 (1961): 133–158.

Goitein, Shelomo D. "The Renewal of the Controversy over the Prayer for the Head of the Community at Abraham Maimuni's time." In *Ignace Goldziher Memorial Volume, II,* 49–54. Jerusalem: Reuven Mass, 1958 [Hebrew].

Goitein, Shelomo D. "The Tribulations of an Overseer of the Sultan's Ships: A letter from the Cairo Geniza (written in Alexandria in 1131)." In *Arabic and Islamic Studies in Honour of H.A.R. Gibb.*, edited by G. Makdisi, 270–284. Leiden: Brill, 1965.

Goitein, Shelomo D. *Jewish Education in Muslim Countries Based on Records from the Cairo Genizah.* Jerusalem: Ben-Zvi Institute and The Hebrew University, 1962 [Hebrew].

Goitein, Shelomo D. *Studies in Islamic History and Institutions.* Leiden: Brill, 1968.

Golb, Norman. "New Light on the Persecution of French Jews at the Time of the First Crusade." *Proceedings of the American Association for Jewish Research* 34 (1966): 1–63.

Golb, Norman. *History and Culture of the Jews of Rouen in the Middle Ages.* Tel Aviv: Dvir, 1976 [Hebrew].

Goldberg, Jessica. "Choosing and Enforcing Business Relationships in the Eleventh-Century Mediterranean: Reassesing the 'Maghribī Traders'." *Past & Present* 215.2 (2012): 3–40.

Goldberg, Jessica. *Trade and Institutions in the Medieval Mediterranean: The Geniza Merchants and their Business World.* Cambridge: Cambridge University Press, 2012.

Goldman, Eliezer. "Authority and Autonomy." In *Between Authority and Autonomy in Jewish Tradition*, edited by Avi Sagi and Zeev Safrai, 32–54. Tel Aviv: Hakibbutz Hameuchad, 1997 [Hebrew].

Gottheil, Richard J. "A Distinguished Family of Fatimide Cadis." *Journal of the American Oriental Society* 27 (1906): 217–296.

Granat, Yehoshua. "The Mixed Blessings of the Western Wind: Ambiguous Longings in Halevi's Alexandrian Poems of Welcome and Farewell." In *Israel in Egypt: The Land of Egypt as Concept and Reality for Jews in Antiquity and the Early Medieval Period*, edited by Alison Salvesen, Sarah Pearce, and Miriam Frenkel. Leiden: Brill, forthcoming.

Greif, Avner. "Contract Enforceability and Economic Institutions in Early Trade: The Maghribi Traders Coalition." *American Economic Review* 83.3 (1993): 525–548.

Greif, Avner. "Reputation and Coalition in Medieval Trade: Evidence on the Maghribi Traders." *Journal of Economic History* 49 (1989): 857–882.

Greif, Avner. "The Maghribi Traders: A Reappraisal?" *Economic History Review* 65 (2012): 445–469.

Greif, Avner. *Institutions and the Path to the Modern Economy: Lessons from Medieval Trade.* Cambridge: Cambridge University Press, 2006.

Grohmann, Adolf. *Arabic Papyri in the Egyptian Library.* Cairo: Egyptian Library Press, 1934.

Gulak, Asher. *The Elements of Jewish Law.* Tel-Aviv: Dvir, 1967 [Hebrew].

Gurevitch, Aron J. *Categories of Medieval Culture.* Translated by G.L. Campbell. London: Routledge and Kegan Paul, 1985.

Hacohen, Elisheva. "The Poetry of R. Anatoly Bar Joseph." M.A. thesis, The Hebrew University of Jerusalem, 1996 [Hebrew].

Halbertal, Moshe. *Interpretive Revolutions in the Making: Values as Interpretative Criteria in Jewish Law.* Jerusalem, Magness Press, 1997.

Halm, Heinz. "Die Fatimiden." In *Geschichte der arabischen Welt*, edited by Ulrich Haarmann. Munich: Verlag C.H. Beck, 1987, 166–199.

Halm, Heinz. "The Isma'ili Oath of Alliance and the Sessions of Wisdom." In *Medieval Isma'ili History and Thought*, edited by Farhad Daftary, 91–115. Cambridge: Cambridge Uiversity Press, 1996.

al-Harāwī, ʿAlī b. Abī Bakr. *Kītāb al-ishārāt ilā maʿrifat al-ziyārāt.* Damascus: IFAO, 1953.

Hasan, Yusuf F. *The Arabs in Sudan.* Edinburgh: Edinburgh University Press, 1967.

Havatzelet, Meir and Uri Melamed. "Commentaries on Alphabets in Psalms." *Peʿamim* 88 (2001): 4–20 [Hebrew].

Heinrichs, W.P. et al., eds. *Encyclopaedia of Islam*, 2nd edition. Leiden: Brill, 1960–2005. 12 vols.

Heller, Chaim, ed. "Introduction." *Maimonides' Sefer ha-Mitzvoth translated by Moses Ibn Tibbon.* Jerusalem: Mossad Harav Kook, 1960 [Hebrew].

Higley, John and Michael Burton. *Elite Foundations of Liberal Democracy.* NY: Rowman & Littlefield, 2006.

Higley, John, and György Lengyel, eds. *Elites after State Socialism.* Oxford: Rowman & Littlefield, 2000.

Higley, John, Jan Pakulski and Włoszimierz Wesołowski, eds. *Postcommunist Elites and Democracy in Eastern Europe.* Basingstoke: Macmillan, 1998.

Hirschberg, Haim Z. *History of the Jews in North Africa.* Jerusalem: Mossad Bialik, 1965 [Hebrew].

Hodgeson, Marshall. *The Venture of Islam: Conscience and History in a World Civilization.* Chicago: The University of Chicago Press, 1974. 3 vols.

Hofer, Nathan. *The Popularisation of Sufism in Ayyubid and Mamluk Egypt, 1173–1325.* Edinburgh: Edinburgh University Press, 2015.

Holt, Peter M. *The Age of the Crusades: The Near East from the Eleventh Century to 1517.* London: Longmann, 1985.

Hourani, Albert. *A History of the Arab Peoples.* London: Faber & Faber, 2012.

Humphries, R. Stephen. *From Saladin to the Mongols: The Ayyubids of Damascus, 1193–1260.* Albany, NY: SUNY Press, 1977.

Ibn al-Athīr, ʿAlī b. Aḥmad. *al-Kāmil fī al-taʾrīkh.* Leiden: Brill, 1870.

Ibn al-Ṣayrafī, Amīn al-Dīn ʿAlī. *al-Ishāra ilā man nāla al-wizāra.* Cairo: IFAO, 1923.

Ibn Baṭṭūṭa, Muḥammad b. ʿAbdallāh. *Riḥlat Ibn Baṭṭūṭa al-musammāt tuḥfat al-niẓār fī ghrāʾib al-amṣār wa-ajāʾib al-asfār.* Beirut: Dār al-Kutub al-ʿIlmiyya, 1983.
Ibn Ḥajar al-ʿAsqalānī, Aḥmad b. ʿAlī. *Rafʿ al-aṣr ʿan quḍāt miṣr.* In Abū ʿ Umar Muḥammad al-Kindī, *Kitāb al-wulāt wa-kitāb al-quḍāt.* Leiden: Brill, 1912.
Ibn Ḥawqal, Muḥammad b. ʿAlī. *Kītāb ṣūrat al-arḍ.* Leiden: Brill, 1938.
Ibn Jubayr al-Kinānī, Muḥammad b. al-Ḥusayn. *Riḥlat Ibn Jubayr.* Beirut: Dār Ṣādir, 1964.
Ibn Kathīr, ʿImād al-Dīn. *al-Bidāya wal-nihāya fī al-taʾrīkh.* Cairo: Maṭbaʿat al-Saʿāda, 1932.
Ibn Khallikān, Shams al-Dīn. *Wafayāt al-aʿyān wa-anbāʾ abnāʾ al-zamān.* Beirut: Dār al-Thaqāfa, 1968.
Ibn Khurradādhbih, ʿUbaydallāh b. ʿAbdallāh. *Kitāb al-masālik wal-mamālik* (= *Liber viarum et regnorum*). Leiden: Brill, 1889.
Ibn Muyassar, Muḥammad b. ʿAlī. *Akhbār miṣr*, edited by Henri Massé. Cairo: IFAO, 1919.
Ibn Rusta, Abū ʿAlī Aḥmad. *Kitāb al-aʿlāq al-nafīsa.* Leiden: Brill, 1881–1882.
Ibn Saʿīd, Abū al-Ḥasan ʿAlī al-Andalūsī. *al-Mughrib fī ḥulā al-maghrib.* Cairo: n.p., 1953.
Ibn Taghrībirdī, Jamāl al-Dīn Yūsuf. *al-Nujūm al-zāhira fī mulūk miṣr wal-qāhira.* Cairo: Dār al-Kutub al-ʿIlmiyya, 1932.
Ibn Wāṣil, Jamāl al-Dīn Muḥammad. *Mufarraj al-kurūb fī akhbār banī ayyūb.* Cairo: Maṭbaʿat Jāmiʿat Fuʾād al-Awwal, 1953.
Ibn ʿAbd al-Ḥakam al-Qurashī, ʿAbd al-Raḥmān. *Futūḥ miṣr wal-maghrib wal-andalus.* Leiden: Brill, 1960.
Jacoby, David. "Byzantine Trade with Egypt from the Mid-Tenth Century to the Fourth Crusade." *Thesaurismata* 30 (2000): 25–77.
Jönsson, Christer and Jonas Tallberg, eds. *Democracy Beyond the Nation State? Transnational Actors and Global Governance.* Basingstoke: Palgrave Macmillan, 2010. 3 vols.
JPS Hebrew-English Tanakh: The Traditional Hebrew Text and the New JPS Translation. Philadelphia: Jewish Publication Society, 1999.
Kahle, P. "Die Katastrophe de mittelalterichen Alexandria." In *Mélanges Maspero IIII. Orient Islamique*, 137–154. Cairo: IFAO, 1940.
Kalfon-Stillman, Yedida. "Medieval Egyptian Dress." In *Masʾat Moshe: Studies in Jewish and Islamic Culture Presented to Moshe Gil*, edited by Ezra Fleischer, Mordechai. A. Friedman, and Joel. L. Kraemer, 237–245. Jerusalem and Tel-Aviv: Bialik Institute, 1998 [Hebrew].
Kalfon Stillman, Yedida.*The Arab Dress: A Short Story from the Dawn of Islam to Modern Times.*ed. Norman A. Stillman (Leiden: Brill, 2000).
Kanarfogel, Ephraim. "The ʿAliyah of Three Hundred Rabbis' in 1211: Tosafist Attitudes Toward Settling in the Land of Israel." *Jewish Quarterly Review* 76 (1986): 191–215.
Katz, Daniel. "Patterns of Leadership." In *Handbook of Political Psychology*, edited by Jeanne N. Knutson, 203–233. San Francisco: Jossey-Bass, 1973.
Katz, Jacob. *Tradition and Crisis: Jewish Society at the End of the Middle Ages.* Translated by Bernard D. Cooperman. NY: NY University Press, 1993.
Kedar, Benjamin Z. "The Jewish Community of Jerusalem in the Thirteenth Century." *Tarbiẓ* 41 (1971): 82–94 [Hebrew].
Kennedy, Hugh. *The Prophet and the Age of the Caliphates: The Islamic Near East from the Sixth to the Eleventh Century.* Harlow: Longman, 2004.
al-Kindī, Abū ʿUmar Muḥammad. *Kitāb al-wulāh wa-kitāb al-quḍāh.* Leiden: Brill, 1912.

Krakowski, Eve. *Coming of Age in Medieval Egypt: Female Adolescence, Jewish Law, and Ordinary Culture*. Princeton, NJ: Princeton University Press, 2017.

LaCapra, Dominick. *History and Criticism* (Ithaca NY and London: Cornell University Press, 1985).

Labib, Subhi Y. "al-Iskandariyya," *Encyclopedia of Islam*, 2nd edition, 4: 137–143. Leiden: Brill, 1960–2005.

Labib, Subhi Y. "Egyptian Commercial Policy in the Middle Ages." In *Studies in the Economic History of the Middle East*, edited by M. A. Cook, 63–77. London: Oxford University Press, 1970.

Labib, Subhi Y. "Kārimī," *Encyclopedia of Islam*, 2nd edition, 4:640.

Landman, Leo. "The Office of the Medieval Hazzan." *Jewish Quarterly Review* 62 (1972): 246–276.

Lecomte, Gérard. *Ibn Qutayba (mort en 276/889): L'homme, son oeuvre, ses idées.* Damascus: n.p., 1965.

Leiser, Gary. "The Madrasa and the Islamization of the Middle East. The case of Egypt." *Journal of the American Research Center in Egypt* 22 (1985): 29–47.

Lev, Yaacov. "The Suppression of Crime, the Supervision of Markets, and Urban Society in the Egyptian Capital During the 10th and the 11th Centuries." *Mediterranean and Historical Review* 3 (1988): 71–95.

Lev, Yaacov. *Saladin in Egypt*. Leiden: Brill, 1999.

Lev, Yaacov. *State and Society in Fatimid Egypt*. Leiden: Brill, 1991.

Lévi-Provençal, Évariste. "Une description arabe inédite du Phare d'Alexandrie." In *Mélanges Maspero IIII. Orient Islamique*, 161–171. Cairo: IFAO, 1940.

Lewellen, Ted C. *Political Anthropology*. Westport, CT: Praeger, 1983.

Lewis, Archibald R. *Naval Power and Trade in the Mediterranean, 500–1100 AD*. Princeton, NJ: Princeton University Press, 1951.

Liebson, Gideon. "Determining Factors in *Ḥerem* and *Nidui* (Ban and Excommunication) during the Tannaitic and Amoraic Periods." *Shenaton ha-Mishpat ha-Ivri: Annual of the Institute for Research in Jewish Law* 2 (1975): 292–342. [Hebrew]

Liebson, Gideon. "*Gezerta* and *Ḥerem Setam* in the Gaonic and Early Medieval Periods." J.D diss., The Hebrew University of Jerusalem, 1979 [Hebrew].

Liebson, Gideon. "The Ban and Those under It: Tannaitic and Amoraic Perspectives." *Shenaton ha-Mishpat ha-Ivri: Annual of the Institute for Research in Jewish Law* 6–7 (1979): 177–202 [Hebrew].

Mahamid, Hatim. "The Fatimid Government from al-Mustanṣir to Ṣalāḥ al-Dīn 1036–1171." M.A thesis, University of Haifa 1988. [Hebrew].

Maimonides, Moses. *Responsa*. Edited by Abraham Lichtenberg. Leipzig: H.L. Schneuss, 1859.

Maimonides, Moses. *Responsa*. Edited by Joshua Blau. Jerusalem: Reuven Mass, 2014.

Maimuni, Abraham. *Responsa*. Edited by Abraham H. Freiman and Shelomo D. Goitein. Jerusalem: n.p., 1938.

Makdisi, George. *The Rise of Humanism in Classical Islam and the Christian World*. Edinburgh: Edinburgh University Press, 1990.

Mann, Jacob. *The Jews in Egypt and Palestine under the Fatimid Caliphs: A Contribution to their Political and Communal History Based Chiefly on Genizah Material Hitherto Unpublished*. Oxford: Oxford University Press, 1969.

al-Maqqarī, Aḥmad b. Muḥammad. *Nafḥ al-ṭīb fī ghuṣn al-andalus al-raṭīb*. Cairo: Maṭbaʿat al-Bābī al-Ḥalabī, 1949.
al-Maqrīzī, Taqī al-Dīn. *al-Bayān wal-iʿrāb ʿammā nazala fī miṣr min al-aʿrāb*. Cairo: [n.p.], 1334/1916.
al-Maqrīzī, Taqī al-Dīn. *Kitāb al-sulūk li-maʿrifat duwal al-mulūk*. Cairo: Lajnat al-Taʾlīf wal-Tarjama wal-Nashr, 1934.
al-Maqrīzī, Taqī al-Dīn. *Ittiʿāẓ al-ḥunafāʾ bi-akhbār al-āʾimma al-fāṭimiyyīn al-khulafāʾ*. Cairo: al-Majlis al-Aʿlā lil-Shuʾūn al-Islamiyya, 1967.
al-Maqrīzī, Taqī al-Dīn. *Kitāb al-mawāʿiẓ wal-iʿtibār fī dhikr al-khiṭaṭ wal-āthār*. Beirut: Maktabat Iḥyāʾ ʿUlūm al-Dīn, 1959. 3 vols.
Margariti, Roxani E. "Mercantile Networks, Port Cities, and 'Pirate' States: Conflict and Competition in the Indian Ocean World of Trade before the Sixteenth Century." *Journal of the Economic and Social History of the Orient* 51.4 (2008): 543–577.
Margariti, Roxani E. *Aden and the Indian Ocean Trade. 150 Years in the Life of a Medieval Arabian Port*. Chapel Hill: University of North Carolina, 2012.
Marger, Martin N. *Elites and Masses: An Introduction to Political Sociology*. Berkeley: University of California Press, 1987.
Martin, Roderick. *The Sociology of Power*. Oxford: Routledge & Kegan Paul, 1977.
al-Masʿūdī, Abū al-Ḥasan ʿAlī. *Murūj al-dhahab wa-maʿādin al-jawhr fī al-taʾrīkh*. Cairo: n.p., 1958.
Matthew, Donald. *The Norman Kingdom of Sicily*. Cambridge: Cambridge University Press, 1992.
Mazor, Amir and Efraim Lev. "Dynasties of Jewish Physicians in the Fatimid and Ayyubid Periods." *Hebrew Union College Annual* 89 (2018): 221–260.
Michels, R. *Political Parties: A Sociological Study of the Oligarchical Tendencies of Modern Democracy*. Translated by Eden and Cedar Paul. Glencoe, Ill.: Free Press, 1949.
Motzkin, Aryeh L. "The Arabic Correspondence of Judge Elijah and his Family (Papers from the Cairo Geniza): A chapter in the Social History of Thirteenth Century Egypt." Ph.D. diss., University of Pennsylvania, 1965.
Nadel, Siegfried F. "The Concept of Social Elites." *International Social Science Bulletin* 8 (1956): 413–424.
Nallino, Carlo-Alfonso. *La littérature arabe des origins à l'époque de la dynastie ummayade*. Translated by Charles Pellat. Paris: Maisonneuve, 1950.
Nanji, Azim. "Portraits of Self and Others: Ismaʿili Perspectives on the History of Religions." In *Mediaeval Ismaʿili History and Thought*, edited by Farhad Daftary, 153–160. Cambridge: Cambridge University Press, 1996.
Neubauer, Adolf. *Mediaeval Jewish Chronicles and Chronological Notes*. Oxford: Clarendon Press, 1887.
Nicholas, Ralph W. "Factions: A Comparative Study." In *Political Systems and the Distribution of Power*, edited by Michael Benton, 21–61. London and NY: Routledge, 2011.
Nicolet, Claude. "Prosopographie et histoire sociale: Rome et l'Italie a l'époque républicaine." *Annales, Economies, Societés, Civilisations* 25.2 (1970): 1209–1229.
al-Nuwayrī al-Iskandarānī, Muḥammad b. Qāsim. *Kitāb al-ilmām bi-l-aʿlām fīmā jarat bihi al-aḥkām wal-umūr al-maqaḍiyya fī waqʿat al-iskandariyya*. Hyderabad: Daʾirat al-Maʿārif ʿUthmāniyya, 1970.
Ostrower, Francie. *Trustees of Culture*. Chicago: University of Chicago Press, 2004.

Owens, E.J. *The City in the Greek and Roman World.* London and NY: Routledge, 1991.
Pareto, Vilfredo. *Treatise of General Sociology, The Mind and Society.* NY: Harcourt, Brace & Co., 1935.
Parry, Greaint. *Political Elites.* London: Allen & Unwin, 1969.
Pellat, Charles. "Variations sur le theme de l'adab." *Corréspondence d'Orient-Études* 5–6 (1964): 19–37.
Petry, Carl F. *The Civilian Elite of Cairo in the Later Middle Ages.* Princeton, NJ: Princeton University Press, 1981.
Phillips, Jonathan. *The Life and Legend of the Sultan Saladin.* New Haven and London: Yale University Press, 2019.
Prawer, Joshua. "Chapters in the History of the Jewish Community in the Latin Kingdom of Jerusalem." *Shalem* 2 (1971): 103–112 [Hebrew].
Pryor, John H. "The *Eracles* and William of Tyre: An Interim Report." In *The Horns of Hattin*, edited by Benjamin Z. Kedar, 270–294. Jerusalem: Ben Zvi Institute and Israel Exploration Society, 1992.
al-Qalqashandī, Abū al-ʿAbbās Aḥmad b. ʿAlī. *Ṣubḥ al-aʿshā fī ṣināʿat al-inshāʾ.* Cairo: Dār al-Kutub, 1913.
Reiner, Elchanan. "Overt Falsehood and Covert Truth: Christians, Jews and Holy Places in Twelfth-Century Palestine." *Zion* 63.2 (1998): 157–188 [Hebrew].
Reiner, Elchanan. "Pilgrims and Pilgrimage to Eretz Yisrael, 1099–1517." Ph.D. diss., The Hebrew University of Jerusalem, 1988.
Rothkopf, David. *Superclass.* NY: Farrar, Strauss & Giroux, 2009.
Russ-Fishbane, Elisha. *Judaism, Sufism, and the Pietists of Medieval Egypt.* Oxford: Oxford University Press, 2015.
Rustow, Marina. "Formal and Informal Patronage among Jews in the Islamic East: Evidence from the Cairo Geniza." *Al-Qanṭara* 29.2 (2008): 341–382.
Rustow, Marina. "Patronage in the Context of Solidarity and Reciprocity: Two Paradigms of Social Cohesion in the Premodern Mediterranean." In *Patronage, Production, and the Transmission of Texts in Medieval and Early Modern Jewish Cultures*, edited by Esperanza Alfonso and Jonathan Decter, 13–44. Turnhout: Brepols, 2014.
Rustow, Marina. *Heresy and the Politics of Community: The Jews of the Fatimid Caliphate.* Ithaca: Cornell University Press, 2008.
Salem, ʿAbd al-ʿAziz. "D'Alexandrie à Almeria." *Revue de l'Occident Musulman et de la Mediterranée* 46 (1987): 64–70.
Sālim, ʿAbd al-ʿAzīz. *Taʾrīkh madīnat al-iskandariyya wa-ḥaḍāratuhā fī al-ʿaṣr al-islāmī.* Alexandria: Dār al-Maʿārif, 1982.
Sanders, Paula. "Fatimids." In *Dictionary of the Middle Ages*, edited by Joseph R. Strayer, 5: 24–30. NY: C. Scribner's Sons, 1983.
Sanders, Paula. *Ritual, Politics and the City in Fatimid Cairo.* Albany, NY: SUNY Press, 1994.
Sartre, Jean-Paul. *Search for a Method.* Translated by Hazel Barnes. NY: Knopf, 1963.
Sato Tsugitaka. "Slave Traders and Kārimī Merchants during the Mamluk Period: A Comparative Study." *Mamluk Studies Review* 10.1 (2006): 141–232.
Sato Tsugitaka. *Sugar in the Social Life of Medieval Islam.* Leiden: Brill, 2014.
Scheiber, Alexander. "Unbekannte Gedichte von Aaron Ibn al-Ammani, dem Freunde Jehuda Hallevis." *Sefarad* 27 (1967): 269–281.

Schirmann, Hayyim. "Poets Contemporary with Mose [sic] Ibn Ezra and Yehuda ha-Levi (III)." *Studies of the Research Institute for Hebrew Poetry in Jerusalem* 6 (1946): 249–339 [Hebrew].

Schirmann, Hayyim. *Hebrew Poetry in Spain and Provence.* Jerusalem: Mossad Bialik, 1959 [Hebrew].

Schwartz, Seth. *Were the Jews a Mediterranean Society? Reciprocity and Solidarity in Ancient Judaism.* Princeton, NJ: Princeton University Press, 2009.

Sela, Shulamit. "The Head of the Rabbanite, Karaite and Samaritan Jews: On the History of a Title." *Bulletin of the School of Oriental and African Studies* 57 (1994): 255–257.

Sela, Shulamit. "The Headship of the Jews in the Fatimid Empire in Karaite Hands." In *Mas'at Moshe: Studies in Jewish and Islamic Culture Presented to Moshe Gil*, edited by Ezra Fleischer, Mordechai A. Friedman and Joel L. Kraemer, 256–281. Jerusalem: Mossad Bialik, 1998 [Hebrew].

Serjeant, Robert B. *Islamic Textiles: Materials for a History up to the Mongol Conquest.* Beirut: Librairie du Liban, 1972.

Shailat, Yitzhak. *The Letters and Essays of Moses Maimonides: A Critical Edition of the Hebrew and Arabic Letters of Maimonides.* Maaleh Adumim: Ma'aliot, 1987 [Hebrew].

Shayyāl, Jamāl al-Dīn. *Aʿlām al-Iskandariyya fī al-ʿaṣr al-islāmī.* Cairo: Dār al-Maʿārif, 1965.

Shayyāl, Jamāl al-Dīn. *Jamāl al-Dīn Abū Bakr al-Ṭurṭūshī: al-ʿālim al-zāhid al-thāʾir.* Cairo: n.p., 1968.

Sherwood, Jessica Holden *Wealth, Whiteness, and the Matrix of Privilege.* Lanham: Lexington Books, 2010.

Shokeid, Moshe. "Clans Indeed? Family and Political Factions in the Adaption to the Moshav." In *The Intercultural Experience: A Reader in Anthropology*, edited by Moshe Shokeid and Shlomo Deshen, 196–209. Jerusalem and Tel Aviv: Schocken, 1998 [Hebrew].

Shoshan, Boaz. "Fatimid Grain Policy and the Post of Muḥtasib." *International Journal of Middle Eastern Studies* 13 (1981): 181–189.

Shoshan, Boaz. "Grain Riots and the 'Moral Economy': Cairo 1350–1517." *Journal of Interdisciplinary History* 10 (1980): 459–478.

Siegal, Bernard and Allan Beals. "Pervasive Factionalism." *American Anthropologist* 62 (1960): 394–417.

Simmel, Georg. "The Stranger." In *The Sociology of Georg Simmel*, edited by Kurt H. Wolf, 402–408. Glencoe IL: Free Press, 1959.

Spiro, Socrates. *Arabic-English Dictionary of the Colloquial Arabic of Egypt.* Beirut: Librairie du Liban, 1973.

Staffa, Susan. *Conquest and Fusion: The Social Evolution of Cairo 642–1850 AD.* Leiden: Brill, 1977.

Steingass, Francis J. *A Comprehensive Persian-English Dictionary.* London: Routledge and Kegan Paul, 1892.

Stern, Samuel M. "Cairo as the Center of the Ismaʿili Movement." In *Colloque international sur l'histoire du Caire*, 437–450. Cairo: al-Hayʾa al-Miṣriyya al-ʿĀmma lil-Kitāb, 1972.

Stern, Samuel M. "A Twelfth-Century Circle of Hebrew Poets in Sicily." *Journal of Jewish Studies* 5 (1954): 60–79, 110–113.

Stern, Samuel M. *Studies in Early Ismaʿilism.* Leiden: Brill/Jerusalem: Magness Press, 1983.

Stillman, Norman "The Jews in the Urban History of Medieval Islam." In *Mas'at Moshe: Studies in Jewish and Islamic Culture Presented to Moshe Gil*, edited by Ezra Fleischer, Mordechai A. Friedman, and Joel. L. Kraemer, 246–255. Jerusalem and Tel-Aviv: Bialik Institute, 1998 [Hebrew].

Stone, Lawrence. "Prosopographie." *Daedalus*, 100.1 (1971): 46–75.

Stroumsa, Sarah. *The Beginnings of the Maimonidean Controversy in the East.* Jerusalem: Ben-Zvi Institute, 1999 [Hebrew].

al-Subkī, Tāj al-Dīn. *Ṭabaqāt al-shāfiʿiyya.* Cairo: Maṭbaʿat al-Bābī al-Ḥalabī, 1935/1324.

Sublet, Jacqueline. "La prosopographie arabe." *Annales. Economies, Societés, Civilisations* 25.2 (1970): 4–79.

al-Suyūṭī, Jalāl al-Dīn. *Ḥusn al-muḥāḍara fī akhbār miṣr wal-qāhira.* Cairo: IFEO, 1321/1924.

Tcherikover, Victor A. *The Jews in Egypt during the Hellenistic-Roman Age in the Light of the Papyri.* Jerusalem: Magness, 1963 [Hebrew].

Tykocinski, Chaim. *The Geonic Regulations.* Jerusalem: Sura, 1960 [Hebrew].

Udovitch, Abraham L. "Formalism and Information in the Social and Economic Institutions of the Medieval Islamic World." In *Individualism and Conformity in Classical Islam*, edited by Amin Banani and Speros Vryonis, 61–81. Wiesbaden: Harrassovitz, 1977.

Udovitch, Abraham L. "A Tale of Two Cities: Commercial Relations between Cairo and Alexandria during the Second Half of the Eleventh Century." In *The Medieval City*, edited by Harry A. Miskimin, David Herlihy and Abraham L. Udovitch, 143–162. New Haven and London: Yale University Press, 1977.

Udovitch, Abraham L. "Merchants and Amirs: Government and Trade in Eleventh Century Egypt." *Asian and African Studies* 24 (1988): 53–72.

Vajda, Georges. "La Mašyaḥa d'Ibn al-Ḥaṭṭāb al-Rāzī: Contribution a l'histoire du sunnisme en Egypte fatimide." *Bulletin d'études orientales* 23 (1970): 21–99.

Veblen, Thorstein. *The Theory of the Leisure Class.* NY: Penguin, 1994.

Walker, Paul. *Exploring an Islamic Empire: Fatimid History and its Sources.* London: I.B. Tauris, 2002.

Weiss, Gershon. "Legal Documents written by the Court Clerk Halfon ben Manasse (dated 1100–1138): A study in the Diplomatics of the Cairo Geniza." PhD diss., University of Pennsylvania, 1970.

Wiet, Gaston. "Les marchands d'épices sous les sultans mamlouks." *Cahiers d'Histoire Egyptienne* 7 (1955): 81–147.

Wilkinson, Rupert. *Governing Elites: Studies in Training and Selection.* NY: Oxford University Press, 1969.

William of Tyre, *A History of Deeds Done Beyond the Sea.* Translated and annotated by Emily A. Babcock and August C. Krey. NY: Columbia University Press, 1943.

Wright-Mills, C. *The Power Elite.* NY: Oxford University Press, 1956.

Yahalom, Joseph. "Maimonides and Hebrew Poetic Language." *Pe'amim* 81 (1999): 4–18 [Hebrew].

Yahalom, Joseph. "Poetry and Society in Egypt: Their Relationship as Reflected in the Attitude to the Secular Poetry of Judah ha-Levi." *Zion* 45 (1980): 286–298 [Hebrew].

Yahalom, Joseph. *Yehuda ha-Levi: Poetry and Pilgrimage.* Jerusalem: Magness Press, 2009 [Hebrew].

Yāqūt al-Ḥamawī, Shihāb al-Dīn. *Muʿjam al-buldān.* Beirut: n.p., 1995.

al-Yaʿqūbī, Aḥmad b. Abī Yaʿqūb. *Kitāb al-buldān.* Leiden: Brill, 1891.

Zeldes, Nadia and Miriam Frenkel. “The Sicilian Trade: Jewish Merchants in the Mediterranean in the 12th and 13th Centuries.” *Michael* 14 (1997): 89 – 137 [Hebrew].
Zinger, Oded. “Social Embeddedness in the Legal Arena According to Geniza Letters.” In *Writing Semitic: Scripts, Documents, Languages in Historical Context*, edited by Andreas Kaplony and Daniel Potthast. Leiden: Brill, forthcoming.

Glossary of Terms

Amīr	ruler, military commander.
Babylonian Yeshivot	two central Jewish institutions of leadership, education and law (Sura and Pumbedita) operating mainly in the area formerly governed by the Sassanid Empire.
Beit dīn	the Jewish legal courthouse. Also the title of the chief justice
Dayyan	Jewish judge, who presides over the Jewish court of law.
Exilarch	or Head of the Diaspora (Rosh ha-Golah). Head of the Jews whose sat in Baghdad and derived his lineage from King David. During the high middle- ages he exercised direct control only over the Jewish communities in the lands of the Eastern Caliphate.
Faqīh	Muslim jurist
Gaon	Head of one of the Yeshivas (in the context of this book: mainly the Palestinian Yeshivah)
Genizah, Cairo	a side chamber in the Ben Ezra synagogue in Fustat where worn written material was deposited since the 10th century. It is the main source of manuscripts relevant to the medieval history of the Islamicate world.
ḥaver	fellow of the Yeshivah, and an honorific title granted by the Yeshivah to people associated with it and to local leaders.
Jāh	prestige, standing
Jāliya	Poll tax paid by Jews and Christians
Jizya	tax payable by non-Muslims
Ketubba	Jewish marriage contract
Maghribis, *Maghāriba*	people whose origins are from the Maghreb, usually meaning anywhere west of Egypt, mainly, the central Southern shores of the Mediterranean (now days Tunisia).
Muḥtasib	a Muslim market inspector also in charge of public morals
Muqaddam	a local leader
Nagid	the leader of the Jews of Egypt and Palestine from the 12th century.
Nasi	Title referring to exilarchs.
Pesīqā	pledge
Ra'īs	Head. Applied to various ranks of leaders.
Rasm, pl. **Rusūm**	taxes or customs
Responsum, pl. **responsa**	the response of a Jewish legal scholar to a query in Jewish law.
Wālī	local Muslim governor. Sometimes head of police

https://doi.org/10.1515/9783110713619-030

Index

Aaron b. Yeshūʿā Ibn al-ʿAmmānī 47, 119–129, 192f., 198, 219f., 260, 265, 277, 293
Abbasids XVIII, 4, 13, 22, 29
ʿAbd al-Karīm al-Bīsānī 25
al-ʿAbdarī, Abū ʿAbdallāh 30
Abiyār 296
Abraham al-Ṣiqillī 85f.
Abraham b. Abī al-Ḥayy Khalīla 14, 297f.
Abraham b. Abū Zikrī 33
Abraham b. Berākhōt b. al-Ḥājja 40
Abraham b. David Ibn Sighmār 83
Abraham b. Eleazar 171
Abraham b. Fakhr 33
Abraham b. Jacob al-Darʿī 108–114, 213–215
Abraham b. Muqillah 132
Abraham b. Nathan Av 238, 249f., 281
Abraham b. Nathan the Seventh 115, 262
Abraham b. Sahlān 39, 65f., 72, 296
Abraham b. Solomon b. Judah 209
Abraham ha-Kohen b. Isaac Ibn al-Furāt 60, 67f., 72f., 75f., 79, 90, 210f.
Abraham ha-Kohen ha-Maʿaravi 172
Abraham Maimuni (Abraham b. Moses Maimonides) 45f., 153, 170f., 173, 175, 181f., 184, 186–188, 190–194, 198–200, 224, 229, 231, 233f., 242, 270, 292, 308
Abū al-ʿAlāʾ 126f.
Abū ʿAlī b. Ḥanikh 184f.
Abū ʿAlī ʿImrān 7
Abū al-Bishr 108
Abū al-Faḍl b. Hibat Allāh 115
Abū al-Faraj Ismāʿīl 305
Abū al-Ḥasan ʿAllāl 307
Abū Isḥāq 77, 130, 132, 284
Abū al-Maʿānī al-Masjūnī 38
Abū al-Maḥāsin al-tilmīdh al-Miṣrī 38
Abū al-Majd b. Abū al-Munā b. al-Dimyāṭī 137
Abū al-Mufaḍḍal (the chief justice of Cairo) 252
Abū Karīm al-Khayyāṭ 307
Abū Manṣūr, the Amir of Alexandria 89
Abū Naṣr al-Ṭabīb 306, 308
Abū Naṣr b. Abraham 18, 128, 130–139, 261f., 282, 290, 295
Abū Naṣr b. Saʿd 307
Abū al-Riḍā b. al-Maghribiyya 157, 239, 288
Abū Saʿd al-ʿAṭṭār 121
Abū Saʿd b. Shardāna 99
Abū Saʿīd ha-Talmīd 161
Abū Zikrī b. Elijah b. Zechariah 188
Abū Zikrī b. Manasseh 108
Abū Zikrī ha-Kohen b. Judah 130, 133, 135f.
al-ʿĀḍid (Fatimid Caliph) 19f , 22
al-Afḍal b. Badr al-Jamālī 15–17, 219
Ahl al-dhimma (“protected people”) XII
Aḥmad b. al-Ḥasan Ibn Ḥadīd, Makīn al-Dawla 16f., 47, 116, 123, 219, 262
Aleppo 10, 20
Alexandria mentioned *passim*
Alhambra 35
ʿAlī Ibn al-Nuʿmān 213
Alptakīn, Nāṣir al-Dawla 15
Amalfi 84
Amalric 21f., 26
ʿAmmār Ibn Ḥadīd 258
Amram b. Isaac of Alexandria 290, 293, 296
Amram b. Joseph 307
Amram b. Nathan 40
Anatolia 6, 85, 295
Anatoly b. Joseph 169f.
Āraḥ b. Nathan the Seventh 17, 45, 115–118, 212, 218, 238f., 262, 269, 306
Asad al-Dawla, Ildegüz 13f.
Ashkelon 21, 101, 255f., 298
al-ʿAṭṭārīn (perfumers)
– Jāmiʿ (mosque) 15, 43f.
– Quarter 86
– Sūq (market) 40, 44
avīzāriyya (compensation bill) 93
ʿAwāḍ b. Hananel 258, 292

https://doi.org/10.1515/9783110713619-031

al-Awḥad, Abū al-Ḥasan ʿAlī 14f.
ʿAyyāsh b. Ṣedaqah 304f.
Ayyubids XXIII, 3, 6, 16, 22, 25, 27f., 42, 44f., 47, 154, 206, 218, 220, 239, 252, 261, 278

Babylonians XVII, 64f., 71f, 142 (see also: Ysehivot, Synagogue)
Badr al-Jamālī (Fatimid vizier) 14f., 44
Baghdad XX, 79, 199, 300
Baltzell, E. Digby XV–XVI
Banū Qurra 8
Banū Sunbās 8
Barakāt b. Harūn b. al-Kūzī 39
Barqa 7, 84, 109, 215–217, 247
Baruch b. Sasson 253
Bashīr Ben Nahum 91f.
Bedouin 6, 10, 14f.
Beit dīn (Jewish court) 80, 94, 171, 326
Ben Elhanan 249
Ben Nahum family 91f., 96f., 100–103, 106, 213, 267, 279
Ben Saʿadyah family 76, 115
Ben Wāfī 244
Benayah b. Mūsā 95–98, 103, 109, 228, 235, 244, 257
Benjamin of Tudela 30, 35f., 45, 48, 142
Berākhōt b. Abraham 38
Berākhōt b. Ḥalfon 178
Berākhōt the Cantor 305–307, 309
Bīr Jabr (neighbourhood) 38, 46
Bishr b. Ezekiel 38, 40
Book/s 13, 18, 46, 78, 121, 130, 140, 146, 171f., 176, 215–217, 242, 287, 290–293, 307
Bourdieu, Pierre XV
al-Buḥayra 8, 10, 20, 229
Burns, James 221
Būsh (south of Cairo) 40
Byzantines 5f., 9, 11, 84, 180, 233, 242, 251 (see also: Edom)
Byzantium 72, 199, 233, 243

Cairo Genizah XIII, XVIII, XIX, XX–XV, 3, 5f., 11–15, 17, 19, 24f., 27, 29f., 32f., 37f., 41, 45f., 53–56, 58f., 80, 111, 115, 121, 127, 130, 140, 168, 173, 182, 206, 219, 228, 241, 279,, 286, 302, 304,
Cairo XIII, XXI, 13, 15, 18, 28, 40, 45, 53, 82, 123, 133, 192f., 197, 201, 207, 213, 219, 245, 250, 252, 261f., 300 (see also: Fustat, al-Qāhira)
Cantor/s (*ḥazzan*) 7, 57f., 62, ,83, 99, 119, 142, 161, 192, 195, 198, 248, 251, 270f., 288, 296, 298, 302, 305–307, 309 (see also: Mawhūb b. Aaron (the Cantor); Meir b. Yakhin (Thābit); Ṣadoq Ibn al-ʿAmmānī; Shelah b. Moses the Cantor)
Captives/Prisoners 6f., 11, 17, 34, 58, 69, 71f., 76–78, 81f., 84–86, 150f., 156, 254f., 259, 262, 265, 295, 298–300, 310
Charity 26, 45, 81, 145f., 174, 199f., 250, 256, 267, 297–299, 310
Christians XII, 9, 15, 23, 25f., 31, 34, 37f., 43, 46, 48f., 133, 167, 169, 178, 207, 229, 252, 255
Cohen, Abner XVI, 278
Cohen, Mark XXII, 153
Crusaders 16, 21–28, 31, 49, 128, 222, 298

Damascus 20,194
Damietta 27f., 99, 134, 213, 252, 299
Daniel, R. 165f.
Daniel b. Azaryah 60, 63, 66–70, 72–79, 87, 91, 101, 153, 210, 268
Darʿa 108
David b. Daniel b. Azaryah 78, 101f., 112f., 140
David Ben Nahum 92, 106
David ha-Levi b. Isaac 83, 262, 298
Dawūd al-Rūmī 216
Day of Atonement 7, 152, 271
al-Dayāmīs (neighbourhood) 40
dayyan (a Jewish Judge) 19, 25f., 38, 45, 56f., 123f., 174, 181, 251, 277
Denia (Spain) 109
Derrida, Jacques XXIV
Ḍirghām Ibn ʿĀmir 20
Divorce 162, 163, 164, 185, 187, 190
Ḍiyāʿ b. Joseph al-Qamrī 38, 98
Dress 82, 225, 280, 301–303, 310

Edom (Christendom) 6, 35, 48, 84
Eleazar, R. 24, 83, 144 f., 220, 236, 270 (see also: Eleazar ha-Kohen b. Judah Sa'd al-Mulk)
Eleazar ha-Kohen b. Judah Sa'd al-Mulk 149–155, 158 f. (see also: Eleazar, R.)
Eli b. Amram 67, 72, 74, 87, 89, 294 Eli ha-Kohen b. Yaḥyā 98
Eli ha-Kohen (*parnas*) 94
Elijah b. Solomon (Gaon) 89
Elijah b. Zechariah 174, 177, 182, 184 f., 188 f., 193, 199, 226, 236, 238, 243 f., 298
Elyakim, R. 170
Ephraim, R. 152–159, 220 f., 230, 239, 247, 254, 265, 288, 298
Ephraim b. Ismāʿīl al-Jawharī 6
Ephraim b. Nissim 291
Ephraim b. Shemaryah 58, 71 f., 74, 81, 255, 295, 298
Etzioni, Amitai 205
Europe XX, 9, 25, 30, 48 f., 160, 167, 169, 173, 177 f., 180 f., 183, 206, 222, 226, 234, 242 f., 266, 277
Evyatar Gaon 94, 101, 112 f., 140, 249
Excommunication 70, 91, 97 f., 157, 185 f., 190, 227–234, 257
Exilarch XVII, 152
Ezra b. Bashīr Ben Nahum 91–92

al-Fāʾiz (Fatimid Caliph) 19 f.
Fakhr al-Dīn (Amir of Alexandria) 25
Fakhr al-Mulk (Amir of Alexandria) 16 f., 117, 269, 306
Faraḥ b. Joseph 10, 12
Fatimids XXI, XXIII, 3–13, 15, 19, 22–24, 27, 42–44, 46 f., 57, 67 f., 75, 79, 106, 131, 150, 154 f., 206–208, 210 f., 213 f., 219 f., 236, 248, 252, 261, 263, 269, 278, 302
flax 253, 286, 304
France 27, 160 f., 167, 188, 233 f.
Fustat mentioned *passim*
Futūḥ b. ʿAllān 280

Gaon (Head of the Yeshiva) 56 f., 60–70, 75–77, 89, 94, 101, 106, 140–148, 155, 207–212, 220 f., 265, 268, 272, 274, 293
Geertz, Clifford 54
Gil, Moshe XXI, 71, 77, 89, 91, 94, 102, 126, 228, 235, 249, 291–293, 304
Goitein, Shelomo D. XXII, XXIV, 3, 7, 11, 26, 40, 46, 57, 59, 94, 121, 126 f., 136, 140, 143 f., 153, 177 f., 193, 197, 207, 235, 241, 251 f., 266, 280, 288, 296
Goldberg, Jessica XX–XXII, 11
Gramsci, Antonio XVI
Greif, Avner XIX–XXI, 279
Gurevitch, Aaron 264, 273

Ḥalfon b. Manasseh 251, 288, 296
Ḥalfon b. Nethanel 18, 122, 126, 130–138, 290
Hananel b. Samuel 280, 294, 301 f.
ḥārat al-Yahūd (The Jewish neighbourhood) 38
Hārūn b. al-Muʿallim Jacob 7
Ḥasūn b. Yaḥyā al-Mahdawī 286
ḥaver (Fellow of the Yeshiva) 56, 60 f., 66 f., 94, 124 f., 157, 184, 209 f., 250 f., 268, 270, 272, 291, 294
Ḥayyim b. ʿAmmār 284
Ḥayyim b. Eli ha-Kohen 14
Hibat Allāh (Nethanel) b. Judah b. Aaron Ibn al-ʿAmmānī 193 f, 201, 284
Hillel b. Bunyās al-ʿAṭṭār 40
Hillel Ibn ʿAwkal 309
Hodayah b. Jesse 181, 185, 194, 233 f.

Ibn Abī Thawbān 5
Ibn al-ʿAmmānī (family) 39, 47, 119 f., 122, , 192, 198, 219 f., 248
Ibn al-Ḥabbāb, Abū al-Makārim 21, 47
Ibn al-Muḥayraq 14
Ibn al-Qāsh (family) 232 (see also: Yeshūʿā Ibn al-Qāsh)
Ibn ʿAmmār, ʿAlī b. Muḥammad 15 f.
Ibn ʿAwf (qadi), Abū Ṭāhir Ismāʿīl b. Makkī b. ʿĪsa 18 f., 42 f., 134
Ibn Ḥabīb (family) 260
Ibn Ḥamdān, Nāṣir al-Dawla 12 f.
Ibn Jubayr 32, 36, , 44 f., 48
Ibn Maṣāl, Najm al-Dīn 20 f.

Ibn Taghrībirdī, Jamāl al-Dīn Yūsuf 4
Ibn al-Tallāj 157, 230
Ibrāhīm b. Faraḥ of Alexandria 9, 64, 262
'Imrān b. Bashīr Ben Nahum 91–92
India XVII, 48 f., 130 f., 280 f., 289
Isaac al-Nafūsī 292
Isaac b. Ezra 131
Isaac b. Ḥalfon 184–186, 188–191, 224, 226, 229 f., 241
Isaac b. Joseph Yerushalmi 124
Isaac b. Sasson 175, 231
Isaac Ben Nahum 92
Isaac Nīsābūrī 252
Ismā'īl al-Qala'ī 108
Ismā'īl b. Abraham al-Tūnī 40
Ismā'īl b. Faraḥ 10, 12, 287
Ismā'īl b. Yūsuf Ibn Abī 'Uqba 5

Jacob, R. (the Judge of Alexandria) 143
Jacob b. Salmān al-Ḥarīrī 8, 9
Jacob Ben Nahum 92, 97 f., 106, 286
Jacob ha-Kohen b. Muvḥar 123
Jalīla b. Abraham 99, 253
Jāliya 244, 258 (see also: Jizya, tax)
Japheth b. Moses 198
Japheth b. Amram al-Jāzifīnī 251, 309
Japheth b. Manasseh Ibn al-Qaṭā'if 251, 288
Japheth b. Shelah 20, 262
Japheth ha-Levi b. Mevorakh 123
Jerusalem XVII, 16, 21, 48, 72, 119, 199, 255 f., 298
jizya XX, 17, 133 f., 136
Job b. David ha-Levi 94
Joseph al-Aḥwal 82
Joseph al-Baghdādī 33, 176, 245–247
Joseph al-Maqdisī 151
Joseph b. 'Allān 280, 301, 308
Joseph b. Gershom 188 f., 230, 233 f.
Joseph b. Isaiah al-Dhahabī 93
Joseph b. Michael 198
Joseph b. Moses the *ḥaver* 294
Joseph b. Mubashshir Ben Nahum 100, 104
Joseph b. Samuel Ben Nahum 92
Joseph b. Shemaryah 8
Joseph b. Yaḥyā 249
Joseph Ben al-Shāmī 132, 138, 295
Joseph Ben Migash 132, 138, 295
Joseph ha-Kohen 20
Joseph ha-Kohen b. Solomon 94
Joseph ha-Kohen b. Yeshū'ā (the Judge) 7, 9, 34, 57–59, 62, 71, 209, 254
Joseph Ibn Kaskīl 294
Joseph Rosh ha-Seder 46
Joseph (Yehosef) b. Samuel ha-Bavli 172, 176
Jospeh Ibn 'Awkal 6
Judah b. Aaron Ibn al-'Ammānī see: Judah the Teacher Ibn al-'Ammānī
Judah b. Ezra 131 f.
Judah b. Isaac (Abū Zikrī) 40
Judah ha-Kohen b. Joseph, "the Rav" 72–76, 78, 80, 90, 98, 105 f., 218
Judah b. Joseph 33, 35
Judah b. Moses Ibn Sighmār (Abū Zikrī) 41, 64, 69 f., 72, 76 f., 80, 86, 261 f.
Judah b. Nathan 103, 111, 283
Judah b. Sa'adyah 93, 115, 258
Judah ha-Kohen Abū al-Barakāt al-Kātib 250
Judah ha-Kohen 'Amīd al-Dawla 149
Judah ha-Levi 19, 47, 119–128, 131–134, 137 f., 266, 295 f., 304, 309
Judah the Teacher Ibn al-'Ammānī 25 f., 33, 120, 172, 173, 175 f., 178, 192–201, 224, 226, 242, 245 f., 266, 271, 274, 284, 293, 295, 298, 300 f., 306, 308

Karaites XVIII, 207, 299
Kārim (merchants) 131
Ketubba (marriage contract) 94, 99, 109
Khalaf b. 'Azrūn 93
Khalaf b. Sahl 12
Khalīj (the canal) 27, 31–33, 47
Khidma XVIII, 150, 273

LaCapra, Dominick 54
Labrāṭ b. Moses Ibn Sighmār 76, 80
Lighthouse of Alexandria 29, 34, 35–36
Liturgical poetry, See: *Piyyut*

Madrasa (religious college) 19, 24, 42–45
Maghāriba XX f., 95, 97, 107, 279

Maghreb XX, 5, 16, 20, 30, 42, 79, 85, 93, 95, 97, 113, 130, 161, 167 (See also: *Maghāriba*)
al-maḥajja al-ʿuẓmā (the Great Royal Road) 37, 42, 44
al-Maḥalla 123, 142, 146 f., 300
al-Mahdiyya 93, 132
Maimonides XIX, 26, 39, 45, 47, 123, 140, 143, 150 f., 158, 160–167, 169–171, 174 f., 181, 190, 222–225, 231, 248, 270, 288, 292, 302
Makhlūf b. Mūsā al-Nafūsī al-Yatīm 8, 9, 288
Mamluks/Mamluk period 3, 28, 30, 44, 53
Manasseh ha-Kohen, Abū Sahl 108
Manasseh the Teacher 22, 149, 250 f., 283
al-Maqrīzī, Taqī al-Dīn Aḥmad b. ʿAlī (Historian) 9, 13, 44 f., 123
Mardūk b. Mūsā 38
Mariotis (Mariyūṭ), Lake 29, 31, 79
Mariut ha-Kohen b. Joseph 94 f., 103, 215
Markets (Sūq) 10, 12, 25, 27, 30, 37, 39 f., 42, 44, 48 f., 96, 98, 117, 212, 214, 237, 244 (see also: al-ʿAṭṭārīn)
Marriage 43, 58, 74 f., 80, 94, 99, 113, 124, 141, 162, 171, 185–187, 190, 193 f., 199, 229–231, 250, 253, 266, 284 (see also: *Ketubba*)
Marx, Karl XIII
Maṣliāḥ, Head of the Yeshivah 228
Mawhūb b. Aaron (the Cantor) 94 f.
Meir b. Hillel b. Ṣadoq 140 f., 143–150, 220 f., 259, 280, 282, 284, 290
Meir b. Yakhin (Thābit) (the Cantor) 178, 192–200, 293, 295, 300, 306
Menahem, R. (Menahem b. Isaac Ben Sasson, the judge in Cairo) 174 f., 192
Mevorakh b. Isaac 13
Mevorakh b. Saʿadyah 16 f., 45, 89, 96, 99 f., 102–106, 108–112, 114 f., 117, 212 f., 215, 245, 252 f., 263, 272, 281, 283, 299, 306
Michels, Robert XIV
Minyat Ziftā 162
Mishnah 89, 140, 283, 293
Mishneh Torah (Maimomonides' Code) 165 f.
Morocco 108
Mosca, Gaetano XIV, 278
Moses b. Japheth ha-Levi Sanī al-Dawla 18
Moses b. Joseph Ibn Kaskīl 87–99
Moses b. Judah b. Saʿadyah 115 f.
Moses b. Khalīfa 301
Moses b. Mevorakh 252
Moses ha-Kohen Ibn Ghulayb 171
Moses ha-Kohen Sanī al-Dawla 102 f.
Moses Ibn Tibbon 292
Moses the *ḥaver* 294
Mosque/s 4, 15, 22, 24, 43–45, 214 (See also: al-ʿAṭṭārīn)
Muʿāmala (business partnership) 9, 78, 98, 196, 273, 293, 297
Mubārak b. Isaac of Alexandria 285
Mubashshir Ben Nahum 91, 93
Mufaḍḍal ha-Kohen 307
Muḥtasib 25, 27, 214, 237
al-Muʿizz (Fatimid Caliph) 4 f.
Munajjā b. Ghallāb 307
Muqaddam 57–60, 116 f., 175 f., 179–182, 185 f., 192, 200 f., 229, 231, 238 f., 242, 244, 248 f., 259, 266, 269–273, 277
Mūsā b. Abī al-Ḥayy Khalīla 7, 11, 33, 97, 291
al-Mustanṣir, Caliph 7, 12–15, 57
Muvḥar b. Ṣedaqa 91

Nagid /Nagidate XVII, 16 f., 45, 64, 89, 98–100, 102–106, 108–112, 114 f., 117, 119, 121 f., 124–129, 140, 142 f., 148, 153,180–184, 189–190, 195, 199, 206, 211–216, 218–220, 222, 226, 232, 243, 245, 252 f., 258–260, 263, 269, 272, 283, 292 f., 306, 308,
Nāḥiyyat Banī Ḥusayn (neighborhood) 37
Nahray b. Nissim 7 f., 11, 29, 33, 35, 72, 74 f., 78–81, 84, 87 f., 90, 92 f., 95, 97 f., 106, 108, 218, 250, 253, 257 f., 262, 281, 286, 291–293, 298 f., 307
nāʾib 109, 111, 114, 130, 132, 213–215, 219 f., 236, 260, 277, 283
Nasi 181 f., 185, 194, 233
Nathan b. Abraham 60 f., 69, 75
Nathan b. Judah 18, 109, 111–114, 213, 215, 247, 270

Nathan b. Nahray 14, 108, 291
nāẓir 17, 150, 236
Nethanel b. Ḥalfon ha-Talmīd 143
Nethanel b. Moses ha-Levi the Sixth 141–146, 148
Nethanel ha-Kohen 82f., 298f.
Nissim b. Shelah b. Mubashshir Ben Nahum 96, 99f., 253
Nissim b. Shemaryah 284
Nizār, son of Caliph al-Mustanṣir 15f.
North Africa XVII, 5, 28, 44, 76
Nūr al-Dīn Ibn Zangi 20, 22
al-Nuwayrī al-Iskandarānī, Muḥammad b. Qāsim 44, 47

Palermo 169f.
Palestinians XVII, 64f., 67, 71–72, 296 (See also: Synagogue, Yeshivot)
Pareto, Vilfredo XIV, 278
Peraḥyah, R. 259, 294
Pesīqā 145, 147, 309
Pinḥas, R. (judge of Alexandria) 26, 31, 160–168, 222–226, 270
Piyyut (liturgical poetry) 121, 128, 172, 194f., 197, 225, 268f., 293, 296
Plague 8, 16, 18, 26, 28, 109, 271
Provence 160f., 167, 169

al-Qābisī 41, 305
al-Qāhira 4, 42 (See also: Cairo)
al-Qamra (quarter) 38f., 237
al-Qarāfa (cemetery, quarter) 30, 39, 45
qaṣaba (quarter) 37

Rabbanites XVII, 207, 299
Ramāda 85
Ratzon b. Fityān 178
Responsa 140, 146, 151, 160f., 195, 198, 222, 291, 293
Riḍwān Ibn al-Walkhashī (vizier) 42
Rīf 82, 132
Rustow, Marina XVIII, XIX

Saʿdān b. Thābit 32
Saʿadyah b. Berākhōt 45, 270
Sabrah family 267f.
Ṣadoq b. Josiah 140
Ṣadoq ha-Levi b. Levi 83
Ṣadoq Ibn al-ʿAmmānī 173, 175, 193f., 200, 242, 308
al-ṣaffayn 41f.
ṣāḥib al-bāb 34
Sahlān b. Abraham 64, 71
Ṣalāḥ al-Dīn al-Ayyubī (Saladin) 21–26, 29, 39–42, 44, 47
Salāma b. Mūsā al-Safāqṣī 35, 41
ṣaʿlūk 285–288
Samuel al-Nafūsī 169
Samuel b. Aaron 33
Samuel b. Hananyah 119, 121f., 124–129, 140, 142f., 218–220
Samuel b. Jacob 177–185, 188, 199, 224, 226, 242, 266, 273
Samuel b. Judah b. Asad 146f.
Samuel b. Judah ha-Bavli 18
Samuel b. Saʿadyah ha-Maskīl 175
Samuel Baghdādī Kohen 300
Samuel ha-Kohen the Judge 181
Samuel ha-Levi of Fustat 268
Sanhūr 260
Sar-Shalom ha-Levi Gaon 143
Sartre, Jean-Paul 54
Schwartz, Seth XIX
Shabbetai b. Nethanel 6, 72, 295
Shaltiel b. Mubashshir Ben Nahum 100, 104
Shawār Ibn Mujīr 20–22
Sheʾerit b. Shemaryah b. Hillel 147
Shelah b. Moses the Cantor 62, 64–66, 78
Shelah (Sahl) b. Mubashshir Ben Nahum 91–106, 213, 215–218, 228, 232, 244f., 247, 253, 257f., 266f., 272, 277, 280, 299
Shelah ha-Levi b. R. Moses the Teacher 124
Shemaryah b. Ephraim 83
Shīrkūh, Asad al-Dīn 20–22
Sicily 20, 23, 130, 169f., 173f., 190, 198, 224, 244, 301
Sijill 252
Silk 39, 101f., 108, 130, 133, 280, 304
Sitt al-Nasab 185f., 190, 198
Sitt al-Rūm 93

Sitt al-Ukhūwah b. Futūḥ 40
Solomon (an Exilarch from Mosul) 152
Solomon b. Elijah b. Zechariah 193, 284
Solomon b. Judah Gaon 60–66, 69, 75, 208–210, 265, 268, 272, 274
Solomon b. Nissim 14
Solomon b. Zechariah 38
Spain 17, 43, 109, 127, 131, 138, 161, 167
Sugar 286
Sulaymān b. Faraḥ 305
Surūr b. Ḥayyim b. Sabrah 266f., 280, 285
Surūr b. Sālim 185
Susa 76, 80
Synagogue XX, , 45f., 56, 58, 67, 83, 96, 104, 117, 145, 150, 152, 166, 174–175, 199, 215, 216, 217, 225, 229, 232, 236, 245, 246, 247, 268, 269, 270, 271, 280, 299, 302
– Babylonian 38, 46, , 152,
– Palestinian 46, 296
Syria 5, 21–23, 40, 47, 101, 142, 148

Ṭāhertī 7, 12
Ṭāhir al-Dimashqī 246
Ṭalā'i' b. Ruzzīk 20
Talmud 87, 89, 140, 140, 163, 167, 171, 233, 240, 284, 291, 293
Taqī al-Dīn Ibn Ayyūb 47
Ṭarkhān b. Salīf b. Ṭarīf 20
Tax XX, 15–17, 22, 24, 40, 95–98, 102, 110, 130, 133, 136, 144, 150, 229, 235, 256–259, 262, 285 (See also: *Jāliya*, *jizya*)
Tinnīs 213, 252, 299
Torah 104, 109, 141f., 149, 151, 153, 166, 169, 171, 215–217, 223, 229, 231f., 270, 283, 290, 292–295, 310
Tripoli 92, 110, 304
al-Ṭurṭūshī, Abū Bakr 43
Tustarīs 262

Veblen, Thorstein XIV
Vineyard 31, 89, 168, 263, 281

wālī (local governor) 18, 20f., 133f., 237f., 261, 263
Weber, Max XIII, 205
William of Tyre 21–23, 31, 48f.
wine 9, 109, 197, 217, 308

Yabqā b. Abī Razīn 84
Yaḥyā al-Munayyir 307
Yāqūt al-Ḥamawī 37, 39
al-Yazūrī, al-Ḥasan b. ʿAlī ʿAbd al-Raḥmān (vizier) 8
Yedūthūn (Eli the Cantor) 296, 305–307
Yeshivot (academies) XVII, 115, 124, 132, 240
– Babylonian XVII, 142
– Palestinian (Jerusalem) XVII, 56, 57, 59, 60, 61, 62, 65–71, 73–79, 81, 83, 87, 89–90, 91, 94, 95, 101–102, 105, 112, 113–114, 115, 140, 141, 142, 146, 148, 157, 206, 207–210, 211, 213, 215, 228, 249–250, 261, 280.
Yeshūʿā b. Aaron Ibn al-ʿAmmānī 245
Yeshūʿā b. Ismāʿīl al-Makhmūrī 7, 108, 292, 304
Yeshūʿa b. Japheth 104
Yeshūʿā b. Joseph 56, 59–91, 208–211, 247, 255, 261–263, 265, 268f., 272, 281, 293–295, 298–301
Yeshūʿā Ibn al-Qāsh 158, 232, 249, 258, 272, 288
Yūḥannā b. Munajjā 37

al-Zanātī 110
Zayn al-Kuttāb b. Eleazar ha-Kohen 149, 283
Zikrī al-Kaʿkī 307

www.ingramcontent.com/pod-product-compliance
Lightning Source LLC
Chambersburg PA
CBHW020828160426
43192CB00007B/567
* 9 7 8 3 1 1 1 1 1 0 6 7 7 *